FULLY HUMAN

The Story of a Man Called

Yeshua

By Douglas R Thompson

Chelsea Press

Fully Human: The Story of a Man Called Yeshua is a work of fiction. Names, characters, (with the exception of some well-known historical figures,) places, events, locales, and incidents are either the products of the author's imagination or used in a fictitious manner. When real-life historical figures appear, the situations, incidents, and dialogues concerning those persons are not intended to depict actual events or to change the fictional nature of the work. In all other respects, any resemblance to actual persons, living or dead, events, or locales is entirely coincidental.

First Edition, Chelsea Press
© Copyright 2018 Douglas R Thompson

All rights reserved.
Library of Congress Control Number: 2018906414
ISBN-13: 978-1-7322437-0-5

Chelsea Press
PO Box 196
Hyattsville, MD 20781

Bookcover design: Randy Fletcher, Exarte Design, Inc.

DEDICATION

I am the "baby" of five brothers, four of whom are still living. They are, from oldest to youngest, Herbert, David, James, and me.

Between Herbert and David, my mother gave birth to my brother John in 1938. I will let David tell you about our brother as it appears on his *Thompson/Smith Ancestry* blog, which he so carefully updates with stories and photos of my ancestors on both my father's and my mother's side. David writes:

> Our second brother, John, had serious mental issues, making it impossible for him to develop. My mother said that he seemed to be normal when he was born, but never really developed at a normal rate. She and my dad spent much of their early lives together taking John from one doctor to another, from one hospital to another, always looking for some sign of progress and hope. My earliest memories included hearing John crying in the back bedroom. My mother said that my first sentence was, "Why is Johnny always crying?" She didn't have an answer, since she didn't know either.
>
> In 1942, with my mother pregnant with her fourth child—soon to be Jim—it became clear that something had to change concerning the care, and ultimately the housing, of John. On February 18, 1942, my mom and dad petitioned the State of Michigan to have their son, John Ellsworth Thompson, committed to the Lapeer State Home & Training School as a "feebleminded" patient. He never developed mentally any further during the 22 years he was there. My parents occasionally visited him, but those visits proved to be very hard for my father.

John left his body in 1964.

We four brothers have been very lucky. We have all had an abundance of opportunities and adventures throughout our lives. Each of us has been blessed with so many things, from families and careers to health and prosperity. I often wonder what John would have become had he not been afflicted with whatever it was that prevented him from leading a productive life.

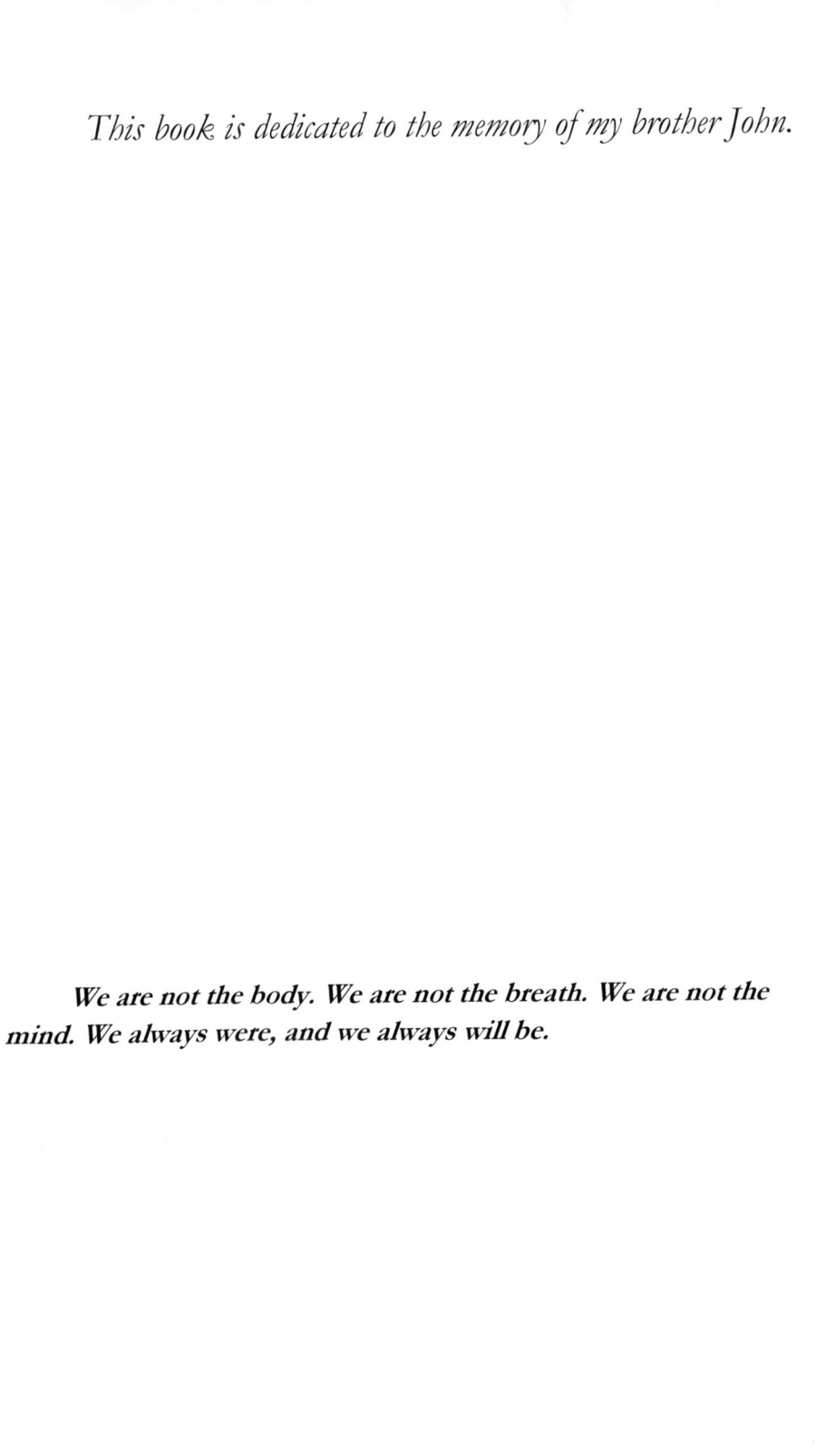

This book is dedicated to the memory of my brother John.

We are not the body. We are not the breath. We are not the mind. We always were, and we always will be.

Table of Contents

Prologue xiv
1 (The Samaritan and the Traveler) 3
2 (Yeshua begins his tale) 9
3 (A week earlier) 13
4 (Yeshua confronts the bully) 25
5 (Yeshua's mother and father) 29
6 (First encounter with the poor) 35
7 (Another encounter with the poor) 43
8 (Ephrayim's compromise with Yeshua) 47
9 (Yeshua fails at carpentry but makes new friends) ... 51
10 (Tahmid's meeting with Mara) 57
11 (Ephrayim and Yeshua both make a decision) 61
12 (Bacha teaches Yeshua how to fight) 65
13 (Yeshua's brush with death) 69
14 (Yeshua returns home) 75
15 (A reunion with Efah) 79
16 (Ephrayim in Sepphoris) 83
17 (Patanjali's vision) 91
18 (Yeshua's real father - Yosef) 95
19 (Vijayananda arrives in Egypt) 101
20 (Journey to Jerusalem) 103
21 (Arrival) 107
22 (Passover ceremony) 113
23 (Yeshua decides to stay) 117
24 (They meet at last) 123
25 (The decision is made) 127
26 (The journey begins) 133
27 (A voyage and a storm at sea) 137
28 (Pirates and the final leg of the journey) 143
29 (Yeshua meets Patanjali) 149
30 (The palace and Prince Hala) 155
31 (First lessons in Kriya Yoga) 161
32 (Another meeting with Prince Hala) 163
33 (Ephrayim and Mara wonder) 167
34 (Aharon's success) 169
35 (Yeshua learns a lesson about the opposite sex) 171
36 (Yeshua completes his training in Kriya Yoga) 177
37 (The White Priests) 185
38 (A harsh lesson in Brahminism) 189
39 (A healing chant) 193

40 (Issa heals) 199
41 (A warning from Jnyaneshwar) 203
42 (Teaching the working class) 205
43 (Issa faces Indian justice) 209
44 (Ephrayim and Mara prepare to move) 215
45 (Issa scorns the worship of idols) 219
46 (Issa meets Kapaali) 221
47 (Going to prison) 229
48 (Near death and a new destination) 233
49 (Help from the Buddhists) 241
50 (A decision to stay and learn) 247
51 (Issa begins healing and being healed) 251
52 (Aharon's divorce) 259
53 (Issa decides to leave) 261
54 (A last meeting with Patanjali and a farewell to India) 267
55 (Parting with Bacha) 275
56 (Meeting Yochanan the Baptizer) 279
57 (Yeshua and Yochanan forge a friendship) 285
58 (Yeshua meets Semadar and visits the wilderness) 291
59 (Semadar shows feelings toward Yeshua) 301
60 (Semadar becomes Yeshua's first disciple) 303
61 (Yeshua's decision to leave) 307
62 (Into the wilderness and temptation) 315
63 (His ministry begins) 321
64 (Curing the leper and making the lame walk) 331
65 (A spy is summoned) 337
66 (Filippos witnesses the sermon on the mount) 343
67 (Learning mashals and the spy reports back) 347
68 (Semadar finds Yeshua) 353
69 (A reunion) 359
70 (Seeing Efah and talking to Ephrayim) 363
71 (Efah's uncle) 367
72 (Yeshua brings Leviy the tax collector into his following) ... 369
73 (Filippos finds something useful for Aharon) 373
74 (The disciples get new names) 379
75 (A storm in the Sea of Chinnereth) 385
76 (Yochanan the Baptizer is arrested) 389
77 (Sending his apostles out to teach) 393
78 (Aharon's meal with Herodias) 395
79 (Yeshua in Samaria and the woman at the well) 399
80 (Filippos leaves Aharon while Yeshua finds Bacha) 403
81 (Mattiyahu and Yehuda face danger) 407

82 (Filippos finds Yeshua) 411
83 (Yochanan is beheaded) 415
84 (Feeding the thousands) 419
85 (Aharon tries to turn away Yeshua's followers) 423
86 (Yeshua rebukes the Pharisees and scribes) 425
87 (Making a deaf man hear) 429
88 (The Sadducees meet Yeshua) 433
89 (Aharon's plan, and Yeshua's experience on Mount Tabor) 437
90 (Yeshua struggles with the concept of a Messiah) 441
91 (Yeshua raises the dead) 445
92 (A dream within a dream) 449
93 (Yeshua foresees his death) 453
94 (The money changers at the temple) 455
95 (Yeshua's transformation) 461
96 (Aharon springs his trap) 469
97 (The arrest of Yeshua) 475
98 (Filippos plots to save Yeshua) 481
99 (Pilate agrees to judge Yeshua) 485
100 (Sending him to Herod) 489
101 (Pilate's plan fails) 493
102 (Bacha and Miryam console one another) 497
103 (Final victory) 501
Epilogue 509

Preface

Two books started me on my own journey to write this novel. One of them is entitled *Jesus for the Non-Religious* by John Shelby Spong, former Episcopal Bishop of Newark. In his book, he strips away all the mythology of Jesus written in the four gospels and ends up describing a very human, very Jewish, and very great spiritual leader.

The second book is entitled *The Unknown Life of Jesus Christ* by Nicolas Notovitch. This is alleged to be a true account by Nicolas Notovitch of his travels in Ladakh, where he was shown an ancient Buddhist manuscript detailing the travels throughout India of a famous saint from the west whom they called Issa. It accounts for the years between twelve and thirty that are missing from the biblical accounts of Jesus.

As a yoga teacher and lover of Eastern philosophy, I decided to spin these two books into a story, along with some of my own ideas. I imagined a child prodigy who was as comfortable with Brahmanism and Buddhism as he was with his own Jewish religion.

I hope you will enjoy reading the journey of Yeshua as much as I enjoyed developing and writing it.

Douglas
April, 2018
Hyattsville Maryland

Acknowledgements

Owning a yoga studio in Hyattsville, Maryland (Yoga Space), teaching eleven classes per week there, and teaching four classes per week at the George Washington University in Washington, DC, doesn't leave a lot of free time for writing. Lucky for me, I have been blessed with a wife of forty-seven years, Gloria, who takes it upon herself to quietly work in the background—answering phone calls, handling crises, managing the studio and its books, organizing my schedules, keeping anybody from needlessly bothering me, and making both our house and our business run seamlessly. Thank you, Gloria, for making all my dreams come true.

I would also like to acknowledge some of the help I had in researching and describing some of the events in Yeshua's life. First, I would like to thank Jayaram V, a prolific writer about Hinduism, self-help, and spirituality. He is also the president and founder of hinduwebsite.com. He helped me as I tried to describe India as it existed two-thousand years ago. He gave me lots of information on some of the prevailing customs and religions of that time.

Next, I would like to thank Aaron Bourn, a former yoga student and current psychologist who treats PTSD in persons who have returned from Iraq or Afghanistan, as well as their families. I wanted Yeshua to be a person with real problems. Aaron helped diagnose and prescribe treatment for Yeshua as he coped with these problems in a time when psychologists didn't exist.

Finally, I would like to thank the many people who read my manuscript and offered edits and suggestions. Especially my friends in the Hyattsville Writers Group.

Introduction

This book was meant to bring to life the character, Yeshua, who struggled with real human issues throughout his short time on this earth. In the process, I hope to create a person you will grow to love as much as I do.

The book is divided into four sections. The first section begins when Yeshua is eleven years old and follows him through a year of life in Nazareth, a journey to India, and the beginnings of his training in the Eastern philosophies. The second section follows him through India as he learns and as he teaches. The third section brings him back to Israel and follows his three-year ministry. The last section depicts the tragic ending of his life.

Some of the characters in India are real-life historical figures. There really was a King Hala who ruled the Satavahana Empire in India from the years 20 – 24. The commander-in-chief of his army was Vijayananda. And although Patanjali, the author of the *Yoga Sutras*, was believed to have been born a century after Yeshua, nobody knows for sure. I took the liberty of having him alive when Yeshua was in India.

My online research of Israel has shown that the Nasi, or Prince of the Great Sanhedrin, at the end of Yeshua's life was Rabbi Gamliel the Elder. Rabbi Yochanan ben Zakkai was the Av Beit Din (father of the court). Other historical figures come from the Gospels of the New Testament.

In his book, *Jesus for the Non-Religious*, John Shelby Spong tells us that the names of Yeshua's parents could very well have been fictionalized: "Neither parent receives any mention in any written material available to us prior to the eighth decade of the Christian era." I therefore chose the name "Mara" for Yeshua's mother.

I have chosen to use the Hebrew version of names in this novel. The name Jesus, for example, is written as Yeshua. Below are, in alphabetical order, the Hebrew names of the characters, along with familiar places, and names of books in the Bible, and their more familiar English equivalents.

Hebrew Name	English Name
Aharon	Aaron
Andres	Andrew
Ben-Ragash	Boanerges
Cephas	Peter
Chanan	Annas
Chavvah	Eve
Devarim	Deuteronomy
Elazar	Lazarus
Filippos	Philip
Hoshea	Hosea
Leviy	Levi
Mal'akhi	Malachi
Mattityahu	Mathhew
Mikha	Micah
Miryam	Mary
Miryam of Magdala	Mary of Magdala
Mishlei Shlomo	Proverbs of Solomon
Moshe	Moses
Nachum	Nahum
Naomiy	Naomi
Ovadyah	Obadiah
Sea of Chinnereth	Sea of Galilee
Sea of Salt	Dead Sea
Shemot	Exodus
Shemuel	Samuel
Shimon	Simon
Tehillim	Psalms
Tzefanyah	Zephaniah
Yaaqob	James
Yechezqel	Ezekiel

Yehuda	Judas
Yesha'yahu	Isaiah
Yeshua	Jesus
Yishmael	Ishmael
Yochanan	John
Yo'el	Joel
Yonah	Jonah
Yonatan	Jonathan
Yosef	Joseph
Zekharyah	Zechariah

"To be human is to be beautifully flawed"

— Eric Wilson, *October Baby*

Prologue

**Nazareth, Israel
AD 63**

Filippos and Bacha sat on a beautiful green hillside overlooking the town of Nazareth, in the same spot where they had sat each summer since Yeshua's death thirty years ago. As soon as the weather turned warm, Bacha would travel from his own Samaria to visit with Filippos, who now made Nazareth his home. Filippos liked this spot because, although they could see Nazareth below them and even some of the people moving about the town, they were alone. Except for the occasional fox or wild goat that scurried by, they were free to just sit and be with one another, uninterrupted.

But the tranquility of this particular late summer afternoon was interrupted, as Filippos turned to Bacha and said, "You know he failed."

"Who failed?" Bacha asked.

"You know who I mean." Filippos retorted, "That filthy *ben 'avah marduwth*! Son of a bitch!"

Filippos looked intently into Bacha's eyes, his own filling with tears, and continued, "He truly believed he destroyed our master, our teacher, our Yeshua. Ten years, he said. Ten years before Yeshua would be completely forgotten by mankind. Can you imagine that? He told me so. He bragged about it. But here we are, thirty years later. I ask you, Bacha, who is remembered and who is forgotten? He failed, I tell you. Nobody remembers that ben 'avah marduwth, but everyone remembers Yeshua. Everyone speaks about Yeshua almost as if he were still alive. The only thing that ben 'avah marduwth did was to kill Yeshua's body. "

Filippos was silent for a moment, and then continued. "Yeshua always used to say to us—remember? 'We are not the body. We are not the breath. We are not the mind. We always were, and we always will be.'" As he spoke, Filippos watched Bacha close his eyes and recite along with him with reverence, as if they were quoting scripture. Filippos continued after a brief pause, "I can still hear Yeshua saying that. For people like you and me, it's *faith*. It's something to *try* to believe. For Yeshua, it was merely a statement of fact. He was so certain, Bacha. So damned certain."

Filippos tasted salt on his lips and broke eye contact. He knew Bacha would not want to see him in tears. Instead, he gazed blurry-eyed at the long scar on Bacha's left arm, the scar that, in an odd way, had started Yeshua's incredible journey. He tried as best as he was able to keep his voice from wavering as he spoke. "I wish I had known him as long as you, Bacha. I wish I could have been in India with the two of you. I wish with all my heart that I had never done those things I did ... before."

Bacha turned toward him, and it appeared to Filippos that he looked straight into his heart and sensed the shame and the hurt inside. *Can Bacha do that, too?* Filippos thought. *Yeshua certainly had that power.* Bacha placed a strong hand on Filippos's shoulder. "In India, Yeshua and I learned that a sin need not be forgiven, only that it not be repeated. Patanjali even called them mistakes, not sins.

"At the end, you loved him too. You came to me to help him. You did everything you could to save his life and, truth be told, you almost did. Once you change direction, Filippos, once you begin walking down the *right* path, don't ever look back. He taught us that too. How I miss him as well." Bacha shook his head from side to side. "Oh, how I miss him."

The two aging men struggled to get up from the tree under which they were sitting. The sun had made its way to the west, and soon it would be dark. They leaned on each other as they slowly hobbled down the path toward Nazareth. A flock of birds in the vast reddish-orange sky before them created mesmerizing shapes and beautiful patterns in the air. There were thousands of birds, small dots in the sky suddenly merging into huge dark oval shapes, swirling around and around and, just as suddenly, splintering back into individual dots, like wisps of smoke dissolving into nothing. Back and forth they soared, sweeping the sky like a painter's brush, their endless shapes appearing and disappearing on the horizon as if by magic. Now they broke into two groups, each making a different pattern, only to majestically merge back into one. Bacha and Filippos paused and watched in wonder. It was as if the birds were dancing a ballet in celebration of the setting sun.

I. YESHUA

"Yeshua" is a Hebrew name, which has been transliterated into Greek. The English "Jesus" comes from the Latin transliteration of the Greek name.

Bethadonai.com

1 (The Samaritan and the Traveler)

It was midmorning near the town of Samaria on a cloudless sunny day, peaceful and serene, not at all the kind of day you would expect such a thing to happen. This part of Samaria was a mostly forested area filled with oak, carob, and pistachio, and a dense undergrowth of myrtle. The Samaritan hid in the tall green grass that lined the path on both sides, waiting for the traveler to pass by. He would never know what hit him. A short time ago he had spotted this person from behind, off in the distance. Even from this far back, he recognized the traveler as his adversary, and quickly moved off the road. Once there, he crouched and ran parallel to the road, as fast and as quietly as he could until he was way ahead of him. The tall grass kept him from being seen throughout his run. Now he waited. Now he was the predator awaiting the prey. He couldn't be sure that he hadn't been heard as he ran by. If so, his plan would be foiled. He held his breath as the traveler neared. He couldn't see him clearly through the grass, but he could hear his footsteps. His heart was beating fast as the traveler came closer. Now they were right next to one another. *He has no idea I'm here*, the Samaritan thought. *I have already won.* He silently waited as the sound of the footsteps moved past him. Now the traveler walked further down the path, unaware of the danger that awaited him. The Samaritan smiled.

Slowly, ever so slowly, he silently parted the grass and crept out into the road behind his victim, his muscles tense. The traveler seemed quite oblivious. And then, with a sudden burst of energy, the Samaritan swiftly ran, jumped, and tackled him, throwing him to the ground with a loud "Ha!"

"Leave me be, thief. I have no money," he heard the traveler yell.

"Yaish, what are you talking about?" Then, spinning him around face up, the Samaritan's eyes and mouth became wide like three huge circles as he gripped the sides of his own head with his hands. "What? You're not Yaish."

"Who are you? What do you want?" the traveler cried out. He was desperately trying to wiggle his way out from under the Samaritan who had him pinned quite soundly.

The Samaritan stood and sized up the stranger he had just subdued. "Who am I? Well, I say who are you? You are not from around here, of that I am certain."

The eleven year old child stood and brushed himself off. "My name is Yeshua, and whoever you are, you had no reason to do what you just did." His knees were bent, his hands resting on them, and he was breathing hard and fast as if he had been the one who had been running.

"Well, Yaish, uh, Yeshua, I'm sorry. But from the back you look just like my friend Yaish."

Yeshua caught his breath and straightened his body. "Well, if that is how you treat your friends, remind me never to become your enemy."

The two of them laughed, the tension broken. "Bacha, by the way," the Samaritan said. "My name is Bacha. Yehsua, follow me. There is a shady spot near some water, and we can sit and talk, uh, that is, if you want to talk. I wouldn't blame you if you didn't."

"No, I would like that, Bacha. Let's go to your shady spot and talk."

As they walked, Bacha explained, "Yaish and I are always sneaking up on each other and jumping on one another. He got me the last time near this very spot, and I vowed revenge. It's a little game we have played since we were children. That is why I did what I did. The two of you really do look alike from the back."

It was good to get out of the hot sun. They sat on two stumps in the shade of the forest, by the water, and cooled their feet in it. Bacha looked closely at Yeshua. No, from the front he definitely did not look like Yaish. He had black curly hair like Yaish, but that's where the similarity ended. Yeshua had a protruding nose, not flat like Yaish's. And his skin was light colored. Yaish's was a darker brown. Yaish had brown eyes, Yeshua had blue-gray ones.

"Where are you from, uh, Yeshua?"

"I am from Nazareth of Galilee. I have come here to meet Samaritans. You are the first."

Bacha's eyes and mouth opened once again. "You are from Galilee? And you come to Samaria? Are you crazy?"

A duck came out of the water and boldly walked toward the two boys. Yeshua bent down, scooped the duck into his lap and began nonchalantly petting it. The duck did not object, and nestled into Yeshua's arms.

"What? How did you do that just now? I've never seen anyone do that before. Why is that bird not flying away?" Bacha was moving his head back and forth, first staring at the duck, then staring at Yeshua, and then back to the duck again.

Yeshua smiled and said, "I have a way with animals, Bacha, birds in particular. I've always liked birds. But tell me why I am crazy for coming to Samaria?"

"Because they hate the Jews, that's why."

Yeshua looked at Bacha and tilted his head. "You are a Samaritan, Bacha. Do you hate me?"

Bacha picked up a stick and began to draw circles in the dirt, looking down as he drew. "Me? No, I don't hate anyone. But the others—well, many of the others, they don't like Jews. I hear the way they talk about Jews around town. Especially Jews not from Samaria. I would strongly advise you not to go there."

Now Bacha put the stick down and looked up toward his new friend. "Why did you come all the way here? You could have met Samaritans much closer to your Nazareth. Like Dothan. Why didn't you go there?"

Yeshua gently set the duck back into the water and the two watched as it paddled away from them, creating a graceful wake behind it. "I needed time to think, Bacha. I just needed some time to myself. And so I—I just kept walking."

Bacha understood this need well. Although he was only fourteen years old, he had the need to be alone many times. But sometimes he needed a friend. This was one of those times.

"Yeshua," Bacha said, "are you hungry? I live not far from here. You could eat with me. "

Yeshua's face brightened. "That would be wonderful. Will your parents mind?"

The smile on Bacha's face dropped. "I don't have parents. I live by myself."

As they walked, Yeshua put his arm on Bacha's shoulder. "I'm sorry, Bacha. I didn't mean to make you sad. What happened to them?"

Bacha quietly gathered his thoughts. "My mother died giving birth to me, and my father died five years ago, when I was only nine. When my father died, I went to live with my uncle. He seemed nice enough at first, but he drank. And when he got drunk he got very mean. He beat me, Yeshua, and I mean hard. And sometimes he would do worse. Do you see this scar on my left arm? He did that with a knife one night when he was drunk."

Yeshua gazed at the long, jagged scar that went from Bacha's elbow almost down to his wrist. He shivered and turned away.

Bacha continued. "And that's when I left him. I went into the forest and built a house. Well, I didn't build it all by myself, I had lots of help from some of my adult friends who look out for me. It's where I live now. We're almost there."

Bacha's house lay hidden inside a grove of trees. It was a simple square structure having one floor. It spanned about ten feet in each direction: length, width, and height. The height was actually only about eight feet, but a two-foot parapet wall surrounded the roof. The walls of the house were stone, and quite thick. Bacha told him it had taken him and his adult friends more than a year to build it. He had fully grown chickens, some baby chicks, and a lone rooster. When the baby chicks became old enough to produce eggs, he would use the rooster to produce new chicks and kill the older chickens for their meat. Meantime, with the rooster confined, he would have a daily supply of eggs. He would then repeat the process. Outside the grove of trees a garden thrived where he grew vegetables, melons, and wheat. The water they had cooled their feet in flowed nearby, and he would fish there often. He needed nothing more, and except for when he got lonely, he enjoyed living on his own.

"Do you ever get frightened?" Yeshua wanted to know.

"Never. Well, almost never. I used to worry that my uncle would come after me. So I made a plan to hide from him. Come, let me show you."

The two walked a short distance from the house, out of the woods, and near the bottom of one of the many hills of Samaria. "There it is, Yeshua."

Yeshua looked around. "There is what? I don't see anything."

Bacha laughed. "It's right there in front of you. Look again."

Yeshua looked around in vain.

Bacha walked to a pile of large rocks near the base of the hill and stooped down. He pulled aside a flat slab of nari stone, exposing a hole in the ground. It was big enough for someone to get into, crouch down, and pull the stone back over the hole. And the stone was light enough that one person could easily move it. Bacha showed Yeshua. Once he was inside and pulled the stone cover back in place, unless you knew what your were looking for, you saw nothing. Yeshua tried it for himself. "Perfect," Bacha called out after he had replaced the stone.

"Where did you find such a light stone?" asked Yeshua after he had crawled out.

"It was originally a tombstone I found not far from here, but the tomb had been robbed, and there was nothing inside. Because it was so light, I got the idea, and dragged it here. This is *my* tomb," Bacha said with a laugh.

The sun began to set, and Bacha said, "Yeshua, if you want, you can stay with me tonight. I have another mattress, and if you are hungry, we can have eggs and bread. I also have some figs."

"You are very kind, Bacha," Yeshua said. "Yes, I would like that very much."

After they ate, Bacha lit a lamp, and they talked long into the night. Although they had only met a few hours ago, they were forging a deep friendship and acted as if they had been together all their lives.

"What's it like having a mother?" Bacha asked. "I never had one, but I always wanted to learn what it was like."

Yeshua's voice quivered as he spoke. "Well, she's very pretty, especially her ears. She has a gentle voice, and when she laughs, her nose wiggles." Bacha waited to hear more, but Yeshua stopped talking.

"Go on. What's she like, Yeshua? I mean, what's it like to be with her?"

Now Yeshua's voice became loud and angry. "I can't really tell you more, Bacha. I have a mother, true, but she never has time for me.

Never! It's always, 'Yeshua, go see why your brother is crying; Yeshua, come and feed your sister; Yeshua, watch over your family, I need to go out.' Everybody in my family gets plenty of love and attention from my mother, but not me. I'm just the slave. She says it's because I'm the oldest. My stepfather is always either out on a job or working in his shop in the back of the house. He's a carpenter. But that's fine. We don't get along anyway. I wish my real father were still alive. He died before I was born. But my mother doesn't talk about him either, so I don't know what he was like. I'm sure he was better than my stepfather, though."

A brief silence settled over them. Bacha quietly started again. "We have much in common, you and I. My mother died during childbirth, and your father died before you were born. I have an uncle who I don't get along with, and you have a stepfather who you don't get along with. It seems like we both are not so lucky when it comes to parents. But you know what, Yeshua, living on your own, it's not such a bad thing. I have friends my age, and I have adult friends, plenty of them. And I'm happy. You should think about living on your own if you are so unhappy."

The sound of Bacha's voice seemed to calm Yeshua down. After finally finding nothing further to say, Bacha spread out Yeshua's mattress. It was filled with sheep's wool, and very soft. The gentle sounds of the forest—the crickets, the owls, the wind blowing through the trees, the distant howl of the occasional wolf—all merged into nature's nighttime song, putting Bacha and Yeshua to sleep.

2 (Yeshua begins his tale)

Yeshua awoke early in the morning and was momentarily confused by his new surroundings. Then he remembered. He had run away from home and was in Samaria. He had made a new friend, Bacha. He looked over to see Bacha still sleeping. Bacha had a long face with big ears, a round flat nose, and a mouth that seemed to be in a perpetual, toothy grin. He had short, thick, jet-black hair and was quite stocky. There was something about him that said "friendliness." Even in his sleep he looked like everyone's best friend.

Yeshua thought more about what had brought him here. He thought about two nights ago when he overhead his stepfather, Ephrayim, talking to Mara, his mother. Ephrayim was going to take Yeshua and his brother Jaaqob out of school for a year in order to save money. He vividly remembered overhearing his stepfather's words: "And it will only be for one year. If Yeshua wishes it, he can go back to school next year, and still help me part time. Yaaqob, too, if he so wishes. Between the two of them, for a full year I will have one full-time carpenter! We will make enough money to feed our family; both my oldest sons will learn a trade; and I might even have money enough to make a down payment on a workshop for my business."

Perhaps to spite his father, he chose Samaria to run away to. The people of Galilee despised the Samaritans, not even wanting to breathe the same air as they did. Yeshua did not know why. And so besides spiting his father, he would satisfy his curiosity. He would meet these Samaritans. Aside from his initial encounter, he found the first one he had met to be a very likable person.

Bacha awoke and grinned at Yeshua. "Did you sleep well?" he asked.

"I slept very well, Bacha. Thank you."

"Well, what are we going to do today?" Bacha's question seemed to Yeshua to be an invitation to stay longer.

"I'm happy to do anything you would like to do, my friend."

Bacha thought and then replied, "Let's eat first, and then, if you don't mind, I would like to learn more about you. Why did you come here? Why don't you get along with your parents? Won't they be worried about you? Things like that."

This was not what Yeshua would have opted to do, but he had make the offer, after all, and it was now too late to back out.

Bacha put some wood in the oven outside his house and began to make bread, just like Yeshua's mother made it. "Hey Yeshua, since you get along so well with birds, why don't you gather some eggs from the hens over there."

After retrieving four eggs, Yeshua returned, and the two sat down to eat. They had fresh-cooked bread, eggs boiled in water, a fresh melon, and some berries.

As they ate, Bacha began questioning Yeshua. "So tell me first of all, why did you run away?"

"Because I had to," Yeshua said loudly.

"Calm down, friend. You don't need to yell at me. I just asked a question."

He won't understand, Yeshua thought. *Nobody understands*. "I told you I don't get along with my stepfather, right? He has been trying and trying for three years to get me to learn carpentry. I hate carpentry. I hate it." His voice was rising again. "And I'm only eleven years old. He actually wanted me to become a carpenter at age eight. Can you imagine that?

"The only thing I like is going to school and learning the scriptures from Rabbi Towbiyah. It's what I'm really good at, Bacha. I love learning from him. We have great discussions about the Torah. But my stepfather was going to take me out of school and make me learn carpentry. He was going to take me away from the one thing I love the most and make me do the one thing I hate the most. That's why I ran away."

"And you couldn't talk to him about it? You couldn't make him understand?"

"No. He won't listen. He never listens." Yeshua's voice was even louder than before.

Bacha reached over and placed a hand on Yeshua's shoulder. "It's all right, Yeshua."

Something in Bacha's voice and demeanor calmed Yeshua down like no one had ever been able to before. Not even his mother.

"I'm sorry for yelling," Yeshua said in a much softer voice. "I have a hard time keeping from getting angry. I've had it as long as I can remember. Even when I was six. Even when I was five. I can't remember too much before then, but my earliest memories are of being angry."

"And so your stepfather was the main reason you ran away. Other than that, were you happy?"

Yeshua controlled his voice this time, although he still felt a little angry. "There is a bully in town named Efah. He always beats me up. He humiliates me in front of the other children. He spits on me."

"And do you fight back?"

"Bacha, I don't know how to fight. Besides, fighting with fists is not something I am interested in doing. I just want to be like all the other children. They think I am a bastard, you know. I'm not, but they all think I am. I don't know if you do this in Samaria, but in Galilee we are called by our father's name. My name would be 'Yeshua son of,' and then whatever my father's name was. My mother won't tell me what his name was, so I don't know what I would be called. But when someone wants to call you a bastard, they will use your mother's name instead, as if to say you don't have a father. Efah calls me 'Yeshua son of Mara.' And then the rest join in and call me the same thing. "

"And that's when you fight?"

"That's when I get beat up."

Bacha laughed, but stopped when he saw the distraught look on Yeshua's face. "I'm sorry for laughing at you, Yeshua. But won't your mother and stepfather be worrying about you right now? Have you ever run away before?"

"Yes, I ran away once before. And yes, they are probably worried about me. But—but I just don't care. Well, I care what my mother thinks but not my stepfather."

Yeshua took a deep breath and then began to tell Bacha things he had never told anyone before.

11

3 (A week earlier)

Nazareth, Israel
AD 8 - Yom Rishon (Sunday)
Yeshua's age: 11

Will this be the day it happens? One day is all I ask, Lord. Just one day without anger.

Yeshua sat in his classroom at the top of a hill, two miles outside of Nazareth, and set his resolve.

"Yeshua!" Rabbi Towbiyah abruptly interrupted his thoughts. "Please tell us where the following comes from, and what it means: 'Life for life, eye for eye, tooth for tooth, hand for hand, foot for foot.'" The rabbi was fat, like Yeshua's Uncle Yo'el, with silver hair and an equally silver beard. He paced in front of the class as he spoke, his belly bouncing up and down, his face drawn into a childish grin.

Yeshua stood and stretched his spine, making himself as tall as he possibly could, thrust his chest out, folded his arms, and lifted his head with an authoritative air. He replied in a boisterous voice, "Rabbi, you forgot 'burning for burning, wound for wound, stripe for stripe.' It comes from Shemot, the second scroll of the Torah, and it has to do with vengeance."

There were five rows of five chairs in the classroom and a long table in front of each row. Yeshua always sat in the aisle seat in the front row, nearest to the rabbi, and more often than not, there were several empty seats between him and the next boy. He looked around the classroom for approval, but was met only with the other boys' rolling eyes. He once again saw that his memory and knowledge of the Torah would impress no one but Rabbi Towbiyah. Such was always the case. But arguing scripture with the rabbi was one of his few pleasures.

"Vengeance?" Rabbi Towbiyah prompted with lifted brows. "Vengeance, you say?"

Yeshua was ready and eager to engage him. The rabbi always argued with him and questioned him more than any of the other boys in class.

"Well, it is written in Shemot that if two men are fighting, and by accident they hit a woman who is growing a baby inside her, and that baby is born before its time, the woman's husband may go to the judge and ask for money. The judge will decide if the price he asks is fair, and if it is, the man who hit her has to pay that amount to the husband. But if something really bad happens, such as the baby or the mother dying, then the man must be given a punishment equal to all the hurt he has caused. More than just money—vengeance. He will be put to death. Eye for eye. Life for life. This is plainly wrong."

"Why do you say that?" the rabbi asked, no longer grinning.

Yeshua took no notice of the change in the rabbi's demeanor. "If the baby dies, the man is guilty. Of that there is no doubt. Punishment is warranted. But to kill a man for something he did by accident is not fair punishment."

The rabbi's eyes narrowed and he spoke sternly. "These are the laws of God that have been handed down to us by Moshe. They are to be obeyed, Yeshua, not questioned."

It was happening again. It welled up deep inside him. Anger. Raw anger. He did not understand where it came from, but as far back as he could remember, which wasn't very far for a child of eleven, he had harbored this feeling. He had been angry at one time or another at most of the adults in his life and many of his peers. It invariably happened when they told him he was wrong. But this time he caught himself. He saw that he was breathing hard—the first sign that he was going to yell or shout—and he took a deep breath. He would not let the anger overpower him now because he was trying to go a whole day without it happening. But he wasn't going to back down either.

He took his most authoritative stance, shook back his curly black hair with a toss of his head, and pierced the rabbi's eyes with his own bluish-gray ones. "Where is it written, Rabbi, that on the Sabbath, picking grain to eat is 'work,' and therefore a sin?" Yeshua often did not come straight to the point. His first words would sometimes seem to answer an unasked question.

He continued, "It would seem that the laws of God today are what the Pharisees say they are, not what Moshe said. Moshe told us that it was a sin to work on the Sabbath, but it was the Pharisees that told us that picking grain to eat was work. The Pharisees argue about the laws of Moshe all the time and often contradict one another, do they not? Who is right? Who is wrong?

"Moshe never said that a man should be put to death for accidentally causing a baby to be born dead. The Pharisees said that. This is vengeance, not justice. I say that even if the baby is born dead, killing the man who hit her doesn't bring the baby back. I think his own shame and guilt over what he has done is punishment enough. Don't you?"

There was an uncomfortable silence in the class. All the other boys were looking at one another. Yeshua felt his face growing hot. *What have I said wrong? Why is everyone so quiet?*

After a moment, Rabbi Towbiyah shifted his stance and began again. "And yet, you are now doing what you accuse the ... Pharisees are doing, are you not? Who is interpreting the laws of Moshe now?"

Yeshua's face remained hot, and he noticed the whole classroom leaning forward as if to hear his every word.

"Tell me, Yeshua, I hear that Efah sometimes picks on you after school. If he strikes your right cheek without reason, do you want him to be brought to justice according to the laws of Moshe, or would you too interpret his laws differently? Perhaps you would simply turn your left cheek as well?"

Yeshua bristled at the mention of Efah's name. He was one of the older boys who came to class later in the day. Yeshua raised his voice, close to yelling, but not quite. "He does more than hit me on the right cheek, Rabbi. He also calls me the son of Mara!" Since his stepfather, Ephrayim, was not his real father, Yeshua did not wish to be called the son of Ephrayim, and had never called himself that, but even *that* would be preferable to the spiteful way in which Efah used his mother's name to essentially call him a bastard.

This brought a round of laughter from the rest of the classroom and a stiffening of Yeshua's posture. He turned toward the class and stomped his foot hard on the ground as if to silence them, which only made them laugh harder. He had lost his daily battle. The morning had hardly begun, and he was already seething with anger.

Yeshua's mother had told him that she was carrying him inside her when her husband—his real father—died. He was aware that most of Nazareth didn't believe that she had ever been married, but he believed what she claimed. She never spoke about his father to him, or to anyone else, though he longed to learn more about him. He didn't even know his real father's name. Whenever he asked her about him, she simply said that his father was in heaven, and that was that.

"Quiet, children," admonished the rabbi, "Quiet! So, Yeshua, according to the laws of Moshe, what should then be done to Efah? Tell us."

Losing his internal struggle with anger made him momentarily unable to think. "I ... I don't know, Rabbi. But I know that vengeance is wrong." Then, quickly regaining his composure, he added with conviction, "We are told so by the Lord in the scrolls of Devarim, Rabbi: 'It is Mine to avenge; I will repay. In due time their foot will slip; their day of disaster is near and their doom rushes upon them.'"

Rabbi Towbiyah sighed and slowly shook his head from side to side as he often did when Yeshua used scripture to answer the argument but missed the point. He placed his pudgy hand gently on Yeshua's shoulder. It suddenly became clear to Yeshua. This was not about Efah at all. It was about the Pharisees. In the course of their discussion, and in his verbal contempt toward the Pharisees, he had insulted his teacher in front of the rest of the class. Rabbi Towbiyah was, after all, a devout Pharisee. Too late for an apology. Yeshua bowed his head.

Yeshua was sullen for the remainder of the school day. Whenever Efah's name was mentioned, it brought up memories of past beatings that gave him knots in his stomach.

***

As Yeshua walked home from school, these unhappy thoughts of his last encounter with Efah continued to run through his mind. His friend David walked along side him. Like most of the other children whose parents allowed them to speak to Yeshua, David would be kind and friendly when they were alone together, but if they were in a group and Efah began his taunts, David often joined in.

It was just two days ago, that Yeshua and David had walked down this same hill as Efah and his friends were walking up it. Efah was a bully, plain and simple. His face was long, like someone had stretched it, and he seemed to wear a perpetual scowl. He had a mean streak that always turned in Yeshua's direction. He remembered it clearly. Efah began his favorite taunt:

"Hey Yeshua, where is your father?

"Whom are you the son of?"

And then in a singsong voice, "Yeshua, son of Mara! Yeshua, son of Mara! "

As he continued the refrain, Efah's friends joined in. Other children who heard the noise came to watch, and after looking at each other and back at Efah, they too joined in. Even David added his voice.

Yeshua, son of Mara! Yeshua, son of Mara! Yeshua, son of Mara! Ha-ha-ha-ha!"

Yeshua was so enraged that he screamed, his face burning, and ran headlong into yet another beating from Efah. As in all the previous beatings, Yeshua did not know how to fight and just tried to shake Efah, but it ended the same way—him lying on the ground with Efah standing over him.

And then came the worst part. "Accch—ptoo!" Efah bent his sneering face close to Yeshua's and loudly spat on him, causing the rest of the boys to laugh and cheer and wave their arms. Once they had all left, Yeshua rolled on his side, drew his knees to his chest and his head to his knees, wrapped his arms around his shins and cried, not from the physical pain, but from the humiliation.

What am I to do? he thought as this unhappy memory of two days ago repeated itself over and over. *They are all against me. Not just Efah and his friends—everyone. Even David sometimes. If I tell Mother or my stepfather, they would surely speak to Efah's parents, and that would only make it worse for me when I saw him again. What am I to do?*

"Yeshua," David said, "tell me a *mashal*." This brought Yeshua out of his foul mood. He was now the *other* Yeshua—not the angry one but the kind and gentle one who only those close to him saw. He turned to David and smiled, placing his arm around him.

At least David is my friend, Yeshua thought. Then, correcting himself: *At least today he is my friend.*

Yeshua loved the mashals, or parables, contained in the scriptures, and he loved to tell and explain them. But many were too complicated to explain to David, because very few eleven-year-old boys understood them as well as Yeshua did. The two boys settled beside the road, in the shade of a tree. Yeshua thought of a simple mashal from the prophet Yesha'yahu and quoted it.

Shall the plowman plow all day to sow? Shall he open and harrow his soil? Is it not so? When he smoothes its surface, he scatters the black cumin and casts the cumin, and he places the prominent wheat, and the barley for a sign, and the spelt on its border. And He shall chasten him justly, he whose God directs him. For not with a grooved implement is black cumin threshed, neither does a wagon wheel turn around on cumin, but black cumin is beaten with a staff and cumin with a rod. Bread grain is crushed but it is not threshed forever, and the wheel of his wagon shall break, and its separators, he does not crush it. This too comes forth from the Lord of Hosts: He gave marvelous counsel, made great wisdom.

"What does it mean, Yeshua? Tell me. I don't understand farming." David always asked Yeshua to explain things to him, which made him a special friend. And perhaps this was why Yeshua had never asked him about why he joined in with the other children when they were making fun of him. Maybe he just wanted to keep this part of their relationship intact.

"David, you tell me you like to watch your mother cook. Tell me how she makes her bread."

David was quiet for a moment, and then he said, "Well, first she takes some flour. Then she takes some water. Then she mixes them together."

Yeshua interrupted him to ask, "Is the water heated first, or is it cold?"

"It is cold, of course. She adds some salt, just a little, and kneads it until it is smooth. If it is too sticky, she adds more flour. If it is too dry, she adds more water. She lets it rest for a short time, and then she pinches off a small amount and flattens and stretches it into a really thin round. Once she has about three or four rounds, she puts them in the oven."

Again Yeshua interrupted. "Does she heat the oven first, or does she put the rounds in the oven and then heat it?"

"She heats the oven first, of course. The bread has to be put in a hot oven, or it will not bake right."

"Does she cook the bread for the same amount of time it takes for you and me to walk from the temple to our houses?"

"No! It would burn if she left it in that long. It is a much shorter time before the bread is crisp. She knows exactly when to take it out of the oven."

Yeshua smiled. "So you see, David, everything she does has to be done in the right order and for the right amount of time, or the bread will not turn out right. The farmer has to do things right, too. The prophet Yesha'yahu says the black cumin is beaten out with a staff, not threshed. Otherwise, it won't turn out right. Just like your mother's bread wouldn't turn out right if she put it in a cold oven, or if she let it cook too long."

"Yes. I see that now, Yeshua. But what does it mean?"

Yeshua continued. "The prophet Yesha'yahu is telling us that God also does things very carefully and in the right order, and instructs us to do the same. You and I might not understand why something is happening, but it *has* to happen that way. If something bad happens today, we might not understand why, but maybe in time, something good will come to pass. And that good thing could not have happened unless that bad thing happened first."

"How can something good come of something bad?"

Yeshua thought for a minute. "When I was only six, I heard the screams of my mother giving birth to my sister. Mother was in our sleeping chambers on the second floor and I was on the ground floor. But I heard the screams. She was in great pain at that time, and it frightened me. Is pain a good thing, David? Maybe you think not. But soon, my sister was born and mother was no longer in pain. Now she is happy. It has to happen in that order. That's what the prophet Yesha'yahu is saying to us. Remember the last words of the mashal: 'This too comes forth from the Lord of Hosts: He gave marvelous counsel, made great wisdom.'"

Now David understood. Yeshua could make more sense than Rabbi Towbiyah, or the prophet Yesha'yahu for that matter. Sometimes even Yeshua had trouble understanding the prophet Yesha'yahu.

They sat in silence for a moment. Yeshua thought, *I have to ask*.

"David?"

David cocked his head.

"Why did you make fun of me with the other boys when Efah taunted me two days ago?"

David bowed his head as if looking for something on the ground.

"Come on, David. Tell me."

David stood suddenly, stared at Yeshua, and raised his voice. "Why can't you be this way—the way you are with me right now *all* the time, Yeshua? Why do you always have to act so ... so superior in the classroom?"

Yeshua stood as well. "What do you mean, superior?"

"You know what I mean. You puff up your chest and lift your head like you were the rabbi instead of Rabbi Towbiyah. You know all the answers. And you let everyone in class know that you know all the answers. You act like you are better than us. But you're not."

"I don't mean to, David. But when it comes to scripture, well, I ... I really do know all the answers. They just come into my head. I don't even have to think. Rabbi Towbiyah challenges me, and I enjoy the challenge."

"Well, I hate it when you are like that, Yeshua. I hate you at those times. That's why I join in with the others." David pushed Yeshua away from him.

Yeshua's anger burst forth. "Yeah? Well at least I don't make fun of you for being short."

"Yeah? Well at least I have a father!"

David turned and ran. Yeshua stood in shock as he watched his only friend running away from him. Hot tears burned in his eyes as a lump of regret formed in his throat. *Have I lost another friend?* He slowly made his way home, a heaviness in his body, and a knot deep in his stomach.

***

As Yeshua walked into the house, his mother was waiting for him with some bread and honey. Her face glowed a little more than usual after baking the bread, and Yeshua took notice. He guessed she was pregnant again, although she hadn't yet begun to show. He knew all the signs. He already had three younger brothers—Yaaqob, seven; Yosef, six; Shimon, four; and one sister, Miryam, aged three—so he had seen the changes in his mother before and was old enough to remember them.

"Yeshua, this afternoon I need you to watch the children. Your father is busy, and I need to go to Esav's farm to buy some food."

Another chore, he thought. Being the oldest child, Yeshua bore more responsibility than his siblings. He resented that his mother never had time for him, save for handing him a piece of bread and then giving him a task. For as long as he could remember, she was either pregnant or caring for her newest baby. It seemed to him that the only attention he got from her was being asked to help with chores. Not that he minded helping; he just wanted some of what his mother seemed to have in abundance for her younger offspring.

Yaaqob and Yosef, who were also in the room, stared at him without saying anything. He felt like a stranger, not a brother, as he glanced over at them. If he felt close to any of his siblings, it was probably Yaaqob. They often played the mill game together, using stones and lines in the dirt, and during these times Yeshua enjoyed being with his nearest brother. But as close as they were, Yeshua still felt disconnected. Whenever Yaaqob played with his friends at being adults, he got to call himself "Yaaqob, son of Ephrayim." And although Yeshua hated the taunts of the other children, "Yeshua, son of Mara," he would never refer to himself as "son of Ephrayim," because he was not. He wanted to be the son of someone, but he didn't even know his own father's name. His mother had never shared that with him. And so Yaaqob would always be the son of Ephrayim, and Yeshua was the son of no one—except Mara.

"Oh, and Yeshua, your father wants to talk to you," his mother said in a slow and very firm voice as Yeshua sat in the front doorway eating his bread and honey. He kept eating, but felt his stomach churning. Whenever his mother used *that* tone, he sensed what was coming.

He finished his bread and slowly walked around back where his stepfather was busy building a table. "Hand me that hammer, Yeshua," Ephrayim said without looking up.

"Yes, sir." he replied, handing Ephrayim the hammer and immediately stepping back.

He never said, "Yes, father," although he was well aware of how much strain his words carried. Ephrayim showed no reaction to this.

"Yeshua, come sit by me. We need to talk."

Yeshua sat as far away from Ephrayim as he could without displaying disrespect.

"Yeshua," he began, "you are now eleven years old. It is time for you to stop fighting me and learn the carpentry trade. You are my oldest son, and it is fitting for you to follow in my footsteps, as I followed in my own father's footsteps at your age."

Yeshua looked his stepfather in the eye and shook his hair back. "I am my mother's oldest son. Yaaqob is *your* oldest son. Why not let Yaaqob follow in your footsteps?"

"Yaaqob will also be my apprentice. But you are the eldest. I will first teach you what you will need to survive. Unless you have a trade, you will have no food to eat. Is that what you want? Do you want to starve to death?"

Yeshua folded his arms and tilted his head. "Have you not seen the birds in the fields? They have no trade, and yet they have food to eat and a warm place to raise their children. They know that God will provide for them."

Ephrayim was beginning to breathe faster, his face turning red, his voice rising. "Yeshua, we are grateful for the help that God gives us. But one way that God helps us is to give us the ability to help ourselves. We learn a trade, we earn money, and we provide for our family."

"And so shall I. But it will not be as a carpenter."

Ephrayim slammed his hammer down on his workbench. "You will be a carpenter. You are my son, and I am now telling you, not asking you. I will teach. You will learn."

Yeshua's voice too got very loud. "I will not learn. I will never be a carpenter."

As both their voices got louder and louder, Yeshua glanced over his shoulder into the house and watched his mother crying as she always did when the two of them argued, then he looked back to where his stepfather had just been. Ephrayim stomped away, shouting, and gesturing with his hands. Yeshua headed to the roof. He spent a good deal of his time on the roof.

Something inside Yeshua told him that carpentry was not his destiny. He had no idea what his destiny was, only what it wasn't.

What he really wanted right now was to just be a normal child, like his brother Yaaqob. His classmates would not be his friends, so he had no playmates, his mother would not give him her affection because she was too busy with his little sister, and his stepfather wanted him to be a man. A man? He was only eleven years old!

4 (Yeshua confronts the bully)

As Yeshua sat on the roof, calming himself down from this incident, his thoughts turned from his stepfather back to Efah. His stepfather he seemed to be able to sidestep, but Efah? Efah was different. He thought of the sixteenth Mishlei Shlomo. In verse seven it said: "When a man's ways please the Lord, he makes even his enemies to be at peace with him." *I do try to please the Lord. Well, I do argue with my stepfather, and that probably doesn't please Him. But in other ways I try to please the Lord. So why is Efah not at peace with me? Perhaps the Lord wants me to first make peace with Efah? And if it works with Efah, maybe I can do the same thing with my stepfather.*

The more he thought about it, the more he thought this would be the right course of action. *I will have to find Efah alone, though. He will be home from school by now.*

Yeshua knew that Efah's home was just south of Nazareth, near the border of Samaria. Yeshua and David had once gone to the border in hopes of seeing a Samaritan. Many awful stories had been told about Samaritans, and he and David wanted to see one. They both wondered if Samaritans looked different than they did. They never did see one, but on the journey back they saw Efah going into his house. They were glad Efah didn't see them.

Yeshua quietly came down the ladder to see if his stepfather was still gone. He was. "Where are you going, Yeshua? " Mara asked as he started toward the door.

"I'm just going out for a walk, Mother," Yeshua replied with a half-truth.

Mara started to say something, and then stopped. After a pause she said, "Fine, but don't be too long. It will be dark soon."

Yeshua nodded his head and walked quickly out the door. His mother was right. It would be dark soon, so he had only a short time to accomplish his goal.

What will I say to him? Yeshua thought as he walked south at a quick pace. *"Efah, I have come to make peace with you." No, that's no good. "Efah, it is time for us to talk." That's better. And then what do I say? I just don't know. Maybe it's better to just wait until I see him, and say the first thing I think of.* Yeshua continued in this manner all the way to the house Efah lived in.

As Yeshua arrived he saw that Efah was with several friends and it looked like they were doing some planning. Efah would say something, and they would all nod their heads and laugh. He quickly hid behind a tree and waited for his heart to stop pounding in his chest. After a moment, Yeshua quietly moved from tree to tree, getting nearer and nearer, trying his best not to be seen. He stopped when he was close enough to hear what they were saying and listened intently.

Efah told his friends, "I'll start with 'Son of Mara,' and you all join in, as usual, and then when I say 'Now,' we all jump him. Everybody gets to hit him once. Make it a good one—a really good one. We'll send the bastard Yeshua home looking like he was attacked by wolves! Even his mother won't recognize him."

Efah and each of his friends stood in a circle and held their fists in the air, one touching the other. "Tomorrow, Efah, tomorrow." they all said as they left.

One of them was heading straight toward the tree Yeshua was behind. With no time to hide somewhere else, Yeshua shuffled around the tree to the other side as Efah's friend approached. He wasn't seen, but he realized he was now in clear sight of Efah. His heart began to pound again. Efah's friend was almost out of sight, but if Efah looked his way, he would be found out.

So be it, he finally thought. *This is what I came here for. And now he is alone.*

Yeshua took a deep breath and walked straight toward Efah. Efah turned, jumped back, stopped, and then sneered. "Son of Mara? I was just talking about you. Did you come all the way over here for a beating?"

"I didn't come here to fight you, Efah."

Efah folded his arms. "Well? What then?"

Yeshua answered, "I came to talk."

Efah boldly stuck his finger on Yeshua's nose. "You and I have nothing to talk about."

"We have to talk about fighting. Efah, why must you always fight with me? I have done nothing to you. From the first day you came to school you have been fighting with me."

Efah placed his hands on his hips. "Fight with you? Hah! It's only a fight if you fight back."

Yeshua held his hands out on either side of him, palms face up. "But I don't even know how to fight, Efah."

"I know. And I keep trying to teach you, but you just don't learn."

Smack! Efah suddenly slapped Yeshua hard across his cheek. Yeshua rubbed at the sting on the side of his face, his eyes and mouth wide open in disbelief.

"See? Even now you don't learn. Now go back home before I teach you some more."

Efah lunged toward Yeshua, fists drawn, and Yeshua backed up, quickly turned and walked away hoping Efah would not jump him. He turned and started to say something about knowing what Efah and his friends were up to, but thought better of it.

Efah was just standing there staring at him. "See you tomorrow, Son of Mara," Efah shouted. "Be ready to learn." He laughed as he swaggered to his house.

Yeshua was shaking as he walked. Efah always scared him. *What now?* he thought. *I can't go to school tomorrow. What am I going to do?*

It was rapidly getting dark so Yeshua quickened his pace. *I'll just have to talk to Mother. She'll know what to do.*

5 (Yeshua's mother and father)

After Yeshua left for his walk, Mara sat at her favorite table, sewing the holes in her children's tunics. The late afternoon sun threw long shafts of light through the windows and onto the table.

Ephrayim had returned shortly after Yeshua left. He seemed to Mara to be calmer. He came in from his workshop and Mara paused a moment to look at him. He was still a very handsome man despite being eleven years older than when they had wed. She loved his long, rugged face and his large grayish eyes with deep wrinkle lines on the outside of each, etched from many years squinting into the sun. She loved that he kept his thick black hair and beard cut short. She loved his muscular body and deep voice. But Mara noticed changes in him that were worrisome.

Ephrayim looked over to see her gazing intensely at him, and he furrowed his brow.

"Ephrayim, my love, what has been troubling you lately?" Mara asked.

"What do you mean?" Ephrayim folded his arms and stared at Mara, the color rising in his cheeks.

"Sit, my love, and I will tell you," she answered calmly.

The two sat at the table that Ephrayim had made long ago, the setting of many discussions between the two of them over the years, both pleasant and unpleasant.

Mara pushed her sewing to the side of the table and began. "My love, you used to be so kind to everyone. It was one of the things I loved so much about you. Now ... now you argue with Yeshua all the time and you only show kindness to your new wealthy friends."

Ephrayim's voice became hard. "I argue with my son because he argues with me. He is disrespectful. As for the wealthy, I show kindness to them because we will be wealthy one day."

Mara looked down at the table for a moment and then back up at Ephrayim.

"Yes, my love, we will be wealthy one day. But in the meantime, you ignore the friends we already have."

"No I don't!" Ephrayim replied, avoiding making eye contact.

"You don't? When did you last invite Yaanay—your best friend who helped you so much last summer—to dinner?"

"I haven't invited him to dinner for a while? That means nothing. I haven't seen him for a while."

Mara continued to probe. "When is the last time you invited *any* of your old friends to the house, Ephrayim? We always used to have old friends over."

Ephrayim raised his voice. "You don't understand. If we are to become wealthy, we need to seek new friends—rich friends, people who can be *useful* to us."

Now Mara raised her voice. "And I say to you those people you speak of are not your friends. Trust me. These are the kinds of people I grew up with. I know how they are. I know how they think. They are not your friends. They are not *our* friends."

"Enough! I will hear no more of this. They *are* my friends."

Ephrayim rose from his chair and went to the window; his body tight with anger. Mara went over to him and slowly placed her hands around his waist. Usually he would immediately relax when she did that, but not this time. She tried again.

"Ephrayim, let's not fight. Of course you can have friends who are rich. But let's not forget about Yaanay and the others, all right? They are decent people, and they are my friends, too. You know I don't have many friends in Nazareth."

"You don't understand. I am doing all this for *you*, Mara. One day, when we are rich and living in Sepphoris in a big house, your parents will rue the day they abandoned you."

"Is that what all this is about? My parents are my fight, not yours! Leave them out of your decisions. Whether I choose to be angry with them, or if I forgive them—it's my business. You leave them out of this."

Ephrayim wrested himself from her arms and turned to face her. "You speak to me just like Yeshua does. So now my wife *and* son are against me! We will be rich, Mara. We will live in Sepphoris ... in a big house!"

Mara's body stiffened at the mention of Yeshua. "And *why* do you think he speaks to you the way he does? *Why* do you think he refuses to be your apprentice?"

Ephrayim shook an angry finger at the sky. "Because he is a disrespectful child, that's why."

"Or could it be that he sees through your wealthy friends as easily as I do? Could it be that he wants no part of them? Could it be that *you* are becoming like them and because of that, he wants no part of you? Ask him, Ephrayim. Go ahead, ask him. Ask Yeshua!"

"Ask me what?" Yeshua stood in the doorway looking from one parent to the other. Ephrayim and Mara had no idea how long he had been there, or how much he had overheard.

"We'll speak of this later!" Ephrayim said with a tone of finality in his voice. Yeshua quickly stepped to the side as Ephrayim brushed by him, stormed outside, and once again walked brusquely away from the house with a quickening pace.

"Ask me what?" Yeshua now looked to his mother.

***

Yeshua, having returned from his confrontation with Efah, had been quietly standing in the doorway for some time and listened to almost the entire argument. His mother was right. He hated the strange new rich people his stepfather kept inviting over, and he wanted nothing to do with them.

Only a week ago he heard his stepfather talking unkindly about other people—poor people. Yeshua had never gotten to know a poor person—they mostly lived in another part of town and kept to themselves—but the other day he noticed a poor man walking near the house. He wore dirty clothes and looked pale and sickly. Ephrayim pointed to him and said to Yeshua and his mother, "Look at him! What a waste. If he doesn't want to be poor, all he has to do is work. I started working with my father when I was eight years old. And I have worked every day since. Poor people don't *want* to work. That's the problem. Don't ever go near them, Yeshua. They're crazy. Mean as they are dirty."

"Mother," Yeshua began, "I have something important I need to talk to you about."

"Waaaaah!" Miryam, who had been upstairs napping, suddenly awoke, perhaps roused from sleep by the angry voices below, and began to cry. Mara looked outside for her husband, then she looked at Yeshua, and then with her baby's crying growing more and more intense, she looked to the ladder. Three people needed her at the same time. She picked Miryam. "Yeshua, I ... can we talk later?" she said as she began to climb the ladder. "We'll talk later, I promise."

After a moment, he quietly climbed the ladder enough to see her breast-feeding. Yeshua loved looking at his mother in secret. It wasn't her breasts he looked for; it was her face. Her nose was slightly upturned, unlike Yeshua's, and she parted her hair in the middle, pulling it back to expose her ears. He thought she had pretty ears. Her blue eyes forever gazed at some distant point as if she were watching something far away. Her warm smile was often accompanied by that strange and faraway look in her eye. Her voice was kind, even when she told Yeshua what to do. But it seemed to him, even with her kind voice, that he heard an awful lot of, "We'll talk later."

***

Ephrayim sat on a rock and looked out over the evening countryside, not seeming to take in the beauty of the vista before him. A family of deer was grazing in the distance. The clouds overhead had turned a majestic shade of purple. The fragrance of flowers was everywhere. But all Ephrayim could think about was his wife and oldest son, who didn't seem to understand what he was trying to do for them.

He looked up to see his friend Yannay standing before him. "What's the matter, Ephrayim? You look just like you looked the morning after you and I drank all that wine last summer. Remember?" He was smiling at Ephrayim, but Ephrayim was not in the mood for laughing.

Ephrayim hesitated, wondering what, if anything, he should say to him. But he and Yannay had been through much together, and Ephrayim needed to talk to someone. He beckoned Yannay to sit on a nearby rock, and the two faced each other.

"Yannay, what am I to do? I have five children already and another on the way. How will I feed them unless I make more money than I am now making? I barely make enough right now. What if Mara has another child after this one?"

Yaanay took his sandals off and began to massage his feet. He did that often when they sat. After some time, he said, "Ephrayim, you are a good carpenter, the best I have ever known. You are also a good leader. You know how to inspire workers, myself included, to work hard and get things done. So why don't you find and manage your own projects instead of working for others? Wouldn't that get you the money you need to feed your growing family?"

"You think I haven't thought of that myself, Yaanay? But it seems that to make money these days, you need to first *have* money. I need a bigger workshop. I need a stock of wood and tools. And then, I need to secure those projects you speak of. To do that, I need a reputation. I need to convince others—others with money—that I am capable.

"I invite them to my house. I serve them my wine. I share my dinner table with them. And I am learning to talk they way they talk. But whenever I talk of money, they change the subject. And whenever I try to set money aside, my wife tells me we need the money to feed and educate the children."

Yaanay was a good listener. He knew there was more coming, and so he silently continued to massage his feet as he maintained eye contact with Ephrayim.

"And then there is Yeshua. He refuses to learn carpentry. When I was only eight years old my father began to teach me his trade. I have tried the same with Yeshua, but for the past year he has done nothing but defy me. I don't know how to deal with someone like Yeshua. He is smart beyond his years and always knows how to evade me."

Yaanay put his sandals back on, stood, and placed a strong hand on Ephrayim's shoulder. "My friend, you are the smartest man I know. There is no doubt that you will find a way to feed your family. As to your son, believe me you are not the only person with defiant children. They all learn very early in life what angers their parents, and then they proceed to use that knowledge. I would love to sit here and talk with you more. I haven't seen you in many months and thought you were avoiding me for some reason. But I need to go home while there is still some light. Come visit me any time and we can talk further."

As he disappeared from sight, Ephrayim smiled. In those short moments he had lost most of his anger. *Mara is right. I have been neglecting my old friends*, he thought. *I must invite him to my house again. Mara would like that.*

He sat on his rock and just for a lingering moment longer he dreamt about his business, his obedient children, and his house in Sepphoris—his big house in Sepphoris.

6 (First encounter with the poor)

Yeshua lay awake all that night; the knots in his stomach grew tighter and tighter as he imagined the day that was coming for him. His mother did not make the time for him to discuss his problem with Efah. His stepfather was still angry with him, and he would rather not talk to Ephrayim about it anyway. He tossed and turned for hours before finally crawling up the ladder to the roof. In the heat of the summer, the whole family slept on the roof because it was much cooler than inside the house. But Yeshua would sleep there even when it was cold. He enjoyed the solitude. On the roof, by himself under the brilliant star-filled night sky, he could think.

It was a clear, cool autumn night, the moon almost full. Yeshua knew he would not sleep tonight. How could he face his classmates in the morning knowing they would come for him after class?

For company on this lonely night, he had brought his little pet sparrow to the roof. He looked inside the small box he kept the bird in and wondered what to do. He momentarily distracted himself from his problems with a happy memory. A few weeks earlier, he had been looking for berries in the forest when he had spied the sparrow hopping around with a broken wing. With gentle hands, he'd picked it up and brought it home with him.

"Mother, look. I found a bird that cannot fly. I'm going to help him. Mother, what do sparrows eat?"

"I don't know what sparrows eat, Yeshua," his mother had replied to his questions as she held his sister. "Why don't you go watch them and find out?"

So Yeshua watched the sparrows and saw that they ate worms and bugs and seeds, and that they drank water. He kept his broken-winged sparrow in a box, and he fed it every day. He even had a name for it: Doren, which means "gift."

Now his mind turned back to Efah. Just before daybreak, Yeshua finally decided he would need to run away, at least for the day.

***

Yom Sheni (Monday)

"Goodbye, Doren," he said as he snuck out of the house before anyone else had awoken. The sparrow eyed him suspiciously.

Yeshua wandered through the mostly empty streets of Nazareth and into the nearby countryside. He loved Galilee because of the many fruit-bearing trees dotting the hillsides. Sycamore trees bearing fig-like fruits, and carob and pistachio trees. Almond trees, quinces, and date palms. There was always something falling to the ground to eat. The scent of myrtle blended with anemones, crocuses, and narcissi, filling his nostrils as he walked through the colorful hills and valleys.

Yet, despite the beauty that surrounded him, Yeshua thought only of his loneliness. His shoulders slumped and he felt a deep hollowness in his chest. How he ached to have friends. Each time he argued with Rabbi Towbiyah in class, he secretly hoped the other children would flock to him after school to ask him questions about the Torah. David asked him questions, true, but he was the only one. Yeshua sighed. At least he would not get a beating today. His parents would be angry with him for running away, but that wouldn't happen until later.

Yeshua walked all morning, lost in his own despair. The sun rose high in the sky, and he suddenly felt very hungry. He found berries and ate some figs, drank water from a stream, and sat down under a tree. He hadn't slept all the previous night, and soon he fell asleep, soundly, and for a very long time.

When he woke he was surprised to find it was almost evening; he hadn't planned on being away from home this late. More surprisingly, a small boy stared at him. It took Yeshua a moment to remember his own circumstance. After a long pause, he asked the boy, "Who are you?"

The child replied, "Elan."

"What are you doing way out here in the woods?"

"Waiting for my father to come back." Elan continued to stare.

"Where did your father go?"

"He went with the others. They went to find food."

Yeshua stood up and looked more closely at Elan. The child—Yeshua guessed him to be about six years old—was wearing old and tattered clothes, almost rags. He just stood there and kept staring at Yeshua, waiting for him to speak again.

"Do you live around here?" Yeshua asked.

"We are unclean and live in the forest. Do you live in the forest too?"

Yeshua didn't understand what the boy meant. He replied, "I live in a house. In Nazareth. But today, I have run away."

"Why?" Elan was both full of questions and naively direct.

Yeshua did not answer his question; he didn't want to talk to a small child about his problems at home and at school. Instead, he asked Elan to take him to where he lived. Without fear, Elan took Yeshua's hand and brought him to a clearing not far from where Yeshua had been napping. Several women sat and talked in the clearing and were clearly startled by the appearance of Elan and Yeshua. The women stood, and one of them challenged him, "Who are you? And what do you want?"

Yeshua noticed that some of the women had a few patches of pale-colored skin on their faces and hands, but that held no importance for him. He told them his name and that he had run away from home. The women looked at each other as if they could exchange thoughts, and one finally said, "Yeshua, are you hungry? Our husbands have gone out to find food and will be back soon. I'm sure there will be enough for you. That is, if you don't mind eating with us. Most people do."

Yeshua blinked rapidly. His stepfather's attitude toward poor people had not prepared him to encounter their generosity. How was it that people who were so poor they lived in the forest would offer food to him, a total stranger? In Nazareth most people whispered about him as he passed them by and treated him as if he didn't belong. The kindness of these women stood in stark contrast to all the other adults he knew. More children stood in the clearing, and Elan ran over to be with them. Yeshua stayed with the women.

"Why do you call yourselves 'unclean'?" he asked.

Besides having those few patches on their faces and hands that he had previously noticed, they did not seem particularly dirty.

One of the women replied, "Have your parents never told you about us? We are unclean because we are lepers. Do you know what a leper is, Yeshua?"

Yeshua could not remember his parents talking about lepers, but he recalled some of the children at school talking about their hideous, scaly faces and how their hands and feet fall off so they can't walk. He had thought they were making up stories and so paid little attention to them.

"Will your hands and feet fall off?" Yeshua asked, not sure if he wanted to know the answer.

The eyes of the woman he was talking to grew wide. She stared off into the distance for a moment, then her face returned to normal. "It might happen in time, Yeshua. But you mustn't be afraid of us."

"I'm not afraid," he replied. "Why should I be afraid?"

The woman asked Yeshua to sit and talked to him about leprosy. "Many people believe you can catch leprosy if you touch a leper, so we are banished from the villages. We are certain it doesn't happen that way, because our children are without blemish. But that is why people are frightened of us. Why they cast us out. Whole families are banished from the village, even those who don't have the disease.

"We shout 'unclean' if a villager approaches, to warn them of our presence. That is why we live here in the forest, Yeshua. We can live in peace here. We can raise our children here. And if God wills it, yes, some of us will lose fingers, toes, hands, feet, even arms or legs. But the rest of us are here to help. We take care of each other. Do you see, Yeshua?"

Yeshua was quiet for a few minutes, and then he said, "People can be so unkind. I may not be unclean, but I do know what it feels like to be shunned."

The men returned to the clearing and looked with suspicion at the boy talking with the women. But after their wives spoke to them, they, too, were kind to the young stranger among them. Altogether, there were four families, with seven children among them, aged six through twelve. The men had brought back fresh fish from a nearby river, as well as figs and olives. The women cleaned the fish and put them in a large pot on the fire. There was only one large spoon to remove the cooked fish from the pot and only one plate for sharing.

The lepers had no bread with which to pick up the hot fish, as Yeshua was accustomed to doing, but instead they used bundles of leaves to keep from burning their fingers. As they ate, they questioned Yeshua. Where did he come from? Why had he come here? Wouldn't his parents be worried about him? And Yeshua, in return, voiced all his frustrations: the fights with Efah, the humiliations of being beaten and spat on, the arguments with his stepfather, the teasing by the other children, the looks from the adults. By the time he was done he was sobbing.

One woman came over and put her arms around him, and he wept on her shoulder. With a gentle voice she said, "Yeshua, you were right about people. They really can be unkind." Then she added, "You are aware that your parents will be worried about you?"

Yeshua nodded his head.

"My dear boy, it's too late to go anywhere tonight; it isn't safe. Stay here with us and tomorrow morning at first light, you will go home. Do you understand me? First thing. You have a home and a mother and father who love you and who will be worried about you. And surely not everyone in Nazareth dislikes you?"

"Well, Rabbi Towbiyah likes me," Yeshua said after thinking a moment. "And a few of the other children seem to like me—at least when they aren't with the mean ones."

"So there, you see, Yeshua? You have a home, a family, and you have friends. You have food to eat every day and a warm place to sleep when it is cold at night. And running away from your problems at school doesn't really solve them, does it?"

Yeshua was not as much concerned about school anymore as he was about his parents. He hadn't planned to be gone all night, and he was beginning to realize that his parents would be terribly worried. He wondered what awaited him when he returned. Nothing good, he imagined.

His thoughts were interrupted by one of the men. "Yeshua, you say you go to school."

"Yes."

"And what do they teach you?"

"I study the Torah, and I have learned lots of mashals."

"Wonderful! Tell us all a mashal!"

Yeshua thought about the kindness of these people and remembered the mashal about the ewe lamb in the scrolls of Samael. He knew all the words by heart.

There were two men in one city, one rich, and one poor. The rich man had very many flocks and herds. But the poor man had nothing, save one little ewe lamb, which he had bought and reared; and it grew up together with him and his sons; of his bread it would eat, and from his cup it would drink, and in his bosom it would lay, and it was to him like a daughter.

And there came a wayfarer to the rich man, and he spared to take of his own flock and of his own herd to prepare for the guest who had come to him, and he took the poor man's lamb, and prepared it for the man who had come to him.

And David became very angry at the man; and he said to Nathan: 'As the Lord lives, the man who has done this is liable to death. And the ewe lamb he shall repay fourfold, because he did this thing, and because he had no pity.'

Everyone was quiet, so Yeshua continued, "This mashal is only part of a greater story about King David, but just this much of it shows you the difference between poor people, who treat even a little ewe lamb as if it were a family member, and rich people, who would rather steal a poor person's beloved lamb and kill it and serve it to a rich friend to eat, than give up one of their own. Think of me as that ewe lamb and you as the poor people who treated it like a family member. I will remember your kindness for the rest of my life."

The children looked confused, but the adults all smiled, looked to one another, and nodded their heads. Yeshua told a few more mashals late into the night, explaining their meanings at the end of each one. As the warmth of the fire faded, they all huddled together to sleep. Yeshua slept next to the woman who had been so kind to him.

***

Yom Shlishi (Tuesday)

Before the first light of dawn, Yeshua was awakened by one of the men. Once again, Yeshua's stomach was in knots, this time at the thought of what was in store for him at home.

The man walked together with Yeshua to the outskirts of Nazareth. "You can go the rest of the way by yourself. I don't want to be seen by anyone," he said when he judged they were near enough. "Thank you for your stories, young man. You can visit us any time." The man turned and disappeared back into the forest; Yeshua walked the rest of the way home by himself.

He could tell by the look on his mother's face that she had been crying. "Yeshua! Where were you? We were so worried about you. We have been up all night looking for you. We thought you were ... where were you?"

"Mother, I tried to tell you the day before yesterday. Remember? I said I had something important to tell you. I wanted to tell you that Efah and his friends were going to beat me up after school. I heard them planning it. They said they were going to send me home looking like I was attacked by wolves. I just couldn't go to school, Mother."

Ephrayim came into the house with a worried look on his face, but listened quietly as Yeshua continued. "So I ran away. Then I fell asleep, and when I woke up, it was too late to go home. It was already getting dark."

Ephrayim asked, "So where did you sleep? In the woods by yourself?"

Yeshua knew they would not like what he was about to say. "A little boy saw me and took me to his family and several other families who live in the woods. They said they were lepers. They were very kind to me and shared their evening meal with me. They ..."

"Lepers? You slept with the unclean?" Ephrayim's face was turning red. "If the people of Nazareth find out, they might well cast you out of the village—maybe us too! Did you touch them? Do you have any idea what you have done to your mother and me by sleeping with the unclean? Answer me, young man!" Ephrayim stood for a moment, glaring at Yeshua, and then, when there was no reply, he stomped off to his workshop.

Mara saw her son trembling. "Yeshua, my son, you did the right thing to stay with adults rather than walking home in the dark. Your father can't say it, but I say it to you now."

Yeshua looked off to where his stepfather had gone, and then back to Mara. "Mother, they told me you can't get the disease by touching them. Is that true?"

Mara wrinkled her face as she thought, and then she replied, "No, I don't believe you can get the disease by touching them. But it's probably a good idea not to just the same. Did you, Yeshua? Did you touch them?"

Yeshua shook his head no, even though he had slept in one of the woman's arms.

Mara reached toward Yeshua and stroked his curly hair. "I'm sorry I didn't listen to you that night you came home and said you had something important to tell me. I had no idea you were having such problems with your friends. I'll try to do better next time, my son. I will."

"Mother, why does Stepfather always get angry and then walk away?"

Mara's lips began to tremble. "I don't know, Yeshua. He never used to be like that." She shook her head and stared at the door leading to the workshop. "Something is bothering him, and he just doesn't know how to get rid of it. He is a good man, your stepfather is." Then, after a pause, "He is a good man."

After a moment of silence, Yeshua went to the roof where he could be alone, save for Doren, his little sparrow. He had only been home a very short time, and already it was as if nothing at all had changed. His stepfather was angry at him. Again. His mother promised to make time for him. Again. And he still had Efah to deal with.

7 (Another encounter with the poor)

Yom Revi'i (Wednesday)

When Yeshua awoke, Mara was already up and cooking. "Yeshua, come here. I need to tell you something."

Yeshua approached his mother tentatively.

"I talked to your stepfather last night, and we are in agreement. You are to stay home from school today, and your stepfather is going to talk to Rabbi Towbiyah about your problem with Efah."

Yeshua's eyes grew wide. "No! You don't understand! It will only make things worse."

"It has been decided, son. Your stepfather has already left."

He began to get angry, but he didn't want to let it out on his mother. Instead, he breathed loudly and quickly, his face turning red, his hands clenched in fists. Mara had seen this before. She stroked his head and said, "My son, why don't you spend the day doing whatever you want to do. I have no chores for you today. If you want to stay here and keep me company, you can do that. If you want to go off by yourself, you can do that too."

The gentle sound of her voice calmed him down and he sat in a chair and watched her while she cooked. "Tell me about my father," he said suddenly.

Mara froze for a moment, then turned and said, "Yeshua, you are not yet old enough to understand, and I am not yet ready to speak about it. I will tell you in time, my son, I promise. But please don't ask me to tell you today."

Yeshua's calmness left him as quickly as it began. His voice got louder. "You will not tell me today. So be it. You said I could go off by myself if I wanted to. That is what I want. That is what I will do." He abruptly stood and stomped away, just like his stepfather had been doing lately.

He turned back once and saw his mother watching him. Their eyes met. Then, she shook her head and went back to cooking.

Yeshua had no plans. He just wanted to get away and calm down. *What am I going to do all day?* he wondered. *Maybe I'll visit my new friends in the forest—the unclean.* Just the thought of it made him feel better. He headed off in that direction. But when he arrived, nobody was there. He knew he was in the right place because the remnants of the cooking fire, with rocks all around like makeshift chairs, were still there; he could still recognize the one he had sat on that night as he told the mashals. His friends were no longer there. He called out for Elan, the small boy who had first befriended him, but no one answered. *What now?* he wondered.

On the outskirts of Sepphoris—the principal city in Galilee—there was a district where a lot of poor people lived. They were foreigners, widows, orphans, and the sick and feeble-minded. The laws of Israel commanded that people be generous to the poor, to not leave them to starve. When Israelites harvested their fields, for example, they were supposed to leave the crops that grew at the edges for them. Likewise, the laws stated that Israelites should beat the olives from their trees only once, and when they harvested grapes, they were not to go back over the vines. Anything left over was food for the poor. The laws even stated it was permissible to eat grapes from anyone's vineyard so long as the grapes weren't collected in a basket; grain could be picked from anyone's field, provided it was picked by hand and not using a tool.

Many Galileans followed these laws; but many did not, some even going so far as to chase people from their fields. Enough obeyed the laws, however, that people rarely starved, but neither did they fill their bellies each night. It was not good to be poor in Galilee.

With a newfound curiosity about the poor, Yeshua headed to the eastern edge of Sepphoris, the poorest district he knew. The houses were small and made of mud bricks—unlike the large stone houses in other parts of the city. Nothing seemed clean, and there was a foul stench in the air of feces and urine. Everywhere people looked pale and sickly; some even had skin like the lepers who had befriended Yeshua in the forest. Children huddled together in the streets, largely uninterested in him, but the adults eyed him suspiciously as he passed. Finally, a man approached him and asked, "Are you lost?"

Yeshua didn't know how to answer the question. "No," he tried. "I'm just taking a walk."

"Well, boy, this is not a place for taking a walk. Why don't you go back to your own village?"

"My name is Yeshua."

"Yeshua, then, why don't you go back to your own village?"

"They don't like me there."

The man paused as if to take measure of the child. The expression on his face changed as he asked, "Why don't people like you, Yeshua?"

Yeshua replied matter-of-factly, "They think I am a bastard. The children all call me 'son of Mara.' That's my mother's name. Even the adults call me 'the carpenter's bastard child.'"

The man's eyes softened, and he said to Yeshua, "And what is so wrong with being a bastard? It's not your sin. You didn't ask to be brought into this world this way, did you?"

The man raised one hand high above his head, clenched into a fist, looked up to the sky as if shouting to God, and continued loudly, "What is so wrong with people that they castigate a child—a *child*—for the sins of his parents?" It was such a bizarre sight that people nearby turned to look at him.

Yeshua wanted to tell the man he wasn't really a bastard, that his mother had been properly married but his father had died before he was born. She'd told him so. It was other people who didn't believe the story. But before he could say anything, the man said, "Let me tell you something, Yeshua. Bastards are just like anyone else. Come with me, I want to show you something."

By the afternoon, Yeshua had been introduced to six or seven adults and two children. The man said all of them were without a father when they were born. Yeshua sat with the two children, who were about his own age, talking easily. There seemed nothing extraordinary about them, even though they had no fathers. As they chatted, Yeshua nonchalantly reached into his tunic and pulled out a piece of bread that he had brought from home. The children's eyes grew big, but they said nothing. With the realization that his new friends were hungry, Yeshua broke the bread into two pieces and gave them each half, leaving nothing for himself. Too hungry to notice his selflessness, the children devoured the bread like hungry animals. Yeshua wondered how long it had been since either of them had eaten anything.

After the bread was gone, the three children played leapfrog and ran through the streets, laughing and shouting. This was something

Yeshua had occasionally done with his brother Yaaqob, but never with children his own age. Back in his own neighborhood, he was either made fun of, or the children were instructed by their parents not to play with him. Here, playing with these poor bastard children, Yeshua felt freer and happier than he could ever remember.

As the afternoon wore on, the man who had initially befriended Yeshua approached the children. "Yeshua, you should probably go home now. This is not a place you want to be after dark, and you have a long walk home." Yeshua looked downcast, but the man continued, "You can come back any time you want. See that house over there? That's my house. Just knock, and if I'm not there, ask for Yechezqel. That's my name. I live with my friends. They will tell you where I am. Go now."

Walking back to Nazareth in the late afternoon sunshine, Yeshua noticed a change in his feelings. When he first came to this place, all the adults looked mean and appeared to be suspicious of him. Now he looked at the same faces, seeing the same expressions, and saw only people going about their business. Before, he saw strangeness. Now he saw normalcy. They hadn't changed; he had. Even the stench of this part of the city didn't bother him. He felt very comfortable among the poor.

8 (Ephrayim's compromise with Yeshua)

Ephrayim and Rabbi Towbiyah were sitting in the small chairs the students sat in about the same time that Yeshua was meeting Yechezqel. "How can I help you, Ephrayim?" the rabbi asked.

"Rabbi, I've come to talk to you about Efah."

"What about Efah? What's he done now?" The rabbi did not seem surprised.

"He has been beating up my son, that's what. Yeshua will not be at school today, Rabbi. He overhead Efah and his friends planning to beat him up on his way home from school today and all take turns hitting him. So either you do something about it, or I will."

Rabbi Towbiyah placed a hand on Ephrayim's shoulder. "Ephrayim, calm down. This is worse than I thought. I knew he was taunting Yeshua, and I was trying to help your son with that, but I had no idea … Efah really was going to do that?"

Ephrayim nodded his head.

"Ephrayim, I have had a few similar problems with children over the years. Here is what I propose: I will go speak to Efah's parents tonight after school. I know both of them very well. They are good people. They will know how to discipline him, I promise you. Meantime, let Yeshua stay home for a week. If I know Efah, by the time a week has gone by without your son to taunt, he will find something else to do. I think that should work. And if it doesn't, I will try something else. Perhaps you can spend the time with Yeshua and teach him carpentry. He will soon need to learn a trade."

Ephrayim shook his head. "You have no idea what you are asking, Rabbi. Keeping Yeshua home will be hard enough. He enjoys arguing scripture with you, and speaks so fondly of you. But learning the carpentry trade is something else altogether. He has fought me for almost a year. I never thought it would be so hard to teach my son."

Rabbi Towbiyah brought his face closer to Ephrayim. "Ephrayim, I now tell you something of great importance. Your son is … special. I'm sure you already know that. I have never seen a boy this young with such a mature understanding of the Scriptures. Not just the words, but the ideas they convey.

"Sometimes he teaches me, Ephrayim. I mean that. His understanding sometimes surpasses my own. So I say to you, do not push him so hard to learn a trade. I know that goes against what I just suggested you do. But I didn't know he was rebelling. If he truly fights you about learning carpentry, there may be a reason greater than a young boy defying his father."

Ephrayim raised his eyebrows. "What reason?"

"I think you will not need to worry about young Yeshua. I think he may be a *nabi* [prophet]. I have even started to tell some of my friends who are members of the Great Sanhedrin about your son. They wish to meet him. Not now, when he is barely eleven, of course, but perhaps when he is twelve, and you attend Passover, he can meet them then."

Ephrayim stood. "You give me much to think about, Rabbi. I am a practical man. While I agree with what you say about Yeshua being special, he also cannot go through life without learning some kind of trade. Without a way to earn a living, even a prophet will starve to death. Or he will live his life in the outskirts of Seppheris with the poor. I will try not to be so hard on him, but he has to learn to do something. Carpentry is all I know. So, carpentry it must be. Thank you for your help. I will keep Yeshua home for a week."

***

Yeshua and Ephrayim both arrived home about the same time. The family sat outside and ate a meal together. Neither Yeshua nor Ephrayim said anything about their day. But when the meal was over, Ephrayim said, "Yaaqob, take your sisters inside. Your mother and I need to talk to Yeshua."

Mara and Yeshua sat and waited as Ephrayim gathered his thoughts. "Yeshua, I will come straight to the point. Are you a prophet? The rabbi says you might be."

"A prophet?" Yeshua asked. "No. I'm not a ... I don't think I'm a ... the rabbi told you that?"

Mara added her voice. "Our son? A prophet?"

"That is what he said. Well, he said you *might* be one. But I think if you were, you would know it. Wouldn't you, son?"

Yeshua had no answer.

"More about that later. Here is what else the rabbi told me. He will speak to Efah's parents, and they will speak to Efah. He said you should stay home from your schooling for a week."

"A week? But I need to go to school. What will I do for a week?"

Ephrayim took a deep breath. "This is what you will do, Yeshua. I know you don't want to learn carpentry. But, you see, it is all I know. It is all I have to give you. Do you understand that? Two years from now, when you are thirteen, you will be a man. And a man can do whatever he wishes. But I would not be a father to you if I did not give you the means to make a living."

"But ..." Yeshua began.

"No. Just listen. Here is what will happen. During the morning, when you would normally be in school, you will stay with me. I will teach, you will learn. And in the afternoon you can do what you wish. It is only for a week, Yeshua. A week."

Yeshua had nothing to say. Ephrayim was unsure if he was angry, or resolved to his fate. Finally, Yeshua asked, "May I go to bed now?"

Ephrayim and Mara stayed outside and drank a glass of wine. Mara appeared to be trying to make sense of it all. "Rabbi Towbiyah thinks our son is a prophet?"

"Mara, our son is special in some ways. There is no doubt. But I'm not so sure about being a prophet. Rabbi Towbiyah said I shouldn't push him so much. And maybe I shouldn't. But I just want him to be a carpenter like I am. A good carpenter."

Mara replied, "You have been pushing him, Ephrayim. But I think I understand why. You told me you began learning your trade from your father when you were eight. And you enjoyed it from the beginning. But Yeshua is not like you. He is, well, different. Special, as the rabbi says. I think your decision is a good compromise. I think Yeshua does too. Now let's go to bed."

9 (Yeshua fails at carpentry but makes new friends)

Yom Chamishi (Thursday)

Yeshua was not looking forward to spending the morning with his stepfather. But if he could keep from getting angry, it would make the afternoon go well for him. He had decided the night before that in the afternoon he would go back to Sepphoris and visit his new friend Yechezqel. He did not tell either Ephrayim or his mother what he had planned.

"Yeshua, today we are going to make a scratch plow for a farmer who lives nearby. And we are going to make a yoke for his two oxen. What kind of wood do you think we should use?"

"I suppose we would use a hard wood," Yeshua said.

"That's right Yeshua, we will use oak. It will consist of a pole, a stick for the handle, a blade, which I have already made, and then we will make a horizontal yoke. I thought we would start with something simple."

Yeshua asked, "Why does Moshe forbid us to yoke an ox and a donkey together?"

Ephrayim furrowed his brows. "I don't know, Yeshua. You need to ask the rabbi that."

"Well, it doesn't make any sense. If a farmer has only one ox and only one donkey, why can't he just ...?"

"You are not here to learn scripture, son," Ephrayim interrupted a bit louder than before, "you are here to learn carpentry."

Yeshua sighed. He already missed being in school.

"Now, how long is a cubit, Yeshua?"

Yeshua knew this from school. "It is the distance from my elbow to the tip of my fingers." He had once actually measured out three hundred cubits, the length of Noach's ark, in the dirt in order to see how long it was. He remembered it being very long.

"Very good," Ephrayim said. "In carpentry, however, we measure a cubit as six handbreadths. A long cubit we measure as seven handbreadths."

Yeshua asked, "And what is a handbreadth?"

Ephrayim held up his hand with his fingers together and his thumb turned under. "The distance between four fingers. See? From here to here. Now, Yeshua, take this nail and measure out six handbreadths on that piece of wood by scratching a mark for each handbreadth. Under each mark, inscribe the numbers one through six with that ink over there. This will be your measuring stick. We will then use it to make the scratch plow and yoke."

The talk of cubits brought up another thought from Yeshua. "Why are we not allowed to walk more than two thousand cubits on the Sabbath? If mother were ill, and you needed to bring her to a physician who lived more than ..."

Ephrayim shouted, "I said we are not here to discuss the Scripture. Now do as I say."

Yeshua bowed his head, went to the wood piece on the work bench, and began to measure out six handbreadths. He would ask Rabbi Towbiyah these questions next week.

Things got worse as Yeshua tried to use the saw a short time later. In using his head he was very quick, but in using his hands he was quite clumsy. He was cutting the wood crooked and had not checked the length twice before cutting, as Ephrayim had instructed him to do.

"You did that on purpose!" Ephrayim shouted. "You only measured once. And you cut the yoke too short. I said twenty-four cubits, did I not? Now we have to cut another piece of wood."

The two glared at each other like two fighters trying to frighten each other with their gaze.

"Would my two carpenters like some fresh-baked bread and honey?" Mara grinned and stood in the doorway with her offerings. The smile quickly left her face as she looked from one to the other. "You have been fighting again, haven't you? Must you fight? It is only the first day. My husband, my son, if you are to make it through the week, you both need to try harder. Now let's all go outside and sit and eat and calm down."

Mara did not wait for a response. She quickly turned and left the workroom. Yeshua and Ephrayim continued to glare at each other, and then, in unison, they walked outside and sat. The silence that followed spoke loudly of the tension that had not left either of them. But in their attempt to not change, along with a slight smirk on Mara's face as her eyes rolled from Yeshua to Ephrayim and back again, they finally realized how they must look, and all three of them started to laugh.

After they had eaten, Yeshua said, "It is now the afternoon. May I go?"

"Go, then," said Ephrayim.

Mara placed her hand on Ephrayim'. "Your father says you can go, Yeshua. But tomorrow you must try harder. Promise?"

"Promise," Yeshua replied. He grabbed two pieces of bread from the table near the oven and stuffed them in his tunic as he ran off.

Mara turned toward Ephrayim, cocked her head and waited. "Promise!" he answered.

***

Yeshua would only have a short time to spend in Sepphoris, so he walked very quickly, running at times. When he got there, he was confronted by a boy he didn't know. Something about him scared Yeshua, so he stepped to the boy's side and quickly walked past him.

"Hey, you," Yeshua heard him say. "Yes, you. Don't walk away from me when I'm talking to you. What are you doing here?"

Yeshua felt his heart pounding as he turned. "I have come to see my friend Yechezqel."

"Yechezqel? I know most of Yechezqel's friends, and I have never seen you before. Hey, you look like a rich boy. How much money do you have, rich boy?"

Yeshua didn't know what to do. "Money? I have no money," he said.

The boy drew his face close to Yeshua's and said, "Well, you are going to have to pay me if you want to see Yechezqel."

He pushed Yeshua hard, and as Yeshua stumbled backwards, he felt the hands of someone else behind him, keeping him from falling. He turned to see another boy, bigger than the first; bigger even than Efah. The other boy was grinning. "You better do as my brother says. When he gets mad, I get mad. And you don't want the two of us mad at the same time."

He pushed Yeshua back into to the first boy. Yeshua stumbled into him. "Did you just push me?" the first boy said. He pushed Yeshua back into his brother. "Did you just push me?" the second boy said. Back and forth Yeshua went.

What happened next was so quick, Yeshua wasn't sure what he was seeing. "Look out," he heard one of the boys say. Without a word, the two boys suddenly pushed Yeshua to the ground, turned and ran, as three other boys chased after them. All five turned left at the next street, and then Yeshua heard yelling and cries of pain. When the noise stopped, the three boys who had chased Yeshua's tormentors came back. One of them had some blood on his face and torn skin on one of his knuckles.

"Did they hurt you?" the bigger of them asked.

Yeshua shook his head, indicating no.

"My name is Zamir. These are my two friends Gera and Lemek. We are friends of Yechezqel. You were playing with my younger brother, Aziz, the other day. I saw you. He told me you were nice, and gave him and his friend bread to eat."

Yeshua was beginning to calm down. "Thank you, Zamir. Thank you, Gera. Thank you, Lemek. You saved me. I've never had anyone help me like that before."

Zamir said, "Around here, we look out for one another. And you are now our friend, so we will look out for you too."

Yechezqel suddenly appeared and placed his hands on Yeshua's shoulder. "Good to see you again, Yeshua. Lemek, have you been fighting again?"

The boy with the bloody face and torn knuckles grinned and said, "It was those two bullies. I don't know their names, but you know who I mean. The ones from the west side of the city. They were trying to beat up Yeshua. I don't think they will be back!"

Yechezqel shook his head, half smiling. "You know I don't approve of you fighting, Lemek, but I do approve of you helping those in need."

Others, including Aziz, whom Yeshua knew from before, gathered around. Aziz said, "Hey Yeshua, tell us a story. You told us one the last time you were here."

They all sat down and looked to Yeshua. And so he started to tell the children mashals. Unlike at school, these children loved to listen to him first recite the stories and then explain them. It was like a dream that had come true. Because none of these children had ever been to school, Yeshua found he had to give a lot more explanations, but it came easily to him to use simpler language and simpler ideas.

At one point he stood, and as he did, the two pieces of bread fell out of his tunic and onto the ground. They all looked at the bread, and then back up to Yeshua as if to see what he would do. He picked up the two pieces of bread, held them out in front of him, and then handed them both to the children on either side of him. But instead of quickly eating them, like he had seen them do the other day, each child tore off a tiny piece and then passed the bread to the next child. Everyone ended up with a piece of bread except Yeshua. And then Aziz tore his own piece of bread in two, walked up and handed one to Yeshua. Yeshua was quite moved as they all ate together.

When it was time to leave, Zamir, Gera and Lemek accompanied Yeshua to the edge of town. "I'll be back tomorrow if I can," Yeshua promised.

10 (Tahmid's meeting with Mara)

Yom Shishi (Friday)

Tahmid walked the dusty streets of Nazareth each morning. Although he had a limp from a childhood injury, he enjoyed walking briskly and had not missed a day in the past ten years. He walked faster than some people ran. But even at his fast pace, he noticed things: the smell of the fresh bread being baked at Yochanan's bakery, the songs the birds sang to one another, the ever-changing cloud formations. As he approached the corner of a building, he collided with Mara, who was coming round the same corner from the other side. Mara was knocked to the ground.

Startled, Tahmid reached down to help her up saying, "I'm sorry, madam. That was my fault. Are you …" He stopped midsentence when he saw whom he had knocked over.

"Why don't you watch where you're going, you horrible woman," he said instead, pulling his hand back.

"Tahmid, I'm so sorry," Mara said, rising and brushing off her tunic. Then smiling, she said, "Ephrayim was asking about you just the other day. How are you doing?"

Tahmid ignored her apology and her attempt at conversation. "How I am doing is no concern of yours. You still don't understand, do you?"

"I don't understand what, Tahmid?" Mara shifted her stance, her voice taking a sharp tone.

"You don't understand why the people of Nazareth dislike you."

Mara now stood rigidly, the two cords of her neck jutting out. "I know why the others don't like me. It's because of the lies told of my marriage to my first husband. The lies you …"

"I don't believe for an instant you were married when you conceived that bastard child of yours. You may fool the others, but you don't fool me. I doubt if all the rest of your children are Ephrayim's either. Who knows *what* you do when he is away working. You and that … that Yeshua, don't belong here. That you are even still alive makes a mockery of justice."

Mara wanted to slap him, and slap him hard, but she resisted. *No,* she thought. *That is what he would do. I will not be like him.*

"I'm sorry you feel that way, Tahmid. I will pray tonight for your forgiveness."

"God doesn't listen to unrepentant sinners!"

"I know this, Tahmid. This is why I will pray for *you*!"

Tahmid shook. Spittle formed in the corner of his mouth as he shouted, "Ephrayim was once my good friend. If he had listened to me, he would have never married you."

Mara now stood toe to toe with Tahmid. "Ephrayim is my friend too—my friend, my lover, and my dear husband to whom I have always been faithful. Always! And he certainly knows me better than you do, Tahmid, you and the rest of the unkind people of Nazareth who scorn us. That he didn't listen to you shows his character. That you have been holding a grudge for—what has it been, eleven years? That shows your lack of character. My husband speaks kindly of you sometimes and wonders why you still don't speak with him."

"It's more than a grudge, *Mara,*" Tahmid almost spit Mara's name from his mouth. "I was the one Rabbi Towbiyah sent to Sepphoris eleven years ago—remember? Remember that, Mara? The rabbi wanted to assure the people of Nazareth you were legally married when you became pregnant. And what did I find when I got there? The city official told me he had no record of you having ever married to—what was his name? Yosef? You claimed Yosef had been murdered. But I checked that, too. No record of it! Rabbi Towbiyah—ever your protector—was so taken in by you he convinced everyone it was simply a case of lost records. Some actually believed him. But not me. You deserved to be stoned then, and you deserve to be stoned now."

"And will you stone me, Tahmid, you who are without sin?" Mara picked up a stone and held it out to him, standing even taller than before.

"Are you worried that I might? Well, you should be worried, you evil woman. This is not over, I promise you. Think about that when you pray tonight." Tahmid struck the stone out of her hand with the back of his hand and walked briskly away as the stone hit the ground by Mara's feet.

Mara found a large rock to sit on, placed her head in her hands, and closed her eyes for a few minutes. What *had* happened to those records in Sepphoris? It was bad enough that the town thought her to be a sinner, worthy of being put to death, but they despised Yeshua as a bastard and hated him almost as much as they hated her. She wondered if Tahmid was constantly stirring them up. She could picture his contorted face in her mind, even now. Sometimes she wished she could leave this wretched city, but this is where her husband made his home. It was often said that nothing good ever came out of Nazareth. In Tamid's case, she thought, the saying was true.

As she walked back home she felt more and more alienated. She felt sure that her argument with Tahmid had been overheard and that it would soon be the talk of the town. The people she would smile at would turn their heads and say nothing to her. This was nothing new. She did have a few friends, mostly Ephrayim's old friends, but only a few. She used to be outgoing and longed to join the rest of the women in some of the social gatherings that took place in Nazareth. But she knew she was not welcome.

As she approached home, Yeshua came running outside. "Mother, mother! Look what I taught Miryam to …"

"Not now, Yeshua. I need to lie down upstairs for a little while."

Mara felt guilty about not listening to her son, but she was tired, she had just been insulted and threatened, and she wished to be alone. This incident with Tahmid bothered her more than she thought. She lay in the bed and listened to her daughter Miryam talking to Yeshua.

"What's wrong, Yeshua?" she heard Miryam ask.

"Oh go away!" he yelled. "Just go away and leave me be."

"Yeshua, be nice to your sister," she shouted. Her words broke up as she shouted them, and then she began to cry. It came over her like a wave from the sea. It had all been just too much. Tahmid, the fighting between her son and her husband, having almost no friends, being humiliated, being pregnant again, everything. It was just too, too much.

After she had calmed down, Mara decided not to tell Ephrayim what had just happened with Tahmid. He was having a hard enough time finding work. He didn't need yet another problem on his hands. *Besides*, she thought, *I rarely see Tahmid anyway.*

She looked up to see Yeshua sitting by the ladder that he had quietly climbed. "Come over here, my son," she said. "I'm sorry I yelled at you a moment ago."

He came to her and they embraced. "What's the matter, Mother?"

"Oh, nothing," she began. "Well, it's not nothing. But nothing you need to worry about. A man named Tahmid was mean to me today, that's all."

"Did he hurt you, Mother?" Yeshua looked concerned.

"No, son, he didn't hurt me. He tried to, but with his words. I would not let him. Yeshua, don't say anything to your father. He is also having a hard time, and doesn't need more worries. All right?"

Yeshua said nothing, but after a brief pause, he nodded.

11 (Ephrayim and Yeshua both make a decision)

Yom Shabbat (Saturday)

It was Sabbath evening and it was hot. Yeshua's week at home was up, and he was already thinking about school. He was, as usual, up on the roof, hiding behind the parapet. His mother and stepfather were below, sitting outside drinking a cup of wine. They had brought two chairs from the house and were facing each other as they drank.

"Mara, I'm sorry I've been so upset with everyone and everything lately. I truly am." Ephrayim's head was facing down, but his eyes were looking up at his wife. He looked to her like a child who had just been scolded. He clasped his hands tightly in his lap.

Mara smiled, reached over and took both his hands out of his lap, holding them in hers and replied, "I know you are, my love. I knew it would just take time for you to work through this … this, whatever it is you are going through. It's the way you always do things—slow and deliberate." The two enjoyed a moment of silence as they gazed into each other's eyes. Then they both leaned forward and kissed a slow, deliberate, and loving kiss.

Ephrayim shuffled his feet. "Mara, hear me out. Please don't interrupt me. I have a plan."

Mara set her hands in her lap and waited patiently. Whenever Ephrayim talked about having a plan, it meant more than an idea that had suddenly come to him. It meant that he had been doing some careful and calculated thinking.

"I have been trying to make friends with Shimon and Gilad and Melek because I wanted for us to be rich as they are. I realize now how wrong I was. You were right about those kinds of people. They don't care about me. They only pretend to like me to see if there is profit in it. But I still want to run my own business. Not to move to Sepphoris and live in a big house; not to spite your parents. I want it for me, for us.

I don't care about being rich anymore. I only want to be a good businessman and make enough money to take care of my family. What keeps this from happening is that I barely make enough money to feed my family right now. And with another baby coming, it will only be harder. So here is what I have decided we should do."

Now she would find out his plan. She leaned in toward him, her heart pounding.

"Yeshua is way ahead of the rest of his classmates in school. Rabbi Towbiyah has told me as much. He said our son is, in his estimation, over a year ahead of his class. Yaaqob is also doing better than most, although he is not as gifted in his schooling as Yeshua. So I will take them both out of school for one year. Only one year, Mara."

"No!" she began. "It was only to be for a week. Ephrayim, he is eleven. He only has two years of schooling left."

He cut her off and continued, "Think about it for a moment, love. With the two of them working together as my apprentices, we can save the money we now pay for their schooling, and maybe Yeshua won't be quite so resistant to being my apprentice if his brother is learning at the same time. He has already learned much."

Mara's face softened. She began to see his point.

"And it will only be for one year. If Yeshua wishes it, he can go back to school next year, and still help me part-time. Yaaqob too, if he so wishes. Between the two of them, for a full year I will have one full-time carpenter! We will make enough money to feed our family, both my oldest sons will learn a trade, and I might even have money enough to make a first installment on a workshop for my business."

***

Tears were streaming down Yeshua's cheeks. His hands were both doubled into fists. He heard every word they said from the dark shadows of the rooftop where his parents couldn't see him, and he was certain his mother wasn't going to save him this time. The thought of spending all his time with Ephrayim made him shake. He hated that he would be taken out of school against his will. He didn't even like carpentry. *Why are they doing this? What am I going to do now?*

His stomach was once again in knots as he lay looking up at the stars. He would not sleep much this night. He needed to make a plan. Just like his stepfather, he needed to think things through and formulate a course of action.

He loved his mother and pined for her attention, but he never seemed to get it. He didn't want to be around his stepfather, but he would soon have no choice. He imagined his life becoming nothing more than a daylong argument with Ephrayim, day after day. He loved learning the scriptures that he learned in school, but that was now going to be taken away. The people of Nazareth didn't seem to like him, his schoolmates made fun of him, and he had only one or two friends in this town. There was absolutely nothing left here that made him happy. It felt to him like being squeezed in someone's fist, tighter and tighter. Every direction he turned, there was a wall in front of him.

And worst of all, worse than anything else, he felt anger inside him that he desperately wanted to get rid of, anger that had been with him as long as he could remember. Anger at his stepfather, anger at the children at school, anger at the people of Nazareth who scorned him and his family: burning, raging anger. His only course of action was to escape. Maybe if he ran away from home, he would leave his anger behind him as well. It was worth a try.

But escape where? Where would he go? What would he do? He would need to go far enough away from home that he couldn't be found by his family. That much he knew. The rest of it he couldn't figure out. Well, he would just have to reason that out on the way to … where? His plan was off to a bad start. And now the fear he would lose his nerve crept into his thoughts. If he were going to do it at all, it would have to be tomorrow morning; before he changed his mind. Yes. Tomorrow it would be.

12 (Bacha teaches Yeshua how to fight)

Samaria

Yeshua had told Bacha almost his whole life's story just by recounting the previous week. Now maybe he would understand. After staying up half the night talking, they slept late. The sun had risen long ago. Yeshua sat up in bed, once again forgetting where he was for a brief moment. Bacha stood over him.

"Today, my friend, I am going to teach you how to fight!"

"Bacha, I told you last night about my anger. Why would I want to learn to fight?"

"Yeshua, fighting has little to do with anger. In fact anger can often make you lose a fight. Fighting is simply standing up for what you believe in. Standing up to, uh, Efah. Standing up to anyone who would say something wrong about you or your family. You must learn to do this. Trust me."

Try though Yeshua might to avoid learning to fight, Bacha proved to be persistent. He taught Yeshua how to fall without getting hurt. At first he just threw Yeshua to the ground, showing him how to roll as he landed, and then he started flipping him over his shoulder. He would have Yeshua run toward him, and then use Yeshua's own momentum to flip him over his back and onto the ground. They did just that, over and over.

Next Bacha taught Yeshua how to perform the flip himself. "Whenever someone is running toward you, use that forward movement to bring them down," he said. "They do most of the work all by themselves." Bacha would run toward him, and he would flip Bacha to the ground. He eventually got very good at it.

"What if they are not running toward me? How do I throw them to the ground?" Yeshua asked.

Bacha taught him how to use his opponent's elbow to twist him onto the ground. "If you can get their elbow, you can always control them," he said. "And once they are down, as they try to get back up they will be for a moment unbalanced. Sweep their feet with your foot, and they will fall right back down."

After that, he taught Yeshua how to deflect a fist moving toward him. In spite of himself, Yeshua was enjoying these lessons. Not knowing where the next fist would come from was like a game. Sometimes he would get hit, but Bacha would pull his punch when Yeshua failed to anticipate, so that the impact would not be so hard.

But when Bacha tried to teach him how to throw a punch, Yeshua refused. "You are learning how to fight really well, Yeshua, but you cannot win unless you hit." He threw his fist toward Yeshua, and Yeshua deflected it to his side as if swatting a fly, just like Bacha had taught him.

"If I keep you from hitting me and I make you so tired you can't hit anymore, haven't I won?"

Bacha tried to counter his argument, but Yeshua grabbed his elbow and twisted him onto the ground. Then he pinned Bacha's arms and began tickling him. Bacha, who was bigger and stockier than Yeshua, had no trouble rolling him over, and now he was the one who tickled. Over and over they rolled and tickled and laughed.

When they finally stopped laughing, someone stood over them, eying them. Bacha stood up quickly and then smiled. "Yaish! I want you to meet my new friend Yeshua."

Yeshua stood and pulled back slightly, swallowing hard. So this was Yaish. He could now see how Bacha could have mistaken him for Yaish from the back. They were both the same size, and their hair was almost identical. That was as far as the similarities went, however. Yaish had the same "foreign" look to him that Bacha had. They both had skin that was darker than Yeshua's, and Yaish's nose was like Bacha's: round and flat.

Yaish did not say hello to Bacha's new friend. He looked straight at Bacha, not once making eye contact with Yeshua. "I came to go fishing with you, Bacha. I'll come back later."

And with that, he was gone.

"Excuse my friend, Yeshua. He doesn't like strangers. Never has. He'll get used to you, though. It will just take some time."

Again, Yeshua heard in that statement an invitation to stay longer. Over the next few days their friendship blossomed. Yeshua would go fishing with Bacha, and harvest food from his garden, and find berries in the woods, and they would continue to wrestle and fight and tickle each day. Bacha had much more to teach Yeshua about fighting, although he never got him to throw a punch. Yeshua would occasionally feel like they were being watched, and suspected that the watcher was Yaish, but he never actually saw him.

At night he often thought of his family and what they might be going through, but the pain of separation from them, especially from his mother, was offset by the joy of finally being free of Nazareth and all that it meant to him. The fist he once felt squeezing him, the obstacles that stood in his path everywhere he turned, the taunts of the other schoolchildren: all gone. Almost as if he had awakened from a horrible nightmare. And although Yeshua missed his lessons with Rabbi Towbiyah, he still felt he was now in a better place. This was the right thing for him to do. He was now quite sure of it. He had not felt anger once since coming here. Maybe it was finally gone.

One night when they were talking, Yeshua said, "Bacha, I came here to meet Samaritans. You are the only one I have met. Well, you and your friend Yaish, but I really didn't meet Yaish. I would like to go to Samaria and meet more. Tell me about your people."

Bacha sat in silence for a few minutes. "They won't like you, Yeshua, I told you that before. They will be just like Yaish. Even the ones who look like you won't trust you."

"What do you mean, 'the ones who look like me'?"

Bacha began to tell Yeshua some of the history of Samaria as he understood it. There were two kinds of people: the Samaritans like himself who had always been there, and the Jews who had come there many years ago. The Jews were very strict and very religious. Some had intermarried with the Samaritans, which Moshe had forbidden them to do, and some had not. But even the Samarian Jews didn't like the Jews from elsewhere, especially Galilee. Bacha told him it had something to do with religion, but he didn't know exactly what.

"So if you come to town, you need to say you are from somewhere else, not Nazareth or anywhere else in Galilee."

Yeshua grew very serious and said, "I couldn't lie, Bacha. I can do lots of things, but lying is not one of them."

"I'm telling you, Yeshua, if you want to meet the people of my city, you can't say you are from Nazareth. You just can't."

"What about Judea?" Yeshua asked. "Do Samaritans hate the Jews of Judea as well?"

"They don't like them either. Especially the Sadducees, but not as much as the Galileans."

"So what if I told them I was from Judea? It would be a lesser lie, and I might be able to say that."

"Fine. Tell them you are from Judea, then. Just don't say you are from Galilee."

Yeshua decided upon Bethlehem. He would tell everyone he was born in Bethleham. He knew enough about the city to talk about it with familiarity. But Bacha could see his uneasiness about lying. He would have to stay near his new friend to make sure he didn't get himself in trouble, this was clear.

"Fine." he said. "Tomorrow we will go to the city of Samaria."

13 (Yeshua's brush with death)

Yeshua and Bacha walked down the hill toward the city gate on the west side of Samaria. Bacha said, "The older people still call it Samaria. But about thirty years ago it was renamed Sebaste by Herod."

From the hill they could see a temple and a palace, and off in the distance a theatre and forum. Yeshua was quite impressed with its grandeur. Not like Jerusalem, but quite grand just the same.

As they passed through the gate, the city was a blur of activity, and filled with people who had the same characteristics as Bacha and Yaish. Their skin was darker than Yeshua's, and their noses flatter. Many eyed him suspiciously, but because he was with Bacha, whom most everyone knew, they went about their business.

Bacha, who knew Yeshua was interested in religion, immediately took him to a priest he knew named Joiada. Because he was a priest, and because Bacha knew him well, he felt it would do no harm to tell Joiada where Yeshua was really from.

Yeshua at once began to question him on the differences between their religions. Joiada eyed the child before him. "So tell me, Yeshua, I'm sure you read the Torah. What is the first of the ten commandments?"

Yeshua replied almost without thinking, "I am the Lord your God, who brought you out of the land of Egypt, out of the house of slavery."

"So here is the first difference between our religions that I will tell you about. For us, those words are an *introduction* to the ten commandments. Our first commandment, then, is "You shall have no other gods before me."

"So, then, you only have nine commandments," argued Yeshua.

"No, Yeshua. Our tenth commandment says:

It shall be when your God will bring you to the Canaanite land, which you are going to inherit, you shall set yourself up great stones, and plaster them with plaster, and you shall write on them all the words of this law. It shall be, when you are passed over the Jordan, that you shall set up these stones, which I command you this day, in Mount Gerizim. There shall you build an altar to Yahweh your God, an altar of stones: you shall lift up no iron tool on them. You shall build the altar of Yahweh your God of uncut stones; and you shall offer burnt offerings thereon to Yahweh your God: and you shall sacrifice peace-offerings, and shall eat there; and you shall rejoice before Yahweh your God. That mount is beyond the Jordan, behind the way of the going down of the sun, in the land of the Canaanites who dwell in the Arabah, over against Gilgal, beside the oaks of Moreh, against Shechem (Nablus).

"We followed God's commandment and built a Temple on Mount Gerizim. It was destroyed two hundred years ago, but Mount Gerizim is still a holy place that we visit."

Yeshua said: "But I have never seen that commandment written in the Torah."

"Then come look. I will show you."

Yeshua was puzzled how it could be that two different Torahs existed. As he read their scrolls, he noticed other differences besides the added commandment. There were different spellings of words, but also some of the words were completely different. He wanted to know more.

The kindly priest told Yeshua as best he could of the differences between the Samaritans and the Jews. It was a long and complex history that entailed forbidden marriages, combining of religious practices, separation from the Jews of Israel, unyielding beliefs in the words of their respective Torahs, and fear and hatred of one another. "The thing you should remember, Yeshua, is that our people love God just as your people do. We follow the laws of our Torah, just as you do. There is much more that makes us alike than what makes us different. If you accept that, then you have taken the first step in friendship and healing."

The two had now stepped outside the synagogue, and were discussing some of the differences Yeshua had noticed. Bacha was waiting nearby, anxious to get back home. Yeshua looked over long enough to see his friend pacing, and knew what that meant. They had not eaten before they left, and Bacha had told Yeshua earlier that he always got very irritable whenever he was hungry.

***

"There he is. He's the one." Yaish was pointing Yeshua out to his group of friends. They were far enough away that they were not seen by Yeshua or Bacha. Yaish said something else to them, something that made them all hesitant, but he looked from person to person, and would not look to the next until he got a nod from the one he was looking at. As they left, Yaish took one look back at Yeshua and smiled.

***

It had been a week since Yeshua met Joiada. Bacha promised to introduce him to others. Although he was living with Bacha, Yeshua was beginning to feel totally independent. He now knew that if he needed to, he too could live on his own like Bacha. This made him happy. He still thought about his family from time to time, and wondered if they missed him, and most of all he thought about his mother, but still he had no desire to return home. He was thinking about them less and less. It was working. Still no anger.

It was a cool winter morning. Temperatures would get quite cold this time of year, and Yeshua dressed warmly for his daily foraging in the woods. Bacha had gone into Samaria for supplies. As Yeshua searched the familiar places, he began to have feelings of apprehension. It wasn't that he heard anything, or saw anything; he just felt something was not quite right. He was picking some berries that the deer had not yet found when a loud "caw" from a startled bird made him stand and face the direction of the noise. As the bird flew high in the air, Yeshua could see a group of six boys off in the distance running toward him. "There he is! Get him!" he heard them shout. He immediately ran toward Bacha's house with the six in pursuit. When he got there, however, he thought better of going inside, and kept running past it. Maybe they would search the house first, thinking him there, which would give him time to escape. He had no idea who they were, or why they were chasing him, but he knew he was in great danger.

***

When the group got to the house, the leader beckoned to three of the boys and said, "You three look inside the house. You two follow me." The three continued running past the house and in the direction they had seen Yeshua heading.

Every few minutes, the leader would stop the other two and they would all face different directions and listen for noise. When they didn't hear any after several stops, they concluded that Yeshua must have stopped running and was now hiding somewhere. The leader shouted: "You two stay here and keep listening. If you see or hear anything, yell." He then ran back to the house to see if the others had found Yeshua.

***

Yeshua trembled inside the shelter, listening for sounds of his pursuers. He was lucky he had remembered about Bacha's "tomb." It had taken Yeshua a few minutes to find it, but he had climbed inside it, moved the stone cover back in place, and hoped that he would not be found.

Yeshua heard his persuers' voices coming closer and closer. From what they were saying, he knew they were looking up trees in case he had climbed up one of them to hide and they were looking at bushes for broken foliage, indicating someone had run by. And then the thought came to him: *That's Yaish and his friends out there. Yaish must know about Bacha's hideout. I'm trapped.* Once he heard one of the boys come very close to the hideaway and suddenly stop. Yeshua was sure it was Yaish looking for the hideout. He held his breath, his heart beating faster and faster. Then he heard the person run past him.

Finally, off in the distance he heard someone say, "He's gone. Let's go home. Maybe we scared him all the way back to Jerusalem. If he's still around, though, we will get him for sure the next time."

It was getting dark, and Yeshua feared he would have to sleep in this tiny shelter, because he could never find his way back to the house in the dark. Off in the distance he heard a voice. *They're still looking for me*, thought Yeshua. But as the voice got nearer, he recognized it as Bacha's.

"Yeshua, where are you?" Bacha shouted.

"Bacha, I'm over here!" Yeshua removed the stone from the entrance of the tomb, climbed out, and ran toward Bacha. They hugged each other tightly.

"Now I truly know what it feels like to be an outcast. Yaish and his friends were chasing me. I know it was him. I recognized his voice. I was so sure that Yaish knew about your hideout," Yeshua said. "I thought it was all over for me."

Bacha replied, "No. It has been, up until now, only my secret. I told no one. But you and I share secrets, and I knew I could trust you. So you are the only other person I have ever told."

That night, as they talked, Bacha was very silent and sullen, looking down at the floor as Yeshua talked. Finally, he looked up and said, "Yeshua, I'm afraid you are going to have to go home."

"What are you talking about, Bacha? Go home? I … no, I can't go home." Yeshua had tears in his eyes, as did Bacha.

"Yeshua, my friend, I can't let you stay here. They will be back. Yaish won't give up. I know him. He won't give up until he has found you. There is talk about you in Samaria. Many don't want you here. Yeshua, Yaish and his friends; they want to kill you."

"Kill me? But why? They don't even know me."

"I know. It doesn't make any sense to me either. I honestly didn't know how strong their feelings were about Jews until now. We never really talked about it before, Yaish and the others and me. It just never came up. I never realized their feelings until you came along. It's like I never knew them at all. I would never have believed they could talk the way they do about you and your people.

"Tomorrow, you and I will leave early in the morning. I will walk with you as far as Nain. From there, you can safely find your way back home."

Yeshua was devastated. Going home was going to be a horrible experience. Ephrayim would be furious with him, and facing his mother was going to be even harder. He slept very little that night, in part because of his feelings and in part because he feared Yaish and his friends might come back in the middle of the night.

Morning came, and Bacha and Yeshua headed north toward Nain. It was about a fifteen-mile journey, so it was a hard walk, even for two boys as young and energetic as Yeshua and Bacha. Fear and quickened heartbeats, however, made for a quick pace, and they soon neared Nain. Saying goodbye was very hard for both of them.

Bacha said, "Little brother, you have been a closer friend to me than anyone I have ever known. I don't want to lose that. I want to be your friend always."

Yeshua replied, "Big brother, I feel the same way about you. We have to find a place to meet often. A place where both of us will be safe."

Bacha thought a minute and said, "Yeshua, you are eleven now, aren't you?"

"Yes, why?"

"Next year won't you be going to Jerusalem to celebrate Passover and to celebrate becoming an adult as you reach your twelfth year?"

"In Israel we are considered adults in our thirteenth year. But the twelfth year is also important. So if my stepfather permits it, yes I will attend."

"Well, let's meet there then. I will be going there too. Yeshua, I will wait for you inside the Fish Gate on the northern side of Jerusalem. I will be there early, so look for me as soon as you get there."

It was time to go. Yeshua would walk north to Nazareth and Bacha south to Samaria. "Don't forget, little brother," shouted Bacha.

A flock of birds were flying into the dark forest. "I know, big brother! The Fish Gate," Yeshua shouted back.

14 (Yeshua returns home)

The closer Yeshua got to Nazereth, the more frightened he became. *What are they going to say to me?* he thought. He knew his mother would cry and he knew his stepfather would be angry. Beyond that, he was uncertain of their reaction. He began to feel sick to his stomach. Each step closer to his house brought a new thought. *Maybe going home is a bad idea. But where would I go? What should I do? I just don't know what to do.*

His mother was ecstatic when her trembling firstborn appeared at the door. It had been almost a half year. At first they both just cried and hugged one another. Then she began to shout, "Yaaqob, Yosef, Shimon, Miryam! Come look! Your brother Yeshua has returned! He's home! He's home!"

They all came and stood around him. Yaaqob was smiling, but the other three were looking at him like he was a stranger. Ephrayim's reaction is what Yeshua feared the most. But his mother said that Ephrayim was in Sepphoris trying to secure a business deal and would not be back for a week.

Mara kept touching him, as if trying to convince herself that this wasn't just a dream. "Let me look at you. Have you been eating right? You look like you haven't been eating right, Yeshua. You're not as heavy as you were before. I'm going to fix us all dinner now. I want to see you eat."

Then Yeshua began to talk, but his mother put her finger over his lips to quiet him, and shook her head. "Not now," she said. "Later. First we eat. I'm very angry with you right now, Yeshua, and I need to calm myself down. You have no idea what you put me through. How could you do that to me—to us? What were you thinking? No. You sit. I'll cook. We'll eat. And then you explain to me why you did what you did."

After they had eaten, he sat with his mother and told her all about why he had left. He told her about Bacha, and about his adventures in Samaria. Yaaqob and Yosef sat around him listening intently. He was quite honest about his brush with death, and how Bacha's hiding place had saved him. Mara's eyes grew wide, but she said nothing. Yeshua was purposely avoiding talk of Ephrayim, but he finally asked.

Mara appeared to be gathering her thoughts. Yeshua was familiar with that look on her face. "Your father—and yes, I'm calling him your father, not your stepfather—was as frightened as I was. He spent a lot of time looking for you, Yeshua. He even went to that poor section outside of Sepphoris that you used to visit to see if anyone had seen you. His impressions of the poor have changed since he went there. He met someone there who seems to know you well. His name is Yechezqel."

Yeshua's face lit up. Ephrayim had met Yechezqel! "What did Yechezqel tell him, mother?"

"He was very concerned about you, and told your father about what a bright child you are, and how caring you are of the other children. He told your father about the mashals you tell everyone, and how you share your food with those who have none. Your father was very proud of you, Yeshua. It was a side of you he had never seen before. Yechezqel said to let him know the moment we learn anything of your whereabouts.

"As the weeks went by, we all began to fear the worst. Your father feared you might be dead. He feared you might have been killed by robbers, or attacked by some of the wild animals. But something inside me told me you were still alive. If you were dead, I think I would have known it, Yeshua. I would have felt it inside me."

Yeshua was beginning to face the full consequences of his actions. He was seeing the impact his leaving had had on his family. He felt ashamed. "I'm so sorry Mother. I guess I just didn't think things all the way through. I now wish I would have told you before I left."

Mara was quiet. Yeshua turned to his next younger brouther and asked, "And you, Yaaqob, are you your father's apprentice now?"

Yaaqob lifted his head, and puffed his chest out. "Yes I am. I have decided not to go back to school. I am my father's apprentice and soon I'll be his business partner. We have lots of discussions about the business, father and I."

***

When Ephrayim returned a week later, he was very surprised to see Yeshua. He was angry at first, but not as angry as Yeshua had expected him to be. He didn't yell and then walk away to his workshop like he used to. Ephrayim had changed. He even talked differently. His voice was gentler. And it was as if Ephrayim was treating him more like an adult and less like a child. "Come son," Ephrayim said. "Let's go talk alone." The two of them walked down to the river where Ephrayim used to go when he was angry.

"Yeshua," Ephrayim began, "I should be very angry at you. But I'm just glad and relieved you have returned. Your mother told me some of what happened. If only you had told your brother or even your friend Yechezqel what you were doing or where you were going, one of them could have told us and we wouldn't have worried so much about you. But you were just ... gone. Do you know how that made us feel? Do you have any idea?"

"I'm sorry, Father. I never meant to hurt you or Mother." For the first time in his life, he had addressed his stepfather as "father." Ephrayim seemed to notice and smile.

"Why did you leave us, my son?"

Yeshua confessed. "Do you remember that night when you sat with mother and talked about taking Yaaqob and me out of school?"

"You were listening to our private conversation?" Ephrayim's voice increased in volume.

"I couldn't live that life, Father. I can't live that life. I can't be a carpenter. I know this in my heart. The only thing that ever brought me joy in this town was my school lessons with Rabbi Towbiyah. And you were about to take that away from me."

Ephrayim spoke with a calmer voice now. "Yeshua, do you really think I wanted to bring you unhappiness? I know how much you enjoy school. I just wasn't making enough money to feed us all, son. What was I to do? Would it be better for us to starve? I made the only decision I knew how to make. I did what I thought was right. Tell me, what would you have done if you were me?"

Yeshua groped for an answer, but he knew that there wasn't one. "I guess I would have done the same thing."

"Now that you are back, Yeshua, what will you do? Next year when we celebrate Passover, you will be twelve. Our laws say that when you are thirteen, you are considered to be a man. And yet you have no trade. You have no training. You need to learn to do something. Think long and hard about this. Don't say anything now. But think it through. We will speak again in a week. Now come, let's go home and prepare for the evening meal."

Yeshua was happy that Ephrayim had not said anything about his becoming a carpenter. Ephrayim put his arm around Yeshua's shoulder as they walked back. It felt good.

15 (A reunion with Efah)

The next day Yeshua went to the temple to speak to Rabbi Towbiyah. The morning lessons were over, and in another hour the older children would be coming. The rabbi was happy to see Yeshua safe and sound. He had been terribly worried and had helped Ephrayim search for his son.

They spoke about the two different versions of the Torah, and Rabbi Towbiyah confirmed the priest Joiada's historical explanation of the hatred between the Samaritans and the Israelites. The rabbi also agreed with Joiada's assessment that there were far more likenesses between the two people than there were differences.

The conversation then turned toward Yeshua's schooling. The rabbi asked, "Yeshua, will you be returning to school? I miss our disagreements over the scriptures. You make me think, as I hope I make you think."

"You do make me think. I too enjoy our discussions. As to my returning, I don't know, Rabbi. My father hasn't said anything about school, and I think it is too soon to ask."

"Do you want me to ask him, Yeshua?" the rabbi offered.

"No. Thank you, Rabbi, but this is something I need to do for myself."

Rabbi Towbiyah's face brightened as he said, "Yeshua, I think you are growing up!"

Some of the older children began to enter the temple, so Yeshua said goodbye. He rounded the corner from the Temple and started down the hill to his house when he heard the familiar taunt: "Hey Yeshua! Where's your father? Yeshua, son of Mara!"

Efah was with several of his friends, and they were all smirking, waiting to see what would happen. Yeshua and Efah hadn't seen each other in half a year, but it was as if no time had passed at all. Efah seemed to have grown even taller than he was before. In the past Yeshua would quickly walk away, with Efah and all his friends running behind him taunting him. But this time Yeshua just stood there and said nothing.

"What's wrong, son of Mara? Can't talk today?"

Again Yeshua said nothing, but neither did he move. He just looked straight into Efah's eyes. He could see the confusion in Efah's face. Still he stood there saying nothing, indifferent toward Efah's taunts, almost casual.

Finally, Efah could stand it no longer and swaggered up to Yeshua and pushed him; or at least tried to. Yeshua quickly sidestepped him and Efah only pushed into air. He turned to face Yeshua and this time threw his right fist toward Yeshua's face. Yeshua with one hand grabbed the fist, lifting it high up into the air, and grabbed Efah's elbow with the other. Moving quickly behind him, Yeshua twisted him face-down to the ground. Efah was furious. He turned over and tried to stand, but Yeshua kicked his feet out from under him as he did, and Efah fell to the ground again. He rolled away from Yeshua and shot up. This time he ran toward him the same way that Yeshua used to do to him. Yeshua grabbed his hand, turned his back to Efah, and using the momentum that Efah himself had created, flipped him over his back and onto the ground again. Efah landed hard. There was disbelief in the faces of Efah's friends. Again and again Efah found himself on the ground. Yet not once did Yeshua hit him. When it looked like he could no longer get up, Yeshua simply turned and walked away. He could hear Efah's heavy breathing.

And then it happened. Suddenly Yeshua saw bright white lights and then as suddenly, darkness. When he woke up, he was lying on the ground, and his old friend David, whom Yeshua used to tell mashals to on the way home from school, was next to him. Yeshua felt dizzy and confused, and his head was throbbing. "What in the—what just happened?" he asked as he felt the huge lump on the back of his head with his hand.

"I was watching the whole thing from the corner of the temple. When you walked away, Efah picked up a big stone and threw it at you with his sling. It knocked you out, Yeshua. Your head was bleeding pretty badly, but I stopped it with my tunic. My mother is going to kill me when she sees all this blood on it."

"Thanks, David." Yeshua was still too dizzy to stand so he sat there for a few minutes. There was so much blood on David's tunic that it looked as if he had been stabbed.

"Yeshua where did you learn to fight like that? You were incredible. When Efah threw that stone at you and knocked you down, he turned to his friends and laughed. But they wouldn't even look at him, Yeshua. They were disgusted with him, and just walked away and left him standing there by himself. He stared at you for a short time clenching his fists, and then left. That's when I came over."

Yeshua had unfairly lost a fight, but had gained much respect from Efah's friends. He had also made Efah an even bigger enemy than before. But respect was an important commodity among youth, and what Efah had lost, Yeshua had gained. By the next day, everyone in Nazareth would know what had happened. From that day forward, everyone would see both him and Efah differently.

16 (Ephrayim in Sepphoris)

Ephrayim was sweating as he signed the contract with a trembling hand, though he tried not to let Eleazar see his fear. "There it is, sir," he said as he handed the contract back. "Twenty tables, 120 chairs."

"Very good, Ephrayim. I'll be back in two months to inspect your work and pay you."

As he walked out the door to the workshop Ephrayim was renting in Sepphoris, he turned back once and smiled at him. Ephrayim smiled back. Things did not go the way he wanted them to during negotiations, but Ephrayim, after thinking it over, was willing to take the two risks that Eleazar had written into the contract. One risk was that Eleazar wanted Ephrayim to hire two local workers, Yonatan and Yishmael, who Ephrayim did not know personally, because he needed the job done quickly. Ephrayim much would have preferred to use some of the carpenters he knew in Nazareth. However, he had seen some of the local carpenters' work, and they appeared to know the trade when he met and talked to them earlier. The second risk, and the one that really worried him, was that although Ephrayim himself would not get paid until the job was complete, the workers would only work if they got paid weekly. This meant that Ephrayim needed to pay money up front. He not only needed upfront money for the two workers, but also for the building material and the rental of the workshop.

If it works out, this could very well be the start of the business I once dreamed of, he thought. With Yaaqob still out of school, and Yeshua having been gone for half a year, he had managed to save just enough money that he could now pay these upfront costs.

They would need to make two tables per day for the next ten days. Then, if each person made at least one chair per day, there would be plenty of time built in for any unforeseen circumstances. Ephrayim was going to make sure that this project went smoothly. He had everything planned to the last nail.

Yonatan and Yishmael arrived early the next morning. They each read through the contracts that Ephrayim had written up, and signed them. "Tell me Ephrayim, how do you know Eleazar?" Yishmael wanted to know.

"I don't," Ephrayim replied.

The two exchanged glances, and then looked back to Ephrayim.

"He told me that someone in the government had seen my work, and recommended me. This person, whoever he is, didn't want me to know his identity for some reason."

"Very strange," Yishmael said. "I've never known Eleazar to hire someone he didn't know personally, especially for a job like this."

"Nor do I know anyone in the government," added Ephrayim. "But that is of no matter to me. What matters is that we do a good job. Let's get started."

Yonatan and Yishmael had worked together for many years, and so they needed little supervision. Ephrayim's plans were well designed. By the end of the first day they had two beautiful tables, just as Ephrayim had envisioned.

Since they worked so well together, Ephrayim reasoned that he could leave them with building the tables and he could start on the chairs. They would likely be done long before the two months was up, and Ephrayim would thus save some of the money that would otherwise be spent on labor. Each day when it was time for the midday meal, Yonatan and Yishmael would go off together and eat. This left Ephrayim alone to sit and dream. He no longer dreamed of being rich, or living in a big house. He dreamed of being recognized far and wide for the quality of his work. He dreamed of owning a business with his sons. He even dreamed of Yeshua coming to his senses and learning the carpentry trade. Each day, unseen by Ephrayim, a stranger stood outside the shop and watched.

Although Ephrayim did not mingle with the Romans as the Sadducees and the Herodians did, he did long to be part of the rebuilding of the city. It had been totally destroyed by Varus, the Roman governor of Syria, when Ephrayim was just a child. The city had been burned to the ground, and all the inhabitants who could be captured before they ran away were sold into slavery. This was the Roman answer to not one but two revolts. The first took place when the Roman Senate made Herod "king of the Judeans." He had complete authority over Galilee, but Sepphoris refused to submit to his authority. A bloody siege took place and the first rebellion was quashed. But when Herod died, Judah ben Hezekiah, who was the son of the leader of the first revolt, took more drastic action, plundering the palace of Herod in Sepphoris and arming the city's people. This led Varus to take these final steps.

Antipas, Herod's son, was now reconstructing the city, and would rename it Autocratoris when it was finished, in honor of the emperor Augustus. Not far from Ephrayim's workshop they were beginning work on a huge theater that could seat fifteen thousand people. *Oh, to be part of that*, Ephrayim thought.

On the second day of the third week, Yonatan came in by himself. "Where's Yishmael?" Ephrayim asked.

"He is very sick, Ephrayim. He has fever and can't keep his food down. I don't know when he will be able to come back to work. But I'm sure you and I can get everything done in time."

This was not good news for Ephrayim. He made mental calculations and determined that as long as they worked hard, the two of them just might get the job done in time. And however many days Yishmael was out sick was money Ephrayim would be saving. However, nothing else could go wrong or Ephrayim would indeed have a problem.

Yishmael returned to work in two weeks. But with just three days left before the contract said the job needed to be completed, Yonatan hit his hand with his hammer, breaking bones in two fingers. Ephrayim and Yishmael wrapped the fingers up so that they would heal properly, but Yonatan could no longer work. This was very bad news.

Now it was just the two of them trying to get everything done in time. Ephrayim worked long into the night all by himself for those last four days. He slept in the workshop to save money.

It was the last day, the day that Elezar was to return, and they were not finished. Only three more chairs to go, when they saw one of Elezar's servants coming to the workshop to bring Ephrayim to Elezar's home. Ephrayim looked at Yishmael helplessly. "Go to him, Ephrayim." Yishmael said. "Keep him as long as you can. Meantime, I will finish. Just keep him from coming back too soon. I can do this."

Ephrayim nodded. "Thank you for—"

"Never mind that. No time. Go. Go."

Ephrayim met the servant outside before he entered the shop. Together, they walked to Elezar's house. Elezar was standing out in his front garden.

"Ephrayim, it's good to see you. Is it finished?" he asked as Ephrayim walked through his front gate.

"Of course it is sir, " Ephrayim lied. "Just as I promised."

The two went inside, sat at Eleazar's table, and drank a glass of wine. Ephrayim drank his wine slowly, and tried to engage Elezar in conversation, but Elezar seemed interested in finishing his business. Elezar pulled out his copy of the contract, glanced through it one more time and said, "Shall we go see your work?"

The two of them walked toward the studio, Ephrayim hoping that Yishmael had completed the chairs. Then Ephrayim noticed a billowing of smoke coming from that direction. Many of the townspeople were running toward the smoke, some of them shouting, "Fire, fire!" Ephrayim and Eleazar also ran. It was the workshop! The entire building was burning. The roof had already been destroyed, and the tables and chairs inside were all part of the blazing inferno. Ephrayim gasped as he saw all his work going up in flames. *Who could have done such a thing?* Ephrayim thought. *It had to have been set on purpose. How else could it have happened?* There was nothing that could be done, however, and so they watched helplessly as the fire reached its final end and began to smolder. The workshop was a detached building, so no other buildings caught fire, but its destruction was total. Yishmael was lying on the ground outside the smoldering building, coughing.

Between coughs he said: "Ephrayim. Someone came from behind and hit me over the head after you left, and must have set the place on fire. I would have died in there had Yonatan not come by to celebrate your completion. He saw the smoke and ran inside."

Yonatan, who was sitting next to Yishmael continued, "I dragged Yishmael outside, and ran back in to try and get at least some of the tables and chairs out, but the flames were already too great, and it was too hot and smoky to go back inside."

Ephrayim sat on the ground and slowly shook his head from side to side. All that time, all that money, all that work—gone. Eleazar was angry that he had no tables or chairs. The owner of the workshop would be angry that his property had been destroyed.

Ephrayim filed a report with the town authorities, but there were no witnesses, so nothing could be done. He would not have to pay damages to the owner of the workshop, but he would also not get paid by Eleazar. Eleazar was paying for a finished product, not labor. This meant that the money Ephrayim paid Yishmael and Yonatan out of his own pocket had been lost. The rent money he paid the workshop owner, also out of his own pocket, had been lost. The money he had paid for the wood; lost. Many of the tools he had brought with him, the time and labor he had put into this project—all lost.

Eleazar decided to buy used furniture rather than renewing his contract with Ephrayim, because, he said, he needed to open his restaurant soon, and could not afford to wait until new furniture could be built. And so any chance of recouping any of his financial losses had also been lost. What would he tell Mara?

He slowly began his walk back to Nazareth. Off in the distance, standing in the shadows slightly behind a building, a lone man was watching him go, smiling.

***

It was late in the afternoon, and the sun was beginning to usher forth the warmest part of the day. Mara looked outside to see Ephrayim slowly walking toward the house. Something was wrong. He did not look happy. She had seen that look—drooping chin, mouth open, black half-circles underneath his red eyes—only once or twice before. He also was not carrying his tools. She ran outside to meet him. "Ephrayim, what happened? Where are your tools?"

Ephrayim was a strong man who rarely cried, but on this occasion he began to weep loudly, shaking his fists into the heavens. "I'm ruined!" he cried. "Mara, what are we going to do now? I've lost everything. Everything!"

She took his arm and gently walked him to the house where he sat at the table. He sat with his head in his hands and rocked back and forth.

"Now tell me what happened, my love." She reached across the table and held his hands in hers, looking at him with understanding eyes.

He told her in detail the events, not noticing the agitation that she was now beginning to display. He kept asking aloud, "Who could have done this, Mara? Why would someone do this to me?"

She could hold back no longer. "Tahmid must have done it!"

His eyes widened. "Tahmid? No! Why do you say that? Tahmid would never do such a thing."

Now it was Mara's turn to tell a story. It had been over half a year, but she could quote his exact words, because she had heard them over and over in her head since the day it happened: "This is not over, I promise you. Think about that when you pray tonight."

Before she could even complete her story, Ephrayim forcefully pushed his chair back and started hurriedly for the door. "Ephrayim, wait. What are you going to do?"

But Ephrayim ignored her and left the house. Mara watched as he ran, knowing that nothing good would come of this.

***

Tahmid lived on the other side of Nazareth in a two-story house much like Ephrayim's. By the time Ephrayim got there, he was angrier still. He pounded on the door.

Tahmid's wife, Shoshan, opened it with a perplexed look on her face.

"Where is he?" Ephrayim shouted.

"Where is who?" answered Tahmid, limping around the corner. Ephrayim immediately doubled up his fist and threw it into Tahmid's face with all his might, sending him hurling back onto the ground. There was blood pouring out of his nose and a shocked look on his face.

"If you ever talk to my wife like that again, I'll kill you. Do you hear me? I'll kill you!"

Tahmid rose but only to hold a cloth to his nose. Shoshan stood between them.

"What are you doing, Ephrayim? What's wrong with you?"

"Ask Tahmid. He insults my wife, he insults my children, and he burns down my work in Sepphoris. Your husband is a wicked man."

Tahmid took the cloth away from his nose for a moment and said, "Sepphoris? I was nowhere near Sepphoris. I burned down nothing."

"And you didn't call my child a bastard? And you didn't accuse my wife of adultery? Are you denying you said those things?"

Shoshan said, "Ephrayim, I think you had better leave. And don't ever come back here. I can't believe Tahmid would say or do those things."

Ephrayim was shaking but beginning to calm down. "Tahmid, you and I used to be great friends." He was pointing his finger toward Tahmid's face. "But insulting my family and burning down my work was the last straw. I mean what I say, Tahmid. I'll kill you if you come near my wife again."

***

Ephrayim stormed off, and Shoshan tried to help Tahmid with his nosebleed. He briskly turned away from her, not letting her touch him. "It's her," he said. "She put him up to this. She is an evil woman, Shoshan."

"So you really did say those things to her?" she asked.

"You know the kind of woman she is. All of Nazareth knows. He never should have married her, Shoshan. She should have been stoned to death long ago. Now she has poisoned him against me. You saw that."

The bleeding had stopped, and Tahmid went outside to wash his face. If ever there was even a thought of reconciliation between him and Ephrayim, it was gone now. It was gone forever.

17 (Patanjali's vision)

AD 8
Pratishthana, India

Pratishthana was situated almost exactly in the center of the southern territory of India called the Satavahana Empire. Pratishthana was the empire's capital city and a great commercial center, renowned throughout the West for its exports, especially its textiles. It was here in the great palace of King Aristakarman that Patanjali had a vision that worried him. As with all of his visions, he saw some things, but not all things. On this day he saw two children in a far off Western land. One of these children was destined to become a great spiritual teacher—one of the greatest, or perhaps *the* greatest. He saw the child being turned away by those he sought out to teach him. The older child was a friend and a protector of sorts. And what worried him most was that the children were in great danger.

Prince Hala, who studied the Vedas from Patanjali, was most interested in hearing more. Patanjali's future visions had always come true. He had seen the peace that had come throughout the Satavahana Empire of India before it actually happened, and more recently he saw the impending dangers of war. Invaders from the North would soon be coming, he had warned King Aristakarman. The king also put great faith in Patanjali's visions, and prepared his army for the impending invasion. Prince Hala was next in line to be king. Not yet on the throne, he was already contemplating his legacy. If this person whom Patanjali saw was in fact going to become a great spiritual teacher, and his very life was now in danger, what would be a more fitting tribute to himself than to have arranged the saving of this child's life, and to have him brought to India to achieve his greatness there? Hala's name might well go down in history as the one who saved the greatest spiritual teacher in the world. "King Hala, friend and savior of …"

"Who is this person?" Prince Hala asked. "What is his name? Bring him to me. I wish to meet him."

The prince was used to issuing commands and having them immediately followed. But Patanjali, though he would not directly disobey an order of Prince Hala, could not always make things happen the way the prince would like.

"His name I cannot tell you. I only see what I see, my Prince."

"Well, tell me what you see. What does he look like?" Prince Hala wanted to know.

"I cannot see his face or the face of the other. The older child, the protector, has some sort of mark on his arm, perhaps a scar or tattoo. This I *can* see."

"But where in the West does this child come from, Patanjali?"

Patanjali paused a moment and sat in silence, then replied, "Egypt. No, wait. Not Egypt. But nearby. Yes, the land where the teacher dwells is near Egypt. There will be a great spiritual festival soon in this land. Both the children will be there. The teacher child, the great one, will be turned away by his own teachers. It is at this time that both the great one and the protector will be in danger of being murdered."

Again Prince Hala thought of his legacy. *I must bring about the saving of this child's life. He will be grateful to me, and thus, as he achieves greatness here in India, so will I.* He summoned his most trusted aide, Vijayananda, for the task of finding the child and bringing him back. Like the prince himself, Vijayananda was of the warrior caste, called Kshatriyas, and although only nineteen, was wise beyond his years. He had already traveled twice to this land that Patanjali spoke of, Egypt, by ship, and although he couldn't yet speak the Egyptian language, he could speak fluently a language called Hebrew. It was what many of the ship's crew spoke on his two voyages. In Egypt, in the port city of Myos Hormon, it was spoken as well. Vijayananda had a gift for learning languages, and found learning Hebrew a welcome challenge.

Vijayananda's skin was a beautiful dark brown, and his tall body was muscular. His dark hair was braided and came down to his massive chest. His eyes were deep set, and he had a large, flat nose. Painted on his forehead was an *Urdhva Pundra* (upright lotus). Its "U" shape symbolized the heel of a Hindu god called Vishnu. Its color was white, although it had a third vertical red line going through the center. This identified Vijayananda as a worshipper of Vishnu. As a warrior, Vijayananda was not afraid of the unknown. But to go to Egypt, find a nearby land with an unknown name, find a spiritual festival that he knew nothing about, find a child with a tattoo or scar on his arm whose name he did not know, and find a great teacher who was not yet a teacher and whose name he also didn't know—these were overwhelming challenges he was not prepared for. Patanjali assured him that he would be successful. He didn't trust Patanjali's visions as much as Prince Hala did, but he knew his duty.

"As you command, my Prince. I will set out this very day." Vijayananda was given money for the voyage there and back, and money to pay for the teacher's voyage. Much more money than he needed. But the prince knew Vijayananda would only spend what was necessary. He depended on Vijayananda's warrior-like cunning and Patanjali's meditative insight, and although it might be more than a year before Vijayananda returned, Prince Hala had already grown anxious to meet this young spiritual teacher.

Before he left, Patanjali delivered a strict warning. "Vijayananda, once you get to the festival, find the protector quickly, but speak to no one else. I see great danger there. Even the protector will not see it. Both of their lives will be in your hands."

18 (Yeshua's real father - Yosef)

It was two weeks before Passover, and Mara was resting in the early afternoon when the sun was overhead, making it hard to do any work. Ephrayim was in Bethabara, on the other side of the River Jordan, working with a group of other carpenters on a building that a rich landowner was going to turn into an inn. All the children except for Yeshua were napping. Yeshua sat down next to her on her bed and gave her that look that she knew meant something important was on his mind. This time she would make the time for him, even though she would rather nap. She reached up and brushed his curly bangs off to the side and waited for him to speak.

"Please tell me about my father, I beg you tell me, Mother." Yeshua's eyes were filled with tears, and Mara knew that he was finally old enough to know the truth.

She looked into his gentle eyes and was silent for a moment. Then she said, "If I tell you, Yeshua, do you promise never to ask me again? And do you promise never to repeat any of this, even to your stepfather?"

Yeshua immediately nodded his head. Mara sensed his eagerness and knew that he had desperately wanted to know this for a long time.

"Very well," she began. "I was born in Sepphoris, less than a day's journey from here. I came from a very rich family and lived in a beautiful house. Oh Yeshua, you have no idea how beautiful it was, and how beautiful the city will be once it is completely rebuilt. When I was living there, there were already bathhouses and theaters, and beautiful mosaic floors. The streets where I lived were paved, and the markets were always filled with fresh fruits and vegetables. I had fine dresses and jewelry and everything a girl could ask for.

"When I was fourteen, I met your father, Yosef. That was his name, my son: Yosef. Your father wanted to become a rabbi. He was studying with one of the rabbis in Sepphoris and was learning very quickly. We met at a religious festival and quickly fell in love. But my parents had promised me to a man named Aharon, a very rich man from an aristocratic family, and a wealthy landowner. When they found out about us, my father forbade me from seeing Yosef.

"I had no interest in Aharon and let him and my parents know. My father had the law on his side and could rightfully promise me to whomever he chose. He let me know that at every opportunity. Yosef and I began to meet secretly, until one night we were caught by my father. He tried to have Yosef arrested, but because I was not yet engaged, he had broken no laws. My father insisted that I not see Yosef again. But I did.

"Finally, when he saw that I would not respect his wishes, he gave me an ultimatum. Marry whomever I chose, but if I chose to marry Yosef, I would be disowned. I would have no dowry. I would never be allowed back in the house again. In truth, he could have rightfully even sold me into slavery, and he let me know that too. But I knew he would never do such a thing.

"I loved your father, Yosef. I loved him with all my heart. And so I made the only decision I could. I followed my heart.

"We were wed, but only Yosef's family attended the wedding. My parents were bitter and refused to have anything to do with us. It was on the seventh day of our marriage that a terrible thing happened."

Mara began to tremble, and Yeshua grew very quiet, although he was beginning to tremble too. He stroked her hair and held her hands in his. "Please go on, Mother."

"Your father and I were walking home one evening when we heard footsteps behind us. I turned around, and there he was: a very large man with a hideous face. He had a mean look, and a knife in his hand. I begged him to go away—Yosef did too—but he kept walking toward us. We were backing up as he neared. Yosef pushed me behind him and stood between the man and me. Your father was a beautiful, kind man, Yeshua, but he was not a fighter. The man lunged. In less than the blink of an eye, Yosef was lying on the street with a knife deep in his chest, and blood . . . Oh God, there was so much blood, Yeshua. It ran down the street like rain.

"Yosef's eyes were open but I knew that he no longer saw anything. He was gone forever. I became confused. Why would this evil man do this horrible thing? Did he intend to rob us? No, he took no money. To this day I don't know why he did it, Yeshua. The awful man simply ran away, leaving me alone with my dead husband. Your dear father, Yosef."

Yeshua was trembling. Mara's hands tightened around his, and she continued. "Yeshua, I didn't know what to do. I ran to my parents' house and pounded on the door begging for help. I was shouting, I don't even know what I was saying. But my father's heart was turned to stone, and he told me that whatever happened, it was of my own making. He told me to go away. I shouted again, begging for help, and again he told me to leave. And so I left."

"Why didn't you go to my father's house? Yosef's. His parents would have helped you, mother. I know they would have." Yeshua was breathing quickly.

"I did go there, Yeshua." Mara stroked Yeshua's hair. "Right after my father turned his heart away from me I went. But they were not home. Nobody was home. I pounded and pounded on the door but nobody came. Finally I just started walking."

"I don't even know how I came to Nazareth, Yeshua. I had wandered about for four days. But when I was walking through the streets of Nazareth in a stupor, a kindly old woman by the name of Rachel walked up to me and asked me what the matter was. I couldn't talk, I was too much in shock and in pain, but she saw that I was in desperate need of help. And so she took me to her home."

Yeshua asked, "Was she the same Rachel whom we used to visit before she died last year?"

Mara's eyes filled with tears. "Yes," she said. "Rachel was like the mother I never had. I won't tell you about my mother right now; that is another story. But Rachel was so kind to me. Within a few weeks it became obvious that I was with child. I had *you* inside me, Yeshua. You were all I had left of Yosef, and you were so precious to me." She paused a moment to look into his eyes and once again brush his bangs with her hand. "You still are. I remember shortly before you were born I kept holding my belly as if I were already holding you in my arms. I couldn't wait.

"I had told my story to Rachel and to some of the people of Nazareth, but they were so unkind, Yeshua. Some of them thought I was lying about your father Yosef, and was unwed. Rabbi Towbiyah sent a man named Tahmid to Sepphoris to inquire, but a government official told them that there was no person named Yosef who had been murdered, and as far as they knew, a person named Mara had never married. It was either a horrible mistake, or an ugly lie, but that was what Tahmid told Rabbi Towbiyah.

"The good rabbi took pity on me. He didn't believe me to be a person worthy of being stoned to death. He told everyone that just because nobody named Yosef had been *reported* murdered, didn't mean it hadn't happened. Many deaths took place in Sepphoris that were not reported. And the official only said that 'as far as *he* knew' I had not been married."

Yeshua shook his head back and forth. Now he looked off into the distance, not at Mara, but he seemed to be listening intently.

"Tahmid could have investigated further, and perhaps found the priest who married us, or found Yosef's parents. But his mind was already made up, as was most of the rest of Nazareth. Nobody truly believed me. Although I wasn't stoned, I was despised as a sinner. I felt like even if I went to Sepphoris myself and brought back proof of my marriage, they would all say I had just bribed someone. Nobody but Rachel would look at me or talk to me. It was during the last few weeks before you were born that Ephrayim became my friend. Ephrayim also believed me. He really is a wonderful, caring person, Yeshua, and I hope that you will someday see that.

"Ephrayim made the most beautiful crib for you. It's the one that all your brothers and sisters have since used. And he kept coming around to help me. Sometimes he would bring food for Rachel and me, sometimes he would fix a broken table or chop wood for our fire. And always we would talk and talk on int`o the night. Rachel would leave the door open, and the downstairs lanterns lit, so that nobody would think us to be alone and spread even more horrible rumors.

"And then one day, he offered to marry me. He said that you would need a father, and he was quite willing to be that person. He said he didn't want or need to know anything more about my past. He just knew that he loved me and wanted to be a husband and a father.

"He is *still* trying to be your father, Yeshua. You know that, do you not?"

Yeshua appeared to Mara to be confused. She had given him a lot of information, and she wasn't sure how much he had taken in. He continued to stare into the distance.

Mara grabbed him by both of his shoulders, turned him toward her, and shook him. Now he stared at her. "Yeshua, your stepfather is a very sensitive man. I have spared him all the details about my past that I have just now told you, partly because he would rather not hear about it, and partly because I would rather not think about it. I would ask that you respect my wishes and not bring any of this up again, especially in front of him. All right?"

Yeshua was very quiet for a long time. He then nodded his head yes. Mara waited. She knew he had more to say.

Yeshua suddenly stood, folded his arms, and lifted his head. "Mother, I am going to become a rabbi," he said with great conviction. He even tossed his head with that shake that was so familiar to Mara. "I am going to become the rabbi my father, Yosef, never had a chance to become."

Mara closed her eyes and said nothing.

19 (Vijayananda arrives in Egypt)

AD 9

Vijayananda was happy to get off the ship at Egypt's Myos Hormon. He didn't mind the sea, but he much preferred feeling ground beneath his feet. The city was bustling with merchants and traders. Indian traders were buying gold coins to bring back to their homeland to be reminted into their own coins; spices were being bought and sold; clothing and fine cloth for making clothing were exchanging hands.

Vijayananda moved away from the main crowd. These people would be too busy making money to stop and talk. But further away he would find people willing to converse. Of these, he would need to find those who spoke Hebrew. It would not be hard. Almost everyone spoke a little Greek and a little Hebrew. He bought some bread from a local baker and found him to be quite knowledgeable of events near and far. The man told him about spiritual festivals in Egypt but didn't know much about festivals going on in other countries. He spoke in his own language to a fellow merchant, and after a short exchange, he asked Vijayananda, "You are looking for a spiritual festival somewhere near here, but not Egypt?"

"Yes, that is what I am seeking."

"How near?"

Vijayananda didn't know, so he guessed, "A few days' walk."

Again, the two merchants talked. He then said, "Ah, too bad. There is a festival of great spiritual significance in Judea, in a city called Jerusalem, but it is more than a few days' walk. The festival will take place in fifteen days."

"How far is it?" Vijayananda wanted to know.

"By camel, it is about an eleven- or twelve-day journey."

Vijayananda continued to walk through the city and talk to others, but after some time had passed, he had come up with nothing more. He would have to take a chance that Jerusalem was the place. He found a group of traveling merchants with enough empty camels to take a few people with them. They would leave in the morning. Meantime, because he was thorough, he would continue to talk to others, asking about spiritual festivals in nearby foreign lands. He learned of none. By nightfall, Vijayananda was convinced that if Patanjali's vision was true, it would have to be in Jerusalem that he would find this teacher who was not yet a teacher.

20 (Journey to Jerusalem)

AD 9
Yeshua's age: 12

For Yeshua and his family, the journey to Jerusalem began as it always did. Ephrayim walked in the front, guiding a donkey and a cart. In the cart were Mara and the younger children. Yeshua and Yaaqob walked behind.

"Will your friend Bacha be there?" asked Yaaqob as they walked down the busy road.

"Yes, he promised he would," answered Yeshua.

"Can you trust the word of a Sam-a-ri-tan?" Yaaqob asked, elongating the word "Samaritan."

Yeshua's response was to angrily punch his brother on the shoulder. Yaaqob only laughed and ran a few steps ahead.

"Boys, be nice," Mara cried out.

Yeshua felt ashamed that his family would be among the group who crossed the River Jordan, then followed it south, just to avoid, as many in Nazareth often said, "breathing the same air as the Samaritans." That phrase had never bothered him before, but now that he was friends with Bacha it seemed wrong. He wanted them all to meet Bacha and see that Samaritans—at least some of them—were nice people.

The crowd of Nazarenes now split. Some, including Yeshua and his family, continued east to the river and others followed the direct route south through Samaria. The crowd that traveled through Samaria, however, would avoid its people at all costs.

There were several fords along the river allowing them to cross over to the other side of Samaria and then back just before they reached the Sea of Salt. It had been a dry winter, and the river was almost like a creek in many places.

Yeshua and Yaaqob sometimes played a game on the way to Jerusalem. They would take turns walking backwards, hanging onto the tunic of the other. It was fun, and a little challenging to walk, not being able to see. Yeshua watched the crowd behind him, and saw a tall man with a limp and a woman. He did not know who they were, but they both seemed to know who he was. The couple saw Yeshua, and stopped suddenly. Yeshua watched as they frantically talked to each other, gesturing with their hands toward him. After a brief exchange they turned and followed the crowd traveling south through Samaria. *How strange*, Yeshua thought. Ephrayim was facing forward and missed seeing the pair whom he would have recognized as Tahmid and Shoshan.

Splash! Yaaqob had led them to a mud puddle and sidestepped it at the last minute. Yeshua, walking backward, went right in up to his ankles, and almost fell. "I'll get you for that!" he shouted at his brother. He began to chase Yaaqob.

"Yaaqob! Yeshua! Behave yourselves!" Now it was Ephrayim shouting at them. The two immediately began walking next to each other with red faces as Mara hid a smile and shook her head. Over the next few days there would be revenge, more games to play, and new ways to tease one another. The river was full of twists and turns, and Yeshua enjoyed walking along the river's edge. There was something about being near water that always made him feel good.

That first night, as they sat with many others by the fire, Yeshua and Yaaqob began to talk about Bacha once again. Yeshua said, "Samaritans aren't what we have been told, Yaaqob. I met some who were really nice. Especially Bacha. You'll see when you meet him. He lives by himself in a house that he built with the help of some friends." Yeshua was wishing they were already there.

"If they are so nice, then why did they throw human bones on the temple porches and in the sanctuary and desecrate it six years ago on Passover?" Yaaqob was eager to argue with his brother, citing a true story that was often told in Nazareth.

Yeshua thought about Yaish and his friends who had chased him. "That was only some of them, Yaaqob. They were probably angry for the insult the Jews gave them. Have you not read the scrolls of Ezra? The Samaritans offered to help rebuild the city and the temple years ago, but the Jews refused to as much as let them lift a single stone. And they won't let them enter the inner courts even to this day."

"Well, they won't let us on Mt. Gerizim either. But that's fine with me. I wouldn't want to go there, anyway. They aren't like us at all,

Yeshua. I think they are all a bunch of heathens. I'm glad we are on the other side of the river."

Yaaqob's words hurt Yeshua, but he was more angry at his brother than hurt. "You are always so quick to judge, Yaaqob. Since you dislike Samaritans so much, I won't introduce you to Bacha. He is much more of a brother to me than you ever were. We even call each other 'brother.' He never talked about us the way you do about Samaritans. He was eager to meet everyone in my family. But I will make sure that he never meets you."

No, his anger had not left him. Yeshua had simply avoided situations that brought about his anger while in Samaria. Now that he was back, so was his anger. This time it was pointed at his brother. The next day they would be playing and teasing once again, but their differences had moved them further apart.

21 (Arrival)

The journey from Myos Hormon to Jerusalem was uneventful, and had taken only ten days. Vijayananda had never been so deep into this strange land, but he was focused on his mission. He spoke to no one, and kept to himself.

Jerusalem was a beautiful city. It was not the same kind of beauty he found in his own country, but there was a grandeur about it that captivated Vijayananda. The buildings were all made of huge stones, all of them square and uniform. A huge fortress stood in the northernmost part of the city. It was square in shape, and each of its four corners consisted of a massive tower higher than anything Vijayananda had ever seen. He sensed right away this was where the city was defended. South of the fortress was a temple, the likes of which he had never seen before. The stones of the temple were pure white, with huge columns topped in gold. He marveled at its beauty and resolved that he would further explore the temple later. Right now he wanted to walk the entire perimeter of the city. Working his way around the temple and traveling south, he came to the lower part of the city, where the poor seemed to make their home. Just as in his own India, he reasoned, the rich and poor must not live together. He wondered where the rich people lived.

There were many gates into this fortress city, some of them guarded heavily and some lightly. He would remember which was which, as it might prove useful. As he got to the west side of the city, he noticed that it was at a higher elevation, and the houses were bigger and better constructed. The people were likewise better dressed. This was most certainly where the rich people lived. He walked further north and saw a palace that seemed to be made of one massive piece of white marble. Such a feat would be impossible. How is this so? When he neared it, however, he saw that it was constructed of many huge rocks, each identical to the next. They were fitted together so precisely that the building appeared seamless from a distance. This building too seemed to be military in nature like the fortress where he began his exploration, but it was not nearly as big.

North of this structure was a body of water, its shape perfectly square, just like everything else in this city. He wondered at its purpose, guessing it was drinking water for the city. Finally he reached the north edge, and off to his right was the fortress where he had begun. Good. The city was small enough that he could walk the perimeter many times in a day. This was going to be his strategy. There were so many gates leading into the city, he concluded that if he constantly walked the inside perimeter, passing each of the gates in turn, he would increase his chances of finding the two youths. Even if he missed their actual entry, he might eventually find them inside the city by continuing his vigil.

The festival would not start for a few days, so he would have time to familiarize himself with the area. He not only examined the perimeter, but walked through the upper and lower city, learning the streets and buildings. He had been warned by Patanjali not to talk to anyone once he arrived, which was not usually his way. He would have much preferred to talk to everyone and anyone, just to find out more about the festival, its customs, and the people who would come. But he was a warrior and would follow his duty as he had been instructed. He was wearing clothing that the local people wore, and had removed the painted markings on his forehead, but it was easy to see he was a foreigner. There were very few people who had skin as dark as his. He would have to take the chance that when the crowds increased, he would blend in more.

***

Within a few days, the crowds got increasingly bigger, and Vijayananda was right—nobody seemed to give him as much as a second look. His method was to do three circles around the edge of the city, cross the center of the city north to south, and then walk east to west. He would do this several times a day. According to Patanjali's vision, he was looking for two youths, one older, and maybe with a mark of some sort on his arm, perhaps a tattoo or scar. Unfortunately, everyone seemed to be wearing clothing that covered their arms. No matter, he would keep an eye out for two youths traveling alone, and when and if he found them, he would figure out a way to look at the arms of the older one.

***

Bacha arrived a few days after Vijayananda. He also liked to come a bit early and watch the spectacle unfold. It was not the grandeur of the buildings that captivated him, but rather the human mosaic being built person by person. The tunic coats of the men were made of white cotton and were rather plain, but most of the women had fine needlework in their coats, and multicolor threads. The belts of the women also were more vibrant than those of the men, being made of very colorful silk or wool, sometimes having fringe falling nearly down to their ankles. The outer mantles of both sexes' clothing were of many different colors, as were the headdresses. To sit near the temple, which was the highest elevation of the city, and see this living rainbow merge and grow was a sight to behold. Bacha never tired of it. After enjoying this for a while, Bacha walked northward and found a spot to rest by the Fish Gate, where he and Yeshua had promised to meet. Bacha was quite observant, and noticed a foreigner walking past him several times, always looking around, seemingly searching for something or someone. Bacha wondered who this person was, but mostly he watched and waited for Yeshua. At night, Bacha slept just outside the Fish Gate, along the road back to Samaria, and near one of the many campfires that pilgrims made. Especially during Passover, groups of travelers were welcoming of strangers looking for a warm and safe place to sleep.

There he is again, thought Bacha early the second afternoon. *What is he looking for?* He decided to ask the stranger rather than to just wonder. But as he approached him, Vijayananda suddenly turned in his direction, looked startled, and quickly walked away.

Bacha took that to be a challenge, and began to follow him. He would stay at a discreet distance, but he now wanted to find out more about this strange person.

***

Yeshua and his family arrived about the same time Bacha began following Vijayananda. They, along with the other pilgrims, had been singing the Songs of Ascent (Tehillim 120 through 134), which corresponded to the fifteen steps leading from the Court of the Women to the Court of the Israelis on the temple grounds. It didn't matter from which direction one entered Jerusalem, it was always "up," since Jerusalem and its temple were on the tops of a series of mountains. It was even said by the pilgrims traveling to Jerusalem that they were *going up*. Yeshua and his family approached the city from the south, traveling on the Sea of Salt road, as they usually did, and set up their tent. Yeshua was intent on his mission of becoming a rabbi and quickly went to the mikveh to bathe and purify himself so that he might go to the temple.

One of the scribes outside the temple looked Yeshua up and down. "You can't read the scrolls inside, I'm afraid. Not without permission. Besides, I can probably tell you whatever you wish to know."

Yeshua replied, "I want to read the twelve Prophets. Our city doesn't have any of them."

The scribe smiled. "Do you even know the names of the twelve Prophets, young man?"

The words were barely out of the scribe's mouth as Yeshua blurted out, "Hoshea, Yo'el, Amos, Ovadyah, Yonah, Mikha, Nachum, Havakkuk, Tzefanyah, Haggai, Zekharyah, and Mal'akhi."

"Well, at least you are educated," said the scribe. "Where is your home, young man?"

Yeshua began to feel more at ease. "Nazareth, sir."

"Nazareth? Rabbi Towbiyah?"

"Yes sir."

"You must be the one he has told me about! You are Yeshua?" Yeshua nodded. "He has told me about you many times over the past few years. He says you are gifted. Come back this afternoon, young man, and maybe I can let you see some of our scrolls, and perhaps even talk to some of the Great Sanhedrin. They are not here now, but will be gathered here in the afternoon."

Yeshua was ecstatic. Talking to the Great Sanhedrin was a great privilege for a twelve-year-old boy, and he had many questions for them. He would go to the Fish Gate to see if Bacha had arrived yet, and then wait for the afternoon when he would go back to the temple. But when he arrived at the Fish Gate, he did not see Bacha. He was disappointed because Bacha told him he would come early. Maybe he had changed his mind. Maybe he wasn't going to come at all. But he had promised! Yaaqob would now tease him all the more.

He looked around one more time and then headed back to the temple feeling a little sad, but he quickly forgot his mood when he was allowed inside and got to meet with some of the Great Sanhedrin. He immediately began to ask questions about the Prophets, and the members of the Great Sanhedrin were duly impressed with his understanding of scripture. He seemed to them much older than his twelve years. They began to test him. "Yeshua, tell us about the apple of wisdom and what we may learn from it," one of the members said.

Yeshua began, standing tall like a teacher, and of course tossing his hair back with a jerk of his head. "The serpent was a very crafty animal and asked Chavvah if she was forbidden to eat from any tree in the garden. She told him that she was allowed to eat from all the trees except from the tree in the middle of the garden. She told the serpent that God had said that if she or Adam touched it, they would die. The serpent laughed and told Chavvah that the fruit would not make them die. God just didn't want them to gain wisdom. If she ate the apple she would be as wise as God.

"*That* was the sin, rabbis. Yes, disobeying God by eating the apple was a horrible sin, but believing that she needed to be wiser than she already was, wiser than God had already made her, that was a far greater sin. God has made us all exactly as wise as we need to be."

The members of the Great Sanhedrin looked at one another in amazement. Another asked, "Can you tell us any other examples of this kind of sin? This time don't use your own words, Yeshua, use the words you have read."

Yeshua thought briefly and replied, "From the scroll of Yechezqel we hear the proclamation of God against the King of Tyre:

Thus says the Lord God: Because you compare your mind with the mind of a god, therefore, I will bring strangers against you, the most terrible of the nations; they shall draw their swords against the beauty of your wisdom and defile your splendor. They shall thrust you down to the Pit, and you shall die a violent death in the heart of the seas. Will you still say, "I am a god," in the presence of those who kill you, though you are but a mortal, and no god, in the hands of those who wound you? You shall die the death of the uncircumcised by the hand of foreigners; for I have spoken.

Once again they were astounded. Two of them were reading from a scroll as Yeshua recited its words and nodded their heads as he recited the passage flawlessly. It was as if he had memorized the entire Torah and understood it completely. They continued to probe his remarkable memory and knowledge for a few hours and then told him to come back again tomorrow.

He went back to the Fish Gate and see if Bacha was there. A new group of people was entering, and he hoped Bacha would be among them, but he watched and searched without success. *Big brother where are you? You're still not here*, Yehsua thought. *We made a promise.*

***

Bacha had lost Vijayananda somewhere in the upper city, and was now walking back to the Fish Gate. He saw Yeshua before Yeshua saw him. He jumped on him from behind, just as he had the first time they met. Yeshua immediately recognized who it was, and the two tumbled and wrestled on the ground for a few minutes. Some of the nearby adults were about to break up what they perceived to be a fight, but Bacha climbed on top, pinned both of Yeshua's arms with his knees, and began to tickle him! As the two laughed and laughed, the adults turned and walked away.

"Bacha! You came!"

"Of course I came, little brother. I said I would, didn't I? You still can't fight very well, Yai—, uh, Yeshua. I think you need some more lessons." The two began to wrestle on the ground once again.

***

Vijayananda missed the spectacle, as he was on the opposite side of the city watching yet another crowd coming in from the Sea of Salt road. Several times he had seen two boys together and followed them, but in each case, they ended up being brothers, and when they found their parents, he knew these were not the two he was looking for. Patanjali had said that the two were friends, not relatives. Each day as the crowds got bigger and bigger, Vijayananda's hopes began to fade. Maybe he was at the wrong festival after all.

22 (Passover ceremony)

Because Yeshua was now twelve years of age, he was finally allowed to take part in the Passover ceremony. This was the beginning of his initiation into manhood which would be completed the following year when he was thirteen. It was the early afternoon of the fourteenth day of Nisan, and the slaughtering of the Passover lambs was about to take place. Yeshua and Ephrayim went to the temple. Ephrayim's lamb had been purchased a few days earlier, and his brother Yo'el, who lived in Bethpage, was with them as well. Yeshua's Uncle Yo'el was still fat and reminded Yeshua of Rabbi Towbiyah. The lamb would feed both of their families. Mara and the other children were now on their way to Bethpage to help Yo'el's wife prepare for the Passover meal.

The Court of the Women was also known as the middle court, because it stood between the Court of the Gentiles and the Court of Israel. It was called the Court of the Women because women were permitted to enter but were allowed no farther. This is where those making a sacrifice waited. They had been divided into three groups. The great Nicanor Gates that separated the Court of the Women from the Court of Israel were opened, and the first of the three groups of pilgrims were let in. Ephrayim, Yo'el, and Yeshua were in the first division. When it became full, the gates were closed and locked. One of the priests blew the Shofar, a musical horn made from the horn of a ram. It made a loud high pitched sound.

Inside the temple, Yeshua saw several rows of priests, each holding a bucket. In some of the rows, they held gold buckets, and in other rows, they held silver buckets. They all stood with their backs to the altar, facing the high priest at the other end. The slaughter of the first lamb, as was the tradition, was done by the high priest, and was designated as being for all of Israel. The high priest drew his knife against the throat of the lamb and proclaimed loudly, "It is finished." When Yeshua saw and heard that, he began to tremble with fear. Those words sounded so familiar to him, yet he knew he had never heard them before. He wondered why he felt so frightened. The sweat began to fall from his forehead, and for a brief moment he thought he was bleeding, not sweating. Yo'el noticed his discomfort and whispered, "Are you all right, Yeshua?"

"I'm better now Uncle," he whispered back. "I just felt a little faint for a moment."

When it was Ephrayim's turn, Ephrayim and Yo'el brought their lamb to the front. Yeshua stood at the side and watched. Next year, when he was thirteen, and legally a man, he might be asked to either hold or kill the lamb. Right now he wasn't quite sure if he could do either. The first priest, along with Yo'el, held the lamb as Ephrayim drew his knife skillfully across its throat. It bleated loudly as death came, and Yeshua turned his head away. He was now almost sorry he had come.

He turned and watched as the blood flowed into the first priest's bucket, and when it was full, the first priest passed it to the second priest, who passed it to the third, until it got to the end of the line. The last priest threw the blood on one side of the altar, after passing his empty bucket to the priest in front of him. And so it went: the full buckets passed to the end, the empty buckets passed to the front. The buckets had round, not flat, bottoms so that they could never be set down on the ground. Yeshua was beginning to sweat again.

Meanwhile, the Leviytes were singing the Hallel, (Tehillim 113 through 118.) When they reached the end, they would sing the Hallel again. Most of the time all the sacrifices would be finished before the third singing of the Hallel. Yeshua sang the Hallel along with the Leviytes silently in his mind to distract him from all the blood.

Once the blood had been drained from their lamb, Ephrayim and Yo'el stepped out of the way so that the next group could sacrifice its lamb. Now Yeshua had to help. He and Yo'el helped to tie the lamb to a wooden pole, and they stood, holding the pole on their shoulders, as Ephrayim skinned the lamb and cut out the inside parts that would be burnt on the altar as a sacrifice. These were given to the priest who was in charge of this task, and the skin was offered to the priests as payment, which was the normal practice. The skins were all piled into a corner to be divided among the priests later.

The Passover meal was required, by law, to be eaten in Jerusalem. Over the years, however, the number of pilgrims had grown, making it necessary to extend the boundries of Jerusalem. The boundries now included Bethpage, just east of Jerusalem, which is why Yeshua's family could go to Yo'el's home to celebrate the feast. They would stay there throughout the remaining days of the Feast of the Unleavened Bread, going into Jerusalem each morning and returning to Bethpage each evening.

***

They arrived at Bethpage early in the evening, and Yeshua's family was invited to sleep in Yo'el's upper room, which was actually a roof. During Passover, homeowners would surround their roofs with latticework, making for privacy, and rent them out to pilgrims needing a place to have their Passover meal. Because it was spring, and the weather quite warm, these upper rooms were quite popular among the pilgrims, and profitable for the homeowners. Yo'el and his wife, Naomiy, did not have renters this year, so Yeshua and his family had a place to sleep.

Mara and Naomiy had already built the fire and prepared for the Passover feast. By law, the lamb had to be cooked over fire. Further, it had to be cooked without removing its head, feet, or internal organs that had not been removed for the sacrifice at the temple. It could not be roasted on an iron roasting spit or on a gridiron, so it was usually cooked on skewers of pomegranate wood. It had to be eaten before midnight with unleavened bread and bitter herbs. No bones could be broken. And finally, whatever was left over the next morning was to be burnt and not eaten.

After watching the slaughter in the temple, Yeshua was not hungry for lamb that night. He ate the bread, and nobody seemed to notice that he had foregone the meat. His mind was not in the present, however, but in the future, with thoughts of the temple, and the Great Sanhederin, and studying to become a rabbi, and of course Bacha.

23 (Yeshua decides to stay)

Yeshua hadn't been this happy in a long time. Mara and Ephrayim noticed this, and allowed him to be on his own for the duration of the Feast of the Unleavened Bread. Each morning he would spend with the scribes and members of the Great Sanhedrin discussing the sacred scrolls and the laws of Moshe, and the major and minor prophets. The adults seemed quite taken by Yeshua and his grasp of rather complex meanings within the scriptures. Whenever they would quiz him on a concept, Yeshua would immediately turn it into a mashal, incorporating current events or familiar concepts. He definitely had the potential of becoming a rabbi, and one of the Great Sanhedrin, a man by the name of Nicodemus, was seriously thinking about training him.

The afternoons would be filled with walking and talking with Bacha. What he had learned in the morning seemed to be all Yeshua wanted to talk about, but Bacha was interested in many things, and religious beliefs were among them. Sometimes Bacha would try to stump him with some of the differences between the Samaritan Pentateuch, of which Bacha actually knew very little, and the Torah. But Yeshua always seemed to have the right answer, and was never thrown off by his questions.

"Look! There he is again." Bacha was pointing to Vijayananda, who had not seen them as he walked by. "Every day he walks this way, Yeshua. Not just once, but many times. I'm not sure who he is, but he doesn't look like he comes from around here. See how dark his skin is? One day before we leave, I may find out who he is. Maybe I'll see if he fights as badly as you!"

Yeshua accepted the challenge and the two began to wrestle again. By now the crowd was familiar with seeing the two of them wrestling and paid them no attention.

***

In another corner of the city a meeting was taking place between one of the scribes, Bazak, and a tall man of prominence whom he had met once or twice before. The man was telling Bazak about the child Yeshua. "You know he is a bastard, don't you?" the tall man asked.

"A bastard, you say? Really?" Bazak was genuinely concerned.

Dark eyes peered at the scribe. "Yes he is. And if you watch him in the afternoon, you will see him with one of his friends ... from Samaria! I understand he and the Samaritan have been friends for a few years now."

"I didn't know that. What else do you know about him?" asked Bazak with dismay.

"I know that his father is now dead, and was a Pharisee. And I know that he disobeys his stepfather in Nazareth. His stepfather wishes him to become a carpenter, but he refuses to obey him."

The Pharisees and the Sadducees did not see eye to eye on many things. The Pharisees were meticulous about following the Torah, and wanted nothing to do with the Romans. Most of the Great Sanhedrin, on the other hand, were Sadducees, who maintained great wealth and power by compromising with the Romans. It was becoming harder for a Pharisee to be a member of the Great Sanhedrin, and to openly teach such a person to become a rabbi could strain the teacher's relationships with the Romans.

Bazak had heard enough. He would return to the temple and relay what he had learned from his meeting. He was glad he had talked to his acquaintance, as he was originally reluctant to do so.

***

It was now the twenty-first day of Nisan, and time to return to Nazareth, but Yeshua was firm in his commitment to become a rabbi. "Won't you please come home with us, Yeshua?" pleaded his mother. Ephrayim stood with his arms folded and said nothing.

Yeshua looked straight at Ephrayim as he said, "Please let me stay. Please understand. Don't you know I must be about *my* father's business?"

Mara had told Ephrayim of Yeshua's decision to become a rabbi before they left for Jerusalem, so it came as no surprise to him. Mara started to say something, but Ephrayim tugged on her arm and said, "Mara, leave him. He is now a man and has made his decision. It's time for us to go home." Ephrayim and Yeshua looked into each other's eyes, and this time it felt to Yeshua like two grown men looking at one another. Ephrayim came close so that the rest of the family would not hear, and quietly asked, "Are you certain? Have you thought this through, son?"

"Yes, father," he replied. "Uncle Yo'el has agreed to let me stay here while I complete my studies. Tell Mother I will come home on the day of my birth to visit."

Ephrayim was pleased with this, because it indicated to him that Yeshua was finally thinking and acting like an adult, and that a family member would be looking after him. Yeshua hugged his mother and stepfather one last time, hugged his brothers and sisters, and turned away and left. Now he was truly on his own; his fate was sealed and his new life was about to begin. He would go back to the temple and tell them of his plans.

***

As the festival came to its end and everyone started leaving in large numbers, Vijayananda was quite certain he had failed in his mission. He had either missed the two children altogether, or he was at the wrong festival. *What will I do now?* he wondered. It looked like he had one or maybe two days before the city was empty. The merchants whose camel he had ridden from Myos Hormon to Jerusalem would likewise be leaving in a few days, and he would need to decide whether to return with them and go back home or search further. He would continue his circling and crossing through the city for another day, and would think as he walked.

***

Bacha saw the dark-skinned stranger once again, and vowed that he would not lose him this time. The stranger was circling the city, and now was moving from east to west. Bacha would follow and find out more about him. He had lost the stranger the last time by following from too far a distance. This time he would stay close. He was right there in front of him, and then suddenly he was gone! He had rounded a corner, and when Bacha got there, the stranger had disappeared. Bacha ran down the street, looking left to right at the cross street he came to, but saw no stranger. Suddenly, from behind, a voice said, "Looking for me?" Bacha pivoted to see the man standing before him, tall, muscular, feet wide, fists clenched, with an alert gaze.

"Who are you?" Bacha tried to look as fierce as his opponent, but Vijayananda was clearly bigger, and stronger.

"You are the one who has been following me. It is not you who should be asking questions. You should be answering them instead," the man said.

Bacha's reply was to grab Vijayananda and try to pin him to the ground, but Vijayananda had spent many years training as a warrior, and Bacha was no match for him. In short order, it was Bacha who was on the ground with Vijayananda on top of him. Bacha's robe had been yanked off him in the short fight, and his tunic was torn. That's when Vijayananda saw the long scar on his arm. They both knew who had won the fight, so when Vijayananda suddenly got off of Bacha and stood, Bacha stood too but made no threatening moves.

"Perhaps," Vijayananda said slowly, "I have been looking for *you*."

"We have never met. Why would you be looking for me?"

"It is not you I am interested in. You have a younger friend with you, do you not?"

Bacha wasn't sure what to make of this question. He didn't think Vijayananda had ever seen them together, and grew protective.

"I am alone," he said.

Vijayananda cocked his head and said, "Your eyes betray your lies. I was told you were his protector. But I have no wish to harm him, or you for that matter. I only wish to talk to him. I have been looking for him for many days."

"I know. I have been watching you every day on your search. How do I know you don't wish to harm him?"

"I told you I only wished to talk to him. You must trust me."

"Trust you? I don't even know you. First tell me where you are from, and why you wish to talk to Ye—uh, my friend."

"My name is Vijayananda. I come from a land called India. It is far to the east of your country. I have been sent on a mission to find your friend. He is a teacher, yes?"

Bacha was starting to trust Vijayananda, but he was still a little reluctant to tell him any more about Yeshua. "Maybe he is a teacher. But what do you want from him?"

"Friend," he began.

"My name is Bacha."

"All right, then, *Bacha*. I am here to bring him back to India if he so chooses. I will not force him to come, I only wish to talk to him."

Bacha was not at all sure about telling Vijayananda any more. Yeshua really was like his little brother, more than just a name they called one another, and he felt he needed to know more about Vijayananda before letting him near Yeshua.

***

Yeshua hurried to the temple to see his new teachers. But when he arrived, they were eyeing him as if he were a stranger. The scribe who had first encountered him said, "You are no longer welcome here, young man. Go back from where you came. Go home to Nazareth."

Yeshua could not believe his ears. "But—but I am going to study here. I am going to be a rabbi. Why are you saying these things?"

"We have heard many things about you, Yeshua, none of them good," said another.

"What? What have you heard?" Yeshua's face was hot, and his eyes wide.

"Who is your father, Yeshua?" asked the first scribe.

Yeshua thought a moment, and for the first time was going to acknowledge Ephrayim as his father. "Ephrayim," he said.

"Not him, Yeshua. Who is your real father?"

It sounded so much like Efah taunting him that he was speechless.

"We have heard you are a bastard child. Are you a bastard child, Yeshua? Do you disobey your stepfather? Do you associate with Samaritans?"

Yeshua's face turned red. Why was this happening to him? Everything was working out in his favor. He was finally free of Nazareth and all that it represented to him; he was free to become a rabbi; and now this. It was just as in Nazareth. Did God hate him? He said nothing in reply. With tears in his eyes, he turned, walked away, and slowly meandered through the crowd, toward the Fish Gate. He needed his friend Bacha.

The scribe's acquaintance, the one who had told him about Yeshua, watched from a distance, smiling.

24 (They meet at last)

"Yeshua, what's wrong?" Bacha and Vijayananda watched as Yeshua angrily ran toward them. Bacha's dilemma about the two meeting each other had abruptly been solved, and not in the way he wanted.

Ignoring Vijayananda as if he didn't exist, Yeshua shouted, "I hate them! I hate all of them! Why do these things always happen to me!"

"Calm down, Yeshua. Sit and tell me what's wrong."

Vijayananda stood and watched as the two of them sat, and Yeshua, still not noticing the stranger, told Bacha what had just transpired. *Patanjali was right*, Vijayananda thought. *He was turned away by his own teachers. I'm now more certain than ever that I have found the right person.* As Yeshua told his story, he began to get even angrier, talking louder and louder, and halfway through he suddenly looked up. "Who are you?" he shouted with anger at the stranger.

"My name is Vijayananda, my friend. I have been looking for you. But before we talk further, I wish to show you something. Place your right hand like this." Vijayananda sat in front of them, and curled his index and middle finger over his thumb pad. "It is called a *mudra*. A seal or lock. Go ahead."

The sudden change in topics, and the strange request, seemed to momentarily shock Yeshua out of his foul mood. "A *what*?" he asked.

"A seal. Just try it. It can't hurt. It will make you feel better, I promise."

Yeshua and Bacha looked at one another for a moment, as if deciding whether they should do it or not, and finally Yeshua shrugged his shoulders and looked back at Vijayananda. Both he and Bacha imitated what they saw.

"Now bring your hand up to your nose like this. Now press your thumb against the right nostril and breathe out through your left nostril. Breathe long and slow."

They all three breathed out a long exhalation.

"Now breathe in, but not as long. Breathe in stronger than you breathed out. Now move your hand so that your finger is pressed against your left nostril, and your right nostril is now free. Again breathe out. Breathe long and slow. Now breathe in, short and strong."

They continued to alternate breathing through their left and right nostrils, with the exhalations being longer than the inhalations. After a time, Vijayananda put his hand down and just sat quietly. Yeshua and Bacha did the same. There was a momentary peaceful silence that permeated all of their consciousnesses. It was as if they were the only three persons who existed in the city of Jerusalem.

"Feel better, my friend?"

Yeshua wrinkled his brow and said, "Yes! I feel much calmer. What *was* that we just did?"

Vijayananda replied, "In my country, India, my master has taught me a practice called *Nadi Shodhanam*. It means alternate nostril breathing. We sometimes use it to calm ourselves when we are in an agitated state. Is it not remarkable? I know many such breathing techniques."

"Where is India?" asked Yeshua, now intrigued by the stranger.

"It is far away from here, to the east. It is where I would like to take you, Yeshua, to meet my master, and the prince who has sent for you. My prince has sent me to bring you back to India to study our holy scriptures."

Yeshua was puzzled. "How does your prince know me?"

Vijayananda replied, "My master, Patanjali, has seen you in a vision. He says you will one day be a very great teacher."

Bacha bristled and said, "He saw Yeshua in a vision? Even if such a thing is possible, how do you know he is the person your master has seen? You didn't even know his name until I said it just a moment ago."

Vijayananda looked from child to child and said, "My master said I would be successful in my quest. In his vision, he said the teacher would be at a great spiritual festival. He said the teacher would be turned away by his own teachers. He said that there would be an older child with him who acted as his protector. He said the older child would have a mark on his left arm. It has all come to pass exactly as he has said, has it not?"

Yeshua looked at Bacha quizzically, but neither of them had an answer.

"So you will come with me then?" He said it more like a command than a question.

Yeshua asked skeptically, "What if I said no?"

"What will you do here? In this city you are not liked. In my country you will be welcomed. In this city you cannot study what you wish, as you have just told me. In my country, my master is eager to teach you. Other great spiritual leaders are eager to teach you. You are welcome to learn as much as we have to offer."

Yeshua countered, "But I wish to become a rabbi, not a ... a ... what do you call teachers in your country?"

"A great teacher in India is called a guru. My master sees you as a very great guru. A very great guru indeed."

"A guru, you say? Is a guru like a rabbi?"

"This I cannot say. I can only say that a great opportunity exists for you in India to learn our holy scriptures. Here, there is nothing."

"Can your guru take away my anger? This I want even more than being a rabbi."

Vijayananda replied, "My guru is very powerful. If anyone can do it, he can."

Yeshua talked a bit faster, and leaned forward. "And are your holy scriptures anything like ours?"

"Again I cannot say. My master can tell you, but you will need to come to India to hear his answer. Come to the western side of the city tonight, outside the gates, where the merchants will be camping by a fire. That is where I will be. You can give me your decision then. We will be leaving in the morning."

Vijayananda arose and calmly walked to the west. His walk was slow, yet deliberate. It was graceful like a woman's, but masculine at the same time.

After he disappeared Yeshua looked into Bacha's eyes and asked, "What do you think, Bacha, is he to be trusted, or is this some kind of trick?"

Bacha thought for a moment and then replied, "I don't know, but I think I trust him. I have a feel for this kind of thing, Yeshua. Since I have been living on my own, I sense who to trust and who not to trust. The only person I have ever been wrong about was Yaish."

They decided they would go meet this Vijayananda later at night and at least hear him out. Then they would decide.

25 (The decision is made)

As they sat by the fire and warmed themselves, Vijayananda said to Yeshua, "So if you agree, we will travel by camel for eleven days to Myos Hormon, the great port city in Egypt. From there, we will journey across the sea by ship to a city in my country, India, called Barbarikon. This will take us almost sixty days—longer if the weather is not favorable. Next we will take another ship to the great port city, Bharuch.

"Then we must journey by camel to the capital of my empire, called Pratishthana. All of this will take us yet another thirty days. Pratishthana is where you will meet my spiritual guru. This, Yeshua, is the time I have to teach you my language, called Maharashtri. I cannot teach you everything, but it must be enough for you to converse with my guru, Patanjali, and more importantly, the great Prince Hala, son of King Aristakarman and the future king of the Satavana Empire."

Yeshua's mother tongue was Aramic. He spoke fluent Hebrew, which is what Vijayananda spoke to him in, and he knew a little Greek. But to learn a whole new language and be able to speak it fluently in ninety days seemed a daunting task. Yeshua was also wondering about money. "But how will we pay for all this, Vijayananda? Surely such a journey will be costly."

Vijayananda replied, "The great Prince Hala has sent for you. He has given me enough money to pay for our journey."

And what of Bacha? Yeshua thought. Was he about to lose his best friend and companion after months of anticipation and a scant one-day reunion? The look on Bacha's face convinced Yeshua that he was thinking the same thing. Yeshua rose and said firmly, "I will not travel to India without my friend Bacha. I will not." He folded his arms in defiance. Bacha grinned a grin that Yeshua knew all too well. It meant he was extremely happy. Bacha mimicked Yeshua's stance with folded arms, and now the two of them were shoulder-to-shoulder facing Vijayananda.

Vijayananda was quiet for a moment, and then he spoke. "If I pay for your friend's journey, I risk the anger of Prince Hala. If I come back without you, I still risk the anger of Prince Hala. I must meditate on this."

Yeshua had never seen anyone meditate, nor did he know what the word "meditate" meant, but Yeshua and Bacha watched Vijayananda sit by a tree. He sat tall. He closed his eyes and grew quiet, as if sleeping, but remained frozen in his seated position without moving so much as a finger. Yeshua watched in amazement as more and more time passed without Vijayananda moving. After an hour or so, when he had still not moved, Yeshua and Bacha laid down close to the fire.

Soon they fell asleep. But when they woke up to the early daylight, Vijayananda was still sitting by the fire. Whether he had sat there all night, or went to sleep later and woke up early, Yeshua did not know. Vijayananda opened his eyes, but remained still for a moment, and then said, "So be it. The three of us will travel to India."

The merchants told Vijayananda that they would not leave for another day, because they had unexpected business they needed to take care of. But for certain they would leave early the next morning.

Not far from where they were, two men were huddled behind a large bush listening to their conversation.

***

Vijayananda, Yeshua, and Bacha stayed in the camp as many of the merchants left for the city to conduct their business. Vijayananda told them more stories about India, and Yeshua grew more excited.

Yeshua turned to his companion and asked, "Bacha, I never even asked you before. Are you sure you are willing to come with me to this India?"

Vijayananda turned toward Bacha and watched for his reaction.

"I love my homeland, Samaria, very much, but this sounds like a great adventure that I do not want to miss out on. Besides, wherever my little brother goes, I go!" He once again broke out into his toothy grin.

Yeshua replied, "Very well. We will go. But I have to let my uncle know, so he can tell my mother and stepfather. What should I do, Bacha? If I go to my uncle, I am afraid he will make me stay. But if I don't let him know, he and my parents will worry. What should I do?"

Bacha squinted his eyes and furrowed his brow and then opened his eyes wide. "I know, Yeshua. Send him a message. We can get a sheet of papyrus to write on and a reed pen and ink from one of the merchants, and then I will bring it to your uncle."

"No. He will only come here and take me back. No, it has to be delivered after we are gone. After it is too late."

Vijayananda said, "Perhaps you can find someone to deliver your message to your uncle. He could be instructed not to deliver it until we have left. We have the rest of the day to find such a person."

Bacha and Yeshua both nodded. Bacha then got up and walked over to some of the merchants who had not gone inside the gates. When he came back, he had everything Yeshua needed to write. Yeshua thought a few moments, and then began his message:

Uncle Yo'el

I found out yesterday that the Great Sanhedrin will no longer allow me to study with them. I have found another place to study scripture. Uncle, it is far away from here in a land called India. My friend Bacha will be with me. A man from India called Vijayananda is paying for our journey which will be by a great ship. We leave in the morning.

I am not sure how long I will be gone, Uncle, but I know I am making the right decision. Please let my mother and stepfather know, and tell my mother not to worry. I will see you all when I return.

Peace be unto you,
Yeshua

When he was finished, Bacha said, "Don't worry, little brother. I will go find someone to deliver the message for you. I'll bring him back here."

Yeshua nodded his head but said nothing. It was all happening so quickly—too quickly. He felt as if he was being pushed down a path, rather than choosing it himself. He could feel his heart pounding.

A short time later, Bacha and a boy about the same age as Bacha appeared. "This is Kaleb. He says will deliver your message."

"Do you know him, Bacha?" Yeshua asked.

"I do not. But he—"

"Do you not trust me? Kaleb interupped. "I am a most trustworthy person. Everyone says so. Just ask any of my friends. They will tell you. I am glad to deliver your message. For it is written in

Mishlei Shlomo: 'Do not withhold good from those to whom it is due, when it is in your power to act.'"

Yehsua's eyes grew large and he nodded and drew his face close to Kaleb. "And from Tehillim: 'Good will come to those who are generous and lend freely, who conduct their affairs with justice.'"

Kaleb countered with, "Again from Tehillim: 'Trust in the Lord and do good; Dwell in the land and cultivate faithfulness.'"

Bacha and Vijayananda looked at one another, both with pursed lips, and there was silence for a moment.

"And you will not deliver the letter until tomorrow night?" Bacha asked.

"Tomorrow night. But you must first tell me where this Yo'el lives."

Yeshua said, "Very well, Kaleb. My Uncle Yo'el lives in Bethpage. It is just east of here. Less than a Sabbath day's journey. His house is easy to find. I will make you a map."

On the back of the papyrus that had Yeshua's letter to his uncle, he drew a very detailed map. Kaleb studied it and said, "I can find it. And if I don't, I can always ask someone. I will not let you down, friends." Kaleb stuck the papyrus into his tunic.

"Yes, ask anyone. Everyone in Bethpage knows my uncle."

Vijayananda stood, grabbed Kaleb by the tunic, pulled him to his feet and said, "Come with me."

They walked away from Yeshua and Bacha. When they were some distance away Vijayananda stared at him and asked, "Why are you really doing this? Don't lie to me."

Kaleb opened his mouth to speak, but when he saw the sternness in Vijayananda's face, he closed his mouth and lowered his head slightly. Then in a soft voice he said, "Bacha paid me."

"He paid you, did he? I thought as much." Vijayananda brought his face close to Kaleb's and with a fierce look and fierce voice continued. "You may leave. But know this, Kaleb: If you fail, you will have me to deal with. Do you understand?"

Kaleb's eyes grew wide. "Ye-ye-yes sir. I understand."

"Then go."

Kaleb needed no more prompting, and left quickly.

Vijayananda returned and sat with his new friends. "It is done. He is gone." And then turning to Bacha he continued. "Kaleb says you paid him. How much did you pay him for such a task?"

"Bacha, you paid him?" Yeshua asked.

"Yes, Yeshua I did. I paid him two sheckels."

"Two sheckels?" Yeshua asked. "Why so much?"

Bacha said, "We are going to a new country, are we not? What good is my money there? I paid him that much because I wanted to make sure he would do it. You would do as much for me."

Vijayananda nodded in approval. Yeshua stared off into the distance.

Now it was evening. All the merchants had returned, and in the morning they would begin their journey. As Yeshua lay down to sleep, he looked around for Bacha and Vijayananda. Bacha was there close to him, but Vijayananda was nowhere to be seen. *Maybe he went into the woods to relieve himself*, he thought as he fell asleep.

***

The two men who had been watching earlier waited patiently for sleep to come to the entire camp. Their daggers were ready. They weren't looking forward to killing mere boys, but the stranger who pointed the two boys out, had paid them well.

One of them whispered to the other, "I think they are all asleep. You take the older child, I'll take the younger. We cover their mouths and strike together. Straight to the heart. Are you ready?"

But the second did not answer. He could not. He was lying on the ground with his throat freshly slit, and his eyes wide, staring into infinity. The first looked around whispering, "Where are you?" And then, as quickly as with his friend, he felt one hand go over his mouth, and another with a dagger in it slicing through the arteries in his neck. He gurgled as he tried to breathe, but the only thing that went into his lungs was blood. In seconds he stopped struggling and was still, just like his companion.

***

Vijayananda thought, *Again Patanjali was right in his predictions. He said both children would be in great danger, and that even the protector would not be aware of it. Now I know for certain I have found the right person. I have no more doubts.*

He dragged the men's bodies, one by one, deep into the woods where the animals would devour their remains, and just as silently returned to camp. Yeshua and Bacha were still fast asleep. He remained alert the rest of that night, but resolved that he had eliminated the danger Patanjali had warned him about.

26 (The journey begins)

The next morning began the first leg of their long journey, the eleven-day trek southwest to the Egyptian port city of Myos Hormos. The camels would carry them through the desert in the early morning while it was still cool, and then they would stop and rest and eat. In the early afternoon they would resume their travels, and then before the sun went down, they would stop for the night.

"Tell me the numbers one through ten, Yeshua," Vijayananada said during their late morning rest of the third day.

"Ek, don, teen, char, paach, saha, saat, aath, nau, daha," Yeshua replied quickly, holding up a finger for each number.

"*Changla*, good," Vijayananda said back, smiling and placing his hand on Yeshua's shoulder.

He then turned to Bacha and asked, "*Aaple naav kaay?* What is your name?"

"*Mee Bacha*," Bacha replied with a grin.

Vijayananda was happy with their progress for now. But there was still much to learn. It was now time to continue, and the merchants began to mount their camels. Vijayananda stood and said to Yeshua and Bacha, "*Chala Jaauya*. Let's go."

Vijayananda was relentless in his teaching of the Maharashtri language. As in everything Yeshua applied himself to, he was a brilliant student. Bacha was likewise learning quite well. This language was spoken at a rapid pace, and the expression that both Yeshua and Bacha used often was, "*Itkya vegaat bolu nakaa*, don't speak so fast." They both made Vijayananda laugh by saying it very slowly, syllable by syllable.

In the evenings, Vijayananda would mostly speak in Hebrew, and talk about India. These were stories that Yeshua asked many questions about. He said he wanted to learn more about these people he would soon be living among.

***

On the eastern side of the city of Jerusalem, outside the gates, the night fires burned. This was a section that most pilgrims avoided. It was filled with the kind of people you did not want to meet late at night. Some were drinking wine and laughing, talking much louder than they needed to. Others were drunk and passed out. Men and women were openly kissing. Foul language and the smell of vomit filled the night air.

Kaleb sat in front of his night fire with his friend Yan and smiled. He reached into his tunic and came out with two shekels. He stuck them into his eye sockets and made a crazy face. "Hooo. Hooo. Look at me Yan. I'm an owl."

"Where did you get those?" asked Yan.

He removed the coins and said, "Wouldn't you just like to know. Perhaps I got them from a stranger while inside the city." He waved them in front of Yan's face.

Yan reached for them as Kaleb quickly pulled them back.

"Are they real? Let me see them."

Kaleb handed him one of the two coins. After examining it, he handed it back.

"And so what did you have to do for them, Kaleb?"

Kaleb reached into his tunic again and pulled out a piece of papyrus. He examined it briefly and then waved it slowly back and forth in front of Yan with the same crazy face he had made before. Yan followed the back and forth movement with his eyes. Suddenly he tossed it into the fire and watched as it blackened, curled and jumped about like a wounded animal, all the while getting smaller and smaller.

"I don't understand," Yan said.

"It is written in the scrolls of Micah. 'Put no trust in a neighbor; have no confidence in a friend.'"

Yan looked puzzled.

"From Tehillim, 'It is better to take refuge in the Lord Than to trust in man.'"

Yan looked even more puzzled than before.

Kaleb picked up a stick and stirred the ashes that were once a piece of papyrus.

"Nothing, Yan. I had to do nothing for them."

***

It was the evening of the sixth day, and sleep had come to everyone. Everyone, that is, except for Yeshua. He tossed and turned in the sand. Sleeping in the desert was not something he was getting used to. Although the days were hot, at night it got quite cold, much colder than in Galilee, making it hard for him to sleep. He rose to his feet and began to pace, hoping that he would soon be warm enough, or tired enough to lie back down and fall asleep quickly.

The two-foot-long peten, or, black desert cobra, waited silently in the sand. The merchants and camels were encroaching on its territory, which made it as unsettled as Yeshua. It had been looking for prey when Yeshua came near, which caused it to stop. It would watch in silence, but if necessary, it would bite.

Yeshua, unaware of the danger, was walking directly toward the cobra. As his feet moved nearer and nearer, the cobra's coiled body was tensing to strike. One more step and it would spring into action. It opened its mouth, its fangs exposed. Suddenly, Yeshua was forcefully thrown sideways to the ground. It made him cry out, and everyone in the camp awoke. Vijayananda was quickly on his feet and ready for whatever danger there might be. It was Bacha who had thrown him to the ground and was now standing between Yeshua and the snake. The snake hissed loudly and tensed even more, its reptile eyes now keenly focused on Bacha. The two eyed each other, neither of them moving, for a brief moment. But when no more threatening moves were made, it turned and slithered off in search of a meal.

It turned out to be the light of the full moon and the quick action of Bacha that saved Yeshua. Bacha was a light sleeper, and when Yeshua arose, it woke him. As his eyes adjusted to the moonlight he had seen the snake and then noticed Yeshua's path toward it. No time to shout to Yeshua; Bacha acted immediately.

One of the merchants said to Bacha, "You are lucky he didn't strike. The bite of the black desert cobra brings death, even to humans."

Vijayananda grabbed Bacha's arm, gripping it firmly and said, "*Dhanyavaad*. Thank you."

On the eighth day of their journey, Vijayananda said to the two of them, "My two friends, once we board the ship I will speak *only* in Maharashtri. You must both promise to do the same. It is the quickest way to learn, I promise you. It is how I learned your Hebrew language."

***

The talk of the ship brought the reality of what Yeshua was about to do closer to his mind. He was about to leave his country with a stranger he had only met days before. *Am I doing the right thing? It's not too late to change my mind. How long will I be gone? What if I want to go home once I am there? Will they let me?* These and other thoughts raced through Yeshua's mind. Bacha too was quiet, and Yeshua was certain that similar thoughts were going through Bacha's head. Once they were on the ship, and the ship was sailing out to sea, it would be too late to go back home; at least until they arrived at their destination. If he was going to change his mind, it would have to be done in the next three days.

***

On the tenth night, Vijayanada sensed reluctance in both of them. He knew he needed to give them more assurances.

"Yeshua, Bacha, tomorrow we will be in Myos Hormon. We will board the ship and prepare for our journey across the great waters. You must be brave. Yeshua, remember what I promised you: that you will be welcome in our country, that you will be able to learn the sacred texts from my master and from others, that you can learn all that my country has to offer. I was told you would become a great teacher. I see this. Even as I teach you, you teach me. I see the seeds of greatness in you.

"And you, Bacha, you have shown courage and strength of character. Patanjali told me that in his vision, you were the teacher's protector. I have seen this with my own eyes. I saw as you placed yourself between your companion and certain death in the shape of a snake. Yeshua is lucky to have a friend such as you, Bacha. I know that you will always look out for him. Part of my mission is to keep Yeshua safe from harm. I feel at ease that you are here too. You make my job easier."

Vijayananda looked from one to the other, searching their eyes for doubt. He saw none. He seemed to have quelled their fears for now. All was well.

27 (A voyage and a storm at sea)

Yeshua had been on what he thought was a large boat before in the Sea of Chinnereth, but he had never in his life seen such an enormous ship. It was written in the Torah that the size of Noach's Ark was three hundred cubits in length. This ship looked to be at least half that size. On each side of its prow were huge carved figures of a winged woman Vijayananda told him was Isis, the protectress of sailors. All along its hull were swan lamps that would be lit up at night. It had a huge square mainsail in its center, and near the prow was a smaller sail that Vijayananda called an aremon. Large pennants were attached to the mastheads. The ship was elegant, colorful, and ornate. It was named *Gaulus*.

On board were armed guards and four teams of archers, ready to defend the cargo against pirates who roamed the eastern coast of the Red Sea waiting for the chance to plunder any ships that strayed from their course and enslave anyone whom they rescued from shipwrecks. The pirates mostly went after smaller, less well-guarded vessels, but often they would band together and take on a large ship such as the one Yeshua and Bacha were boarding. They would often seize the cargo, kill all the crew and passengers, and sink the ship. But these guards were quite capable of defending this ship, and in the five years the Gaulus had been traveling back and forth, it had never once been threatened.

Also on board were pilots, sailors, lookouts, and helmsmen. There was a staff of carpenters and sailmakers as well, in case repairs were needed during the voyage. Yeshua thought to himself that if he had decided to become a carpenter, and he had known about these ships, this is where he would have plied his trade.

Once all the cargo had been secured, they would travel southeast down the Red Sea, stopping along the way in Muza, Aden, and Cane, each time bringing on more cargo and passengers, and then begin the twenty day journey northeast across the ocean to Barbaricon. It was not an easy journey, but May to September was the best time to travel. Rarely did ships sail to the east during the winter months. Of those that attempted the journey, many did not come back.

Yeshua, Bacha, and Vijayananda would share a small cabin. The neverending comings and goings of people and supplies seemed a mass of confusion to Yeshua and Bacha, but Vijayananda was right at home amidst the chaos and appeared to have many friends aboard to whom he spoke during loading.

At last the ship was ready to sail. There were two other ships traveling the same route, the *Ponto* and the *Corbita*, and all three vessels kept in sight of one another so that pirates would be less likely to attack. Yeshua liked being on the sea. He liked the rolling of the waves and the tremendous feeling of power that the ship seemed to convey. Each time he would say something to Bacha in his own tongue, Vijayananda would stop him and make him say it in Maharashtri. Often as Vijayananda listened to the two of them talking, he would begin laughing and correct them. "You are saying the right words, but you are saying them in the wrong order," he would sometimes tell them. "But each day you are getting better."

He taught Yeshua and Bacha several breathing practices during the voyage, and something he called *Naul*. He would bend his knees, half-squat, resting his hands on them, and then produce a strong exhalation, causing his stomach to move in. Next he would hold his breath while trying to inhale, which would draw his stomach in and up under his ribcage. Then he would rotate his hips and cause his stomach muscles to undulate making it look as if there was a creature inside him trying to get out. He explained that Bacha and Yeshua needed to learn this because it would stimulate the digestive fire, removing toxins, indigestion, and constipation. Often on sea voyages, passengers would experience constipation, and Vijayananda wanted to keep Yeshua as healthy as he could. All three did yoga poses each morning to keep them limber. Yeshua wanted Vijayananda to teach him meditation, but Vijayananda firmly said, "This must be learned from Patanjali."

It amazed Yeshua to be on a body of water so vast as the Indian Ocean. And as they neared the middle of their voyage, the southwest winds picked up and blew strongly and endlessly. Vijayananda told them these were called monsoons, and they would not stop blowing for the rest of their trip. The monsoons made for very cold nights. Along the way Yeshua saw many fish he had never seen before, one so large he could not believe his eyes. Vijayananda told him it was called a whale, which now made the story of Yonah and the whale come to life for him. He told Vijayananda and Bacha the story, all in Maharashtri, and was feeling more and more at home with this new language.

***

It was early in the morning, and Yeshua sensed the tension in the crew. Something was wrong. They were all looking and pointing to the clouds in the eastern skies, which were dark and moving to the west—toward their ship. Within a few minutes the skies were completely black, and the winds began to shift, moving from east to west, and the waves grew larger. All the passengers were ordered to go into their cabins and prepare for a storm. This usually meant the passengers should secure anything that could easily break or fall, and pray that they would survive.

The captain had weathered many such storms before, so he knew exactly what he needed to do. For starters, he ordered the sails to be lowered and the foresail hoisted up. This smaller sail would slow the ship's speed and make maneuvers easier. No sooner had that happened when strong gusts of winds began to scream across the right side of the ship, and huge waves began rocking the boat dangerously from side to side. The captain quickly ordered the ship to turn westward, until the wind and waves of the storm came from the stern. The ship would be pushed back toward Cane, but they were far enough out to sea that the storm would pass long before that happened—or so he hoped. The other two ships had likewise raised their foresails and turned westward.

Sheets of rain pummeled the crew. The helmsman, who usually faced the bow of the ship, turned around so that he could watch the direction of the waves coming from rear. He would need to do everything he could to ensure that waves hit the rear section of the ship squarely. Those that didn't would tip the ship sideways, and in either case, the huge crashing waves would send vast amounts of seawater onto the decks.

The fate of the entire ship was now in the hands of the helmsman. The wind blew fiercely into his face, and he squinted to see. If he lost control and the ship turned into the wind, the ship would almost certainly break apart, with the wreckage quickly dragging the ship under. The crew members tied themselves to the bulwarks to keep from being swept off the decks, and bailed the water over the side as quickly as they could.

It did no good for the helmsman to shout a warning of an incoming wave, because the sound of the storm was so great that no one could hear him. Lightning seemed to be everywhere around them; thunderclaps were loud enough to make everyone's ears ring. The captain ordered the rear anchor to be lowered and dragged behind the ship to slow its speed even more.

Vijayananda sat in the cabin stoically with almost no emotion showing in his face as the ship lifted and fell with each passing wave. Even below, inside the cabin, the noise was so loud they could scarcely hear one another speak. Yeshua and Bacha were terrified. "Are we going to die?" shouted Bacha.

"Yes!" Vijayananda bellowed. Yeshua and Bacha's eyes widened in terror as they looked at each other. He then added, "But hopefully not today!"

Yeshua began to grin, but Bacha was outraged. "That's not funny, Vijayananda!" he shouted.

Vijayananda became more serious. He brought his face close to theirs so he wouldn't have to shout so loudly. "Listen to me, my friends. I have been in worse storms than this. The crew and captain have also. And yet we are all still alive, are we not? If the Creator wills it, we will live. If the Creator wills it, we will die. But my master Patanjali promises me that only the body dies. He has told me, just like he will one day tell you, that we are not the body, we are not the breath, we are not the mind. We always were, and we always will be." He then sat back in his meditative posture and closed his eyes.

The ship was suddenly lifted on a huge wave, and crashed down hard into the trough. The crest of the next wave broke above the ship and spilled its foamy content onto the deck, knocking everyone on deck off their feet. Only their ropes kept them from being swept into the angry sea. Yeshua and Bacha huddled together as Vijayananda sat and closed his eyes, moving into meditation. Yeshua had become fixated on Vijayananda's words: "We are not the body, we are not the breath, we are not the mind. We always were, and we always will be." If they survived, he would ask Patanjali more about this. Yeshua watched Vijayananda for the next hour, seeing the calmness in his face even as the ship continued to toss and turn in the storm. This was different from courage. Courage meant that you were frightened but did what needed to be done anyway. Vijayananda showed no such fear. With each crash of lightning, with each roll of the ship, Yeshua and Bacha gripped each other tighter and tighter as Vijayananda sat in meditation.

It seemed like the storm would never end. It was now nighttime, making the helmsman's job almost impossible. He relied more on his instincts than on his eyes, because he could not be sure of what he was actually seeing in the darkness. His instincts were accurate for the most part. But sometimes he was caught by surprise, as a wave would hit the ship broadside.

A huge ripping sound and crack rumbled through the cabin of Yeshua, Bacha, and Vijayananda, and the ship began to toss and turn wildly. They all knew something was wrong. Yeshua and Bacha were now both vomiting, and Vijayananda left them to find out what had happened. When he got to the main deck, he saw it. The main sail had been completely torn away with the force of the fierce winds, the helmsman's rudder was broken in two, and the ship was now at the mercy of the storm. With luck, the aremon at the prow and the anchors at the rear would keep the ship on a straight course away from the wind.

It seemed like an endless night with the sound of crashing waves and winds whistling through the cabin. Yeshua prayed while Bacha cringed with each lift and sudden drop of the ship. Only Vijayananda remained calm.

Then, some time before morning, the skies broke, and the wind and waves calmed. The abrupt silence now seemed like a new, frightening noise. "What's happening?" shouted Yeshua, realizing how loud his voice now sounded.

"We have survived," answered Vijayananda.

"We have survived," Yeshua and Bacha said in unison, hugging one another.

It was over at last, at least for now. Now the sailmakers and carpenters would earn their keep. They quickly set about the task of building a new rudder and repairing the torn sail. Most everyone else came out onto the deck and looked about in wonder.

The joy of surviving the storm was short lived as the news spread that only one of the other two ships they traveled with, the *Ponto*, had made it. Some of the wreckage of the ill-fated *Corbita* floated around them, but no crew or passengers were found—alive or dead. There was a short ceremony on deck to mourn the loss of good friends. One of the crew members, whose brother was on the Corbita, was openly weeping, but abruptly stopped and composed himself as Yeshua approached. Somehow, Yeshua felt, he was constantly being drawn to those in need. In Nazareth, even at the age of eleven, he had been drawn to the poor. Now he was being drawn to those who mourned. He placed his right hand on the shoulder of the man, a fellow Jew, and recited from the scrolls of Tehillim: "Yet I am always with you; you hold me by my right hand. You guide me with your counsel, and afterward you will take me into glory." The crewman nodded his head in agreement and resumed weeping unashamedly, this time into Yeshua's tunic.

Those nearby who had seen this child comforting a grown man gathered around Yeshua, waiting for more words of wisdom and encouragement. He closed his eyes, and the words came forth. "All of you who mourn for the dead, I say put your faith in the Lord. For on this day he will surely bless you and comfort you. He will hold you in his bosom and dry away your tears." This did not come from the scriptures, but from Yeshua. Or, at least, from Yeshua's mouth.

He continued speaking in a voice that did not seem to be his own. It was not only the words he spoke but the way he spoke them that so mesmerized and calmed those who were listening. Bacha and Vijayananda watched and listened in wonder. When Yeshua had finished speaking, there was silence among the crew and passengers who had heard him, save for the occasional sobbing. The survivors were now comforting one another. Vijayananda said, "My master, Patanjali, told me to seek the teacher who was not yet a teacher. But today, truly you have taught us all, Yeshua."

28 (Pirates and the final leg of the journey)

The captain knew the ship had been swept off its bearings and they were now further west than they ought to be. He also feared another storm might come their way. He therefore turned the ship due north. They would need to seek land and then turn and travel southeast down the westward side of India, looking for familiar landmarks. If another storm did come, being close to shore would offer them an escape. This is how the sailors used to travel to the port city of Barbaricon years before; with land always in sight. Being close to shore, however, would make them vulnerable, as India too had its pirates. The archers were on high alert as land was finally spotted.

Vijayananda knew his homeland better than anyone else, and stood with the commander of the archers, watching for danger. It came the next night. The *Gaulus* was not in the lead, and the pirates knew that the last ship was the one to attack. The archers as well as Vijayananda were focused mainly on the shore, watching for signs of danger. The pirates, meanwhile, were waiting on the sea side of the ship. They had been waiting there for hours. They were all dressed in black, their faces were painted black, and their dhows were likewise painted black. Unless you knew what you were looking for, you could look right at them and not know it was anything other than the sea.

The pirate's forte was nighttime, surprise, and hand-to-hand combat. They had no chance against the rain of arrows that would come their way if spotted. They would silently move close enough to throw ropes with grappling hooks up the side of the ship they targated and quickly climb aboard.

Vijayananda sensed it before he saw it. He knew something did not feel right. He began pacing nervously around the ship as he had paced around Jerusalem. He heard the sound of the first hook catching hold and looked down at the sea, into the whites of a pair of eyes looking up at him in surprise. "Pirates on the right side of the ship!" he shouted. All archers immediately raced to the right side of the ship and began shooting arrows downward; hoping at least some of them would find their mark. Shouts of pain let them know of their success. Wooden kegs filled with lamp oil were set on fire and thrown down into the water. The oil began to ooze into the sea, catching fire as it did. The flames reflected into the sea and lit up the surrounding area. The commander could see there were thirty or so dhows, each carrying ten pirates. If they succeeded, three hundred pirates could easily overwhelm the ship. But the surprise was foiled, as they could now be seen.

The first pirate that Vijayananda had seen was now attempting to climb onto the deck. Vijayananda lifted him as if he were a feather and tossed him back into the sea. A few others from the first dhow were now on board. The armed guards were rushing toward them. Vijayananda yanked the knife away from the pirate nearest him and plunged it deep into his neck. None of the other pirates, who were vastly outnumbered, survived the onslaught of the guards. It was over in an instant.

The commander of the archers began shouting orders. Archers lined up in three rows. The first line would shoot, then duck as the second line did the same. Then they would duck as the third line followed. The first line would stand again, and the sequence would repeat itself. An endless volley of arrows would thus rain down on the pirates, giving them no chance to fight back. A shout from the leader of the pirates made those that were still alive turn their dhows away from the ship, slipping into the darkness to regroup.

The sounds of the short-lived battle had awakened most of the passengers, and some had come out to the deck to see what the commotion was about. Others knew, and huddled inside their cabins, fearing the worst. Yeshua and Bacha were standing on the deck when Vijayananda spotted them and shouted, "Go back to your cabin! Now!"

Bacha pulled on Yeshua's tunic, but he resisted. He was too interested in seeing what was happening. Bacha would not leave his friend, and so the two stood on the deck and watched. The fighting had stopped, and the dhows were nowhere to be seen. The archers were now put on high alert, and lookouts were placed on all sides of the ship. Whenever the commander would randomly ring his gong, each lookout, in turn, would shout, "All is well, commander."

Vijayananda took Yeshua and Bacha back to the cabin. He looked very angry. "You must stay here during the night, no matter what you may hear," he said sternly.

He faced each one of them, waiting for a nod of agreement. Instead, Yeshua recited Vijayananda's own words: "If the Creator wills it, we will live. If the Creator wills it, we will die. We are not the body, we are not the breath, we are not the mind. We always were, and we always will be." A grin began to show on his face.

"Yeshua, what I told you before is not to be made fun of. It is true what I have told you. But this does not mean that you give in and simply accept your fate. We have been given ten very important tools by our creator. Five of them move from the external world into the internal world. These are: seeing, hearing, smelling, tasting, and feeling. Five of them move from the internal world into the external world. These are: speaking, moving, grasping, eliminating, and reproducing. You must use all of these tools to survive and live out your Karma."

Yeshua wrinkled his brow. "Some of what you say I understand. But some I do not. Tell me more about Karma."

"Patanjali will tell you all, Yeshua. But perhaps I can tell you a little about Karma. If I throw a rock into the air, what will happen to that rock?"

Yeshua countered, "It will fall back down."

"Correct! And if I throw it really high?"

Yeshua thought a moment, and then said, "It will still come down. It has to. It will just take a little longer."

"Good! Now, if I throw a small rock into the air, will a large rock come down?"

"No. The rock doesn't change size."

"And if I throw a large rock into the air, will a small rock come down?"

"The answer is the same, Vijayananda."

"That is one aspect of Karma in its essence, Yeshua. If you perform a good deed, eventually that good deed will come back to you, just as surely as if you threw a rock into the air. It might come back quickly, like the first rock I asked you about, or it might take longer, like the second rock I asked you about. In our beliefs, it might even not return until another lifetime. But come back it will. The same thing happens with bad deeds. Every bad deed you perform will eventually come back to you. All is in balance. Just like the size of the rocks, a tiny bad deed will return an equally tiny one. A great good deed will return a good deed of equal size."

Yeshua was quiet as he thought about the concept of Karma. "This Patanjali will teach me more about all this?"

"He will teach you that and much, much more, Yeshua. But you need to listen to what I tell you and obey, in order that you live long enough to be taught!" Now it was Vijayananda grinning. The three of them shared a laugh, and then Vijayananda returned to be with the archers. This time Yeshua and Bacha remained in the cabin.

As they neared Barbaricon, Vijayananda became even more intent. The next leg of the journey would be on another ship, and then by camel, and he would once again have to be extra vigilant and protect Yeshua against any harm that might come his way.

***

The next ship they boarded was much smaller, not unlike ones that Yeshua had traveled in before on the Sea of Chinnereth. This would be a shorter journey, about five or seven days, and a much safer one. They hugged the coastline of India. There were not many pirates in this section, and the seas were mostly calm. On this ship, they slept on deck, under a huge tarp to protect them from rain and occasional spray from waves that splashed up the side of the hull.

The realization of how far away from home he now was began to sink into Yeshua's mind, and he grew anxious as the sights on the coast got stranger and stranger. He began to wonder if he had made the right decision.

At last the journey over water ended at another port city called Bharuch, but the next and final trek by camel would cover almost three hundred miles southeast and take yet another sixteen to twenty days to complete. They were all weary of traveling and wanted to arrive at their destination.

One night, as they sat by the fire, Yeshua and Bacha began to talk about their families with Vijayananda. Yeshua talked about his mother, and his brothers and sisters. "You speak of everyone in your family except for your father. Why is that?" asked Vijayananda.

Yeshua grew angry, something he had not done since their journey began. "My father was murdered before I was born," he said.

"I never got to meet him. I never got to learn from him. He was taken from me. It was so unfair."

"So your mother raised you on her own?"

"I have a stepfather," Yeshua replied curtly. "His name is Ephrayim."

Although he had learned that Ephrayim wasn't such a bad person after all, he still lamented the fact that his own father had been murdered. He really didn't want to talk about Ephrayim. The tone of his voice must have delivered that message, because no other questions were put forth.

Bacha then told Vijayananda of his life growing up, and how he had gotten the scar on his arm that first brought him to Vijayananda's attention. After he was done he asked, "So, Vijayananda, tell us about your family."

Vijayananda told the two of them that he was born into the warrior caste. His father was a warrior, and his father's father before him was a warrior. He was brought up in the city of Pratishthana, and had lived around nobility all his life. His mother was a dominant figure in his life, and he loved her for her kind and gentle ways. But his relationship with his father was of the best he could imagine. His father was a very demanding person, wanting his only son to be a great warrior. He was very hard on his son, but when Vijayananda did something really well, his father would slap him on the back and say, "Well done, young warrior. Well done." Vijayananda spoke with such admiration of his father that Yeshua wanted him to stop, and yet at the same time, wanted to listen to him all night. He was very jealous, but Vijayananda was the first person he had ever known who gave him insight as to what it was really like to have a father—a real father; not a stepfather. It sounded so wonderful, so unlike his own life.

The towns and villages they passed through gave Yeshua a glimpse of the people of India. There was a lot of poverty, yet people seemed complacent in their surroundings. It was almost as if, despite their few possessions, they were content to simply have a place to sleep at night and enough food to feed themselves. Of course there were also people who didn't even have enough food and who slept on the streets at night, and this reminded him of the place outside Sepphoris where Yeshua had made friends with Aziz, Zamir, Gera, Lemek, and of course Yechezqel. The rich lived apart from the poor and seemed unconcerned about their plight.

Yeshua noticed a few men, and even some women wearing saffron colored robes, and sitting wih bowls that they would wait for people to fill with food. Vijayananda explained that these were sannyasins or, in the case of females, sannyasinis: people who renounced all worldly and materialistic pursuits and chose to dedicate the rest of their lives to spiritual pursuits. Among them were older people, but also many young monks. It appeared to Yeshua that the rest of the population felt obligated to feed these people—even the poor would put food in their bowls.

As they got closer and closer to Pratishthana, Vijayananda seemed to grow more and more excited. For him, it was a return home; For Yeshua and Bacha, it was another unknown destination. If anything, they both grew more apprehensive.

29 (Yeshua meets Patanjali)

AD 10
Yeshua's age: 13

It was almost evening, and they had finally reached their destination, the home of Patanjali. He lived in a commune of sorts on the outskirts of Pratishthana. There was a large group of houses built in a circle, facing one other, leaving a communal center in which there was a large garden, many beautiful trees, a bathhouse, and a well. There was also a small ornate temple.

Vijayananda tied up the camels and guided Yeshua and Bacha through a small entryway between two of the homes. The houses were square, and constructed of baked bricks. Patanjali's house was bigger than the one in Nazareth in which Yeshua lived. It was located on the eastern side of the commune. Vijayananda said that when meditating, it was helpful to face east, and the room that Patanjali meditated in was on the east side of the house. Vijayananda asked Yeshua and Bacha to wait while he summoned his master. He went inside, and a moment later came back out.

"My master is currently in Samadhi, the deepest of all meditations. If you promise to be very quiet, I will show you." Vijayananda beckoned Yeshua and Bacha to the house. "You must remove your shoes before going in," he whispered.

Yeshua and Bacha removed their shoes, and the three of them quietly entered. Inside the house, on the eastern side, they went into the meditation room. Patanjali was a striking figure with brown hair streaked with gray. Some of his hair hung down below his shoulders, but most of it was braided above his head, in the shape of a high crown. He had three wide white horizontal bands of paint across his forehead, with one red streak going vertically from the bridge of his nose up to the top of his head. His beard was white. He was dressed in a saffron-colored robe and wore several large necklaces made from the dark red seeds of some plant unknown to Yeshua. He sat absolutely straight and absolutely quiet, just like Yeshua had seen Vijayananda sitting that night in Jerusalem and throughout their journey on the ship. But two things were different: Patanjali's face thoroughly defined calm and peacefulness, much more than Vijayananda's, and his entire body seemed to glow. There was a definite, visible aura of light surrounding him. Yeshua had never seen such a thing before, and was amazed. He wasn't at all sure if he was just imagining it, but when he looked at Bacha's face, he knew his friend saw it too.

After some time, Bacha and Vijayananda left, but Yeshua remained. He noticed something else that he had never experienced before: He could actually feel calmness and peacefulness exuding from this strange and holy man. And so he sat and watched the aura shimmering around Patanjali, feeling this strange man's emotions clearly.

Yeshua knew from watching Vijayananda that one could sit in meditation for a very long time, and so after watching Patanjali for a while, he started to get up and leave. But it was then that Patanjali opened his eyes. He at first looked at nothing at all; his eyes were open, but they were glazed and unfocused. And then he turned toward Yeshua. Upon seeing him, he smiled and gently said, "You are the one from the West. The one I have seen in my visions. You have come."

"Vijayananda has brought me here."

Patanjali rose, walked toward Yeshua, and examined him more closely. "Yes, I can clearly see the greatness in you already, young man."

"Yeshua, sir. My name is Yeshua."

Patanjali replied, "You will have a new name soon, young man. It is a custom in my country that a spiritual leader, upon taking his vows, divorces himself from his past, including his name, his family, and all his friends."

"Even Bacha?" Yeshua asked.

Patanjali had not seen the other child, and seemed puzzled. "More about that later," he replied. "Come, let us drink some tea."

Yeshua followed, and soon the four of them were sitting on the floor, drinking a kind of tea that Yeshua had never tasted before. It had lemon and honey in it, and smelled of other spices that he could not identify. He found it most pleasant.

When Patanjali heard Vijayananda's reasoning for bringing Bacha to India, he was in agreement that he had done the right thing. He knew that Prince Hala would likewise agree, especially if Patanjali himself told the prince. Patanjali then said, "Yeshua, tomorrow you must meet our future king, Prince Hala. It was he who paid for your journey—for both of your journeys—and he will be anxious to meet you. I will send word that you have arrived."

"To meet me? Why would your Prince Hala wish to meet me?"

Patanjali closed his eyes and said, "The prince knows from me that you will one day become a great teacher, and he wishes to learn from you, and also to help you grow."

Yeshua looked perplexed. "Learn from me? Help me grow?"

Patanjali smiled at him and said, "Young man, are you not anxious to learn of spiritual matters?"

"I am going to become a rabbi like my father tried to become before he was—um—before he died."

"It's all right, young man. I have seen in my mind that your father died a violent death. I know how it must hurt you inside. I can help you with that. And so tell me, you came to this city where the festival took place in order to begin your studies as a rabbi?"

"Jerusalem. Yes."

"And why did you not do so, my young friend?"

Yeshua began to grow agitated as he thought back on how he was mistreated by the Great Sanhedrin. "They would not let me," he finally replied angrily.

"And are you still interested in learning to become a rabbi?"

"Yes, I am."

"Here in India," Patanjali said, "we know much about spirituality. We have explored it deeply, and practiced it for many thousands of years. We have found that although different people wear different coats, they look the same underneath those coats. And although there are many names for many religions, likewise underneath they are all very much the same. What a rabbi may learn in the West is not so different from what Hindu priests learn here in the East. Let me recite a part of the *Aitareya Upanishad*, one of our holy scriptures. Tell me if it perhaps sounds like something from your own religion."

Before the world was created, only the Self existed.

Nothing whatsoever stirred.

Then the Self thought, "I will create a world."

And so he brought forth out of himself all the worlds.

High above the sky was Ambhas.

The sky itself was Marichi.

The earth was Mara.

And the waters below, Apa.

Yeshua was quick to make the association. "In the beginning," he burst out, "when God created the heavens and the earth, the earth was a formless void and darkness covered the face of the deep, while a wind from God swept over the face of the waters. Then God said, 'Let there be light'; and there was light. And God saw that the light was good; and God separated the light from the darkness. God called the light Day, and the darkness he called Night. And there was evening and there was morning, the first day."

Patanjali was pleased. "See, Yeshua? Different coat; same person!" He continued, "The Self then thought: 'I have created the worlds. Let me now create guardians for these worlds.'"

Yeshua excitedly countered, "Then God said, 'Let us make humankind in our image, according to our likeness; and let them have dominion over the fish of the sea, and over the birds of the air, and over the cattle, and over all the wild animals of the earth, and over every creeping thing that creeps upon the earth.' Different coat, same person!"

They continued in this fashion for a time, Yeshua becoming more and more enchanted with this strange Indian man called Patanjali. Eventually the exchange came to an end, and for a while there was a poignant silence. "Tell me again why your prince wishes to meet me," asked Yeshua.

Patanjali closed his eyes for a moment, and then opened them and said, "Yeshua, you are destined to become a great teacher, and very soon. I have seen this in my own meditation."

"Sir, can you really see these things through meditation?" Yeshua asked.

Patanjali replied, "How do you think Vijayananda was able to find you? Do you think you were singled out by Vijayananda by accident? No. He found you only because I told him where to look. One of the many things you will learn from my teachings, Yeshua, are the 'Siddis.' This is a Sanskrit word that means 'powers.'

"When you reach the end of your training, you will possess powers that most adepts, when they reach such a state, are taught to ignore, because they can corrupt a person. You, however, are different. I see in my mind that you are completely pure. You could never be tempted to use such powers for your own gain. In fact, there will come a time when you will willfully give them up in order to reach the highest state of enlightenment, which we call 'Kaivalya,' which means 'liberation.' Greater than Samadhi, it is a stage that even I have not yet reached."

Yeshua asked, "Was that glowing light around you as you sat in the other room one of those powers?"

"Oh, that," Patanjali said almost dismissively, "Yes, my young friend. Trust me, you too will do that. It is not so much a power that one uses, but something that seems to just happen when you have attained deepness in your meditation. It is a sign that you are progressing on the path. Think of it as an acknowledgement from—um—*God*, as you say."

Yeshua beamed. He already liked this place and these people. He was eager to learn and began talking faster and faster. "Please tell me about your holy scriptures. What are they called? Who wrote them? Will I be allowed to read them? When can I begin learning?"

"Slow down, my young friend. You will learn soon enough. Let us simply enjoy the evening together. Tomorrow you will meet Prince Hala, and the day after that you will begin your training. Together we will study and practice what I teach: Kriya-Yoga. I have no holy scriptures here, but after you have learned what I have to teach you, you will travel about this country and learn from other teachers. They will teach you the Vedas, and, within the Vedas, the Upanishads. This wisdom has been passed from teacher to teacher for many thousands of years. We are only now beginning to write them down for future generations. Perhaps they will let you see some of these writings. You will learn many things. And you will begin teaching here in my country.

"And you, Bacha. Do you also wish to learn Kriya-Yoga?"

Bacha grinned his unique grin and said, "Whatever Yeshua wishes to learn, I wish to learn too."

Patanjali said, "Very well. You may learn in my classroom, with other students. Yeshua I will train privately. You are the protector, yes? Show me your arm that I may see the mark I saw in my vision."

Bacha showed him the mark, and Patanjali grimaced. "That mark came from violence. I am sorry, Bacha. I hope you have made peace with the person who did this to you."

"That person is my father. Yes, I have forgiven him in my mind, but not in person. He's drunk most of the time, and I stay away from him."

Vijayananda, as if trying to turn Bacha's thoughts away from painful episodes, then told Patanjali about how Bacha protected Yeshua from the snake, and how skillfully he did it.

"Good, Bacha. Perhaps you can learn from Vijayananda some of his skills as a warrior," said Patanjali.

"I would like that," Bacha replied, looking at Vijayananda. "I would like that very much."

Patanjali abruptly stood and walked toward the door. "Come, let us go out and watch the sun go down together, and then sleep. Vijayananda will bring you, Yeshua, and you, Bacha, to the guest house where you will spend the night."

Yeshua had many more questions for Patanjali, but thought it best to save them for the next day.

30 (The palace and Prince Hala)

Yeshua and Bacha slept in the guesthouse on soft, comfortable beds. Yeshua was more tired than he had imagined, and when he awoke, the sun had long risen over the horizon. Next to his bed was a table, and on this table someone had placed a clean white robe. It was obviously meant for him to put on.

Bacha, who had been outside, stood at the door in a matching robe and said, "Yeshua, they bathe in *hot* water here! Come, there is a tub ready for you. It has sweet smelling oil in it they call sandalwood. The others are already up."

After bathing and putting on his white robe, Yeshua joined his friends and Patanjali. His skin was smooth, and his hair was shiny from the oil. Patanjali announced, "Prince Hala will provide our morning meal today at the palace. We are expected soon."

Yeshua said, "Please tell me again why a prince would want to meet me."

"There is another one of the Siddis that you will one day possess. It gives one the ability to see both past and future, and I told Prince Hala that a great teacher was going to come from the West and live among us for a time. I told him that this teacher would eventually spread his message of peace throughout the world. Prince Hala's father, King Aristakarman, has created peace throughout the Satavahanan Empire, but there is now talk of war. Prince Hala finds that most troublesome, and wishes to learn the ways of peace. That is why he studies with me. And when I told him of you, he wished to meet someone who would one day become a great messenger of peace. He wants to learn whatever he can from you."

Patanjali knew there was more than just that. He knew of Prince Hala's desire to create his own legacy, but this was a private matter. Besides, the prince really did wish to learn the ways of peace. Nothing he had just told Yeshua was a lie. The vows he had taken would not allow him to lie.

"Don't be afraid, Yeshua. He is only a few years older than you, and he knows how to find out what he wants to know. He will ask you questions, and you will answer truthfully. That's all you really need to do. Now come. It's time for us to depart."

***

Patanjali, Vijayananda, Yeshua, and Bacha all walked the short distance to Pratishthana. Yeshua marveled at the many-colored clothing that people wore throughout the town. It was much more colorful here than Passover in Jerusalem. The palace was a work of splendor and stood many times bigger than the temple in Jerusalem. A yellowish-brown wall completely surrounded the palace, and each of its four corners sprouted huge cylindrical columns. The top of each column housed a smaller columned kiosk, and each was topped with an onion-shaped dome.

Once inside the protective wall, the palace could be seen in all its glory. The turquoise and gold palace door was arch-shaped and stood sixteen cubits (about twenty-four feet) tall and eight cubits wide. The top of the palace had a massive onion-shaped dome with an ornamental finial on top. The base of the dome was banded with multicolored polished stones that glistened in the sunlight.

Upon their arrival, Patanjali said, "Yeshua and Bacha, it is the custom to not only remove your shoes when entering my house, but when entering anyone's house. The palace is no different. We will leave our shoes at the top of the stairs. When you meet the prince, you must place your hands like this, and bow like this." Patanjali placed his palms together in prayer position, placed them on his forhead, and bowed gracefully from the waist. Yeshua and Bacha both mimicked him, and Patanjali nodded his head in approval. Vijayananda smiled.

The inside of the palace was even more beautiful than the outside. All along the walls of the palace halls were huge, multicolored statues of strange creatures that Yeshua had never seen before. One had the body of a human and the head of an elephant. Many had four arms, some had eight arms. One angry-looking demon-like figure had a sword in one of her four hands and a severed head in another. This one, and some of the others, were frightening to Yeshua.

The four guests were escorted down a long hallway and into a room where a young man sat with two guards on either side of him. He rose, and the quartet bowed to him in unison. He immediately fixed his gaze on Yeshua. "You are the great one from the West?"

Prince Hala was tall, with flowing jet-black hair and deep-set eyes. He was dressed in a golden robe and wore many bracelets and necklaces adorned with jewels. Although he wore the look of nobility, he had, in fact, a friendly face. Yeshua replied, "Prince Hala, I come here as a student. If Patanjali says I will some day become a great teacher of peace, I find no reason to doubt him. I have already seen some of the things he can do. But to be honest, I do not feel greatness within me yet."

The prince laughed, rose, and placed his arms around Yeshua's shoulders. It was unheard of for a nobleman to treat a stranger in such a familiar manner. Patanjali and Vijayananda looked questioningly at one another. "Very well, student, let us have some food and talk."

Yeshua had never been served food by servants before, and felt somewhat uncomfortable at being treated like nobility. But the food was both tasty and plentiful. As the trays were constantly placed before them, Yeshua took more sweets several times. Whenever the prince wanted the servants to leave, he would flick his hand at them dismissively. They would back away from him, bowing several times as they did, before turning and quickly leaving.

"Tell me a story from your land," Prince Hala said. "Patanjali told me weeks before your arrival that he had a vision of you being a great teller of stories."

Yeshua looked questioningly at Patanjali, wondering just how many powers this man possessed. But there was something more pressing on his mind. Something had deeply bothered Yeshua as he observed this land from the ship, and then from the camel ride. There seemed to be different classes of people here, in some ways similar to Israel, but in other ways completely different. It was during the journey by camel he had seen someone who appeared to be very poor actually prostrate himself on the ground when others who appeared to be very rich walked by. That he had never seen in his own land. The rich person seemed to ignore the gesture as he walked past. And the rest of the people seemed to accept this spectacle as being normal. Because he was so new to this country, he did not ask Vijayananda about it, but it continued to bother him, and now he wanted to know. He would try to find out, and then use it to create a mashal.

"Before I tell you a story, may I ask you some questions about your land?"

Patanjali and Vijayananda nearly jumped out of their seats. One did not talk this way to nobility. If the prince wanted to hear a story, you told him a story. And you certainly did not ask a prince to answer your questions first.

But Prince Hala did not seem to be the least bit offended. He even smiled as he gestured with his right hand. "You may ask your questions, Yeshua."

Yeshua described what he had seen on his journey and asked who this person might have been who prostrated himself.

"Ah! In my country we have people who are lower than the lowest caste called Chandala. They are not to be touched, Yeshua. The name Chandala means 'untouchables.' Even their shadow is not allowed to cross that of a Brahmin. That is why they prostrate themselves until the Brahmin passes. It must have been one of them you saw."

Yeshua didn't know what a caste was, or what a Brahmin was. "I don't understand. Who are these Brahmins?"

Prince Hala replied, "The Brahmins are the teachers of the Vedas, our most sacred scriptures. They belong to the highest caste."

Yeshua had seen in his own country those regarded as the most holy, the Sadducees in particular, showing no regard toward the poor. Now it made a little more sense to him. He began to formulate his mashal, but he needed one more piece of information. "And do Brahmins only associate with other Brahmins, or are there people they consider to be their friends or their neighbors?"

The prince thought a moment and replied, "The Kshatriya, the caste to which I belong, are the second-highest caste members and are well versed in our holy scriptures. We are taught by the Brahmins. I suppose the Brahmins and the Kshatriayas might be considered neighbors. Patanjali is a Brahmin, and he and I are friendly toward one another. And now, enough questions. Tell me a story."

Yeshua began:

A certain man was traveling from Barbarikon to Pratishthana, and he fell among robbers, who both stripped him and beat him and departed, leaving him half dead. By chance a certain Brahmin was going down that way. When he saw him, he passed by on the other side of the road. In the same way a Kshatriyan also, when he came to the place, and saw him, passed by on the other side. But a certain Chandala, as he traveled, came where he was. When he saw him, he was moved with compassion, came to him, and bound up his wounds, pouring on oil and wine. He set him on his own animal, and brought him to an inn, and took care of him. On the next day, when he departed, he took out two coins, and gave them to the host, and said to him, "Take care of him. Whatever you spend beyond that, I will repay you when I return." Now which of these three do you think seemed to be a neighbor to him who fell among the robbers?

Before he could help himself, Prince Hala blurted out, "The one who showed mercy on him. The Chandala."

Yeshua gestured with his hand as he had seen the prince doing when dismissing his servants. "Go then! And be like the Chandala!"

Prince Hala laughed aloud at this. Yeshua's timing and his gestures were impeccable. "Be like the Chandala—a wonderful story! You must tell me more, Yeshua."

Bacha grinned at Yeshua's mashal. Patanjali and Vijayananda were flabbergasted. Yeshua, by mimicking him, had just openly insulted the prince, and yet Prince Hala was laughing.

For the remainder of the morning Yeshua told more and more mashals; some from the scriptures and some, which he created on the spot, like the one about the Chandala. They were filled with lessons of peace and love and goodwill. Yeshua made his audience laugh; he made them cry; he made them think; and he proved himself to be an expert storyteller. Prince Hala, Patanjali, Bacha, and Vijayananda were all captivated.

Soon it was time to go, and after bidding the prince farewell and promising to visit again, they made their way back to Patanjali's house. Once outside the palace, Patanjali said, "Yeshua, perhaps you are not familiar with our land and our customs, but certain things you must learn. What you did; what you said to the prince, was insulting. You made him answer your questions before telling him what he wanted to know. This is arrogance. You made fun of the way he orders his servants. That was rudeness. He laughed this time, but these things could just as easily have landed you in prison, or even worse. He has paid of his own money to bring you here; he has paid money for your friend Bacha to be here only because you refused to come unless he came too, and yet you repaid him with insults and arrogance."

Yeshua's face turned red. He felt embarrassed, but also he felt anger at being admonished. This was the kind of anger that he often felt in Nazareth. This was the kind of anger that sometimes made him yell. Bacha saw the look on his face, and rubbed his hand on Yeshua's shoulder. Yeshua calmed down a little, but there was still anger in his voice. "You should have told me," he said. "You only told me to answer the questions presented to me by the prince, and to be honest. You never said I was not allowed to ask him questions."

"You have much to learn, young man; starting with your manners!" Patanjali said loudly and curtly. They walked the rest of the way to Patanjali's home in silence.

By the time they reached the house, both Yeshua and Patanjali were calmer. "Perhaps you are right, young Yeshua," Patanjali said. "I only assumed you knew how to act in the presence of royalty. Vijayananda and I have lived among royalty all our lives, so for us it is second nature. We will talk more about the prince and the caste system later. For now, let us eat our evening meal."

After they had eaten, Patanjali said, "Yeshua, tomorrow we will begin your training. One of my students will come get you a few hours before the sun rises. This is the time each day when we do our first meditation. You will say nothing. I will sit, and you will sit like I do. When I bow, you bow. I will chant, you will listen. Soon you will know the chants and may join in. Close your eyes, but open your mind. We will sit in meditation until the sun comes up."

Yeshua went to bed very excited that night. His training was finally going to start. That night he dreamed of the strange creatures he had seen carved in the palace.

31 (First lessons in Kriya Yoga)

Morning came all too quickly, and Yeshua was not ready to be awakened. But as he was shaken awake by one of Patanjali's students, he remembered the instructions that he was not to talk. Together, they walked to the house and to the meditation room where Yeshua had first seen Patanjali. Patanjali lit a small bundle of something that Yeshua was unfamiliar with. The sweet-smelling smoke rose in thin strands, filling the room with its fragrance. They knealt, facing east, and Patanjali placed his palms together on his forehead and bowed his head to the ground. Yeshua did the same. Patanjali then began a chant that started with the sound "*om*." He had a deep and resonant voice. After that, they sat. Yeshua tried to sit tall like Patanjali, but found it hard to do for very long. When he closed his eyes, he remembered being told to open his mind. And he did. Exactly what happened next, Yeshua didn't know, but *something* happened; something that made him feel so calm, so at ease, that he felt like he could sit for days without moving.

As the sun began to light up the room, Patanjali ended their meditation by once more kneeling and bowing. Yeshua did likewise. This was followed by yet another chant. How had this time gone by so quickly? And then they both walked outside into the morning. The first lesson was taught while walking. This would become their daily custom. Master and student, walking and talking. Patanjali said, "Yeshua, repeat after me: '*Yogas citta-vrtti-nirodhah*.'"

Yeshua repeated the strange-sounding phrase. Patanjali began to expound on those words. "*Yogas*, Yeshua, comes from the root word *Yug*, which means to join. Yoga joins, or unites ourselves, with our highest nature. To do that, we come to the second word, *citta*. Citta is a product of consciousness. You will learn much more about citta as our lessons progress, because it is a very complex subject. For now think of it simply as 'mind.' This will make it easier to understand. The third word is *vrtti*. In one sense it means movements, modifications, or fluctuations. Later today, or perhaps tomorrow, we will learn of the five vrttis that we need to conquer. The last word is *nirodhah*. It means 'to restrain, to control, or to inhibit.' Thus this first lesson means, 'Yoga is the restriction of the fluctuations of the mind.' Does that make sense to you, Yeshua?"

Yeshua was quiet for a moment. He turned to Patanjali and asked, "So Yoga is thinking about nothing?"

Patanjali laughed. "Nothing is a thought, like any other thought. Yoga is much deeper than that. Tell me, how did you sleep last night?"

Yeshua answered, "I slept very well, Master Patanjali." For the first time, he was addressing him as master, as he had heard Vijayananda address him earlier.

"And how do you know that you slept well?"

Yeshua was stumped.

"You know because you were *aware*. You were aware of the thought of nothingness. Otherwise, it would seem like you closed your eyes to blink during the darkness, and when you opened them it would be light. To truly still the mind requires time and patience. Even when you *think* your mind is still, it is not—at least not yet. With this first sentence, Y*ogas citta-vrtti-nirodhah,* I have now told you the end result of our lessons. This is the direction we are moving toward. To get there is where the real work is. It will be extremely hard, Yeshua, and it will take a very long time. Do you think you can do it?"

Yeshua stood back up and replied, "I will try, Master. I will try as hard as I can."

They had talked for less than an hour, but Patanjali had given Yeshua much to consider. He was quiet most of the rest of the day, in deep thought.

From that day forward, Patanjali and Yeshua meditated three times a day. The morning meditations were the ones that Yeshua always enjoyed the most. Patanjali's body would glow in the darkness with that strange aura some of the mornings, but Yeshua soon learned to ignore it just as Patanjali did.

Sometimes in the afternoon, Patanjali would leave to go to the palace and teach Prince Hala. Yeshua often wondered if Prince Hala was learning the same things he was. Maybe someday they could discuss their lessons.

32 (Another meeting with Prince Hala)

A month had passed and Yeshua sat in the palace courtyard. The king's warriors were practicing fighting with swords. Yeshua sat and watched them as they knocked each other down and pretended to strike a death blow to the heart. It was not what he really wanted to watch, but Prince Hala had invited him. He had learned from Patanjali that an "invitation" from the prince or the king was, in fact, a polite demand!

Prince Hala was fighting with Vijayananda, and there were several others fighting, including Bacha. Because Bacha had expressed an interest in learning on the first night they arrived, Vijayananda had requested that Bacha be given some training in the ways of fighting. Bacha had shown some of his own techniques to the teachers, including some he had taught Yeshua when he first met him, and they were duly impressed. In this mock battle Bacha was losing. His sword techniques could not begin to match those of his opponent, who had been taught to fight with a sword since he was seven years old. Time after time Bacha ended up on the ground with a sword pointing to his heart or his neck. But when they changed from swords to hand-to-hand combat, he did much better, combining his own techniques with those he had been taught. Bacha had learned many things in his warrior schooling, including all the pressure points in the human body, and now knew how to end a person's life with a single blow to a certain spot.

There was no doubt in Yeshua's mind that the man he was looking at, who sat nearby, was Vijayananda's father. This man smiled whenever Vijayananda was victorious, and frowned whenever he was knocked to the ground. Such pride in his son's accomplishments reminded Yeshua of the father he never had. Ephrayim would likely have shown pride if he had built a perfect table or chair for him, but it wouldn't be the same; at least not in Yeshua's eyes. No, he longed for the father he never had—a father he had created in his mind, a father much greater than Yosef probably actually was.

Mara had never told him what his father looked like, so it was only in Yeshua's imagination that he existed. He imagined Yosef to be tall and muscular, with a thick brown beard. He could be brusque like

Vijayananda's father, but he could be as kind as Patanjali. Everyone in town loved and respected him, and whenever he and his father walked the streets together, Yeshua felt everyone's eyes admiring the two of them. He was Yeshua, son of Yosef. He would say that over and over in his head: *Yeshua, son of Yosef.*

After training was over, they ate lunch, and then Prince Hala invited Yeshua to his study. "Tell me about your upbringing, Yeshua." Prince Hala made it sound more like a command than a request.

"There is not a lot to tell. I was born in Israel, in a city in Galilee called Nazareth. My father was murdered before I was born." Yeshua paused for a moment.

"I'm so sorry. How terrible for you. Please go on."

"My mother married again shortly after I was born, and my stepfather wanted me to become a carpenter. I fought with him about it for almost three years."

Prince Hala's face softened. He said, "My father too wants me to be something I don't wish to be. I am next in line to become king of the Satavahana Empire. My father wants me to become a great warrior. He watches me each time I fight in the courtyard. I would rather keep the peace if possible. To be king is a great honor. But my interest is in spiritual matters and poetry. That's not something most great warriors spend their time with. I have started compiling poems and have even written a few. Would you like to hear some of them?"

Yeshua said that he would. Prince Hala recited several verses to him, giving him some of the background of each poem before he recited it. He had a soft voice when he spoke the words, quite unlike the commanding tone he used otherwise.

Yeshua understood the words, and appreciated the rhythmic meter—a special type called Arya-meter—of the poetry, but a lot of the subtleties of the poems were lost on him. There was much too much history and Indian culture that he could not possibly understand yet.

"You said you are interested in spiritual matters also?" Yeshua asked.

"Yes. I am quite well versed in the Puranas. Do you know what they are?" As if he knew that Yeshua had never heard of them, the prince continued, "These are stories about our deities. We have many of them, and I know a lot of them and can recite them by heart."

The prince's face suddenly brightened and he said, "Yeshua! Let me tell you a story from a great scroll called the Mahabharata. The story is called the Bhagavad Gita. It's not a Purana, but it is a story that can be useful to both of us. There is a boy named Arjuna, and just like us, he is being forced to do something that he really doesn't want to do. In his case, he is being forced to fight to the death against his cousins and his uncle and many friends and teachers and shopkeepers whom he knows. He is a boy of great peace, and doesn't want to fight. Lord Krishna, the other main person in the story, is going to teach him how to perform his duty by fighting, and at the same time preserve his peaceful ways."

"That doesn't sound possible," Yeshua said.

"Ah, but it is. Maybe after I tell you the story, you will do your duty by going back home and becoming a carpenter, while still becoming a great teacher. Such things are possible."

Yeshua bristled at the suggestion. "Becoming a carpenter is not my duty! My real father was going to become a rabbi ... um, that's like a spiritual teacher or priest. But he never got the chance to do it. If he were alive, I am certain he would want me to become a rabbi as well. And so this is what I am studying. This, I believe, is my duty. I have been told there is much to learn in your country. I hope to learn it. Your teacher, Patanjali, is instructing me in Kriya Yoga. After that, I don't know. He will tell me where to go in order to learn other things. He has also told me I will begin teaching here in your country."

But Yeshua was captivated by the Bhagavad Gita as Prince Hala began to tell more of what Lord Krishna says to Arjuna, "This body-bearer in everyone's body is eternally undestroyable, O Descendant of Bharata. Therefore you should not grieve after any and all beings. Seeing your righteous duty you should not tremble, for there is nothing better for a warrior than a righteous battle. Happy are the warriors who find such a battle that has come of its own momentum and is like an open door to heaven."

The Bhagavad Gita contained seven hundred verses. The lessons contained in it were much more than lessons for Arjuna and his situation. The battle described in the story could be more than a physical life-and-death battle, but a symbol of the series of struggles that each person goes through in life. Yeshua saw how this story was not unlike the mashals he had learned to tell, although they seemed to be somehow different. There was much more to them than the mashals he had learned. And they seemed to have greater power. Some of Lord Krishna's lessons that he imparted to Arjuna were about yoga, and Yeshua saw many similarities between that and what Patanjali taught him.

When it came time for Yeshua to leave, he asked the prince if he would tell him more of the story the next time he visited. "Of course I will, Yeshua. And you can tell me something about your religion. I would like to know more about your Moshe. We have much to teach each other."

33 (Ephrayim and Mara wonder)

AD 11
Nazareth, Israel

Ephrayim returned home from the poor section of town, outside Sepphoris. He occasionally went there to see Yechezqel, the man who had befriended Yeshua years ago, and who had since become Ephrayim's friend. Ephrayim's views about poor people had changed dramatically since he had first gone there looking for his son. He had, at first, treated Yechezqel with disdain. But when he saw Yechezqel's genuine concern for Yeshua and his willingness to help look for him, Ephrayim's heart gradually began to soften. Over time, he saw the people here as they really were, not as he assumed them to be. Ephrayim would now donate some of his time and talents to the people who lived there. Today he had helped Yechezqel build a house for a young couple who had no money. The wood and bricks had been donated by kind neighbors in Sepphoris.

"Any word about Yeshua?" Mara asked as he sat down at the table.

Ephrayim sighed and said, "Mara, it's time to finally accept the fact that our Yeshua is dead."

"No!"

"Yes, Mara. You must let him go."

Mara's eyes grew wide, almost wild looking. "I am his mother! If he were dead, Ephrayim, if he were truly dead I would feel it here inside me." She placed her hand over her heart. "He's *not* dead."

"Mara, we've had this discussion over and over. I've looked for him, my brother Yo'el looked for him, Yechezqel looked for him. Rabbi Towbiyah made inquiries throughout all of Israel, and even in Samaria where that boy, Bacha, lived. Nobody has seen or heard of him since we left Jerusalem back when he was twelve. Mara, don't you think if he were still alive, he would have been seen somewhere? Don't you think he would come back, or at least sent word to us? It's been two years now. He's dead, I tell you."

All the while he talked, Mara vigorously shook her head. "Ephrayim, I understand what you say. I'm not denying how things look. I just *know* he is still alive somewhere. You will never be able to convince me otherwise."

Ephrayim stood, looked into her eyes, smiled, and gently placed both hands around her waist. "Very well Mara. He's still alive. If you believe it, I believe it too."

She embraced him tightly, burrowing her head into his strong shoulders, sobbing and saying, "He is alive. He is. He is."

Ephrayim went into his workshop where Yaaqob was busy working. Yosef would be home from school soon, and would work for the afternoon. Yaaqob and Yosef were now Ephrayim's apprentices, and Shimon, who was only nine, was learning as well. Ephrayim had often wondered whether Yeshua really could still be alive. Deep inside him he didn't believe it, but he would keep Mara's hope alive; at least for now. Sooner or later, she would finally give up and accept it. He shook his head slowly from side to side, thinking of what could have been, and went back to his work.

34 (Aharon's success)

It had been fourteen years since Mara disobeyed her father and chose Yosef over Aharon. During that time, Aharon had done very well for himself. He had set his most recent goal to be a member of the Great Sanhedrin, the seventy-one members whot made up the ruling body of Israel, and today it was about to happen. And he would be not just a member but one of the twenty-four chief priests. For others, this was a lifetime ambition, but for Aharon it was merely an interim step. This would bring him one step closer to Herod, who came to Jerusalem often. Herod represented the real power of Rome, and it was power that Aharon was after.

"Aharon, congratulations," said Mered, one of the members of the Small Sanhedrin. He backed away as Aharon neared. Aharon always stood closer to people than they liked, which made them feel a little uncomfortable. This was Aharon's way. He *wanted* others to feel uncomfortable. He could see it in their eyes, and it gave him a feeling of superiority. Although he was smiling, Aharon's hands were tightly closed into fists. He did this often, though he was unaware of it, and it spoke of an unnatural cruelty he held inside him. He was not the kind of person to provoke; you did not want to be on Aharon's bad side.

"Thank you, Mered," he replied in his resonant voice. "I told you this would happen. And in only two years." He wagged his finger in Mered's face as he spoke, which was another way he made others uncomfortable.

Aharon was tall, and always well dressed. He wasn't exactly a handsome man; he had a squarish face with squinting eyes. His lips were thin and his mouth small, creating a perpetual sneer across his face. But his height, his clothes, his well trimmed gray hair and beard, and his mannerisms all spoke of a man of great power.

To become a member of the Great Sanhedrin, one had to have several attributes and accomplishments, and Aharon had them all. He was a direct descendant of his namesake, Aharon, the first priest of ancient Israel, the older brother of Moshe. This was one of the attributes that qualified him to be a chief priest. He was without blemish or lameness. He was an offspring of Jewish parents, he was in the prime of his life, and he was wealthy. All these attributes were necessary.

As for accomplishments, he needed to be a father of a family, so as to be able to sympathize with domestic affairs. After Mara had disobeyed her father and wed Yosef, he had wed another, named Binah, and fathered a daughter, Rachel, who was now eight.

He needed to be knowledgeable in the divine law, secular knowledge, and foreign languages, so that the Sanhedrin would not need to be dependent upon an interpreter. Aharon had studied both Greek and Latin. He chose these languages because they were the languages spoken by the Romans. This would serve him well as he continued his rise to greater power.

Last of all, he needed to be a judge in his native town, and to have been promoted to the Small Sanhedrin, which sat in the entrance to the temple hall. His father had made him a judge, and for the past two years he had been a member of the Small Sanhedrin.

"Aharon, come. The others are waiting." Eylam, one of the Great Sanhedrin, beckoned, and the two of them walked together into the inner chamber of the temple.

It wasn't much of a ceremony, but it was still of great importance. There were five ordained members present, and two nonordained members. The president of the Great Sanhedrin—the Nasi—had given his permission to grant Aharon membership. The seven sat in a semicircle, and Aharon stood in the center. Together, the seven who were seated said the words, "Rabbi Aharon, behold, thou art ordained, and hast the authority to judge even cases involving pecuniary fines." And that quickly, it was over. Each of the seven embraced Aharon and congratulated him. He was uncomfortable with being embraced, but did not show it in his face.

Aharon mentally struck another item off his list. "Will you be staying until Sabbath?" asked Eylam.

"No. I need to return to Sepphoris for a few days. I need to attend to some business. I'll be back before Sabbath."

"Business?" Eylam asked.

Aharon grew tense and tersely replied, "*Personal* business."

Eylam did not press him further.

Aharon mounted his camel and headed north.

35 (Yeshua learns a lesson about the opposite sex)

AD 11
Yeshua's age: 14

The next two years were happy times for Yeshua and Bacha. Bacha continued to spend half of each day learning Kriya Yoga with other students and the other half learning fighting techniques at the palace with Vijayananda. At night, after meditation, he and Yeshua would tell each other of their days and what they had learned.

Yeshua was now being given daily tasks. Some days he would help prepare the food for the next meal. He enjoyed that a lot. Many of the spices, such as turmeric, had medicinal qualities to them as well as flavor. Some days he would bring the clothes to the Nath Sagor lake, wrap them in wet clay, beat the clay off them on stones by the water's edge, rinse them, and then set them on the larger stones to dry. His meditation was progressing, but he found the lessons quite hard. So many concepts, so many meanings. Through the lessons, he was also slowly learning yet another language: Sanskrit.

One day, as he cleaned the clothes by the water, a young girl his age came by. Yeshua had begun to make friends with the townspeople who came to wash their clothes, but it was mostly adults whom he encountered. "You are not from around here," the girl said. "Who are you?"

She was not as tall as Yeshua, and like everyone else in this country, her hair was long and jet black. Not yet a woman, she was, nonetheless, slim and curvaceous. She had rings in her ears, and one in her nose. Her eyes were dark, and she smelled of sandalwood. There was a spot of red on her forehead, between her eyebrows. Yeshua had never seen such a beautiful young girl.

"My name is Yeshua," he said with some hesitation. "And who are you?"

She turned suddenly, as if she was afraid someone was listening, and then turned back and replied, "My name is Chitralekha. Are you the one from the West everyone has been talking about?"

Yeshua came closer to her now. She began to take a step backwards, and then changed her mind. Yeshua said, "I am the one from the West, Chitralekha. I am learning Kriya Yoga from Master Patanjali. Have you heard of him?"

She laughed. "Everyone knows who Patanjali is. He is teaching the great Prince Hala as well." Every few seconds she would turn to look behind her, and then turn back.

Yeshua could stand it no longer. "Why do you keep looking behind you?"

"I am waiting for my brother, Murali. We have been praying at the temple, and when we left, he stopped to talk to some friends. I went on ahead by myself." Off in the distance they both heard her name being called.

"There he is now. I'm coming, brother!" she yelled back.

Yeshua, still enchanted by her beauty, asked, "Will I see you again at the lake?"

She blushed as she lowered her eyes. "Maybe." With that, she ran off to where the voice had been coming from.

***

Patanjali did not look happy as he and Yeshua began their morning walk and lesson. "Yeshua, I have been teaching you as an advanced student, because I thought you didn't need most of the basics. But based on what I have heard, I think we need to focus on some of the early lessons."

Yeshua looked confused, and a bit uncomfortable.

"In the study of Kriya Yoga, there are certain life patterns that you must follow in order to help you tame your mind. We call them the *Yamas* [restraints] and the *Niyamas* [observances]. Perhaps we need to go over them. I will start with the Yama that I think you most need to know about. It is called *Brahmacharya*. It means to walk in the footsteps of Brahma.

"Yeshua, you are in your fourteenth year, and are beginning to mature sexually. For the majority of the population, this is a normal, and perfectly acceptable, condition. But if you are studying Kriya Yoga, and you give in to your sexuality, it can be an impediment to your progress. It needs to be dealt with from the very beginning. This drive that presents itself to you is one of the most powerful drives humans have. It consumes us. And most important of all, it uses a tremendous amount of energy both in the mind and in the physical body, energy you need if you want to reach Kaivalya. Do you understand?"

Yeshua began to blush, knowing that his momentary encounter with Chitralekha had been witnessed and reported to Patanjali. "Master Patanjali," he asked, "is it wrong to talk to girls or women?"

"Talking to anyone is in itself not wrong. Friendship is not wrong. In Kriya Yoga we practice the four right attitudes: 'Friendliness toward the happy, compassion toward the unhappy, bliss toward the enlightened, and indifference toward the wicked.' I only give you a warning about relationships with the opposite sex. You must suppress all sexual feelings and thoughts, at least for a time. You will find that you will be giving up a momentary sensation for a gift that is far greater. If you find yourself slipping in this endeavor, avoid the temptation altogether until you are ready to confront it with strength. It is not only sexual indulgences that I am talking about, Yeshua, it is the craving for *all* sensual enjoyments. The sexual craving is only the strongest of them.

"Do I tell you that you can no longer eat food that brings pleasure to you; that you can no longer enjoy the sweet smell of the lotus blossoms? No. What you cannot have, which is the danger of pleasure of any kind, is the *desire* for its repetition. So in time, after you have tamed your desires, you may freely feel sexual attraction. It is a perfectly normal human characteristic. It is our nature, and we all have it. But to feel it without the desire to act on it, or the desire to repeat even the feeling of it—*this* is what you are striving for.

"So you must now choose, Yeshua. I will give you three days to consider what it means. The next time we talk, you will give me your answer. Either you will continue to study Kriya Yoga, or you will not. It is your decision."

Patanjali abruptly turned and walked the other way, leaving Yeshua, still blushing, alone with his thoughts. He felt as if he had betrayed his teacher, and this did not feel good. But he also didn't fully understand his teacher's anger at him. His meditation was not successful that evening, and he went to bed feeling sad and confused.

Yeshua awoke at the normal meditation time the next morning, but Patanjali was not there. He had gone to the palace and was staying there for some time. As he anticipated, Yeshua was again given the task of washing clothes. Patanjali was making sure he would knowingly make his decision. And as he also anticipated, Chitralekha was there, this time with her brother. The two saw Yeshua walking toward the lake, and ran up to him.

"Yeshua, good morning. I want you to meet my brother, Murali, who also wanted to meet you." Chitralekha looked as beautiful as Yeshua remembered, and he again felt a burning in his cheeks.

Murali made the greeting gesture that was now almost second nature to Yeshua, and the two bowed to each other, their hands in prayer position on their foreheads. "I have heard much about you, Yeshua. They say that you are an excellent storyteller. I love stories. Will you please tell me one from your country?"

As they sat, Yeshua made a point of sitting next to Murali, and not next to Chitralekha. She was a little disappointed, but her face did not betray her. Yeshua chose a theme that spoke more to him than to the two, and he did nothing to give it a more Indian-like flavor:

Then the Kingdom of Heaven will be like ten virgins, who took their lamps, and went out to meet the bridegroom. Five of them were foolish, and five were wise. Those who were foolish, when they took their lamps, took no oil with them, but the wise took oil in their vessels with their lamps. Now while the bridegroom delayed, they all slumbered and slept. But at midnight there was a cry, "Behold! The bridegroom is coming! Come out to meet him!"

Then all those virgins arose, and trimmed their lamps. The foolish said to the wise, "Give us some of your oil, for our lamps are going out." But the wise answered, saying, "What if there isn't enough for us and you? You go rather to those who sell, and buy for yourselves." While they went away to buy, the bridegroom came, and those who were ready went in with him to the marriage feast, and the door was shut. Afterward the other virgins also came, saying, "Lord, Lord, open to us." But he answered, "Most certainly I tell you, I don't know you." Watch therefore, for you don't know the day nor the hour in which the Son of Man is coming.

Murali and Chitralekha looked at each other in puzzlement. Murali asked, "Why wouldn't they share their oil, Yeshua?"

Yeshua looked into the distance, across the lake, and spoke, as if he were speaking to himself. "The story is about heaven, not about sharing oil. It is saying that if you want to live in heaven, you need to begin now. Nobody knows when they will die, so if that is your goal, you must work at it now, not later. The same is so with Kaivalya, or with any other goal you may persue. You must buy enough oil in advance, and not wait until your lamp is dimming. Does that now make sense to you?"

Murali looked confused, but Chitralekha, who knew more about Kriya Yoga than her brother, guessed what he was talking about. She said to her brother, "Murali, please wait here. I wish to speak to Yeshua alone. We will walk down the lake's edge, and will not leave your sight." Murali nodded in agreement.

Yeshua seemed uncomfortable, but Chitralekha put her arm inside his and pulled him along the lakeside until he relented and walked without being dragged. But her body brushing against his was once again awakening feelings that Patanjali warned him about.

"Yeshua, please know this. I ask for your friendship, nothing more. Maybe you don't know our customs, but in my country, our marriages are arranged by our parents from the time we are children. Mine has been arranged for over six years now. The red dot on my forehead indicates this. It is called a bindu. My future husband and I see each other often, and are best of friends.

"You and I have met only once, and for a very short time. Today is only the second time we have met. While I can't honestly say I haven't had certain feelings about you that perhaps I shouldn't have, I can say that just like your own training instructs you to do, I must face those feelings and make them go away. If I thought I couldn't do that, I would avoid you completely. But as you can plainly see, I don't avoid you, Yeshua. And I hope we can continue our friendship. If you choose to avoid me, I will understand why you do it, and I will not be angry at you. But if you ever want a friend, I will always be here waiting."

She then smiled, turned in the opposite direction, and began slowly walking. Yeshua felt a relief, but was still not certain of his own feelings. He quickly caught up to her, and as they walked back toward Murali, Yeshua resolved to thoroughly explore his feelings in his meditations, starting when he returned from washing clothes. He turned to her and smiled.

He had much to learn from Master Patanjali, and Yeshua wanted this more than he wanted anything. He wanted it more than friendship, more than friendship with a female. He had now made a second big decision in his life. The first was in leaving his own country, and now this. There was still a small part of him that looked back and wondered what might have been, but mostly Yeshua was now looking forward. Yes, Chitralekha would be his friend. He would share that with Master Patanjali. But he would do as his master instructed him to and work very hard on the concept of Brahmacharya.

36 (Yeshua completes his training in Kriya Yoga)

Patanjali was back, and Yeshua was excited to tell him his decision. He had even prepared a clever way of showing him. He had thought long and hard about what Patanjali had told him before he left, and those words still rang in his ears: "Do I tell you that you can no longer eat food that brings pleasure to you; that you can no longer enjoy the sweet smell of the lotus blossoms? No. What you cannot have, which is the danger of pleasure of any kind, is the desire for its repetition." As they left the meditation room that morning for their lessons, Yeshua pulled out two oranges. He said to Patanjali, "Master, please let us sit and eat our oranges. I wish to share something with you."

They sat beneath a tree and began eating their fruit. "Master, when I eat this orange I can taste the wonderful, sweet, unique flavor that comes forth. I can taste the texture of the orange on my tongue, and I can feel it sliding down my throat. But I now eat it in two ways. I eat it as if I had never in my life eaten an orange before. And I eat it as if I will never in my life eat an orange again."

Patanjali smiled, placed his arms around Yeshua, and said, "Well done, Yeshua! You have learned your lessons well, and I am very pleased. You understand. You understand. Live your entire life in this manner, and I have no doubt you will follow the discipline of Brahmacharya, and succeed."

***

Another year went by, and Yeshua learned more and more from Patanjali. Chitralekha became his good friend, as did her brother, and Yeshua enjoyed her company, even her sexuality, without once breaking his personal vow of Brahmacharya. She would soon be married, and Yeshua would watch the sexual play and conversation between Chitralekha and her soon-to-be husband with delight. He would occasionally visit Prince Hala, who once introduced him to the king.

And then one day it happened. He was sitting in meditation with Bacha, and when he opened his eyes, Bacha was staring at him with astonishment. "You were glowing!" Bacha said in excitement. "Just like Master Patanjali, you were glowing."

Yeshua had felt it too, but hadn't given it much thought. Now he knew he was, as his master had described it, "on the right path". He was beginning to come to the dangerous part of his training, where he would gain the Siddis.

Patanjali had once told Yeshua that he was a unique individual, not capable of using powers for his own personal gain. He said that Yeshua would always use his powers for the benefit of others. He began their last phase of training with an explanation. "Yeshua, you have now learned *Dharana*, or concentration; *Dhyana*, or contemplation; and *Samadhi*, or ecstasy. You have learned that they are, in essence, one and the same. Each stage differs from the preceding one only in the depth of concentration. But when we evolve through all these three states, all the while aiming them at a particular object or thought, it is called *Samyama*.

"It is through Samyama that you will gain the Siddis that we spoke about. You must learn them, Yeshua, and you must use them to help others. We will begin with a simple Siddi. This is the Siddi of sound. By performing Samyama on sound, you will comprehend the meaning of sounds uttered by any living being.

"Tomorrow we will go together to a town not far from here where they speak a language different from the one you now speak with me. Throughout this country we speak many different languages. We will sit and listen to them speaking. You will perform Samyama on the sound of a person speaking, and be able to know what that person is saying. It will not be a word-for-word translation, but you will grasp the essence of what that person is saying. You will then tell me what you are hearing, and I will know if you have succeeded."

Yeshua was looking forward to this test as they walked through the countryside early the next morning, passing many towns. When they arrived at their destination, it was late afternoon, the time they would normally eat their second meal. Patanjali purchased some food for the two of them, and they sat in the center of town enjoying the ebb and flow of the people as they went about their daily activities. Two men sat near them, also with their afternoon meal, and began talking to each other. Patanjali looked at Yeshua and said, "Here is your test. Listen closely to them, and perform Samyama on their conversation. Tell me what you hear."

Yeshua did as he was told, and was astounded at how easily he could do this, and how strange it was to hear unfamiliar words and yet know what was being said. "Master, they are talking about their work. They are both merchants in this town. One is telling the other that he is not making very much money these days. The other is agreeing."

Patanjali smiled and said, "And so you are now nearing the end of your training with me. Soon it will be time for you to leave."

Yeshua was not pleased when he heard that. But he had been told from the beginning that his destiny was not to stay with Patanjali forever. Still, he had hoped the training would go on for at least a little while longer. He so enjoyed being with his master.

Patanjali looked over and said, "Yeshua, remember your oranges."

The two exchanged knowing smiles.

***

"Tomorrow, Yeshua, we will begin the final ceremony as I have taught you," said Patanjali. "It has been seven months since your final training of the Siddis. You are ready to continue on your journey. It is time."

Yeshua and Patanjali watched the sun go down, as they often did. "Master, I have studied with you for three long years. I am now sixteen years of age. You have taught me so much, yet I feel there is more to learn. I feel ... incomplete."

Patanjali said back to him, "Yes, you do have more to learn, Yeshua—much more. But you will learn it by traveling throughout the Satavahana Empire and visiting other teachers of wisdom. Embrace what you learn, Yeshua. Take everything into your heart as well as your mind."

And so, just before sunrise, Yeshua began. He sat by himself in a small mud hut and fasted there for three days and three nights. It rained the second night, but Yeshua did not notice. He sat in meditation for most of that time. No more did he tire of sitting straight like he did those first months.

On the third night he was not to sleep at all. This would be his vigil. He spent the night reciting the Gayatri Mantra, which Patanjali had taught to him.

The fourth morning came and Yeshua walked solemnly down to the Nath Sagor lake for his ritual bath. After bathing once, he shaved his head, save for one tuft. Then another bath followed.

When he returned, he prepared for and then performed his own funeral rites, throwing rice, but symbolically throwing himself, into the sacred fire that had been prepared for him in his absence. With each handful of rice he would recite aloud the appropriate chant, and end with the word "*Svaha*" as he threw the rice into the sacred fire. The word meant "so be it," and Yeshua translated it in his mind as "amen."

By now, many had gathered to witness this ceremony. The friends Yeshua had made over the years were all there. Prominently in the front of the large crowd was Prince Hala, with a guard on either side of him. Chitralekha, her husband, and her brother Murali were there. They all seemed somber, yet joyful at the same time. It was a very quiet ceremony, but one filled with feelings of happiness and excitement.

And then Yeshua proceeded with his renunciations. He stood, faced his witnesses, and renounced the desire for sex and family. He renounced the desire for wealth and comfort. And he renounced the desire for fame and reputation. He gave his assurances to the people who were gathered that he would do no harm. He assured those present that the whole world was his family now. Prince Hala was pleased that this teacher of peace would soon be traveling throughout his empire, spreading his message. With Patanjali as the prince's teacher, with his own convictions of peace, and now with this stranger from the West teaching his people, Prince Hala felt confident that peace would reign throughout his tenure as king, and felt more certain than ever that he would soon be proclaimed the great benefactor and friend of Yeshua.

For the first time in the ceremony, Patanjali appeared. He sat by the fire and asked Yeshua to come sit facing him. They began to chant the mantra "*om*" together. This was followed by many other mantras Patanjali had taught him. Then, they were quiet. This was meant to be a communication of spirit.

Nine hours had passed since Yeshua began with his bath, and it was now late afternoon. Patanjali broke the silence and instructed Yeshua to give fearlessness to all the people. Yeshua recited loudly,

"There is no fear from me hereafter. No fear shall come from me either to human beings or to animals. I will neither kill a snake nor hit a scorpion, nor attack a human being. No hurt from me will be there be at any time."

Yeshua offered many more prayers, and Patanjali whispered one of the great sayings of the Upanishads into Yeshua's ear, along with further instructions. Yeshua completed his ceremony by putting on a saffron robe, symbolizing the complete burning of his body and signifying purification through fire.

He was now a Sannyasa.

And as he promised when they first met, Patanjali gave him the new name that Yeshua would carry with him throughout India. He placed his firm hand on Yeshua's shoulder and said, "Blessed be thy soul, and attain salvation at the due time—Issa."

II. ISSA

"They taught him to read and understand the Vedas, to heal by prayer, to teach and explain the Holy Scripture, to cast out evil spirits from the body of man and give him back human semblance."

From <u>The Unknown Life of Jesus Christ</u>,

by Nicolas Notovitch

37 (The White Priests)

AD 13
Yeshua's age: 16

It was decided. Vijayananda would go with Issa to help with some of the many languages and dialects he would encounter on the first part of his journey. Issa had learned the Siddi of sound, among the many other Siddis, so he could understand anyone, but he could not speak back to them in their own language. And Bacha, who had learned much from Patanjali—not to the depth that Issa had, but enough to gain a deep understanding of Kriya Yoga—would also travel with him. A Sannyasa usually traveled alone, but Prince Hala wanted to ensure that no harm would come to Issa. Bacha had learned from Vijayananda some of his warrior training, even exchanging with him some of the techniques he knew and had taught Issa, and now felt confident in being Issa's protector. Prince Hala had given them an official paper containing the king's seal granting them both safe passage throughout the Satavahana Empire.

Although he considered himself a completely different person now, it was still with a heavy heart that Issa said goodbye to Patanjali. "I will carry you with me always, Master," he said to his teacher through tearful eyes.

"We will meet again, I promise you, Issa," Patanjali replied. He too seemed sad, his face hiding a secret that Issa could only wonder about.

That having been said, Issa, Vijayananda, and Bacha began their journey to the eastern shores of India. They were going to Juggernaut, in the province of Orsis, to seek out and learn from the white priests of Brahma. Patanjali had given Issa instructions on where to go and whom to seek out on his journeys throughout India, and the city called Kanchipuram was first on the list. Issa, dressed in his saffron robe, carried only a walking stick and a bowl for begging food, nothing more.

"Why are they called *white* priests, Vijayananda?" Issa asked his friend.

"Did you not learn of the castes from Patanjali?"

"I learned their names and their purpose, but not much more."

"What did Master Patanjali tell you about their purpose?"

Issa replied, "He told me that there are Brahmins, the highest caste, who are the priests and teachers. Next come the Kshatriyas, the rulers and warriors. Third come the Vaisyas, who are the merchants. Last are the Sudra, the laborers. But below the lowest caste are the Chandala, who are called 'the untouchables.'"

Vijayananda said, "You are correct. Now let me tell you about our clothing. Different colors of clothing signify the different castes. White signifies the caste of the Brahmins. The Kshatriya red, the Vaisya yellow, and the Sudra black. So the white priests are Brahmin, and thus they wear white."

"And what of the Chandala, Vijayananda?"

"Them? They are so poor that they just wear whatever they can find that others have thrown away. They are dressed in many colors. Some of them wear no clothes at all."

The Chandala reminded Issa of the lepers he had befriended in Israel. The thought of their plight and the plight of the Chandalas here in India made him sad.

***

They continued their eastward journey until they neared the shores of the ocean and came to a city called Kanchipuram. It was here that Issa met his new teacher, an elderly Brahmin priest named Jnyaneshwar. Issa learned from Vijayananda that this name means "god of wisdom." Jnyaneshwar was tall and had white hair, bushy eyebrows, and a full beard. He had many braids in his hair that were wrapped around his head like a hat, but not high like Patanjali's crown. Both his beard and his hair were becoming thin as he aged. And, as Issa had expected, Jnyaneshwar was dressed in white.

Jnyaneshwar had heard much about Issa from Patanjali. He spoke in Sanskrit, but between Issa's Siddi of sound and his limited knowledge of Sanskrit from Patanjali's teachings, they were able to communicate. Of course Vijayananda helped with some of the translating, but for the most part the two spoke without aid.

"So tell me, Issa, what have you learned of the Vedas from Patanjali?" he asked.

Issa had learned very little, as his lessons were all about Kriya Yoga. "I have a limited knowledge of the Upanishads, and I know even less about the Vedas," he replied.

"Hmm. That will soon change. Tomorrow we will go to the burial site of Krishna Dwaipayana Vyasa. His is also known as Viassa-Krichna, Veda Vyasa, Vyasadeva, or simply Vyasa. I will tell you all about this great man. We will begin our studies then."

Jnyaneshwar's school was a small building to sit in during the monsoons, but the classes were mostly held outdoors. Issa, Bacha, and Vijayananda were invited to sleep in the building overnight. After that, their sleeping arrangements would be their own affairs. Many students lived in Kanchipuram, so it was no problem for them. Others slept in the nearby forest. As a Sannyasa, Issa was expected to make the forest his home.

That night Vijayananda asked Issa and Bacha to sit with him for a moment. "My dear friends," he began, "my mission was to accompany you to your destination here in Kanchipuram, to translate for you along the way, and keep you safe. We have now successfully arrived. There is no doubt in my mind that you will be able to continue on your own. After all, you, Issa, are now a Sannyasin. And you, Bacha, are skilled in many of the ways of a Kshatriya. You have a warrior's instinct, for one. You will be able to keep Issa safe from any danger that might present itself when he begins to journey through India to teach. I must go home and continue my duties to Prince Hala, soon to be king."

Issa expected such a thing to happen, but it caught Bacha off guard. "Go home? But we need you, Vijayananda. You have been at our side for many years. You are a good friend. Please don't leave us."

"And you are both good friends to me. I will remember you all my life. But my first duty and obligation is to Prince Hala. He asked that I return. When he becomes king, he has promised that I will become the commander-in-chief of his army—an honored position, and one that will make my parents proud, especially my father."

They stayed up late that night talking and recalling the many adventures they had gone through together. When Issa and Bacha awoke the next morning, Vijayananda was gone.

"I miss him already," said Bacha as he stretched and did some yoga poses that they had both learned from Vijayananda.

"I knew he would have to leave us, Bacha, even before we began our journey. So each night when I went to bed, I slept imagining that he was already gone, and that I would never again see him—not that night, not the next morning. But now he really is gone. Let us now live in the present, big brother. If you have learned nothing else from Patanjali, learn that."

"And do you sleep each night imagining that I won't be here the next morning?"

Issa said, "This is what living in the present means, Bacha. Each moment is precious. Each moment is different. Everything changes, and eventually dies—even us, Bacha. The only thing that doesn't change is the eternal Self who resides in each of us."

"So says Patanjali!" Issa and Bacha were both startled as Jnyaneshwar stood in the doorway. "You will soon learn that in our beliefs, there is only Brahma: One without a Second."

38 (A harsh lesson in Brahminism)

They walked the path to the burial site, and as they approached, Issa saw other students who were already gathered. These were students who wished to become Brahmin priests, and would study with Jnyaneshwar for many years; he required a minimum of twelve. Jnyaneshwar knelt and bowed before the shrine, and the rest of the students, including Issa and Bacha, did the same. Jnyaneshwar walked a respectable distance from the shrine and sat. The others sat facing him and bowed.

Jnyaneshwar's teaching method, unlike Patanjali's, was to ask questions. He began to talk of the famous Katha Upanishad where the child Nachiketa encounters Death, known as Yama. After expertly passing several tests that Yama puts him through, Yama changes his demeanor from a harsh deity to a very likable and delightful teacher. Jnyaneshwar said to his students, "Nachiketa asks Yama, 'How can I know the supreme blissful Self, indescribable, yet known by the wise? Is he the light, or does he simply reflect the light?'"

Jnyaneshwar then asked each student to place the bowl from which they ate and drank on the ground. He walked around filling each with a few drops of water. "Issa, what do you see in your bowl?"

Issa looked at it for a moment and said, "I see water, Guruji."

"Look beyond the water. Tell me what you see."

"I see ... I see the reflection of the sun in the water."

"Good! Do you all see the reflection of the sun in your water?"

All the students nodded their heads in the affirmative.

"So, are there many suns, as Patanjali might have you believe, or is there just one sun?"

The students again chanted in unison, "There is but one sun, Guruji."

"And what do you say to that, Issa? Yama rightfully answered Nachiketa telling him that the Self is the light. The light is then reflected by all."

Patanjali believed, and had taught Issa, the concept of dualism. The Self was described as the knower, and each person contained a Self. He also knew that the Vedas described the concept of One without a Second. But Patanjali had not gone deeply into this subject. Issa thought for a moment and remembered a story that Patanjali once told him. It was about three blind men who came across an elephant, each described his impression of what an elephant was. One of the men was holding the leg and described an elephant as a huge tree. The other was holding the elephant's ear and described the elephant as the leaf of a plant. The last was holding the elephant's tail and described the elephant as a tiny rope.

Issa told his teacher and the students the story in broken Sanskrit, and then said, "Guruji, each of these persons knew the elephant differently. Yet each description was valid within his own understanding. I think, therefore, that you and Master Patanjali are both correct. But I think nobody can truly know the elephant."

Issa was pleased with his answer. But Jnyaneshwar was not! "Young man," he almost screeched, "you are here to learn, not to teach! When your knowledge of the Vedas surpasses mine, *then* you can teach. But not now. Not yet."

Everyone was looking at Issa. His ears turned bright red, and he didn't know what to do next. There was an uncomfortable silence that seemed to last forever.

Finally Jnyaneshwar rose, put his hand on Issa's shoulder, and looking down to him said softly, "But your point is well taken!"

Issa saw what appeared to be a smile on Jnyaneshwar's face, albeit slight, and only for a second. He then went back to teaching as if nothing at all had happened.

When the lessons were done for the day, Jnyaneshwar asked Issa to stay behind a moment. The two sat together by the shrine and the teacher said, "Issa, you are from another country, so I make some allowances for not understanding our ways and our customs. What you did today was to embarrass me in front of my students. This is one of the most disrespectful things a student can do to his teacher. It is like a slap in the face."

"I meant no disrespect, Guruji," Issa said.

"I know you didn't, Issa. But when you disagree with what I say, don't do so publicly. It is a private matter, and I will be happy to argue with you one-on-one in a private setting. My aim was not to discredit Patanjali. My aim was to make you see another way—to see another part of the elephant—which, by the way, is the same story I once told to Patanjali! You have much to learn, Issa, and what I will teach you is in many ways the same as what Patanjali taught you, but in many ways it is different. Don't try to compare the two. And don't argue out of ignorance. You know almost nothing about the Vedas. Spend your time with me wisely, Issa."

Jnyaneshwar then gave Issa his own copy of the Mahabhasya to borrow. It was a scroll on Sanskrit grammer, written by another man named Patanjali who lived 150 years ago. "Perhaps this will help you to speak more correctly. I suggest you study it."

Issa bowed and thanked Jnyaneshwar and then he and Bacha headed to the woods to find shelter for the night. Issa turned to his friend and said, "It looks like I'm off to a bad start."

Bacha replied, "Perhaps. But I think he likes you, Yeshu ... uh, I mean Issa."

As they sat beneath a tree, Issa asked, "What do you think, Bacha?"

"About what?"

"About Patanjali's teachings and Jnyaneshwar's. Patanjali's description of the knower is much like the teachings of the Torah. Moshe calls us the children of God. I understand this concept well. But Jnyaneshwar teaches that we are all one—that there is no separate Self, that there is only Brahma. One without a Second. I have a hard time understanding that concept."

Bacha grinned. "And yet you just had to tell Jnyaneshwar that story about the elephant, didn't you? What did he tell you just before he left? 'Don't argue out of ignorance.'"

Yeshua laughed. "Bacha, you know me all too well. In Israel I was so used to being right all the time. But here it's different. It's not just that we are speaking in a new language. These concepts are so complicated. I remember that Patanjali would sometimes recite a single sentence and I would ponder over it for a week. And now, just when I think I understand, I learn a totally different concept that seems to contradict the ones I just learned. I guess I should take Jnyaneshwar's advice to spend my time with him wisely, and try to keep my mouth from getting me in trouble."

Bacha continued to grin, nodding in agreement.

39 (A healing chant)

AD 14
Yeshua's age: 17

Each day Issa learned more and more about the Vedas. He learned that each Veda had four parts: the Mantra-Samhitas, which were the hymns, the Brahmanas, which explained the Mantras or rituals, the Aranyakas, also called the forest books, which gave philosophical interpretations of the rituals, and the Upanishads. The Upanishads were the most important part of the Vedas. They revealed spiritual truths, both deep and subtle. This is the part of the Vedas that Jnyaneshwar would teach Issa. He would also teach him how Brahmin priests healed the sick.

Jnyaneshwar also began to teach Issa special mantras that were used for specific purposes. One day he took his students to a place where the sick were being tended. One man was said to be possessed of evil spirits. When they came upon him, he was lying down quietly, but when the man saw Jnyaneshwar approach, he stood and began to swear violently. His face was turning bright red, and he was spitting and shouting and jumping about.

The priest asked his students to help hold the man down, and when they had done so, he stooped over and held the earlobe of the man with one hand. "Hold it thusly," he said to his students, "and then whisper the mantra like this." He then brought his face to the man's ear and whispered the mantra he had taught his students. Once he had whispered it, he immediately stood and walked away, knowing what would happen next. The man's eyes rolled upward, leaving only the whites showing, and he ceased struggling, appearing to go to sleep.

When the man awoke a few minutes later, Jnyaneshwar asked him how he was feeling. He was ecstatic. He had been possessed for several months and thought he would never be free, but now he knew that this evil was gone out of his body forever.

"It is not the words themselves, it is how they are said," Jnyaneshwar explained to his class. "It is in the *vibration* of the sounds that the changes occur. You must learn to say them properly. Once you can do that, you will be able to perform such a simple act as casting out evil spirits."

Jnyaneshwar called it a simple act, but there was nothing simple about it. Issa spent a good deal of time perfecting the correct reciting of the mantras, especially those that could heal. Sanskrit was a difficult language, and Issa struggled to get the words just right. Often he would recite them for Jnyaneshwar after class. "Almost, but not quite," he would hear his guru say to him each day. But over time, he was finally able to say the words properly.

Jnyaneshwar would never praise him for doing or saying the right thing. But Issa learned that when Jnyaneshwar paused a short moment and simply said, "Hmm," this was a great compliment. Doing the wrong thing, however, always invoked Jnyaneshwar's wrath. Issa saw that others were yelled at too. It was simply Jnyaneshwar's way of teaching.

According to Jnyaneshwar, doing the right thing was your duty, and required no praise. "Is the finger to be praised for scratching the itch?" he would ask his students. "It does its duty, serving the needs of the body and requires no praise. Praise is a forbidden fruit. As Arjuna learned from Lord Krishna in the Bhagavad Gita, one should never become attached to the fruit of his actions. This is because all actions done by mankind are imperfect. Give somebody a gift with love or kindness, and it will cause that person pain when it is lost or broken. Give up eating meat as an act of practicing nonharming (Ahimsa), and you will still need to kill plants in order to survive. Simply do your duty to the best of your abilities, as Arjuna was instructed to do, and remain nonattached to the fruits."

Issa realized that he had become especially attached to the praise of Patanjali, and his new teacher rid him of that attachment. Issa now knew why Jnyaneshwar had rebuked him for quoting Patanjali's belief in duality that first day. He had seen Issa's attachment to praise and violently chopped it away. It was a valuable lesson.

***

Many of the other students had previously studied with their teachers much longer than Issa had studied with Patanjali. But Issa was master of what Patanjali had taught him, and applied himself with fervor to whatever he was taught. He would immediately turn Jnyaneshwar's lessons of the Upanishads into mashals that could be understood easily. He would tell them to Bacha late at night, and Bacha would laugh. They were both speaking to each other in Sanskrit now, and some of the stories Issa told did not readily translate into this complex language.

The students largely ignored Issa and Bacha. They would get together after class and discuss what they had learned, but Issa and Bacha were never invited to sit with them, and the few times they had tried to hoin their classmates, the tension could be felt in the air, to the point that they would finally leave. One or two of the students were friendly and would chat, but mostly Issa and Bacha were estranged from the rest of the class. This did not go unnoticed by Jnyaneshwar.

As their lessons progressed, Issa became more and more proficient, which only made him more disliked by his classmates. One student told him one day, "You can be *like* us, but you can never be *one* of us." It had to do with the caste system, Issa realized. These students were born into Brahmin families and felt superior to all others. Try though he might, Jnyaneshwar was not able to sever their attachment as easily as he had severed Issa's.

One night after Issa recited his mantras to Jnyaneshwar, the teacher asked, "Tell me about your country, Issa. Do the people of the higher castes look down upon the lower ones?"

Issa said, "Guruji, in my country we don't have such a system. But we do have similar problems. In my country we are under occupation by the Romans. It has been that way for many years. Many of my people have become part of the Roman government, serving in a ruling capacity, and are despised by the rest of the Jews.

"We also have several religious groups who do not see things the same way. Some befriend the Romans, and have become rich and affluent. Others detest the Romans and will not compromise with them at all. Still others violently fight against the occupation at any opportunity. We also have a group called the Essenes that has divorced itself from the rest of society and live by themselves.

"These groups often are in conflict with one another. The Sadducees—those are the rich ones I spoke of—look down upon the Pharisees. The Pharisees believe themselves to be spiritually superior to the Sadducees, and look down upon them. And then we have lepers who are cast out of our society and made to live by themselves. And so you see our problems are different, yet in many ways the same."

Issa began to think about the problems that being a bastard, or with being thought a bastard had caused, but didn't share that with Jnyaneshwar. He continued, "It is the belief of the Jewish people that Yahweh—that is what we call God—has declared us the chosen people. One day, it is believed among some, a Messiah will be born who will deliver his people from the oppression of the Romans and establish a kingdom on earth. Some believe that the end of the world is near, and the Messiah will instead establish a kingdom in heaven."

"And what do you believe, Issa?"

"Right now, Guruji, I am a little confused. You and Patanjali have changed my way of thinking so much that I'm not sure what I believe. I believe, to be sure, but I guess I'm not sure *how* I believe. In my country there are stories of people who can cast out evil spirits, but unless you immediately give credit to God, you can be stoned to death for blasphemy. Yet you have shown me that casting out evil spirits is not unlike a doctor fixing a broken leg. Is it the doctor who fixes the leg, or is it God? Should the doctor give God credit?"

Jnyaneshwar thought some, and then quoted from the Chandogya Upanishad: "'In the beginning was Being. Only being. One without a second. Then He brought forth the cosmos out of Himself and entered into it. There is nothing that does not come from Him. He is the inmost Self. He is truth.' So you see, Issa, God is within you, and it is God who heals the broken bones, and casts out the evil spirits. It should be evident to all that it is God. If you and I watch the sun go down over the hills, and the skies slowly change from yellow to red to blue to purple and then fade into darkness, do I need to tell you it is beautiful? No, I do not. Do I need to tell you that it is God who has created such beauty? No, I do not. Words are often worthless. Truth is to be known, not talked of.

"It is so that we often sing praises to God in the Vedas. But we need not openly give God credit with each and every deed that we do. What we must do, however, is not take credit in our hearts for that which God has done. This is what we have most recently been learning about, Issa. Not becoming attached to the fruits of our actions. Soon we will all be going out and practicing our healing skills. This is why we must first learn this important lesson. Do you understand?"

Issa, remembering Jnyaneshwar's words, "Truth is to be known, not talked of," silently bowed to him.

"Hmm," Jnyaneshwar said, and got to his feet and left. Issa smiled.

40 (Issa heals)

AD 15
Yeshua's age: 18

They were to go together in groups of four. Jnyaneshwar sent each group to a different village to heal the sick. The two who went with Issa and Bacha were not pleased to be stuck with the foreigners—the Sudra, as they called them. Normally, a foreigner would be automatically placed in the lowest of the four castes. Prince Hala, however, had given his authority for the Vedas to be taught to Issa, as if he were a Brahmin. This did not sit well with the students, the two who went with Issa and Bacha included. Their names were Hemel, which meant, "made of gold," and Nibodh, which meant, "knowledge."

It was known that Bacha was Issa's protector, thus he was not expected to do any healing, but Issa was indeed expected to perform, and Hemel and Nibodh were anxiously looking forward to him failing. When they arrived, they were brought to the place where the sick dwelled. It was not a place one would choose to visit. The stench of sickness was everywhere, accompanied by much moaning and crying.

Hemel and Nibodh were both brought up among the rich and well-to-do, and were not used to seeing poor, sick people up close. Their discomfort was obvious, and they were literally holding their noses. Issa, on the other hand, had always felt comfortable among the poor. He immediately went to one of the sickest people, an old woman who seemed to cough unceasingly. The compassion in Issa's eyes already put her at ease. Issa remembered the charm against cough from the Atharva Veda that Jnyaneshwar had taught him, and began to softly chant it between her coughing. The chant went:

> "As the soul with the soul's desires swiftly to a distance flies, thus do thou, O cough, fly forth along the soul's course of flight!
>
> As a well-sharpened arrow swiftly to a distance flies, thus do thou, O cough, fly forth along the expanse of the earth!
>
> As the rays of the sun swiftly to a distance fly,

thus do thou, O cough, fly forth along the flood of the sea!"

The woman was quiet for a moment. Hemel and Nibodh seemed disappointed. But then she began to cough again, more violently than the first time. Now Hemel and Nibodh were smiling at one another, planning to report Issa's failure back to Jnyaneshwar at their first chance. The two did not know of the Siddis that Issa had learned from Patanjali, so they were surprised when he placed his hand on the woman's throat and closed his eyes. Slowly her coughing got quieter and quieter, until she stopped altogether. This time it did not come back.

"How did you do that?" asked Nibodh, forgetting for a moment his dislike of Issa.

Issa smiled at him and said, "It was my hand that touched her, Nibodh, but it was God's hand that healed her."

After that, the two were humbled. They were able to finally tend to those who were not as sick as the others, and like Issa, recited healing chants from the Atharva Veda. There was the Prayer to the Kushtha plant to Destroy Fever. There was the Exorcism of Evil Dreams. There was the Expiatory Formulas for Sins. They chanted them perfectly, and their patients seemed pleased. Of course they would not know that day if their chants had worked or not. The fevers wouldn't go away for a week or so. The exorcism of evil dreams would not be known until the next day. And as for the expiatory formulas for sins, well, who would know if they worked?

The journey back to Kanchipuram was quite unlike the silent journey to the village of the sick. This time there was a lot of talking. They asked Issa and Bacha about their country and their people. They were fascinated by their travels across the ocean. But Issa knew that this was a temporary friendship. Once they were back among their friends, they would turn against these foreigners once again.

That night Issa again sat with Jnyaneshwar. There was something that puzzled him. "Guruji, why did some of the sick respond to chants, and others needed me to use the Siddis?"

Jnyaneshwar replied, "Issa, you will find that a person's faith is most important to their healing. If they are of great faith, and truly believe that the chants will cure them, then that faith will only add to the power of the chants themselves. If they are not of great faith, and do not believe in the powers, they may not get better. It is always best to test their faith first, because with faith, they can cure themselves. Only use your Siddis when you are sure they are required. You did the right thing in that village, Issa. You began with the chants."

They continued to go once a week into the surrounding villages and tend to the sick. Issa noticed something that bothered him. Many of the poor possessed idols to which they would pray. In his own religion, in the scrolls of Shemot, Moshe angrily confronted his followers who had made a golden calf to worship while he was in the mountain praying. The story was long, but the lesson of not worshipping idols was an important one.

The Vedas also taught against idol worship. The White Yagur Veda clearly stated, for example, "No one should make an idol of the Spirit (God) who is invisible and effulgent and whom no one has really known."

When he asked Jnyaneshwar why idols were allowed, he said, "The Vaisya and Sudra are not educated like the Brahmin and Kshatriya. For them, an abstract 'God' who cannot be seen, heard, touched, tasted, or felt is an impossible concept. They simply cannot understand this, Issa. Therefore, we give them idols so that they may concentrate their minds on idols, and thus ascend to God. Each idol contains some visible aspect of God, such as wisdom or strength, and makes God's own wisdom and strength known to them. So they are not praying to an idol instead of to God, they are praying to God *through* an idol. Do you see the difference?"

"But Guruji, they are being preyed upon by unscrupulous sellers," Issa said. They spend their money on idols instead of food. They are being told that if they pray to these idols, they will receive food, or wealth."

"Yes, we have snakes among the saints, Issa. There isn't much we can do about that. But the idols have an important place in our culture."

Issa was not totally convinced.

41 (A warning from Jnyaneshwar)

A year had passed and it was now time for Issa to begin a new chapter in his life. He had learned Kriya-Yoga from Patanjali. He had learned the Vedas, and within them the healing chants, and the Upanishads from Jnyaneshwar. He had even learned some healing mantras that were not in the Vedas, which were passed on to very few. Now he would begin traveling through the villages and teaching according to his own ways. This is what Prince Hala wished him to do. This is why he was brought to India.

Jnyaneshwar knew that Issa's journey would be fraught with danger, and so as they sat together for the last time, Jnyaneshwar gave his final thoughts to Issa and Bacha. "Because you know so little about my country, my two friends, let me tell you some things that you will need to know as you begin your travels. It is about our caste system that so perplexes you. You will be traveling to many villages, and you will find each village different. Some, especially those that have Brahmin priests who live nearby, are very strict about caste. Just to give you an example, in some places, if a Sudra overhears the reading of the Vedas, the law provides that molten lead be poured into his ears. If he recites a verse from the sacred scriptures, his tongue is to be split. And if he memorizes any of the Vedic text, the law provides that his body be cut in two."

Issa and Bacha stared at one another, eyes open wide, mouths agape. "They would really do such things?" Issa asked.

Jnyaneshwar replied, "Between you and me, these laws were written to strike fear into the Sudra, so that only the Brahmin would be able to perform the many Vedic ceremonies and teach the wisdom contained within them. It would, therefore, keep the Vedas uncorrupted and pure, as the Rishis [the ancient teachers] handed them down to us over these many years. The purity of the Vedas is what I wish to preserve, Issa, which is why my training is so long and so difficult. Unfortunately, there are places where such punishment is actually handed out. I have seen it with my own eyes."

"But not all places?" Yeshua asked.

"You will find villages where the people have never submitted to the Brahmins and their laws. They have their own unique forms of worship, some of them based loosely on their own understanding of the Vedas. And you will find other villages where the caste system is observed, but not to the extreme of cutting a body in two.

"So I give you a warning. According to our caste system, you two are Sudra. Make sure you understand the villages you go to before you begin teaching. I would not like to see you with your tongue split!

"The stories that you tell, Issa—mashals as you call them—are filled with wit and wisdom. You have even learned to teach some of the essence of the Upanishads, without reciting the actual words. But again, beware. There are those who will see through these stories and think you are teaching a corrupted version of the Upanishads. This can be very dangerous to you. Make sure you know who your friends are, and make sure that you, Bacha, know who your enemies are. You will have plenty of both."

Issa and Bacha bowed to Jnyaneshwar, arose, and began their new journey. From behind they heard Jnyaneshwar one last time say, "Hmm."

42 (Teaching the working class)

AD 16
Yeshua's age: 19

Issa and Bacha headed north toward Kashi. Patanjali had told Issa to visit that city at least once in his journeys. Issa was now nineteen years of age, and felt as if he was finally ready to teach on his own. The sun was bright—so bright it made Issa's saffron robe look white from a distance. When three Chandala, walking in the opposite direction saw Issa walking toward them in his apparent white robe, they assumed him to be Brahmin and immediately lay facedown. They had been taught that if even the shadow of a Chandala touches a Brahmin, he would be polluted. Issa saw this and walked over to them. He said, "Please get up. There is no need for you to lie that way."

They lifted their heads toward him but remained where they were. One of them said in a frightened voice, "Why are you talking to us? Don't you know we are Chandala?"

Issa sat down next to them and said, "And I am a sannyasa, not a Brahmin. Let me tell you through a story what God thinks of Chandala. A father once had four sons. One of them worked hard, married a beautiful woman, and bought a big farm that had seven cows and four goats. They produced four children.

"The next son worked hard, married a beautiful woman, and bought a medium-sized farm that had four cows and two goats. They produced three children.

"The third son worked hard, married a beautiful woman, and bought a small farm that had two cows. They produced one child.

"The last son worked hard, married a beautiful woman, and they lived on the grounds of a rich man, where he tended the rich man's farm. Although they tried, they did not produce any children.

"Now I ask you, which of his sons did the father love the most?"

By this time, they had all stopped lying prone, and were sitting by him. One of the men thought a moment and said, "He loved them all equally."

Issa smiled. "You have answered correctly," he said. "And so it is that God establishes no differences between any of His children. They are all equally dear to Him—Brahmins, Kshatriyas, Vaisyas, Sudras, and even Chandalas."

They were now looking at one another and smiling, although still a little nervous. The man who had answered the question said, "Nobody not a Chandala has ever talked to us like that before. Who are you?"

"My name is Issa, and I have come to teach you."

"What is it you are going to teach us, Issa?"

"I have come to teach the truth. You have already learned your first truth: that God loves all His children equally. And here is the second: you must all do likewise."

Issa looked deeply into each of their eyes for emphasis. Then he said, "Come back here tomorrow, and bring your friends. I will teach you more."

They all bowed with respect and left. After they had gone, two men appeared from behind a bush. One said, "We heard what you said, and would like to learn more. Would you teach us too?"

Issa opened his arms as if inviting a hug and said, "Of course! Bring all your friends as well."

"Can we come at a different time than the Chandala? We are of the Sudra caste, but we don't usually mingle with the Chandala."

Issa looked a little angry and said, "Did you hear anything I said to them? Did you not understand? God loves all his children equally. And likewise, I love you all equally. If you wish to hear me, you must sit next to the Chandala, who, after all, are God's children, are they not?"

The two looked at each other, said nothing, and slowly walked away.

Issa turned to Bacha and said, "It looks as though I will only be teaching Chandalas tomorrow."

***

The next morning Issa sat where he had last encountered the men and waited. He did not have to wait long. Almost fifty persons appeared. The crowd was mostly men, but among them were a few women and children. Much to Issa's surprise, he recognized the two who had left without speaking yesterday. The crowd was clearly divided into two groups, and Issa knew that they were consciously seperating themselves. "Which of you are Sudra?" Issa asked.

The bigger of the two groups raised their hands. Issa asked three of them to come forward. When they did, he had them kneel and look down toward the ground. He drew a circle in the dirt. "For a moment, I ask that you not look up. Look only at the circle."

He then brought several people up to the three men, one by one, and had them stand inside the circle. All the three men could see was the feet of the people whom Issa brought up to them. "Look only at their feet," Issa admonished them. "Now tell me, is this person a Sudra or a Chandala?" One of them started to look up, and Issa firmly held his head. "Only the feet," he repeated.

"We can't tell by looking at their feet."

"So are you saying that the feet of a Sudra, and the feet of a Chandala are the same?"

"Well, I suppose their feet are the same, but..."

Issa cut them off. "What about their hands? Could you look at only their hands and tell which were Sudra and which were Chandala? How about their elbows? Are the elbows of a Sudra different than the elbows of a Chandala?"

As the crowd was taking it all in, Issa asked the men to stand back up. He then went around to the crowd, quickly directing them one by one. "You, sit here." A Sudra would sit where he was instructed to sit. "And you sit here." A Chandala was seated next to him. "And now you. You sit here."

When Issa was done, he began teaching. He used mashals and taught them all about treating each other as equals. Although they began the morning feeling a little uncomfortable, it took very little time for them to feel at home with one another. They were learning to look each other in the eyes and laugh together at some of the stories that Issa told.

"Come back tomorrow and I will teach you more. But please," he paused a few seconds for emphasis, "come together!" They all laughed and walked back toward the village. The Chandala lived outside the village, but they lived very close.

Issa turned once again to Bacha and said, "Soon I will have the Vaisyas here as well!"

"That might be a little harder to do, Issa. But if anyone can do it, you can."

They headed toward the village. They would wait until everyone was finished eating, and then beg for their evening meal. On this night, many Sudras were anxious to share food with them.

43 (Issa faces Indian justice)

Bacha did not need to worry about the Vaisyas. Each day as the crowds grew, the curious from inside the village began to gather, at first standing outside the circle with arms folded. But over time, they too sat with people they would normally not have anything to do with.

"What can you tell us about the Vedas, Issa?" one of the villagers asked. This was an uncomfortable subject for many, as they had been warned of the consequences of hearing the words or reciting them.

Issa thought a minute and then said, "I will tell you two stories. Here is the first. Two fish were talking to one another. One said, 'I have heard about a great thing that is called water. Have you heard about it?'

"The other fish said, 'Don't you know, water is all around you. It is inside you and outside you. It exists everywhere.'

"'Where? I am looking but I don't see it.'

"The first fish then said, 'It can't be seen by any fish. But believe me, it exists everywhere.'

"And here is the second story. A son is learning a lesson from his father. His father tells him to put some salt in a container of water and bring it to him the next day. When he does, his father asks him where the salt is. He tells his father that he can't see it. His father then asks him to sip the water. 'How does it taste, my son?'

"The son says, 'It tastes salty.'

"The father pours half of it onto the ground. 'Take another sip,' he commands. The son again says, 'It tastes salty.'

"The father says, 'It is true, then. The salt is everywhere in the water.'"

Issa stopped for a moment, giving the crowd time to think about the two stories. He then said, "Can anyone tell me what these two stories have in common?"

A woman rose to her feet and said, "Teacher, I think they are both telling us the same thing. They are both saying that God is everywhere."

Issa beamed with delight. "This woman has truly heard the message in the stories. One of these stories is taken from one of the Upanishads found in the Vedas that you are forbidden to hear. One of these stories comes from me. I will not tell you which is which, but I will tell you this: God does not fear your knowing that He is everywhere. Why should he? God does not fear your understanding things about Him. Why should he?

The Brahmins and the Kshatriyas, on the other hand, would withhold this information from you. I have been told that they consider you to be unable to understand this simple message: that God is everywhere, yet cannot be seen, heard, smelled, touched, or tasted. They say that you are uneducated and unable to grasp its meaning. And yet, you seem to have all understood it perfectly. You have understood it by hearing a story that I told you, and you have understood it by hearing a story from the Upanishads."

The crowd began buzzing with excitement. "Tell us more about God, Teacher."

Issa closed his eyes. "God is the Eternal Judge and Spirit. He alone creates the whole. God has existed from eternity and will exist without end. He has no equal in the heavens or earth." His words were interrupted by the sound of a metal object falling on stone. Issa saw that someone had by accident dropped an idol. Issa stared at the man as he picked it back up and continued, "And He does not share His power with inanimate objects such as the ones you buy and keep in your houses. God alone possesses supreme power."

With this revelation, the crowd began to grow uneasy. Some of them had worshipped idols all their lives. Issa continued, "Do not worship your idols, for they can't hear you. Instead, do these simple things: Harm no one. This is called Ahimsa [non-harming]. Help those who are poorer than you. Assist those who are weak. Those things that others have, be they gold or fancy houses, do not covet them. This is called Aparigraha [non-possessiveness]. By doing these things you are learning to love God with all your heart and with all your soul and with all your strength and with all your mind."

Each day the crowds grew larger. Issa was also tending to the sick, using the chants he had learned and the Siddis he had obtained. This alone increased the crowd's numbers. But as they grew, their purchasing of idols diminished. Many were going so far as to throw them away. And Issa was now beginning to draw the attention of the upper castes.

By order of the chief Brahmin, two Kshatriyas dressed themselves in simple clothing and sat inconspicuously in the back of the crowd. They were prepared to spend days listening to Issa speak, but on the very first day they heard what they came to hear.

A Sudra stood up and spoke. "Issa, you tell us to help those who are poorer than us. But what of those who are richer? The Brahmins and Kshatriyas do none of these things you say. We, the Sudra, have no rights, no privileges. We are not allowed to read or learn the Vedas. We are forbidden to recite the mantras. We cannot enter temples. The only thing we can do is to serve. We are the slaves of the Brahmins and Kshatriayas. We are their barbers. We are their cobblers and blacksmiths. I understand that this is the way of things, but is it right?"

"Perhaps," Issa began, "in the next incarnation, you will be a Brahmin or Kshatriya, and they will become Sudras. How will you then treat them? Will you deprive them of their happiness as they do to you?"

Issa looked around him, seeing some faces that appeared unconvinced. "Have any of you ever heard this story?" he asked. "There was once a famous Brahmin who wished to perform a sacrifice for his ancestors. This particular sacrifice involved beheading a goat. He commanded his students to take the goat to the river and prepare it for the sacrifice.

"As the students were washing it, they suddenly heard laughter. They looked around, but saw no one. Then they heard it again. They finally realized that it was the goat that was laughing. But it sounded so much like human laughter that they were astounded. One of the students grew angry and said, 'Stop laughing. You are going to make the Brahmin very angry.' The goat indeed stopped laughing but now began crying. Once again, it sounded just like a human.

"The students quickly took the goat to the Brahmin and told him all that had happened. The Brahmin asked the goat why it was laughing. Much to the amazement of everyone, the goat began to talk. 'I was laughing because I remembered my past lives. You see, I was once a Brahmin like you many years ago. I too wanted to perform a sacrifice for my ancestors, and I beheaded a goat. When my life ended, my karma was to live five hundred lives as a goat. Each life would end in my being beheaded. I have lived those five hundred lives, and after today I can finally be born again as a human.'

"The Brahmin then asked, 'You have told me why you were laughing, but now tell me why you were crying?' The goat looked into the eyes of the Brahmin, its own growing soft, and said, 'I was thinking of you.'"

The Kshatriyas exchanged glances and rose to report back to the Brahmin. One said to the other, "We are to be reincarnated as Sudra? Did he really say that?"

"And what of the Brahmin being reincarnated as a goat?" the other asked. "Wait until we tell him that!"

The next morning as Issa and Bacha sat in the clearing waiting for the crowd to arrive, two men dressed for battle approached them. Bacha immediately recognized the dress, as he had seen it in his own training in the courtyard of the king with his friend, Prince Hala. These were Kshatriyas.

"Come with us," one said gruffly. Without waiting for an answer, they grabbed Issa and Bacha and marched them into the village.

Inside the temple a stately Brahmin, also ornately costumed, sat waiting. Issa and Bach were pushed to the floor in a kneeling position.

Bacha reached into his tunic and pulled from it the paper with the king's seal, granting them safe passage. "Put your paper back. I know what it is. I know all about you two. You are Issa and Bacha, the two Sudra from the West." He spit out the word "Sudra" with great disdain. "Now know this: I am the chief Brahmin of this village and many surrounding villages. The land you stand on belongs to me. You are both trespassers. I am within my rights to have you killed, but I have decided I will not, at least not now. My guards are now going to escort you to the edge of my land, and you will not come back. If you do, you will not live to see the next day. No discussion. Now go."

The two guards once again unceremoniously pulled Issa and Bacha to their feet and pushed them out the door. They walked many miles before the guards stopped. The guards said nothing, simply staring and pointing in a northern direction. Issa and Bacha looked at one another and slowly walked away. When they turned around to look, the guards were gone.

"Was it something I said?" asked Issa.

"That wasn't funny, Issa. That was scary. You must learn to take

212

care in your talk of idols and your stories about reincarnation. I cringed when you told the people about Brahmins becoming goats and Kshatriyas becoming Sudras. Do you really need to say those things?"

Issa bristled. "I say those things that need to be said. When Moshe came down from the mountain and saw his people worshipping the golden calf, he too was angry. And as he told the story written in our holy scrolls, so was God!"

"Idols are one thing, little brother. Reincarnation is another. You are not hearing me."

"Bacha, I hear you clearly. Now hear me. These people of the upper castes, some of them, are treating the lower castes like animals. I know what that feels like, Bacha. That was my entire life in Nazareth; the life of my whole family. Some of them are bullies just like that boy Efah whom I told you about and just like your old friend Yaish. I will not back down from bullies."

Bacha watched his friend, now filled with anger. "Sometimes," he said quietly, "it's better to back down in order to live to fight another day, Issa. You heard them. They will kill us if we go back. Let's just move on to another village and try again."

Issa was slowly beginning to gain his composure. He sat on a rock. "Perhaps you are right, big brother. You just don't know what it does to me when I see others being mistreated, though. Many times when I speak, I feel as if God is speaking through me. But then, other times, there is this … this other voice inside me. The voice of anger? I don't know what it is, Bacha. I only know that it too wants to be heard, and sometimes I can't tell the difference."

Issa got up from the rock, put his arm around Bacha's shoulder, and the two of them began to walk farther north.

44 (Ephrayim and Mara prepare to move)

Nazarath, Israel
AD 17

It was a late summer afternoon in Nazareth, and the fragrant smell of myrtle filled the air. Inside Ephrayim and Mara's house, however, there was no talk of the aroma of shrubs or flowers. They sat at their table, both staring not at each other but beyond each other and into nothing.

Ephrayim finally said. "Mara, it is time to pack our things. We have no choice in the matter."

Mara was still staring into nothing and simply repeated his words. "Yes, love. It's time to pack our things."

"I was so sure it was Tahmid who kept doing awful things to us, Mara. Burning down my work, stealing my tools, turning business men away from me. But since he has been dead for two years, and these things keep happening. Who is doing these things to us, Mara? Who is out to get us? Who wants us to be poor?"

Mara faced her husband. "I was sure it was him as well, Ephrayim. You don't think his wife Shoshan could be ..."

"No." Ephrayim interrupted. "I can't believe she is capable of doing such things."

"No, neither do I, love. I just can't think of who else might have something against you."

"Or against you," Ephrayim countered.

Mara drew her head back and widened her eyes. "Or against me," she finally said. She looked off into the distance once again.

Ephrayim continued, "Our children have all grown up and left us, except for Shlomit and Yehuda. We are poor, Mara. We must face it. We are living in a house big enough for nine people, and we are but three. With the money we will now have by selling the house and moving into a smaller one we should have enough to live on our own for a few more years. I'm sure our other children will look after us. Even if bad things keep happening."

He sighed as he looked over at the stand by the window with a candle on it. He noticed that Mara was staring at it as well. Each year at this time Mara lit the candle at night. It was nearing Yeshua's birthday. He had once promised Ephrayim that he would come visit on his birthday. Those were his last words when they left him in Jerusalem. She would let the candle burn all night each night in case Yeshua came back home then. He would see the light in the window in the dark, and know she had not given up hope. Eight years. Eight long years since his mysterious disappearance, and still she did not give up hoping.

Hope is what Ephrayim desperately needed. But try though he might, he was not feeling any. At least he had his family, he thought. Whoever was ruining him hadn't taken that away from him; at least not yet.

"What could have happened to him, Ephrayim? Why haven't we heard from our Yeshua?" Mara laid her head on the table and sobbed.

This was a familiar scene, but Ephrayim knew this was not the time to point out what was obvious to him. He too had wondered what had happened to Yeshua for a few years, but had long accepted the fact that his son was dead. There had been so many bad feelings between the two of them, and he wished with all his heart that they could have resolved their differences. But it was not to be.

He walked over to Mara's side of the table and gently stroked her back as she continued to sob. "Come love. Let's go for a walk," he said. "We both need to get out of this house for a bit."

"You're right," she answered. She stood and faced him. "Let's walk." Then, wiping her red eyes she continued, "Let me wash my face first, though. I must look a mess."

Ephrayim placed his hands around her waist and said, "You look as beautiful as the first day I met you."

"Just the same," she said, now smiling and playfully pushing him away, "give me a moment, and then we can go."

When she was ready, they walked through Nazareth and up one of the many hills that surrounded the city. A gentle breeze cooled their faces as they climbed higher. "Are we doing the right thing, Ephrayim?" she asked. "Our son Yaaqob did offer to let us live with him and his family."

Ephrayim held her hand as they continued walking. "Yes, love. We are doing the right thing. We don't want to bring Yaaqob into our troubles. So far our enemy has limited his hatred to me. I'm so afraid that if we moved in with Yaaqob—well, who knows what might happen to him or his wife, or our grandchildren? We are doing the right thing."

As they reached the top of the hill they were met by someone climbing the other side. "Yechezqel, what a pleasant surprise. What brings you here?" asked Mara.

Yechezqel opened his arms wide. "I came looking for you, actually."

Ephrayim was puzzled "Is something wrong?"

"Nothing is wrong, my friend. I'm glad Mara is with you. I wanted to show something to both of you. Come. Let's go to the house you are going to move into."

"Why?" asked Ephrayim.

"You will see. Stop asking questions and just come."

Ephrayim and Mara looked at one another, and then back at Yechezqel. "As you wish," said Ephrayim, "let's go."

They returned down the hill and into the section of Nazareth they would be moving into. Their new house was in fact an old house. Its previous owners were in the exact opposite circumstances. They were young, their family was growing, and they were looking for a larger house. They had been gone now for a week.

"Look," Mara shouted. "Someone is inside our house."

Before Ephrayim could start running blindly toward it, Yechezqel grabbed his robe with one hand, and Mara's with the other. Then he said, "Stop it. It's all right. You'll see."

As they came to the house, all their friends poured out, one by one. Many of the people whom Ephrayim had helped build houses for outside Sepphoris were there. Their friend Yannay and his wife were there.

"We came to welcome you into your new house," Yanny said. "May you live in peace and happiness for many years." Mara was sobbing again, but this time they were tears of joy.

Yechezqel then said, "Before we eat the feast we have prepared for you, I have one more surprise. Ephrayim, come around to the back of the house."

Ephrayim was stunned. There, behind the house was a brand new workshop almost exactly like the one that stood in back of his old house.

"Look inside, Ephrayim," said Yanny, who had joined them.

Inside the workshop were many new tools. Yechezqel said, "For all the good things you and Mara have done for all of us, this is our gift back to you."

Ephrayim, who was generally ready to speak on a moment's notice, was speechless. Though he had known for a long time, it was clearer than ever before: He was richer now than he had ever dreamed of. His life was filled with people who loved him and cared about him. And this gift of his new workshop was much greater by far than the business he once dreamed of. He now knew that he and Mara would be fine. Even if his unknown enemy continued his quest of hatred, it could not take away the love and happiness he felt today.

45 (Issa scorns the worship of idols)

AD 19
Yeshua's age: 22

Not all of the villages they came to were under the domain of a harsh Brahmin. They encountered many Brahmins who knew of Jnyaneshwar and welcomed Issa and Bacha into their villages and into their homes. They also found villages that did not have any Brahmin leaders at all. It was here that they were especially welcome and where it was easiest to get different castes to sit together. Many had done so even before Issa and Bacha came.

Each village had sick people, and when they learned of Issa's ability to heal, they often came to him from a neighboring village, pleading for him to come there next. Issa was beginning to make progress.

Much to the dismay of the Brahmins, however, Issa continued to teach occasionally against the two upper castes, and mostly against the worship of idols. Though he wished to rid himself of it, the anger that burned inside him would sometimes come out. In one of his teachings he said:

> God the Creator has *never* shared his power with inanimate objects, as you have been taught. He alone is omnipotent.
>
> With a single thought He created this world. With a single thought He separated the waters from the land. Into each of you, He has breathed a part of Himself.
>
> He has subordinated unto you this earth, these waters, these beasts.
>
> But the anger of God will soon be let loose upon all mankind; for they have forgotten Him and filled their temples with *abominations*, and worship creatures which He has made subordinate to you.
>
> To do honor to stones and metals, mankind has sacrificed human beings, in whom dwells Gods own spirit.
>
> Those who work by the sweat of their brow are

humiliated to acquire the favor of an idler who sits and watches.

    I say unto you, those who deprive their brothers and sisters of divine happiness shall themselves be deprived. The Brahmins and Kshatriyas shall become the Sudras and Chandala.

    In the day of the last judgement the Vaisyas, the Sudras, and the Chandala will be forgiven, and the Brahmins and Kshatriyas shall be punished.

Whenever he spoke in this manner, it would be followed by a very uncomfortable silence as the crowd looked around hoping that they were not being overheard by spies. This was not the Issa they wanted to hear. It was the other Issa, the one who laughed and told mashals and made them understand the love of God, whom they wanted. Once his anger had dissipated, the old Issa always did come back to them. But he was beginning to make some powerful enemies.

46 (Issa meets Kapaali)

The monsoons were beginning, and Issa and Bacha looked for a cave to spend the night. There they would be dry from the hard rain that was now falling. They shortly found one, but now they needed to make sure a wild animal had not already claimed it. As his protector, that was Bacha's job. He found a sturdy stick and sharpened the end with a small rock until it was quite pointed. He walked near the cave and began shouting and making noise. He then threw a rock inside the cave.

He knew that if a mountain lion appeared, he would have to make himself look bigger. He would raise his arms with spear in hand and appear as threatening as he could. This would usually send the lion running, unless it was a mother with her babies inside. But if a bear appeared, he would try to make himself small and nonthreatening. He would avoid any eye contact at all with the bear. He knew that eye contact was a sign of confrontation, and he knew full well what the outcome of a confrontation with a bear would be. If it were a smaller creature, he would be able to ward it off with the stick if it ran toward him. It was a risky proposition in any case.

A rustling from inside the cave made Bacha tense in anticipation, and then the cave's inhabitant came out. But it was neither a lion nor a bear, nor any other wild creature. It was a small man, dressed in an old, tattered saffron robe. It was another sannyasa. He looked at Bacha, and then Issa, dressed in his own saffron robe, placed his hands in prayer position on his forehead, bowed and said, "Om Shanti."

Issa came forward, feeling somewhat embarrassed, and exchanged the same greeting. Issa asked if the two of them could share his cave for the night, and he beckoned them inside. "Please forgive us for disturbing you," Issa said. "We wanted to make sure the cave was not occupied by wild creatures."

The old man laughed. "I have sometimes been called a wild creature, but I have never had anyone yell and throw stones at me before! My name is Kapaali. It was given to me by my master when I became a sannyasa. It means Lord Shiva, because I am a worshipper of Shiva."

Issa said, "My master, Patanjali, gave me the name of Issa. I don't know what it means."

Kapaali smiled and said, "It sounds a little like Isha, which means auspicious one. Perhaps you misheard. You have studied the Isha Upanishads, have you not? It is also a name attributed to Lord Shiva, so if Isha is actually your given name, you and I are connected in more ways than one. You were very lucky to be trained by Patanjali. He is a very famous teacher."

Issa made a mental note to ask his master about the name the next time he saw him. But for now, he would be known as Issa. He had used that name for a number of years, and nobody had ever questioned him.

"And who are you?" asked Kapaali, turning to Bacha.

"My name is Bacha, and I am a friend and protector of Issa."

"Oh, so you are Kshatrya?"

Bacha looked to Issa, and Issa answered for him. "We are both from a country that is far away to the west of your country. Bacha has been my protector since I arrived here."

"Foreigners? Wonderful! I suspected as much by the way you look and talk. You must tell me all about your country tonight. I'm afraid I have no food to share, and I doubt if anyone in the village would be out in the monsoon. Perhaps tomorrow we can find something to eat in the woods."

Issa was not troubled by this, but he knew that Bacha did not do well with hunger.

Kapaali was genuinely interested in the religion of Israel, and Issa shared with him a great deal. After some time Kapaali said, "Your religion is not very different from some of the beliefs of our various cultures. You describe your people's belief that the end of the days is near. It is our belief that we are near the end of the Kali Yuga, the last of the four cycles of the life of the universe. After that, the universe will be completely destroyed, only to be born again as we start the next cycle with the next Satya Yuga."

Issa listened intently. "How do you know we are near the end of this Kali Yuga?" he asked.

"It is said in the Mahabharata that many things will foretell the beginning of the end of this Yuga. Rulers will levy taxes unfairly; they will no longer feel it is their duty to promote spirituality; people will have evil thoughts, such as thoughts of murder for no reason, and see nothing wrong with that way of thinking; lust will be acceptable by society; sin will increase as virtues decrease; people will take vows, and then break them almost immediately; the use of drugs and mind-altering drink will increase. These are just a few omens which all seem to be transpiring—at least in my country."

"Many of those things are happening in my country as well, Kapaali. Perhaps the end of the days is closer than we think," Issa said.

Bacha was quiet. Issa knew this usually indicated that he did not agree, but did not want to argue. Bacha would usually lose arguments with him, especially ones about spiritual matters.

Kapaali then asked Issa where his wanderings might take him. Issa explained that he had learned the Vedas, with emphasis on the Upanishads from Jnyaneshwar, and wished to teach the concepts, if not the words, to the lower castes. He also told him that he was teaching people to throw away their idols.

"Oh, that is a dangerous thing to do, my friend. You will make great enemies."

Issa and Bacha told him of their previous encounter with the head Brahmin of the village they had been forced to leave. "You are lucky they didn't kill you," said Kapaali.

Issa asked, "What is it that you do? Do you teach?"

Kapaali smiled and tilted his head from side to side. "Yes and no. I follow the teachings, but I don't call myself a teacher. I wander about, learning when I can, and helping where I can. I study the Self. Svadyaya, as it is called. In this village they asked me to teach them, so I simply shared with them what I know. In the last village I was in, they needed a carpenter, so I helped them build."

Issa saw an opportunity to learn more about idols, because although he thought it wrong for people to worship them, he really didn't understand all there was to know about them. Kapaali agreed to help him understand.

"What do you know about the Bhagavad Gita, Issa?" he asked.

"Prince Hala has told me much of the story. I find it to be delightful."

"And did Prince Hala tell you about when Arjuna wished to see Lord Krishna in his true form?"

Issa replied, "We never got that far. I am hoping to find a scroll somewhere and be able to read the entire thing."

Kapaali said, "I can't help you there, Issa. But I can tell you that Lord Krishna gave Arjuna his wish. He gave him a divine eye through which he could see the true form of the Lord. Do you know the result? It was so utterly terrifying that Arjuna asked that he once again see Lord Krishna in the form he previously saw him. It was too much for him to see Him in His true form. He preferred the human form. In essence, the idol. Now let me ask you a question. Do you pray to God?"

Issa said, "I pray to God daily."

"And what does God look like? Describe God to me."

Issa was quiet for a moment and then said, "I cannot. We are taught in the Vedas that God cannot be seen, heard, touched, tasted, or smelled. And yet, God is everywhere. Everything you see is God. Everything you hear, touch, taste, or smell is God."

"Even the idols?" asked Kapaali pointedly.

Issa was silent. "Issa, we don't actually *worship* idols in this land. We worship God *through* idols. The Bhagavata Purana tells us of eight kinds of images made from eight different materials that are all fit to worship. They are stone, wood, metal, earth, paint, sand, clay, and the mind. Yes, the mind.

"You can build a mental image of God and worship that image. For us, the idol is like the human form of Lord Krishna. It is familiar. It does not terrify us. It is a *symbolic* representation of an aspect of God. It is sacred, just as the temples in your own land are considered sacred. You worship God inside a temple, do you not? Your temple is your idol. It is an idol that you crawl inside in order to feel close to God.

"It is not so different from our own idols, Issa. You don't belittle God when you worship him through an idol. But you do belittle Him when you question the faith of the devotees who see Him in a stone or a statue. If you believe that God does not exist in that idol, you are limiting God to those places that *you* believe He exists.

"Imagine a huge mountain, Issa. At its base there are many paths. Some wish to climb it from its northern face, others its southern face. Still others, its eastern or western faces. At first, they are far apart. But as they climb higher and higher, the diameter of the mountain narrows, and thus the climbers become closer and closer. They soon begin to realize that it is but one mountain they are all climbing. It is the same mountain.

"And when they finally reach its top, there is no longer any distance at all between them. They have become one. We have become one. Jews and Hindus climb the same mountain, Issa. Those who worship idols and those who do not likewise climb the same mountain. We all just need to climb high enough that we can see one another."

Issa felt ashamed as he wiped a tear from his eye. He had just learned another valuable lesson. He realized how wrong it was of him to teach against idols. He vowed he would not make that mistake again.

***

The following morning it was still raining. Bacha was quite hungry, and as a result, quite irritable. "How long do these rains last?" he asked Kapaali angrily.

"Sometimes they go on for days at a time, Bacha. But often they will stop for a time during the late morning."

Issa stood at the entrance to the cave. He was soaking wet.

"When did you go out, and why?" Bacha asked.

Issa held out his begging bowl. It was filled with berries. "I knew you would be hungry, Bacha, so I thought I would find us something to eat. God has provided. Enjoy."

He set the bowl down and began to move deeper into the cave. "It is time for my morning meditation."

When he came back an hour later he looked relaxed. He put his hand on Kapaali's shoulder and said, "Thank you for telling me about idols, Kapaali. I have much to be ashamed of. I should have listened more carefully to Jnyaneshwar. He too tried to tell me, but my stubbornness kept me from hearing."

The rain had stopped, and the sun was now shining. "Come, my friends," said Kapaali. "Come to the edge of the village and I will introduce you to some of the people who live nearby."

The three walked the short distance to the village's edge, where there were several poor families of farmers harvesting the dung from the cows. Before the monsoons, they had formed them into patties, stacked them, and put a hay roof over them. The sun had dried them over the hot months, and they could now be used for heating and cooking. But the rains would soon make them useless, so the last of the patties needed to be gathered while the sun was out. They had regular customers for the dung in the village.

"Namaste, Kapaaliji," one of the villagers shouted as the three arrived. The children all ran up to him and tried to be the first to jump into his arms. Kapaali knelt on the ground and became a horse, and two of the children rode on his back. His robe became muddy as the children laughed and shouted, but he didn't seem to care. "Issa, you must always have children around you," he said as stood and hugged the children. "They will keep you honest! *Always* let the children come unto you."

Issa and Bacha were introduced, and Kapaali said that Issa would teach them today. They didn't seem to be excited by this, but said they would tell the others. When it came time for Issa to speak it was raining again, so the small crowd went into a house that was used for a schoolhouse. Kapaali sat with the crowd as Issa came to the front. He spoke of the complexity of various religious rules and the simplicity of finding God. As he spoke of loving one another, and helping one another, and loving those who hate you, the listeners grew quieter and quieter. He spun some of his mashals into his talk, which delighted everyone. Even the children were paying attention.

Issa did not speak of bringing Vaisya, Sudra, and Chandala together to hear him this time. He would gradually and skillfully make that happen in subsequent talks. Right now he was winning the Sudras' hearts, and they were anxious to hear him speak again. One of the farmers invited Kapaali, Issa, and Bacha to his house to eat. The farmer's family had sold the last of their cow dung, and at least for a few days, they would live like the Vaisyas. Issa learned from them that this village too was on land owned by a Brahmin. He was called Prabal, and his name meant "mighty." He was described as a strict follower of the laws. This troubled Bacha, but he was quiet. He would just have to make sure Issa didn't get into trouble again.

That night, as they sat in the cave, Kapaali said to them, "As you well know, Issa, we Sannyasa must change our residence during the rainy season. You have come here, and I will go south. I can see that the people here like you. They know that I must leave, so when I don't show up tomorrow, it won't be a complete surprise to them. I only caution you not to cross Prabal. He is indeed mighty, and not as benevolent as the last Brahmin you angered."

47 (Going to prison)

It had happened again. Over the course of a few weeks, Issa had managed to get the Vaisya, the Sudra, and the Chandala all to sit together contentedly. One day, Issa talked to the crowd for so long that it was nearing the time that most of them would eat, but they were too engaged in his stories to think about food. Finally, a small girl came and sat on Issa's lap. Issa had taken Kapaali's advice about children, and found it to be good advice. He smiled at her, and she looked up to him and said loudly, "I'm hungry!"

Issa had with him a few pieces of Indian bread called chapatti, stuffed with vegetables for his own meal. Someone had given him some the night before, and he had not eaten all of it. He looked around and found a basket. He said, "Let us make a miracle today. We are all of different castes, and yet we sit together as one. That is already a miracle, is it not? Let us ask God to bring forth enough food to feed everyone right here, right now. I have brought with me two chapatti with vegetables. I will place them both in this basket. I now give it to you."

He gave the basket to the little girl sitting in his lap. "Take some out for yourself, but leave some for others. The rest of you, listen closely. When the basket is passed to you, if you have brought food with you, please place some of it in the basket for others. If you have no food, you may take some from the basket. When it comes back to me, if there is still food in it, I will eat with you."

Now the basket began to pass from person to person. The crowd buzzed with excitement as each person either removed or added to its contents. A few minutes later, when it finally came back to Issa, it had more food in it than when it first started its rounds. Much more! Issa held the basket for everyone to see. "There are almost one hundred people here, and you have all been fed by my placing only two chapatti in the basket! You have indeed performed a miracle!" Everyone cheered.

He then spoke of one of the Niyamas that Patanjali had taught him called Samtosa, which meant contentment. This was coupled with the Yama he had taught them earlier called Aparigraha, which meant nonpossessiveness. There were five Yamas, sometimes called the restraints, and five Niyamas, sometimes called the observances, that he had learned from Patanjali. He was teaching them to the people one by one. "If you can learn to not be envious of those things your neighbor has, and be content with what you yourself have, you can be happy. In the Jewish faith of my country we believe that there is enough for everyone. You need only believe, and ask for God's help. Remember, though, that God will just point you in the right direction. It's up to you to provide the labor. That is why He gave us hands and feet."

"What is the meaning of this?" The magic moment was broken by Prabal, standing at the door of the schoolhouse. The Chandala all immediately fell to the ground, face down. The Sudra and Vaisya separated. Prabal watched the commotion, then shouted, "Have you all forgotten what today is? Why are you Vaisyas not in the temple?" It was the day for the village to partake in the Pitri-yajna, the offering of libations of water to ancestors in gratitude. Less than half of the Vaisya were in the temple.

"And who are you?" Prabal was looking straight at Issa. Bacha pulled out the decree from the king granting them safe passage throughout the Satavahana Empire. Two Kshatriyas appeared behind Prabal, and one came forward, grabbed the document from Bacha, and presented it to Prabal. He looked at it, sneered, and said, "You two will go with my guards. You Vaisays will go to the temple. The rest of you, go home!"

Issa and Bacha were taken to the village prison. They were thrown in with about seven other men, and the door closed loudly. One of the prisoners stood up and said, "You are foreigners. Who are you and why are you here?"

"My name is Issa, and this is my friend Bacha. As to why we are here, I'm not really sure."

The other men began laughing. The one standing said, "You may never know. Sometimes we are locked up for being drunk, like Tejal here, and sometimes we are locked up for not paying enough taxes. How can we pay taxes if we are in jail and not allowed to work? But I suspect you have done something to anger Prabal. That is usually what lands you in jail."

Bacha told the men what had happened. They looked at one another, their eyes sharing a silent secret. They seemed a little frightened. Bacha continued, "We will be freed soon, though. I have presented them a document that grants us safe passage through this empire. It has the king's seal on it. They won't ignore that." Again the men exchanged glances.

It wasn't until the next day that Issa and Bacha were taken to another building. Prabal sat in an ornate chair, and they were made to kneel, as they had the last time they had met with a Brahmin land owner. They were both hoping for the same outcome as the previous encounter.

Prabal narrowed his eyes and said, "Where did you get that document?"

"Prince Hala obtained it from his father, the king, and gave it to us," replied Bacha.

"Oh, I see. So you are friends of Prince Hala as well as the king," Prabal said in a most sarcastic tone. "Your document does not fool me, foreigners. I have seen forgeries that were much better written than this. I will send a courier to Pratishthana and see if this document is legitimate. If it is, you can continue on your journey. If it is not, your journey may very well end here! Meantime, you will be my guest." Once again, Prabal spoke with sarcasm dripping from his mouth. " You have already met my other seven guests."

Issa and Bacha were returned to the prison.

48 (Near death and a new destination)

AD 20
Yeshua's age: 23

Over the three months they remained in prison, Issa and Bacha made friends with their seven fellow prisoners. Issa taught them daily, and often, as he was teaching, the guards would gather near, pretending to conduct business. If Prabal was in town they would not dare be caught listening, but often, when Prabal was elsewhere, and the prisoners were outside planting, weeding, or digging up crops in one of Prabal's many fields, they would sit nearby when everyone paused to eat, listen, and even ask questions. The prison guards were Kshatriyas, and Issa's grasp of the Upanishads astonished them. Most of the prisoners were Sudra, but no one seemed to mind that Issa openly shared his wisdom.

The prisoners were fed only enough food to survive and to work. Most of the time they were fed twice a day, but sometimes only once a day. The prison had only one window, with metal bars across it. It faced the south so as to allow the sun to enter throughout most of the day. It was one of Prabal's cruel ideas: Whenever the prisoners were not working outside the prison, they would face unbearable scorching heat inside.

During this time they would sit very still. Issa would often meditate during these times. Two of the prisoners asked Issa to teach them to meditate, and they would sit together in a corner and learn. The other five thought meditation a waste of time, and would sit in the opposite corner and talk among themselves, sometimes quite loudly. This became very distracting for the two meditation students, and they often looked to the corner with anger in their eyes and tension in their bodies. Issa saw the problem, and taught the two the yogic skill of *pratyahara*, which he described as withdrawl of the senses. "It's not that you don't hear them talking," he explained to them one day, pointing to the other five, "just that you don't assimilate the words."

"I don't think I understand," one of the prisoners, Tejal, said. "How is such a thing possible?"

"Do you hear the birds right now, Tejal?" Issa asked.

Everyone became quiet and listened; even the five in the opposite corner. The birds were actually quite loud. Tejal said, "Well, now that you have said it, yes, I hear them."

"And yet a moment ago you did not. Were they not singing a moment ago?"

Tejal paused and thought. "I suppose they were singing a moment ago. It's just that I wasn't paying attention to them."

Issa smiled. "And so, my friend, you were practicing pratyahara without even knowing you were doing it! The difference is, when you are actually practicing pratyahara, you are not paying attention *mindfully*; with a *purpose*."

As the weeks went by, the two students became more and more adept at sitting with eyes closed and going deeper into meditation. Soon several of the other prisoners, seeing the change in their two friends, began to sit with them and learn from Issa.

***

When Issa and Bacha were finally summoned by Prabal, they hoped that the investigation had been completed and they would be set free. But Prabal stood over them and said, "As I suspected, your paper was a forgery! You do *not* have permission from the king to wander through this country."

Issa and Bacha stood there with eyes wide and mouths agape, and both now knew that no investigation had been initiated. This was the reaction that Prabal seemed to want, because his cruel smile grew. They prepared for the worst. "I have spoken to the leaders of the surrounding villages, and it seems that you have been causing trouble wherever you go. I have learned from others in the area that you have spoken openly against the Brahmins, although you yourself have been taught by one.

"You have spoken against our sacred idols. You have stirred up the people and caused them to turn their hearts against the Brahmins and the Kshatriyas. You have caused different castes to sit together who never should have sat together; this I have seen with my own eyes. It is therefore my judgment that you be taken from this village and have your tongue sliced off, so you may never again spread vicious lies. It would best that you then return to your own country. You are not welcome here. Your friend, Bacha, will suffer the same fate for failing to stop you."

Their hands were tied behind their backs, and one of Prabal's guards tied a long rope from Issa to Bacha, and grabbing the front of it, lead them through the village for all to see. Bacha, however, was not going to let this terrible deed happen if he could help it. Up until now, he had been very passive with the authorities he had come in contact with. But this time, he would become the protector that he was tasked to be. He began turning and stretching his hands, gradually creating more space. With each twist and turn, the space got a little bigger. But as hard as he tried, it was simply not enough to slip his hands through the rope.

As they were paraded through the village, everyone came out to watch. Many of the onlookers were the sudras who had heard Issa speak. A group came running up to the guard who was leading them and asked, "Why are you doing this? These men have done no harm."

"Stand back or you will feel my sword," the guard shouted, placing a hand on his weapon, as the crowd moved back. During the commotion, someone had slipped something into one of Bacha's bound hands. He almost dropped it, but managed to hold on. *What is it?* he wondered. As they continued their march, Bacha felt the sharpness of one of the long thin edges of a knife.

They continued outside the village until they came to a clearing where the guard would do his deed. As he stood between Issa and Bacha to untie the long rope, Bacha made his move. He had successfully used the knife to free his hands a few minutes before and was waiting until they were alone. Before the guard could react, he lunged forward and knocked him to the ground. As the guard tried to pick himself up, Bacha kicked him with an upper thrust to the chin as hard as he could. It was a blow he had learned in the courtyard of the king, and it snapped the guard's neck with a loud crack, killing him instantaneously. The guard lay on the ground staring into infinity, his mouth open and his body twisted into a grotesque shape.

"Noooooo!" shouted Issa. "You didn't need to do that, Bacha. Why did you do that?"

"I *did* need to do that, little brother. If we escaped and he was still alive, he would die a miserable death at the hands of Prabal and the other guards. It was the only humane thing to do."

235

Issa sat at the dead guard's side, and with tears streaming down his cheek, he chanted some Vedic verses for the dead. Bacha beckoned him and he slowly stood and followed his friend and protector. But where would they go? Their paper was gone, they no longer had the protection of the king, they were now fugitives, and Bacha was a murderer. Surely they would be hunted down.

"Now what, Bacha?" asked Issa. "Now what?" This time he seemed to ask it of himself as he slowly shook his head from side to side. "Now what?" he asked again in almost a whisper.

"I have a plan, little brother. We must travel north. We are close to the border between the Satavahana Empire and the Kushan Empire. I have seen maps in the palace. Once we have crossed, we will not be followed. These two empires are not exactly friendly with one another. The Kushans, I have heard from Vijayananda, are trying to seize more territory."

Issa was numb. As they journeyed further north, day after day, he said nothing. It was as though his tongue had actually been cut off. Bacha had never seen him so saddened. Perhaps it was time to go home. They could work their way west to the Silk Route and back to Israel. But this was not the time to broach the subject. Maybe in a week or two.

They both saw smoke rising in the distance and Bacha thought that perhaps a battle was being fought. But as they neared, Bacha recognized it as a cremation being conducted along the banks of the River Ganga. They were nearing the great city of Varanasi, still not far enough north to be out of danger, but perhaps a chance to rest for a day. Issa had still not spoken. Each night Bacha had tried to engage him in conversation, but Issa's eyes looked glazed, and Bacha feared greatly for his friend and companion.

As they sat by the water's edge, looking out, someone suddenly placed some food in Issa's begging bowl. "Namaste," the stranger said, bowing. Issa didn't seem to be aware of him.

"Namaste," Bacha replied. "Please forgive my friend. He is going through a hard time."

"Is your friend Hindu?" asked the stranger.

Bacha once again turned protector. He couldn't be sure if this was a spy already looking for them. He knew that there were many

Buddhists in Varanasi, so he replied, "No, he is Buddhist."

"As am I! My name is Haroon. I am a Bhikkhu [monk], and I am on my way to Kapilavstu to hear the great Munish give Buddha's famous discourse on Turning the Wheel of the Dharma, the Dhamma Cakka Pavattana Sutta.

Bacha sensed this man was telling the truth, and thought that if the authorities were looking for a duo, a group of three would look less suspicious. "That is where I am taking my friend," Bacha lied. "He is not well, and I'm hoping Munish can help him. He has stopped talking suddenly, and I am sure he is not doing it on purpose. There is something very wrong with him."

Issa looked at Bacha with a puzzled expression, but said nothing.

"Are you not able to speak, sir?" Haroon asked Issa.

But Issa, glancing once at Haroon, turned back and continued to look at Bacha and remained silent.

"Well, if anyone can help, Munish can. Are you Buddhist as well?"

Bacha knew he could not pose as a Buddhist to another Buddhist, since he knew almost nothing about them. "No, but I am considering becoming one."

"It will be the best decision you have ever made, I promise you," said Haroon cheerfully. "Come, my friends are waiting."

Better still, thought Bacha. *In the midst of a group of traveling Buddhists will surely be a safe place to hide.*

There were about twenty people altogether, most with shaven heads. These were the bhikkhus, the ones who had taken vows. The rest were either practitioners of Buddhism or those hoping to soon become bhikkhus. Haroon introduced Issa and Bacha and explained to the group that Issa needed Munish's help. Each took their turn walking beside Issa and smiling whenever he looked at them. They all seemed genuinely concerned for Issa's well-being. Bacha was no longer in the protector mode. He felt very safe. The journey was almost two hundred miles and would take many days. They began their trek north, into the Kushan Empire, and Bacha began to feel even more at ease.

***

They had not traveled far when one of the Bhikkhus noticed several Kshatriya guards ahead. They were carefully watching everyone who passed by.

Bacha had relaxed too soon. Their new friend Haroon told them that Buddhists were not well liked by the Kshatriya and many Brahmins. "They usually call us 'shavelings' because of our shaved heads, and want us to be gone as quickly as possible. They do not appear to be looking for Buddhists. Perhaps if the two of you have shaved heads and wear tunics like ours, we can pass by unharmed." Clearly, Haroon knew that it was Issa and Bacha whom the Kshatriyas were looking for, but he made no mention of it.

"I don't know," said Bacha. "We may get all of you in trouble."

"Have faith in Buddha," Haroon replied.

After shaving Issa and Bacha's heads, the Buddhists found extra tunics for the two of them. Issa still had not spoken. In another time, the two would have found the sight of each other with shaved heads very funny, but not this time.

"And now you must learn a Buddhist chant. We will all chant it as we walk in columns of two," Haroon said. "This irritates them even more. They will be glad to have us pass them by."

With that, Haroon taught Bacha a simple chant. Issa was still not speaking. "What if they see he is not chanting?" asked Bacha.

"Buddha will watch over us. You will see." Haroon seemed sure of himself, but Bacha was apprehensive.

They formed columns of two and began their chanting and walking. Bacha placed himself on the side that the guards were on, so that it would be even harder to see that Issa was not chanting.

"Move along, shavelings," shouted one guard as they filed by. The other guard had moved to the opposite side of the columns, much to the dismay of Bacha.

"Stop!" he shouted. He was looking directly at Issa. Bacha was sure it was all over.

"Why are you not chanting that ridiculous chant with the others? Answer me!"

Bacha's mind was churning. He had to do something quickly. But before he could do anything, Haroon came to the guard and said, "This man has taken a vow of silence. He has not spoken for over a year. He has committed himself to silence for three years to honor the Enlightened One, and cannot answer you without breaking his vow."

Issa was staring at the guard with a puzzled look on his face. *Please stay silent*, Bacha pleaded to Issa in his mind. *Please don't talk now.*

The silence continued, as the guard kept staring at Issa. The air was thick with tension as everyone held their breath. Then, in the blink of an eye, the guard's posture suddenly changed from rigid to loose. "Move along then, shavelings," he shouted. "Go quickly."

The group began their chanting again and Bacha and Issa walked in step with the others. He wished they could walk faster, but knew that would arouse suspicion. The guard continued to scrutinize them for a few minutes and then turned to examine the next group of people who walked by. Except for the Buddhists, they seemed to be pulling up everyone's sleeves and looking at their arms. *They are looking for my scar*, thought Bacha.

"Did I not tell you to have faith in Buddha?" Haroon was smiling and moved back to his position in the group. Even after the crisis had passed, they continued to chant. Bacha too.

49 (Help from the Buddhists)

Munish was a very short, pudgy man with a shaved head, dancing eyes, and a delightful smile. He made it a point to personally welcome each person who came to Kapilavstu to hear him talk. When he came to the group that Issa and Bacha were in, his face changed from happiness to concern. He walked straight up to Issa and stared at him for a moment. Issa stood there with vacant eyes.

"This man is very ill," Munish said to Bacha, who was at his side. "Please bring him to my cousin's house."

The entire group escorted Issa and Bacha a few blocks from where Munish was going to talk. He was brought inside a small house and placed on a comfortable bed. Munish's cousin, whose name was Samik, sat on the bed and felt Issa's pulse as Issa gazed at him with a blank stare. Munish asked, "Who is he, and who can tell me what has happened to him?"

A great change was coming over Bacha. He normally viewed strangers with some skepticism, Bacha had never before felt so at home with the people he had surrounded himself with. He knew with all his heart that they meant no harm to Issa. He sat with Munish and Samik and told them the entire story, including his killing of the Kshatrya guard. Munish's eyes widened as Bacha talked, but he said nothing. Bacha also told him about their adventures up until this point: being found by Vijayananda in Jerusalem, Issa's training by Patanjali, his learning the Vedas and Upanishads from Jnyaneshwar, his teaching the poor, and his remarkable Siddis, especially his power to heal.

Munish had closed his eyes as if in deep meditation. When Bacha had finished, he said, "Bacha, thank you for telling me this. Your Issa is indeed a very special person, maybe even the next Buddha. But right now he needs care. My cousin is an Ayurvedic doctor, and will look after him. He is in capable hands, I can assure you.

"Issa is not the only one who needs help, however. You too are in great need. You are either holding back, or are unaware of the great pain that is inside you. You have killed someone. This, I can see, is not in your nature. The kind of help you need can be found by learning of our ways. Please come and hear my talk this afternoon. Listen to it carefully."

Bacha was reluctant to leave Issa. But Issa didn't seem to

recognize him anyway, and he was with a doctor. Samik said that he had seen this condition before, recognized its cause by the story Bacha told, and knew how to treat it. So Bacha went back to the assembly with Haroon to hear Munish give his discourse.

By the time the talk began, there were well over a thousand people gathered. Munish began with the words that started every discourse of Buddha's: "Thus I have heard." He then spoke for more than an hour about the four "Noble Truths" that he had once told his very first disciples.

When the talk was over, Bacha sat with Haroon to discuss what they had just listened to. Haroon asked, "So what did you think of the Dhammacakkapavattana Sutta?"

Bacha was excited. "This I can understand, Haroon. I cannot yet pronounce the name of it, but it is a little long, is it not? Dhamma ... cak ... pa ... pa ... Sutta."

Haroon laughed as Bacha continued. "None of the philosophy of Brahmanism made much sense to me. But this—this is clear. It is simple and straightforward. Buddha is speaking of the middle way, the path between the two extremes."

"And what are the two extremes, Bacha?"

"Sensual pleasure is at one end and self-mortification is on the other. And by following the middle path, and not veering toward either extreme, one becomes awakened. Am I right?"

Haroon nodded his head. "Yes, Bacha, one becomes awakened. This in turn gives rise to vision. Vision leads to knowledge, knowledge to peace, peace to direct knowledge, direct knowledge to enlightenment, and enlightenment to Nirvana. Perhaps you are becoming awakened, my friend."

"Perhaps I am, Haroon."

When they finished their discussion, Bacha went by himself back to the house where Issa was staying. Issa was asleep. Samik told him that he had given him medicine that would keep him asleep for several days. This was part of the cure.

"What is it that caused this to happen?" Bacha asked.

"Bacha, your friend, who is a great man of peace, has seen someone killed in front of his very eyes." Bacha cringed when he was reminded of that horrible incident.

Samik continued. "He knew that this person was killed in order to protect him. In his mind, he feels as responsible for the killing as if he had done it himself. This is the main cause of his nonresponsiveness. Then there is this: the path he was taking, that you both were taking, was quite suddenly cut off. In a matter of seconds he changed from being a teacher, friend of Prince Hala, welcome throughout the Satavahana Empire, to a fugitive who could no longer teach there. It is as if he no longer had a purpose. Or so he thinks right now. It was all too much for his mind, and so it simply shut down."

Bacha, almost shouting, said, "It had to be done, Samik. They would have cut our tongues out!"

"Calm yourself. I make no judgments, Bacha. I am just explaining how your friend must feel. I have seen this in soldiers returning from great battles where there was lots of bloodshed, especially young soldiers who had never before killed or seen someone killed. Your friend will wake up soon, and he will begin to be himself in a few weeks. But it will be some time before he is completely well.

"You can do nothing for him now, Bacha. Come back in a few days. He will need to see you when he is awake. Be prepared. He still might not recognize you right away, but you are an integral part of his cure."

Bacha returned to the assembly and found Haroon. "How is your friend?" he asked Bacha.

"Asleep."

"Good. Munish's cousin will take good care of him."

Bacha put a hand on Haroon's shoulder "I want to learn more about Buddha."

"Munish will speak again tomorrow. Come now and join me and my friends. We will find some food in the forests and a place to sleep. Buddha will provide."

Bacha stayed awake for a long time that night, thinking of Issa, thinking of Buddha, thinking about Samaria for the first time in a very long while, and wondering what was going to happen next. He also wondered how it was possible for him to feel so completely changed about things after listening to one discourse by Munish. The words of Buddha pulled him strongly. Would he feel different tomorrow?

***

By the end of the second discourse, Bacha had no more doubts about his transformation. He spoke to Haroon about it after the crowd had dispersed. "Haroon, I think I would like to become a Buddhist."

Haroon slapped his own cheeks with his hands and asked, "And what made you decide that, Bacha?"

"That day when I took the life of another, it affected me much more than I let on. I have never killed anyone before. I have fought before, with my fists, but never killed. You just can't imagine what that makes me feel like. It's horrible.

"When I became Issa's protector, I knew what it meant. I knew I might need to kill in order to protect him. And I thought I was prepared for that. I wasn't, Haroon. I only remained strong after that incident because I had to. And now that Issa is in good hands, I have come face-to-face with my true nature. I thought about it long last night. and it became clear to me. I am not a warrior, Haroon. I could never be one."

Haroon probed. "And yet, Issa relies on you to be his protector, does he not?"

Bacha thought before he spoke. " I will gladly be Issa's companion, as I have been all these years, and I will always stand between him and an enemy. But as for killing, no! I can never do that again. I will never do that again."

They both went to tell Munish, who was delighted, yet did not seem surprised by Bacha's sudden decision, having seen such things before. But he too had questions. "Bacha, tell me, if you wish to remain here and study Buddhism, and Issa wishes to go back home, what will you do?"

Bacha was quiet for a moment, and then spoke. "I will stay. But if I know Issa, he will not wish to go home. In fact I'm sure of it. He will want to study Buddhism too. That is, once he hears some of Buddha's discourses. It will be so. You will see."

Munish was quiet for a moment, and then said, "Very well, Bacha. You will train with the group of followers who have committed themselves to becoming Bhikkhus. You will be training in the great monastery, Nigrodharama. Buddha himself took residence there in the first year after his Enlightenment."

The next morning, Bacha was summoned to Samik's house. Issa

was awake! Bacha ran to his bedside, and much to his delight, Issa smiled and asked weakly, "Bacha, it is you?"

It was the first time he had heard Issa speak since the incident. Samik had warned him not to engage in any conversation relating to the traumatic event that had caused his illness. He and Samik would walk that path together in time.

"It is indeed me, Issa. How are you feeling?"

Issa began to sit up, and then quickly laid back down. "A little dizzy perhaps," he replied.

After a few moments of idle talk about the weather and the food Issa had been eating, Samik came in and said, "Thank you for coming, Bacha. Issa now needs his rest. Please come back tomorrow at the same time."

"See you tomorrow, little brother," Bacha said as he rose and headed toward the door.

Being called "little brother" caused Issa to open his mouth for a moment and look as if he was about to speak. Bacha and Samik waited to hear what he would say. Then he smiled faintly, raised his hand in farewell, curled up, and closed his eyes.

50 (A decision to stay and learn)

AD 21
Yeshua's age: 24

Issa's recovery took almost a year. He had begun his meditation practice once again, and Munish was pleased to see him occasionally glowing. Munish convinced Issa that he should not resume his teaching for a while. If he remained hidden for some time, Munish opined, the search for him and Bacha might diminish.

Munish and his cousin Samik had not met Issa before, so they were unaware of the transformation that had taken place in him. Issa was not as sure of himself as he had once been. He did not speak with as much authority, and his voice was softer.

Bacha was progressing in his studies in Buddhism, and Issa was beginning to face the anger he held inside him all these years. He was now more than twenty years old, and this anger had been inside him as far back as he could remember. Munish helped him to understand some of it, but knowing its root cause and eliminating it, he knew, were two separate things.

Today, Issa did not want to think or talk about his anger. Bacha was visiting, and he wished to talk to his friend. "So, Bacha, tell me some of the things you have learned about Buddhism." Issa knew his friend was eager to tell him some of what he had learned.

Bacha said, "Do you remember how upset both you and I were with the caste system?"

"It still bothers me, big brother," Issa replied.

"Well, it bothered Buddha too! Let me tell you a story I have learned about him. It is called the Vasala Sutta"

And so Bacha began:
> Thus have I heard:
> There was an occasion where the Blessed One was living near Savatthi at a place called Jetavana, in the Anathapindika's monastery. In the late afternoon the Blessed One dressed himself, took his bowl, and entered Savatthi for alms. During that time a fire was burning, and an offering was being prepared in the

house of the Brahmin Aggikabharadvaja. The Blessed One, while begging for alms, came near the Brahmin's house. When Aggikabharadvaja saw him, still some ways off, he said to him, "Stay there you shaveling! Stay there you wretched monk! Stay there you Chandala, you Outcast!."

When the Blessed One heard him, he replied, "Dear Brahmin, do you know who is an outcast, and what makes him an outcast?"

"No Venerable Gotama, I do not know. It would be good if you would explain this to me that I might know."

"Listen then, Brahmin. Pay attention to what I say.

1. "If any person is angered, holds hatred in his heart, hesitates to speak well of others, is perverted in his views, and deceitful, know this person to be an outcast.

2. "If any person kills another, be they once born or twice born, and has no compassion for living beings, know this person to be an outcast.

3. "If any person destroys and besieges villages and markets, and becomes known as an oppressor, know this person to be an outcast."

It went on like this for another 17 verses. Then, it came to the lesson to be learned:

21. "It is not by birth that a person becomes an outcast. It is not by birth that a person becomes a Brahmin. It is by deed that a person becomes an outcast. It is by deed that a person becomes a Brahmin."

Issa was enthralled with this story, and delighted in the fact that it was Bacha who was telling it with sincerity. "Oh what a wonderful story," he said.

"The Buddha also believed in the commonality of all castes. I am so glad we have found this place, Bacha. I too will study this Buddhist doctrine. It is perfect in its simplicity."

As they spoke, Bacha grew silent and the expression on his face changed.

"Bacha, what's wrong?"

"Little brother, I'm still pained by the circumstances that led us here. I have taken the life of another human being, which is the greatest and gravest of all sins. I have turned you into a fugitive. I have prevented you from teaching. I have wronged you, Yeshua. I have wronged you horribly. For the first time in my life I feel as if I am a sinner." He spoke Issa's given name, Yeshua, for the first time since his little brother had taken his vows.

Issa placed a hand on Bacha's shoulder and said, "Bacha, did you not listen to the story you just told?" Issa found some of the self-assuredness he once had. "The Brahmin saw the error of his own ways, admitted them, and was accepted into Buddha's order. You have done the same. Bacha, truly I say to you, because of the repentance I feel in your heart, on this day your sins are forgiven."

Bacha began to weep. He felt the weight of everything he had just confessed to begin slowly dissolving from his heart. He felt as if God Himself had just forgiven him, not Issa. He began to feel radiant.

"Bacha, now it is you who is glowing!" Issa was smiling at him.

He now understood fully what Issa had felt like when this first happened to him eight years ago. As Patanjali had told them, it was an acknowledgement from God that one was on the right path.

The two sat as one in holy silence, looking into each other's eyes for a long time.

51 (Issa begins healing and being healed)

AD 22
Yeshua's age: 25

Munish and Issa sat together in the monastery where Bacha was now studying and drank tea.

"I'm glad you are feeling better, Issa," Munish said.

"Your cousin has helped me through a very difficult time in my life, venerable sir. He has helped me to resolve my past. But now I wish to focus on the present. I am aware that this is the focus taught in Buddhism as it is likewise taught in Brahmanism.

"Although I have learned much from my Brahmin teacher, Jnyaneshwar, and more so from my first teacher and master, Patanjali, I now wish to learn about Buddhism. One of the issues I have never resolved with Brahmanism, although I have begun to understand it, is the caste system. Bacha has told me the Vasala Sutta, and I am delighted to know that your Buddha also had issues with the caste system. I wish to know more about him."

"And I wish to teach you," Munish said. "Word of your powers of healing and your deep love and affection for the poor and the lower castes has already spread throughout India. You seem to be able to teach not as a Brahmin, nor as a—what do you call them in your country—oh yes, a rabbi. Rather, you teach as simply a loving, caring human being, and in turn are well loved by our people. This is also how we teach Buddhism. I think you will find many similarities between our teachings and your own.

"Most of our teachings are written in a language called Pali. You will need to learn how to speak it and read it. But from what I have heard, your mastery of both Maharashtri and Sanskrit is admirable. So I don't think you will have any trouble.

"As you learn, and as you begin to go outside this monastery and teach, you will need to keep your head shaven. This is not only our way, but it will further protect you from those who might be looking for you. Your vows as a Sannyasa will remain intact. Our own vows do not violate anything you have already committed yourself to. Do you have any questions?"

"How shall I address you, venerable sir?"

Munish replied, "I am sometimes called *Acharya*. My Buddhist title is *dev:koti*, which, as you will soon learn, means "teacher" in Pali. So, you may simply call me teacher. Anything else?"

Issa thought a moment and then asked, "How is my big brother Bacha doing, reverend Teacher?"

Munish grinned. "He is doing quite well, Issa. He is a serious student, and is driven to learn as much as he can. He too is learning Pali. He wishes to become a Sramana, which is a wandering ascetic monk who has taken the vow to follow the ten percepts of Buddhism."

"And what are the then percepts of Buddhism, reverend teacher?" Issa's curiosity of religious beliefs was coming back.

Munish recited the ten percepts for Issa. "I will abstain from harming living beings; taking things not freely given; sexual misconduct; false speech; intoxicating drinks and drugs causing heedlessness; taking untimely meals; dancing, singing music, and watching grotesque mime; use of garlands, perfumes, and personal adornment; use of high seats; and accepting gold or silver."

As the ten perceps were being recited, Issa closed his eyes, enjoying the good news about his friend and companion, the taste of the tea, the pleasant conversation with Munish, the beautiful day, and the beginning of the next chapter in his life: Buddhism. Outside, the sound of chattering birds could be heard in the surrounding trees.

***

The first time he entered the clinic where the sick were being kept, Issa began to have doubts if he could still channel the power of healing through his body. There were so many people suffering, and he had not laid hands on anyone for a long time. But as soon as he made eye contact, it was as if no time at all had passed, and his doubts were drowned in his compassion.

He went to the person who was looking at him and asked, "Please tell me why you have come."

She was a tiny woman, but her voice was loud and clear, like a ringing bell. "I have come to see you. They told me you were here. I have heard all about you. You are the one who cures the sick with his touch."

Issa answered, "Only God can cure the sick."

"But I have heard!"

Issa shook his head. "Please tell me what is wrong with you."

She looked confused. "Are you that person I have heard about, or are you not?"

Issa smiled, placed his hand on her shoulder, and said, "I am a servant of God. Sometimes I am used by Him to cure people. But it is not me who cures. It is God. And so it is not me whom you should seek, it is God."

She hesitated a moment, and then began to lift up her robe. As her legs became exposed, he saw that the left one was discolored in shades of red and purple, and almost three times as thick as the other. She stared at him as he looked closely at her leg.

"Well, can you cure me or not?"

He looked at her a moment, rose, and said, "I cannot."

Now the others were beginning to gather closer. They murmured with one another about the saint from the west having lost his power to heal.

He continued, "But God can. I will wrap your leg in a clean cloth. You must then ask God to help. In the morning, I will unwrap it. If you truly believe that God can help you, then the discoloration will be less. After that, we will deal with the swelling."

She now began to cry. "Then I will not be cured."

"Why is that?" he asked.

"It is because I have lost my faith. I lost it when my husband died. Where was God then? Where was God when he was suffering? Why didn't He save my husband?"

This was what Issa was waiting for. He had seen into her heart, and now he could begin to heal her. He stroked her head and said, "I have been told a story about Buddha much like your own. A woman came to Buddha once, because her loved one had died. Not her husband, but her only child. She begged Buddha to bring him back to life. Buddha gave her an empty begging bowl and told her to beg for a bowl full of rice. When she returned with the rice, he would grant her wish. There was one stipulation: She could only obtain rice from families who had not been touched by death.

"She eagerly departed with the bowl and visited almost every house in the nearby town. But in each house, you see, she learned that they too had suffered loss. Some had lost sons; some had lost daughters; some had lost mothers and fathers. Some were still grieving. Three days later she returned with an empty bowl, placed it at Buddha's feet, and said, 'Forgive me. Now I understand.'"

The room was filled with silence, because everyone had stopped to listen to this story. Issa continued, "We grieve when our loved ones die, because we think we have lost something. But we haven't. Our life in these bodies is but temporary, my dear. Eventually they all wear out. As will yours. As will mine. It is only your husband's body that is gone. It is not such an important thing. It was just a body. Your husband is still here." He took her hand and placed it over her own heart. "Don't you even now feel his presence?"

She held her hand to her heart for a moment, and than began to smile. "Oh, thank you, Issa. Thank you. I do feel his presence. Please forgive my rude behavior before. I was just angry."

Issa knew all about anger. He considered his own anger as he began to quietly and carefully wrap her leg. As he neared completion he said, "You must have loved your husband very much." He wiped a fresh tear from her eye and rubbed it into her swollen leg. Then he covered it with the remaining bit of bandage. "What I said to you just now about asking for God's help—that can come later. You should do that, for certain, but not tonight. Talk to your *husband* tonight," he said to her. "Just talk to him. He will hear you."

Issa squeezed her hand and moved to the next patient.

Munish watched as he skillfully moved from person to person, seeming to know exactly what each of them needed. Munish also knew that this was what Issa needed. He was still not ready to go out and teach again, but he was ready to heal the sick. Clearly the Siddis that Patanjali had taught him, as well as his own unique relationship with God, were all intact. But he was not yet fully healed.

When the day was done, he and Munish sat and drank tea together as they often did. "Issa," Munish said as he placed his cup down, "will the first woman you saw have a good leg tomorrow?"

They looked into each other's eyes. Issa said, "She could not be healed, honorable teacher, until she healed her own heart. That she will do tonight. She will talk to her departed husband. And by doing so, she will be talking to God. As you have taught me, God is the ocean, and we are the waves. When we talk to the waves, do we not also talk to the ocean? Yes, the discoloration will be less tomorrow. Then the swelling will gradually decrease. She will be completely healed in two weeks. Healed in her body, healed in her mind, healed in her spirit. It is so." Issa now spoke with complete assurance. Munish nodded.

"Issa, you too have some healing to do. It is why I have not yet sent you out into the world to continue your teaching. Do you know, Issa, that you have nightmares almost every night?"

This came as a surprise to him. He often woke up tired in the morning, but he was unaware of the reason. "Why do you say that?" Issa asked.

Munish replied, "Bacha tells me that he often hears you crying out in the night, and sitting up suddenly with sweat running down your forehead. When he rushes to your side and asks you what the matter is, you say nothing. He is worried about you, Issa, and has come to me. I have spoken to my cousin Samik, and he says you must come back to him for treatment. Your powers are truly great, but it is said that physicians cannot heal themselves.

"You will continue to study the ways of Buddha and learn the Pali language, and you will continue to heal the sick, but you must go to Samik each night. The two of you will talk, and he will give you medicine that will help you sleep through the night. The medicine is not the cure, Issa. Just like the woman you helped this morning, the cure is inside you. Samik will help you find it."

***

"Do you remember any of your nightmares, Issa?" Samik was prodding.

"I don't actually remember the dreams themselves, but when I am awake first thing in the morning, I am thinking about Bacha killing that man, as if I had been thinking about it for a long time. That must be what I am dreaming about. And I can't help feeling that it was my fault that the man died. I was responsible."

"How could that be, Issa?"

"I know it doesn't make any sense, Samik, but that's how I feel. I would do anything to bring him back; anything! Patanjali once told me stories of raising the dead, or of a guru leaving his own body to enter the body of a younger person who was dead. Perhaps if I talked to him

...."

Samik was pleased with Issa's response. He was making progress. When he first arrived, and finally began talking again, Issa kept saying that maybe the guard was still alive. He said that perhaps Bacha had just knocked him out. But of course he knew it was not so.

Shortly after that, he accepted the guard's death, but he then turned to anger. He had confessed his anger to Samik in their many sessions, anger that someone was dead, that his teachings had come to an end, that he would be misunderstood by everyone in the Satavahana Empire, including Patanjali, even anger at Bacha. Now he was entering a new phase. He was, in effect, bargaining with God. Samik knew this, too, would fail, and he would soon become saddened by all that had happened, realizing that he was powerless to change the past. Once that was over, Issa would finally come to peace. It would not be long now.

Samik also saw an anger in Issa that was not related to the tragedy. This was a much deeper anger, something that had been there a long time. But that could wait. In the Ayurvedic discipline that Samik was trained in, the diagnosis was that Issa's vata was provoked. Vata is the air element, and Issa was showing all the signs of a vata imbalance. This was quite common in traumas such as the one he had gone through.

During the day, Issa would need to drink Brahmi tea with honey and milk. This would carry the herb deep into the tissues and create in him a state of balance and peace as well as clarity. At night he would drink a cup of warm milk with ashwaganda and a small amount of nutmeg and honey. This would help him sleep. He was continuing his daily meditation, and Samik prescribed several pranayama (breathing) exercises and some restful yoga poses. All of that, along with daily discussions with Samik and other discussions with Munish, would bring this imbalance to a close.

Samik continued with their talk. "I understand from my cousin that you are going to the clinic to help the sick. How is that going?"

Issa relaxed his posture, realizing at the same time that he had been tense since the beginning of their talk. "Helping those in need brings me closer to God, Samik. Teaching and healing are what I was put on this earth to do. I am quite sure of that now. Munish thinks I should wait a while longer before I continue teaching, but I sometimes feel like a caged animal yearning to be free. I'm not sure how much longer I can hold myself back."

"But you are still learning from my cousin, are you not?"

Buddhism was, for Issa, in many ways so different from Brahmanism. He had taken the essence of the Upanishads into his heart, and used their lessons to create his own. But Buddhism seemed so much simpler. The castes were accepted as being a part of the Indian culture, but their importance was largely ignored.

Issa also found many similarities between the teachings of his Jewish religion and that of Buddha. According to Rabbi Towbiyah, whom he had recently begun thinking about, Jews were supposed to lead their lives as if God were watching them at all times. Everything one did was done in the presence of God.

In Buddhism, Issa learned of the concept of mindfulness, which meant being aware of everything you do, everything you say, everything you think. There was an entire sutra on mindfulness of the breath called Anapanasati. In Buddhism, mindfulness was the equivalent of the Holy Spirit.

"Oh yes," Issa repied, "I am learning new things every day. I can now speak and read Pali quite well, and Munish has let me read all the sacred scrolls that he has. Some of them I read over and over because they are so full of wisdom. I would like to have met Buddha in person."

"As would I, Issa, as would I."

Their time together for this day was nearing an end, and Issa prepared to go to the Nigrodharama monastery for more lessons with Munish. He would sit with Bacha and they would discuss what they had learned after the lessons were over. It was so different for both of them to take on their new relationship as fellow students. It brought them even closer together than when they first began their journey. But although their relationship was different, Issa still called Bacha "big brother," just as Bacha called Issa "little brother."

Issa walked the dusty road to the monastery thinking about the Anapanasati and reciting one of the many breathing mindfulness exercises: *Breathing out long, I know that I am breathing out long. Breathing in long, I know that I am breathing in long.* Over and over he brought those words to his mind with each in-breath and each out-breath. There was nothing else. There was only breath. It was total focus. It was walking meditation.

As he neared the monastery, the woman whose leg he had wrapped came running up to him. "Issa, my leg is well, and I have found my faith again. You cured me! Look!"

With excitement, she lifted her robe enough to show him her leg, which looked just like her other leg now. "I have shown everyone. I have told them of your great powers."

Issa said, "Let me tell you this again. It was not me who did the healing. It was God."

"Yes, it was God. I am going to my village now to show the others what you did."

Before he could correct her again, she ran off. He smiled, shook his head, and continued his journey to the monastery. *Breathing out long, I know that I am breathing out long. Breathing in long, I know that I am breathing in long.*

52 (Aharon's divorce)

Sepphoris, Israel
AD 22

Aharon had told his wife that they were going to town to shop. She and Rachel dressed appropriately, and the three of them made their way to the town's center. When they arrived, two of Aharon's business friends were standing there with a look of anticipation on their faces. Binah, sensing what was about to happen, grabbed Rachel's hand.

Aharon raised his voice to a volume that could be heard from a distance, his public speaking voice. He said, "I, Aharon, son of Zerach, do hereby declare that you, Binah, daughter of Shamiyr, son of Obadyah, are not my wife, nor am I your husband." He handed her a bill of divorce, *sefer keritut*, which said the same. Binah had long expected it, but still, the humiliation of having it declared in public caused her to weep. Aharon then attempted to hand her the required half a mina of silver as she shook her head in shame.

"No!" She cried. She held her fists tight, until Aharon pried her hand open and placed the money in it. All those nearby were now watching this event unfold.

Rachel, who was not expecting this, stood between her parents, and faced Aharon, almost shouting. "And what of me? Do you divorce me as well? Am I no longer your daughter? Or are you going to sell me as a slave?"

Aharon stood defiantly with his arms folded. "You will go with your mother."

Rachel snapped back at him, "Good! You have *never* been my father. Who needs you anyway? I don't! Come, mother. Let's go to Grandfather's house. He's been more of a father to me than—than *him*." She tugged on her mother's arm, and Binah, after a brief resistance, walked away with Rachel. They now walked down the street arm-in-arm, holding their heads high, turning from left to right to stare back at the onlookers, who now turned their heads down to avoid eye contact.

Aharon turned and went back to his house. He would pack up the few items that belonged to his now ex-wife and daughter and have one of his workers bring it to Binah's father's house. He was now free.

As he headed home, his friend Amos, who had been one of the witnesses to the divorce, began walking toward him from behind. Aharon, upon hearing the approaching footsteps, abruptly turned, his fists clenched, his eyes wide. Amos, startled, took two steps back.

"Oh, it's you," Aharon said.

"Aharon, is it official? Your promotion, I mean?" Amos stepped closer, but not too close.

Aharon smiled. "Was there ever any doubt? Herod personally appointed me mayor of Sepphoris. I dined with him three days ago, and that's when he gave me the title. You will soon see posters declaring it in all the public places."

Amos offered his hand. "Congratulations, Aharon. If anybody deserves it, it's you."

Aharon continued his journey homeward. As he walked the dusty streets, he admired himself. *Judge of Sepphoris, member of the Small Sanhedrin, member of the Great Sanhedrin, city administrator of Sepphoris, and now mayor of Sepphoris, friend of Herod. Yes, I've done very well for myself. Very well indeed.*

He was also glad to finally be rid of Binah and Rachel. The marriage had always been a marriage of convenience. He could not have become a member of the Great Sanhedrin without first being married and having a child. And now he no longer needed either of them. *Let her father take care of her now. And that brat Rachel as well.*

53 (Issa decides to leave)

AD 26
Yeshua's age 29

Issa and Munish sat in Munish's home. Five years had passed since Issa began his lessons in Buddhism. Issa brought his teacup to his lips. *How did the time go so quickly? I have learned so much from Munish. I studied Ayurvedic medicine with Samik. I am now teaching and healing the sick. And yet...*

His thoughts were interupted by Munish. "Issa, it seems it is almost time for you to leave me. Yet I feel you have questions. Am I right?"

"Yes, reverend teacher." Issa paused a moment to gather his thoughts. "My master Patanjali taught me Kriya Yoga and when I was finished, I put on a saffron robe and called myself a Sannyasa. My guru Jnyaneshwar taught me as a Brahmin Priest, and when I went out to serve the people, I would often wear a white robe. And now I have studied Buddhism and shave my head and wear the robe of a Buddhist priest. I'm very confused. I'm not sure what I am anymore. All the teachings I have learned seem to blend into one in my mind. I see little difference in them. You are about to send me into the world—as what? A Buddhist? Is that what I now am?"

Munish smiled. "Issa, you will be known in this region as *our* Buddha. But, no, you are not a Buddhist. Look outside and tell me what you see."

"I see the beautiful tree, reverend teacher."

"And what is the purpose of the tree?"

"To provide shade for us in the hot season? To give its leaves to the ground in the fall that other things might grow? To provide wood for building things, and to burn to keep us warm in the cold season?" Issa asked.

"Yes, that is the purpose of the tree according to others. But what is the purpose of the tree according to the tree?"

"I ... I'm not sure, reverend teacher."

"The purpose of the tree is to be the tree, Issa! It doesn't need to try to be anything else. And in the same way, your purpose is to be yourself. Not a Buddhist. Not a Brahmin priest. Not a Sannyasa. Not an Ayurvedic physician, although Samik has told me you have learned enough to become one. In the Avatamsaka Sutra we talk about *apranihita*; aimlessness. There is no need for you to run to foreign lands, Issa. No need to strive or struggle or search. Everything you need for your own happiness is right here." Munish touched Issa's heart with his hand. "Just be. This is the deepest practice of meditation. Just be. There is nothing to do, nothing to plan, nothing to realize. Your purpose is to be you."

It was all beginning to make sense now. The different ways he had been taught—they were all concepts that he knew even before he learned them here in India. He would go home and teach his own people now. He would teach from his heart. He would use the lessons of the Torah and of the prophets, but he would be teaching in a much different way than a Rabbi. He would fulfill his purpose by being himself.

He suddenly yearned to be back home. True, he had been turned away by the religious authorities and scorned by the people of Nazareth, but that was so long ago. He was different now. He wanted and needed to be among his own people, the people of Israel. Munish saw it in his face. He was pleased, and yet sad that he would soon be losing a dear friend.

They sat in silence for a long time as Issa began to journey home in his mind. He was a thousand miles away by the time their teacups were empty.

Issa spoke to Bacha that night. "Bacha," he began, "I'm ready to go home. I would like us to journey together, but if you wish to remain here, I will understand. I have found what I was looking for. There is a great need inside me to return to Israel."

"I've been ready for a long time, Issa. I was just waiting for my best friend to feel the same way. I sensed it was happening. I could see it in your eyes. And I too have found what I was looking for. I too long to be home, in Samaria. This Buddhism is now embedded deep in my heart. I will bring it back to Samaria and share it with those who will listen. Who knows, maybe even Yaish will embrace it and shave his head!" They laughed together for a while.

Issa thought back to those times in Samaria when they were but children. He was so happy that they had found each other and had journeyed together for so many years. And now they would again journey together, perhaps for the last time.

***

Outside the great monastery, Nigrodharama, the place where Buddha once resided, and the place where Bacha and Issa studied, lay a beautiful garden. It was here that a crowd had gathered to say goodbye.

"I give you my blessings, Issa. I give you my blessings, Bacha." Munish placed his hands on the shoulders of the two as they knelt.

It had been five years since Issa and Bacha had taken refuge with Munish, and he felt that Issa had sufficiently recovered and was now ready to spread the word. He would not teach it as Buddhism, Munish knew, but Issa had the unique ability to gather up the essence of the teachings of India, be they yoga, Brahmanism, or Buddhism, and skillfully blend them into anyone's system of beliefs. The ease with which this saint from the West taught and tended to those in need reminded Munish of Lord Buddha himself. In some places, he was already being called an incarnation of Buddha. If he chose to stay in India, Munish was certain many more would call him such. But he knew, just as Patanjali knew, that Issa was not destined to blossom in their country. No, he would return to his own country, Israel, and shine like the light of ten thousand suns. Bacha would spread Buddhism in its true form into Samaria. Bacha had been a good student, and Munish was happy.

"Be careful, both of you," he said to them. "You have many friends in this country, but you still have powerful enemies. Word has reached me that they still look for you in the Satavahana Empire. Buddha will look after you, but please, make your way out of India as quickly as possible."

Issa and Bacha stood and turned to the many who had gathered to say goodbye to them. Samik was there, as were most of the students of the temple. Many of the local villagers who had been cured by Issa or who had listened to him speak were likewise there. Bacha wore his Buddhist robe and kept his head shaved, but Issa was once again wearing his saffron robe and had begun to let the hair on his head and his beard grow. Although the robe labeled him as a Sannyasa here in India, it was similar to the clothing that he had once worn in Israel. He had no other possessions.

"Samik, I can't thank you enough for teaching me so much about Ayurveda and Ayurvedic medicine, and especially all of your help in making me well." Issa and Samik held each other's arms.

"It is my purpose, Issa. I was happy to be of service. I'm only sorry I couldn't help you with whatever it is buried deep in your mind that I was unable to penetrate."

"It's all right, Samik. Knowing that it is there is the first step toward healing, is it not? Whatever it is brings out my anger. Buddha maintained that anger is the most toxic of all emotions; the harm it causes by far exceeds all other afflictions. It is the hardest one to subdue and the most difficult to cure."

"You have learned your lessons well, Issa. I have no doubt you will one day cure yourself of this affliction; this deep anger. And now, I have a gift for you."

"A gift?"

Samik handed Issa a cloth sack. "It is filled with medicine that you are now very familiar with: herbs, spices, plants, oils, things that will be of help to you in your Israel. There are even some seeds for growing your own medicinal plants. I chose things that grow here, but that I have been told do not grow in your land."

"Samik, I could not ask for a more thoughtful gift. I will think of you each time I use something from it."

After meandering through the crowd saying farewells, Issa and Bacha began their long journey northward. As soon as they were out of sight of the crowd, Bacha began dancing in front of Issa like a child. "Issa, we are going home! Are you as excited as I am?"

Issa was solemn. "This land has been my home longer than Israel was. I have learned so much from these people, and have been guided by them. Yes, Bach, I am happy to be going home, but I am sorry to be leaving my second home. Patanjali, Jnyaneshwar, and Munish were all like fathers to me. The people of this land have been so giving. The poor especially have shown me hospitality and respect. Even during my fits of anger, they did not turn away from me. They are my family now. I will miss them very much."

Their voyage home would take them through the Himalayans into Bod (Tibet.) There they would turn west and make their way back to their own Israel. It would be a long and difficult journey. They would travel the Silk Road, the trade route that many merchants still used to go back and forth between Egypt and India, though their numbers were decreasing as more and more ships made their way between the two countries at much faster speeds.

54 (A last meeting with Patanjali and a farewell to India)

Something seemed to be bothering Issa; Bacha could see it in his face. He had seen it many times before and knew the look well. Whatever it was would come out soon. They had reached Srinagar, which was near the border between Bod and the Indo-Parthian kingdom. Issa suddenly stopped and shouted, "Patanjali!"

Bacha opened his mouth to speak, as Issa continued with great intensity, "We must go to Pratishthana, Bacha. Long ago I made a promise to Patanjali that I would return when I was twenty-nine. That is now my age. I cannot break my vow of Sattya [truthfulness]."

Bacha knew his protest would be futile, but he voiced it nonetheless. "Issa, as Munish has told us, they are still looking for us in the Satavahana Empire. They know that we have shaved our heads and practice Buddhism. Your hair is beginning to grow back, but I am still a shaveling. They will be out looking for us. And remember, I too have taken vows. I can no longer be your protector if it means harming another human being."

"Bacha, if you wish, you may continue your journey home. I will be sad, but I will understand. You too must understand. This is something that I must do."

As Issa turned south toward the Satavahana Empire, however, Bacha turned too. He would not leave his friend and companion to face the dangers of being captured, even if it meant he might be captured as well. Nobody knew who killed that guard seven years ago, but they likely suspected that Issa could not take a life, but that he, Bacha, could. Whatever fate had in store for them, his would be more harsh than Issa's. Of this he was certain. However, they traveled together as they had done for so many years side by side.

They talked of Buddha and Patanjali and Brahminism. They also talked about Galilee and Samaria. Issa was slowly turning his thoughts westward. Many conversations began with, "Remember that time when …" These were happy times for the two of them, but it felt like the end of a piece of their lives was unfolding, an ending and yet a new beginning. But the beginning of what? Their happiness and melancholy were mixed with angst and uncertainty.

It was on the fourth day in the late morning that their worst fears were realized. Men on horses—Kshatryas—were racing directly toward them. There could be no question who they were after; there was nobody else around. Issa and Bacha in turn were swept off the ground and onto the horse of a warrior. The group of warriors now quickly turned around and thundered farther south with their two prisoners. Bacha's and Issa's eyes met, each seeing the terror in the mind of the other. Bacha thought, *If I confess my crime, and truly state how sick Issa became, will they spare his life? I hope so. I can't let my friend die for something he didn't do.*

Soon they were in a camp and dragged off the horses by the warriors and into a tent. The warrior who was apparently in command stood with his back to them. "So, shavelings! You have come to face your fate, have you?" His voice was brusque, his stance, even from the back, was imposing.

Issa replied, "I have come to see my master, Patanjali."

Still with his back to them the warrior said in a much softer voice, "Your command of Maharashtri is quite impressive for foreigners. You must have had an *excellent* teacher." And then he quickly spun around to face them.

"Vijayananda! Is it you? I don't believe it," Bacha shouted. His fear was suddenly replaced with happiness. Issa was smiling too, but it was almost a knowing smile, and Bacha wondered if Issa had used his Siddis.

"Believe it, my two bald friends, it is me. Patanjali knew you would be coming back this year, and so I have had my spies out looking for you. Be glad it is I who found you. If it were someone else you would now be in prison awaiting execution. I apologize for your swift ride, but we needed to get you here quickly, without being seen."

Most of what they told Vijayananda over tea and sweets he already knew. Between his spies and Patanjali's own remarkable Siddis, he had pieced together the story. The only part he didn't know was the trauma that Issa had experienced and that it took such a long time to overcome.

Vijayananda came straight to the point. "You cannot go to Pratishthana, my friends. It is far too dangerous. Besides, Patanjali is not there. Knowing of the danger you would face, he planned for this over a year ago. My duty was to look for you and stop you before you got to Pratishthana."

"Where is he, then," asked Issa?

"He is in Taxila."

**

Issa faintly remembered Patanjali once telling him about the capital city of Gondophares, founder of the Indo-Parthian kingdom. It was a place of great learning. Brahmins and Buddhists alike traveled there to learn from prominent and well respected teachers recognized as authorities. Taxila was also where students went to study the Eighteen Silpas [arts], including hunting and archery. It had a famous medical school and law school. It even taught military science. Because of this, the city was always filled with many different people from all over India and neighboring regions. It was a place where two Buddhists could easily blend in without raising suspicion. This is why Patanjali had chosen this place. He would teach there for several years and then return to his own Pratishthana. And it would be here in Taxila that he would say goodbye to his dear student, Issa.

Issa turned his thoughts toward Hala, the prince who had brought him here so long ago, who had befriended him and sent him out to teach peace throughout India. "And is Prince Hala now king?" he asked.

"He was king for only four years, Issa. He is now married to a beautiful woman named Lilavati, daughter of the king of Ceylon. I had the honor of introducing him to her."

"Tell me truthfully, Vijayananda, did he speak unkindly of Bacha and me when he learned what happened?" Issa was concerned about Hala's feelings toward him and ignored the news of his marriage.

"No. To be honest with you, Issa, he never mentioned you again. His duties as king quickly overwhelmed him. He had time for nothing else. He was not able to keep the peace as he intended, and needed to fight in some pretty big battles. We sometimes fought side-by-side, and he fought well, I have to say.

"He maintained his interest in the arts throughout his reign, but after compiling and composing the Gatha Saptasati, he was never again able to devote his time to his passion. Now he is devoted to his wife. He gave up his throne, in part, to spend more time with her. Mandalaka is now our king, but I fear his reign is coming to an end as well."

"Then he must have been disappointed that I did not spread peace throughout his land. This is what he wanted me to do."

"Issa, listen to what I say. When a farmer plants his seeds, he does so knowing full well that they will not all grow into vegetables. Some will not grow at all. Some will grow but be devoured by birds and insects and wild animals. Those that don't grow do not concern him. Nor does he consider their non-growth to be a failure. It is just the way of things. To Hala, you were such a seed. He tried many things to achieve his goal. He spread many seeds. In the end, not enough seeds grew to bring about a lasting peace. But he never blamed you for this."

Issa was relieved to hear this. "And now he is married, you say? I hope he has found happiness, Vijayananda. In the short time I knew him, I knew that being king was not something he looked forward to."

Issa and Bacha learned that their friend Vijayananda was also now married and had two sons and one daughter. After serving as commander in chief of King Hala's army, he retired to serve as the head of the palace school that trained warriors. The current king, Mandalaka, was very happy with him, but what would happen once his reign ended, Vijayananada didn't know.

"Tomorrow we will travel by horse, north to Taxila. This will get us there quickly. At several places along the way I have fresh horses waiting to carry us farther so that we need not spend valuable time letting the horses rest. Our haste will aid in keeping you two out of sight until we reach the city. Sleep well, my friends. We leave at the crack of dawn."

***

They traveled all the way to Taxila in a bouncing, blistering blur of speed the likes of which neither Issa or Bacha had ever experienced. They would dismount in one town, only to mount the fresh horses waiting for them mere seconds later. They only stopped at night to eat, and sleep a few hours.

By the time they reached their destination, Issa was exhausted. It was early afternoon, but he could have easily slept until the next morning. They bathed in a nearby river and Vijayananda escorted them to the town's center. A class of students were just coming out of a building, and behind them, talking to one of them, Issa recognized his

Master, Patanjali. He appeared to have aged more than the fourteen years they had been apart. He walked more slowly, and used a walking stick. He was now thin and hunched. But his face was unmistakable.

"Issa! You have come!" Patanjali said with a radiant smile. Issa ran to meet him. In pure Indian custom, he fell to his knees and placed his forehead on Patanjali's feet.

Patanjali pulled him up and said, "Issa, let me look at you." He held him by both his shoulders and stared into his eyes. "Yes, I can see the changes in you. Soon it will be me who kneels at your feet. Soon it will be me calling *you* 'Master.'"

"No, Master. You will always be my teacher—my heart teacher. You have no idea how often you talked to me when you weren't even there these past years. I felt your presence always."

"Very well, Issa. As you wish. And you, Bacha, I see a great change in you as well. You are now Buddhist?"

"Yes, Honorable One. I have taken my vows, and I will bring this great message of peace to anyone in my home of Samaria who will listen."

The four of them—Patanjali, Vijayananda, Issa, and Bacha— slowly walked back to the water, where they sat and talked of old times and new adventures. There was so much to share, but so little time to share it in. When the talk turned to Jnyaneshwar and Issa and Bacha's time with the Brahmins, Issa began to grow uncomfortable. He would start to talk, and then stop. Finally he could hold his emotions no more.

Issa sobbed, "Master Patanjali, I wanted so much to please you. But I have much to be ashamed of. I disrespected your idols, I was placed in jail ..." And now he came to the real cause of his discomfort. "Someone was killed because of my doing."

When he said that, it was Bacha's turn to grow uncomfortable. His face grew beet-red, and he twitched uncontrollably.

Patanjali's gentle hand rested on Issa's trembling shoulder, and he smiled at Bacha at the same time. "No, Issa. I know all about this—this incident. Don't blame yourself. You are living out your karma, as you, Bacha, are living out yours. Everything you did in this land, you were meant to do.

"You did some things that turned out badly, it is true, but you *learned* from them and did many good things as well. The good you have done here far outweighs the bad. People will remember you kindly, I promise you, especially the poor. You have grown in wisdom, Issa, and are now ready for greatness. Your journey has not yet ended, but it is not destined to end here. Your true greatness will soon shine in your own land like the light of a thousand suns.

"And to you, Bacha, I say: What you call *sins* in your land we call *mistakes* in our land. To make a mistake is human. To repeat a mistake is the sin. Your duty was to protect Issa, and so you did. And then you changed, Bacha. Not only do I tell you that you will not repeat your mistake, I tell you that you are no longer capable of such an act." Bacha had been looking down at the ground, but lifted his head and nodded slightly.

Then, turning to Issa once again, Patanjali said, "Issa, listen to me carefully." Patanjali stared at him intently, and Issa knew that this was very important. "You still carry inside you the last vestiges of anger. One day soon they will awaken and be cast out of you forever. On that day you will finally be ready to achieve what you have sought from your practices here: Kaivalya.

"But to be able to sit in such a state, there is one more thing you must do. Once all your anger has been removed, you must willingly give up the Siddis, the powers that you now possess. Only then is this greatest of all states possible. You will know all this when it is the right time, and you will clearly remember this conversation. We will say no more about it.

"Now go. I give you my blessings, Issa."

As they neared the top of the first hill, Issa looked over his shoulder one last time to see his friend and master, Patanjali, once a strong and robust teacher and now a thin and frail old man with a melancholy smile on his face, waving to the two of them. Issa paused a moment to store this memory deep in his heart. He looked about absorbing everything: the sun beginning its decent into the west where he was headed, the beautiful surrounding countryside, the fragrant smell of the nearby flowers, the sounds of the birds and crickets, the soft breeze wafting across his face. Once again looking at Patanjali, he waved back, and knew he would never see his master again.

And so Issa and Bacha began their long journey home. They would travel the Silk Route west, finding merchants to journey with. There was safety in numbers, and since Bacha could no longer be the protector he once was, this was the best way to travel.

55 (Parting with Bacha)

AD 27
Yeshua's age: 30

It had taken them nearly a year. They traveled with merchants for most of their journey, but they were alone for the last month. When they saw the Jordan River, they knew they were home. If they had traveled more westward than southward, they would have come into Israel closer to the Sea of Kinneret, and much sooner. But when they forded the Jordan River, they found themselves near Jerusalem.

Although it had been seventeen years since they had departed, the lush landscape and the familiar smells of spring, especially the myrtle, brought a sense of familiarity to the eyes and noses of both Issa and Bacha. As they sat under an oak tree and ate their midday meal, Issa asked his friend and companion, "Bacha, what happens next? Will you stay with me, or go to your own home in Samaria?" He already knew the answer, but asked it anyway.

Bacha said, "Issa, you've shown me so much over these past seventeen years. We've both grown, and I so admire the person you've become. You are so different from that twelve-year-old child I once knew.

"But my journey leads me northwest to my own Samaria. I love my country, Issa, and I love my people just as much as you do yours. I will continue to keep my head shaven, and follow my teachings as I travel around Samaria spreading the word. We won't be far from one another, you and I, and I'm sure we will cross paths often."

"You say I'm different, Bacha. How so?" Issa gazed at his friend as a gentle spring breeze wisped across their faces, filling their noses with the smell of lilies and hyacinth from some distant meadow.

"When I first met you, you were so quick to anger," Bacha said. "Remember at Passover in Jerusalem yelling about the Great Sanhedrin who turned you away? You were so angry you didn't even notice our friend Vijayananda while you yelled. You were also very bullheaded about some of your beliefs. You often argued with Jnyaneshwar even when you knew you were wrong. When we were alone and you let your defenses down, I could see how unsure you were of yourself.

"But over the years you have grown more and more confident in yourself, and less and less angry. It still comes out now and again, but mostly you seem to have that part of yourself under control. When I first met you, you were a child and a student. Now you are a man and a great teacher.

"You've taught me so many things, my little brother, I can't begin to tell you. Truth be told, it was you, not Munish, who turned me away from being a warrior. That day, when I killed that man and I saw your face, I knew I had done a great wrong. As we made our way to Kapilavstu, I felt like I had killed you, Issa. I felt like I had deprived the entire world of a man whom they deserved to have.

"Part of my own recovery was to recount all I had heard you say as we wandered through India. It was as if I had heard all the words, but they had never settled into my heart. Once I let you in, I changed. I knew I could no longer harm another human being. I knew I wanted to be like you. I wanted to be a teacher of great peace and love. So while it was Buddhism's simple message that gave me the tools I needed to teach to my own people, it was you who brought me to it."

Tears were rolling down Issa's face. "Thank you for that, Bacha. You're still my big brother too. You know me better than anyone else. You know my weaknesses as well as my strengths. You've changed me as well. I always admired your strength of character and your ability to read people, knowing from the onset who were to be trusted and who were not. I admired your courage as you moved unafraid from one place to the next. I was always filled with fear when we went to a new home. You went with certainty. And so I watched and learned from you. Some of those things you see in me, Bacha, are just a reflection of yourself."

Now it was Bacha with teary eyes. They both knew that their time together was at last over. Issa's final words to Bacha were that since they were back in their own countries, he would once again take the name of Yeshua. Yeshua is what he was called before he left and what he would now be called. He wanted to embrace his Jewish heritage, and his Jewish name was part of it.

"I don't know, Issa ... I mean Yeshua," Bacha began. "When we first met I had a hard time not calling you Yaish. When I finally got used to calling you Yeshua, Patanjali changed your name to Issa. After some time, I learned to call you that, and now you are going back to Yeshua? I don't know. Maybe I'll just stick with 'little brother!'"

The two laughed, embraced one last time, and Bacha set out to Samaria. Yeshua gazed up at the blue sky and smiled. The future light of a thousand suns began to glow.

56 (Meeting Yochanan the Baptizer)

A heavily bearded man came out of the woods and stood directly in front of Yeshua. He was a strong man, with dark, wild, matted hair and a rugged face that showed he had spent lots of time in the sun. He would have been a scary figure if not for his demeanor, which seemed gentle and non threatening. "Where are you going, friend?" he asked with a smile. His voice was quite deep and loud.

Yeshua thought for a moment. Where *was* he going? He wasn't quite sure.

Before he could answer, the stranger once again spoke: "My name is Yochanan. Some call me Yochanan the Baptizer. Who are you?"

"My name ... Issa—uh, Yeshua. My name ... is ... Yeshua," he replied.

Still smiling, Yochanan asked, "Are you from around here, Yeshua? Your accent is strange."

Yeshua struggled to speak in Hebrew, a language he had not spoken since he was twelve. "I ... born in Nazareth, but ... but been away a very long time." He paused and thought some more. Then he continued while nodding his head, "Now I am home."

Yochanan asked, "Do you have a place to stay tonight? If not, you are welcome to stay with us."

With us? Yeshua looked around but saw no one except Yochanan. *Perhaps Yochanan is married*, he thought.

"I would like that. Thank you."

The smile never came off Yochanan's face. "Come with me, then. I'll introduce you to my family."

The two walked down a twisting path toward the Jordan River, and there, by the river's edge, were nine or ten tents, and about thirty men, women and children. They appeared to be fixing their evening meal. Yochanan pointed toward them and said, "There's my family!" Then shouting, "Everyone! Meet my new friend, Yeshua. Welcome him to our family."

As Yochanan and Yeshua got nearer, the crowd all greeted Yeshua as if he were an uncle or a cousin or a brother. He had experienced this in India, while he was teaching, but never in Israel. He felt more at home than ever before. All he could do was grin and stare at everyone as they hugged him and greeted him. Finally, he said to them all in the same slow, staccato voice he had talked to Yochanan with a few moments earlier, "I have been away a very long time. I ... not speak Hebrew or Aramaic for ... many years, since I was twelve. Please help me as I learn once again."

"Where have you been?" one of the crowd asked.

"In a land far to the—to the ..." Yeshua pointed eastward. Someone said, "east."

"Yes, east. A land to the east of Israel, called *India*."

The one who asked him the question, a rather tall woman, continued her inquiry. "I've heard of that land. It's where nard, that ointment that the rich rub on their bodies, comes from. I hear it smells very nice. And why were you there?"

Because of the Siddis he had learned in India, and because he had known Hebrew as a young child, Yeshua had no problem understanding what his new friends were saying to him. It was in speaking that he had problems. Yeshua said, "It's a long story. Telling it ... help me learn to speak better. If you want to hear it, I will tell you tonight at your ... fire."

Yochanan put his arm around Yeshua's shoulder and said, "He is our guest, my friends. Let him rest and eat and drink before we ask him too many questions."

Yochanan brought Yeshua to one of the tents and said, "You can sleep here tonight. This is my tent, and as you can see, there is plenty of room. Why don't you rest for awhile? You look tired."

Something about Yochanan reminded Yeshua of Bacha. Perhaps it was his good nature, or perhaps because he always seemed to be smiling. Yeshua wanted to learn more about him. He was obviously the leader of this group of people. He would find out tonight.

Yeshua lay in the tent and closed his eyes, but after a few minutes, although he was tired, he found he could not sleep. So instead, he sat and meditated. He brought his mind to the present moment and rested it there without thoughts of the past, or anticipation of the future. He felt at peace.

When he was done, he softened his gaze as he slowly opened his eyes. Yochanan was sitting by him. "What was that you were doing just now?" he asked. "You were sitting with no movement for such a long time. Were you praying?"

"No. Not praying exactly. In India it is called *Dhyana*, meditation."

Yochanan wrinkled his brow. "And what is this meditation?"

Yeshua struggled for Hebrew words. "In meditation you do not hear, or ... or smell, or ..." Yeshua pointed to his tongue.

"Taste?"

"Yes, taste. You do not taste. You do not feel touch. You want nothing. You do not ... think. But you are not asleep. You are very awake. You are one with God. I do this always between the first and second sleep each night. Other times too. But always then. It is much ... better at that time. Better is not the right word, but I can't remember. This better meditation is called *samadhi*."

When he was younger, Yochanan thought he was the only person who woke up in the middle of the night—every night. Later he learned that many others did the same, and used that time between their first and second sleep for reflection.

Yochanan stroked his beard a moment, and then said, "What you describe sounds like *suwach*."

"Suwach?" Yeshua did not remember the word.

Yochanan replied, "Suwach is a profound state of reflection. Like when you are pondering or considering something really important."

"Yes. Suwach. It is close, but meditation is still different. I can teach it to you."

Yochanan's face grew serious for a moment, then his smile reappeared. "I think you and I are destined to teach each other many things. I barely know you, Yeshua, and yet I feel as if I have known you all my life. I know nothing about you, and yet I sense something in you that is special. Yes, I would like to learn this meditation. And hopefully much more once you remember more of your Hebrew. But now it is time to eat. Are you hungry?" Yeshua nodded.

They washed their hands in the community wash basin and sat at the table. Yochanan sat at the head, the place of honor, and Yeshua sat to his right, also a place of honor. Yeshua had forgotten just how good the food was here in Israel. Not spicy, like he was used to eating in India, but plain and wholesome. Spread over the long wooden table were plates filled with fresh fruits and vegetables, and bread and goat's cheese. There was a stew made from lamb, and there were locusts. Yeshua remembered how locusts, to him, tasted like shrimp, and how much he liked them as a child. There was also red wine.

Before they ate, they all joined hands and Yochanan spoke: "Lord, we thank you for these gifts that you give to us tonight. May we be nourished with your food, and with your wisdom. And may we always be mindful of those who are less fortunate than we are, and help them in whatever way we can."

After dinner, everyone helped cleaning up. Not just the women—everyone. Yeshua joined in, as did Yochanan. By the time they were done, the community fire had been started, and everyone moved close and found a place to sit. Yochanan stood in front of them with his back to the fire and said, "Tonight we welcome our special guest, Yeshua. He has promised to tell us of his journeys. I think we are in for a treat."

Where to begin? Yeshua thought. He didn't want to talk about his painful childhood, and so he started with his travels across the Indian Ocean on the great ship the *Gaulus*. He told them of the storm at sea, and of the pirates. He told them about Vijayananda and Patanjali and Jnyaneshwar and Munish. As he spoke, Hebrew words came back to him more and more quickly. Whenever he stumbled over a word, which was often, someone would help him. But his voice was slow and disjointed. Then he began to tell them about what he had learned in India. He tried to speak of the similarity of beliefs of yoga and Brahmanism and Buddhism and that of his own Jewish heritage, but without an adequate command of the language, it came across sounding very strange. This, however, made Yochanan sit up and pay attention even more closely.

When Yeshua was done speaking, everyone sat quietly. They were polite, but clearly Yeshua's struggles with Hebrew made his stories difficult to listen to and comprehend. One of the listeners broke the silence, asking, "What is this *yoga* you speak of?"

Yeshua smiled, his eyes closing, his mind traveling a thousand miles to the east, and remembering his very first lesson with Patanjali when he was but twelve years old. "Yoga is a stillness of the ... the, uh, movements of the mind."

"What does that mean?" the listener asked.

Yeshua replied, "David tells us in Tehillim 46." When speaking about scripture, his words were clearer and he spoke with much more assurance. "David says, 'Be still, and know that I am God.' Talking—I mean, uh, language—is something that was created by man, don't you see? When we communicate with God we need no such thing as language. It is in the silence that we speak to God. It is in the silence that God speaks to us. No words are necessary. No thoughts are necessary. Yoga trains us to find this stillness in our minds so that if we wish, we can communicate with God."

No one asked questions after that, and after a few minutes Yeshua said, "If you wish, I will tell you more tomorrow night." A few nodded their heads politely. Others looked at each other and rolled their eyes. The time for talking was now over. They all stared into the waning, crackling fire, its magical warmth and orange glow drawing their deepest thoughts from them. Over the course of the next hour, one by one, they silently arose and went to their tents.

Soon it was just Yochanan and Yeshua. "Let's go to sleep, Yeshua." Yochanan got to his feet, as did Yeshua. As they quietly walked to the tent, Yeshua resolved to relearn Hebrew as quickly as he could.

57 (Yeshua and Yochanan forge a friendship)

The next morning Yeshua arose and looked for Yochanan, but he was already gone. One of the children, Binyamin, tugged on his tunic and said, "If you are looking for Yochanan the Baptizer, he is up the river, that way." He pointed north.

"Thank you, my young friend," Yeshua said, resting his hand on Binyamin's head.

Yeshua had not yet done his morning meditation, but he was curious. He walked the river's edge, thinking back on the times he had walked on the other side of this same river on his way to and from Jerusalem during Passover. How small it looked to him now that he had seen the Indian Ocean, and how large it had looked to him when he was a child. After walking a few minutes, he came across a large crowd. They had all come to hear Yochanan speak, and he was standing at the water's edge teaching them. Yeshua sat and listened.

Yochanan's voice was like thunder: loud and angry. "Every valley shall be filled, and every mountain and hill shall be brought low. The crooked shall be made straight, and the rough ways shall be made smooth. And all flesh shall see the salvation of God."

Yochanan paused and gazed out at the crowd. Now his voice had more anger in it. "Oh generation of vipers, who warned you to flee from the wrath to come?"

Several of those listening had red faces and looked down. A few others stood and went away.

He continued: "Bring forth therefore fruits worthy of repentance."

Maybe Patanjali was wrong, Yeshua thought. *Maybe it's Yochanan who was meant to be the great spiritual leader.*

Yochanan then said, "So who among you wish to have your sins washed away in the waters of the Jordan River?" A great number of people, maybe fifty, stood. Yochanan walked into the Jordan until he was waist deep, and beckoned. The first who came out to him was a woman. He seemed to ask her a question, but Yeshua could not hear what he asked. She nodded her head affirmatively, and Yochanan held her in his arms like a baby, and dipped her completely under the water. He immediately brought her back up, and the change in her was dramatic. She was laughing and crying at the same time. Her face was beaming, her eyes glowing. She lifted her hands toward the sky and laughed even louder. The people on the shore all shouted, "Praise the Lord." She danced through the water back to the dry land, and hugged everyone near her.

Each person who entered the water gave a similar reaction to this ritual. Some were dramatic, like the first woman, others more subdued. But they were all clearly transformed and elated when they emerged from the water. Something had happened to them.

Off in the distance was an iron chariot with cushioned seats and three beautiful stallions at its front. Several Roman soldiers were guarding it. Yeshua scanned the area, and there, by the water's edge, a Roman sat in an ornate chair, with two guards, one on each side. The chair looked out of place in this bucolic setting, but so did the Romans and the chariot. The man in the chair leaned forward as Yochanan lowered each person into the water, and watched keenly as they came out, as if he were looking for something.

When the last person had been dipped into the Jordan, Yochanan waved to the crowd, and they began to disperse. The Roman in the chair beckoned him, and the two talked for several minutes. Then Yochanan bowed to him and walked southward, back to the camp. The guards with the chariot brought it to the river's edge and loaded the chair into it, and they all climbed in. The man who had been sitting in the chair sat in a throne-like seat at the back, as the Roman at the chariot's front gathered the reins. Off they went in a spectacle of noise and speed. Those who had not yet left stood and watched in awe.

Yeshua continued to have doubts about his mission. It appeared to him that Yochanan was doing what he had hoped to do. The people in India had listened to him and loved him. But the people here in Israel seemed to want to follow Yochanan.

Yeshua caught up to Yochanan, and the two walked back to the campsite together. "I saw you in the back listening. What did you think?" Yochanan asked.

"I understand much more than what I can say. Soon I will be able to speak clearly in Hebrew. What you said to the crowd, Yochanan, was much the same as I have said to people in India. It was like hearing my own words—uh, thoughts. Only you say them much better. You must tell me more about yourself."

Yochanan told Yeshua he had been an Essene for a short time. "I thought I had found what I was looking for, but it was really just more of the same. Rules and rituals, and talk of being the chosen people. I don't hold much to rules or rituals." Yeshua nodded his head in agreement. "As for being the chosen people, I respect our heritage, I really do. But between you and me, Yeshua, I don't think we Jews are the chosen people. I don't think any people can make that claim."

Yeshua stopped him and said, "You are wrong, Yochanan. We are *all* God's chosen people. All of us."

"Even the Romans?" Yochanan was smirking, with his arms folded, but seemed to be testing Yeshua's convictions.

Yeshua remained serious. "Yes, even the Romans. If we fail to love those who hate us, we fail to be more like the God whom we worship."

Yeshua quickly walked in front of Yochanan, turned and stopped, causing Yochanan to stop as well. Yeshua asked, "Why did you call your people vipers?"

Yochanan laughed. "I was not calling my people vipers. Did you see some of them stand and leave when I said that?"

Yeshua nodded.

"Hiding among the crowd were Pharisees and Sadducees. I know who they are. They come to find fault with my words. Often they argue with me and rebuke me. Others come to be baptized just as a caution. They think I am wrong, but just in case I'm right, they want to be looked favorably upon by God."

Yochanan shook his head back and forth. "Vipers."

They resumed walking the shore in silence for a moment, then Yeshua asked, "Who was that Roman who sat in a chair listening to you?"

Yochanan stumbled and almost lost his balance. "That, my friend, was Herod Antipas. Many call him *King* Herod, but he is, in fact, just a Tetrarch. Still, a very powerful man. It is best to avoid him unless he asks to talk to you. He seems interested in what we do here, but I feel he is just making sure I am not preaching rebellion, and that we will not cause him trouble. He comes here often. He has a wife,

Herodias, who trusts us even less. She is more openly contemptuous of us. If you see her with him, stay as far away as possible. I only talk to him because he asks to talk to me."

"What do the two of you talk about?"

"He is mostly interested in miraculous events. He has heard stories of certain Jews performing them—making the blind see, making the deaf hear, raising the dead. He watches as I baptize people to see if anything miraculous is going to happen. He—"

Yeshua interrupted. "Baptize? Is that what you call what you were doing in the water?"

"Yes. It is symbolic of cleansing sins. Not the constant daily bathing like the Essenes; or the ritual purification in the Mikveh that we undertake before entering the temple, just a one-time cleansing. It's a way of beginning anew, sin-free. And as you saw, although it is just symbolic, those who are baptized feel the burden of sin actually lifted from them. That's what makes them so happy."

Yeshua thought of the Buddhist woman who had lost her faith. By wrapping her diseased leg and directing her to talk to her dead husband in her heart, he helped make her well. Different, and yet not so unlike what Yochanan had done. He told Yochanan the story in his stilted Hebrew, and then said, "The power of faith is the miracle that Herod fails to see. It can mend a leg, or cleanse people of their sins."

Yochanan replied, "And now it is me that seems to be hearing an echo! You and I think so much alike, Yeshua. Perhaps you are the one."

"The one?" Yeshua wrinkled his brow.

"I have always felt that I have been making way for someone else. Someone greater than me. A Messiah. Maybe it is you." Yochanan looked intently into Yeshua's eyes.

Yeshua's face grew red, and he looked away. "You are such a great teacher, Yochanan. That was a big crowd who listened to you today. And I love the way you tell a story. Your voice carries the way mine does not. No, I don't think I am greater than you. Maybe it is you that is a Messiah."

"We'll see, Yeshua. As for your voice, simply stand higher than everyone, and they will be able to hear you better. Ask them to sit, while you stand. If you are by the water, and there is a boat that you can stand on, do so. If you are by a hillside, go partly up the hill, while they remain at the bottom. Your voice will be heard, I promise you. I always find the people sitting farthest away from me, and imagine that I am talking just to them. I watch their faces to see if they seem to hear me. If they lean forward, I know I need to speak louder."

Yeshua sat under a tree by the tents after their return. He was so sure of himself before he met Yochanan. He was certain that his mission was about to begin. Patanjali himself had said as much. Now he wasn't sure at all. *Maybe I need to learn from Yochanan first, and then begin my teaching. I wish Bacha were here. He would know what to say.* He went to bed that night full of doubt. He would confront it between his first and second sleep, when he meditated.

58 (Yeshua meets Semadar and visits the wilderness)

It had been a week since Yeshua's arrival. His Hebrew was coming back to him more and more quickly. He still hadn't spoken Aramaic, but decided that he should first get his Hebrew back. He had heard several in Yochanan's family speaking his old familiar Galilean dialect of Aramaic among themselves, and decided he would go to them later to help him relearn his language of origin. He had also decided to spend more time with Yochanan, and learn from him.

"Come, Yeshua, we are going into the city to help the needy." Yochanan was tugging on Yeshua's tunic.

"Help the needy?" Yeshua stood as he questioned Yochanan.

"We go into the surrounding cities each week on the fifth day and help our brothers and sisters in need: the poor, the sick, the old—anyone in need. We bring them food. We tend to their wounds. We pray for them. In the evening I preach to all who will listen. Then, on the sixth day, we return home."

"I am with you," Yeshua said with conviction. "What city are we going to?"

"Today we go to Ephraim."

"Ephraim? Isn't that in the desert of Judea?"

Yochanan was packing food and supplies into a sack. "It's on the eastern edge of it. You have heard of it?"

"Yes. I have an uncle and aunt from there. I'm sure they are both dead by now. They were quite old when I left Israel to go to India."

"Well, we can see if they're still alive when we get there. Let's go."

Yeshua helped Yochanan load the sacks onto a wagon, and they, and ten others, headed west toward Ephraim, the mules pulling the wagons.

As they walked, Yochanan said to Yeshua, "The desert is really quite beautiful. It is where I go whenever I need to think or pray. I like to go farther south where it is much more isolated. I would like to show you some of the places I go sometime. I think you would like it there."

"I think I would like that very much, Yochanan. Maybe you and I could do that on our return to the River Jordan?"

Yochanan nodded in agreement.

As they reached the edge of the city, the poor came in great numbers, begging for food. Yochanan and his family had learned that it was important to be careful how food was dispersed. If done wrong, panic would ensue, and the hungry would turn on the givers and on each other. The more desperate they were, the more likely panic would follow.

"Stand back! Make a line!" Yochanan shouted. "There will be plenty for everyone, I promise."

There appeared to be about a hundred people. Five men stood arm-in-arm between the crowd and the wagon containing the food, keeping people from jumping on the wagon and taking more than what was to be allotted to them. But today, there was no danger. The people of Ephrain did as they were told and stood in a long line. One by one, they received a portion of food that would feed them and their families. Yeshua helped hand the food out. Some had words of thanks, some seemed embarrassed and said nothing, and others snatched the food out of the giver's hands with an angry look on their faces and quickly left.

When the last person had been given food, they packed what remained and headed into the city. Yochanan led the mules and said to Yeshua, "The center of town has a meeting hall. There will be more hungry people there. This is also where they will bring the sick."

"Good. Take me to the sick, Yochanan," said Yeshua. "I can be of greatest help to you there."

"Are you a physician?"

Yeshua smiled. "God is the physician. My body is simply one of His instruments. I have learned a great many healing techniques in India, and look forward to using them."

When they arrived, it was as Yochanan had said. Another forty or fifty people were gathered, waiting for food, the sick were inside lying on beds or sitting on the ground. Yeshua immediately went to them. He began treating wounds, using plants from a bag he carried with him.

It was a common practice to use cabbage with warm water as a poultice to treat wounds, but Yeshua had learned much from Samik the Ayurvedic physician before he left India and had plants with him that nobody had ever used in Israel before. He spread some plants on one person's wounded leg, wrapped it in a cloth, and then poured warm water over the cloth. The man's eyes seemed to show a lessening of pain, and he smiled at Yeshua.

"Pour warm water over this cloth again tonight before you go to bed, and tomorrow, take the cloth off," Yeshua said. I will give you some of these plants. Wait until the afternoon and do the same thing I just did. After three days, your wound should be healed."

A woman began screaming, and everyone looked in her direction. One of the sick said to Yeshua, "That's Semadar. She's possessed. Better not go near her. She scratches and spits."

Yochanan was nearby and added, "Yes. She was here the last time we came. Nobody seems able to help her."

Yeshua quietly walked in her direction. "Yochanan, Abraham, help me hold her down."

As the three neared, her eyes widened, and her face contorted as she screamed louder and louder. She struck out at them with her long fingernails. It took the three of them to hold her down. Yochanan asked, "And now what, Yeshua?"

Yeshua was unsure if a mantra he had learned in India would have the same effect on an Israeli, but Jnyaneshwar had assured him that it was the vibration of the sound that helped bring about the cure. He held her earlobe and whispered the healing mantra into it.

Yochanan and Abraham stood up wide-eyed and with mouths open as Semadar immediately ceased her struggling and closed her eyes. Yeshua stayed at her side for a few minutes.

She opened her eyes, looking around her as if she were lost, and asked, "What happened? Where am I?"

Yeshua held her hand and said, "You are safe now, Semadar. You are among friends."

"Who are you?"

Yeshua smiled and said, "My name is Yeshua."

She looked puzzled. "You talk strangely. You aren't from around here, are you?"

"I am from Nazareth," he replied.

Her face brightened. "And I am from Magdala." She began speaking to him in the Galilean dialect of Aramaic spoken in Nazareth, but Yeshua put a finger to her mouth to quiet her. "Please speak to me in Hebrew, Semadar. I have been away a long time and have not spoken in Aramaic for many years."

She began to speak again, this time in Hebrew, but again Yeshua interrupted her. "Semadar, you need to rest. We will talk again, I promise. But right now, you need to sleep." He whispered another mantra into her ear, this time assured of its result, and she once again closed her eyes.

As Yeshua went from person to person, Yochanan and the others watched. They too, attended to the sick, but they all watched what Yeshua was doing. When they were finally done, Yochanan said, "You are truly a gifted physician, Yeshua. And what you did to Semadar ... I've never seen that before. Do you know that several priests have tried to help her to no avail? What exactly did you do?"

"Not what I did, Yochanan, what God did. I told you, I am just an instrument."

"Well, I am anxious to see what else you can do—uh, what else God can do!"

***

It was early morning, and the sun had scarcely journeyed above the horizon. The carts were loaded, and Yochanan and his helpers began their walk home. Semadar, whom Yeshua had cured, was going to come with them and join their family. She seemed eager to walk next to Yeshua. She was short, like Yeshua, and slender. As they walked east toward the River Jordan, she asked in Hebrew, "So, Yeshua, why have you not spoken Aramaic so long that you need to relearn it?"

Yeshua turned toward her. She was much prettier now that she was no longer sick, and had had time to clean herself. She needed to cut her deep red hair short because it had become so matted that it was impossible to comb out. Even so, she was striking. Her face was without blemish, and her eyes were a beautiful shade of green. "I have lived in another land, India, since I was twelve. I have only been back here for a week."

"I want to thank you again for what you did for me. I have been sick a long time. Where did you learn how to do that?"

Yeshua reached for her hand to help her over a fallen tree in the road. "I learned many things in India, including that. But Semadar, we should always attribute such things to God. God works through us, if we let Him, but we should never take credit for His work."

Semadar looked into his eyes longer than she should have, and Yeshua turned his own toward the ground, blushing slightly, as they continued walking. "Tell me about yourself. You are from Magdala? The town on the northwest shore of the Sea of Chinnereth? I was there once when I was a child."

"Yes, that is the one. When I became possessed by evil spirits last year, my parents sent me here to be cured by a priest who is supposed to be an expert at that sort of thing. But he could not help me. He called in some of his fellow priests, but they could not help me either. My parents are wealthy, but they learned that there are things money cannot buy."

Yeshua smiled at that last remark. "If your parents truly learned that, then they are very smart. Many wealthy people never see that truth. At least I found it to be so in India. Were you a happy child?"

Each time she would stumble, Semadar would reach out for Yeshua's arm, and he, in turn, would reach out toward her. "Yes, I was a very happy child. I lived in a beautiful home next to the water, I had everything I could ever want—yes, I was happy."

"But?" Yeshua sensed there was something she was holding back.

"When I became old enough to marry, my father offered me to a man named Shimon. He was nice enough, but not my idea of a husband."

"And so you married?"

"Yes. He died two years ago. He was sick for three months, finding it harder and harder to breathe. It was difficult to watch. After he died, I found myself feeling happier than when he was alive. Why is that, I wonder?"

"Maybe you were happy that he was no longer in pain?"

"Yes, that must be it." Semadar didn't seem to answer him with much conviction, but Yeshua knew she would tell him in her own time. She continued, "What about your childhood?"

Yeshua was quiet for a moment, and spoke in a lower voice than before. "Semadar, I'm not ready to talk about my childhood. Some day

295

I promise I will tell you everything, but for now, I would request that you not ask me again."

The change in mood brought with it an uncomfortable silence. After some time, Yeshua said, "Semadar, Yochanan is going to help me. He and I are going into the wilderness, and will meet you all at the River Jordan when we have spent some time there. I should go let him know that I am ready."

"Are you angry with me, Yeshua? I didn't mean to pry."

"No, no, Semadar." Yeshua placed his hands on her shoulders, like he had seen his stepfather do to his mother. "Don't feel like you have done anything wrong. I have enjoyed our talk, and I really want to talk more to you. You can help me learn Aramaic once again. I would like that very much. Will you help me learn when I return?"

Semadar nodded her head but said nothing, and Yeshua walked quickly to the front of the wagons where Yochanan was. "I am ready," he said.

***

As the rest of the group continued east, Yochanan and Yeshua turned south, going deeper into the wilderness. "This is like a second home to me, Yeshua," Yochanan said as they trudged through the sand. The sun painted their surroundings in shades of reddish-orange and bluish-gray. "Do you see that peak off in the distance? The one that stands much taller than the rest? That's where we are headed. Once there, we will turn east, toward the Sea of Salt. Remember this, if you ever come back here."

The two were quiet as they walked, conserving their energy. They stopped once to drink water from their skins. Yeshua just sipped it in order, he reasoned, to conserve. "No, no," Yochanan said to him. "Don't sip. It won't nourish you if you only sip. Drink only what you need, but *drink*."

Yeshua did as Yochanan said, and they continued toward the distant mountain. It took longer than Yeshua expected, and he was feeling the effects of this physically demanding walk through the heat of the desert. As they turned east, Yochanan said, "Don't worry. We are very near. See those two mountains now that stand side-by-side, and look like they are the same size? Just beyond them is the Sea of

Salt. We walk in that direction, toward the point between them, but we won't go all the way there."

After another hour, Yochanan said, "We are here, Yeshua. My cave." The mountain that stood before them was not very high, and a few feet up was a huge circular opening. They hoisted themselves up and went inside. It was a respite from the hot sun.

"You need to concern yourself with four things when you are alone in the desert, Yeshua: food, water, fire, and shelter. The least important is food. You can go without food for two or three weeks if you need to. I have done so myself. Bring food with you, by all means, but know that you can do without it. I can also show you how to find food out here if you have none. But after a day without food, you will no longer feel hungry.

"Next is shelter. This cave has been my shelter for as long as I have been coming out to this desert wilderness, since I was a child. And now it belongs to both of us. Use it whenever you like. Fire at night is important. It not only keeps you warm on cold nights, it keeps the animals away. But you know that. It is the same whether you are in the desert or not. That leaves the most important thing: water. Come, my friend. I will show you where you will always find water."

Yeshua wasn't looking forward to yet another walk so soon after the one that brought them to the cave, but Yochanan promised it would be worth it. The two walked east toward the Red Sea. Because it was now early afternoon, the sun was moving behind them. Yochanan, who was very much at home in this place, quickened his pace. Looking behind, he saw Yeshua struggling to keep up. "Come, Yeshua. It's not far now."

They arrived at a steep drop off into a valley, which Yochanan began to work his way down. Yeshua followed, stumbling as he went. "Getting back up is a little harder," Yochanan yelled back, "but we're not going down much farther."

Yeshua noticed that the air was much cooler. After a few more moments of descent, Yeshua saw where Yochanan was bringing him, and why the air was cool: A huge pool of water lay at the bottom of the rocks they were climbing down. Yochanan dropped his robe, dove into it, and swam to its center. "Can you swim, Yeshua? It's deep here, and you will need to."

Yeshua's answer was to drop his robe and dive in after him. They laughed and played as if they were children. After some time, they swam back to the pool's edge and pulled themselves up.

They sat in silence for a moment, catching their breath. Yochanan turned to Yeshua. "Here you can both drink and bathe. This pool is always here, and always full. It is pure, not salty. I have been here at all times of the year since I was eight years old. But we have come here late in the day, and we need to get back before it gets dark. I just wanted you to see where it was. And now you know. Fill up your water skin, and let's get back to my cave."

The climb back up was, as Yochanan warned, a bit harder. The sun was moving quickly toward the western horizon. But the water had refreshed them both, and they arrived at the cave just as darkness began to swallow up the desert. Yochanan worked diligently to light the fire, and when he had, Yeshua helped slowly stoke it with larger and larger pieces of wood. "Where did you get this wood, Yochanan?" Yeshua asked.

"I'll show you tomorrow. Now you need to do something for me."

"What is it, Yochanan?"

"Teach me this meditation you have spoken of."

Yochanan did not need much instruction. He had likely meditated before without knowing what it was called. Yeshua taught him the sound of *om*. He gave Yochanan instructions on how to out-trick the monkeys of the mind. "The mind does not like to be watched, Yochanan. Whenever it tries to make you think, simply watch it instead, without judgment. It will soon enough stop trying. Once it is quiet, watch your breath. Become aware of each breath you take. Even count your breaths if you wish. But as soon as you get to five, go back to one. Soon you will stop counting on your own. Now, in this beautiful silence, become aware of the present moment. Know that you and God are one."

Yeshua no longer felt unsure of himself. He felt like he had felt in India. The two sat in meditation until the fire was almost out. Neither of them spoke after this. Yochanan stirred up the red-hot ashes and threw some more logs on them, and when the logs had caught fire, they both went to sleep.

Morning came, and Yeshua was, as usual, awake first. He smiled at Yochanan as his friend sat up and rubbed his eyes. "Did you sleep well, Yochanan?"

"I slept better than I ever have before. Does meditation do that to you?"

"It can, Yochanan. You should make time to do it every morning and every evening. And, if you are like me, you will do it between your first and second sleep."

"I think I just had one long sleep last night, Yeshua. I think I needed it."

Yeshua sensed there was something on Yochanan's mind, but waited quietly until Yochanan was ready. After some time, Yochanan spoke. "Yeshua, why did you not try to find your aunt and uncle in Ephraim? And why have you not talked about your parents? Are they alive? And if they are, don't you want to see them again?"

Yeshua answered, "When I gave up my name in India and became Issa, I gave up my former life—my family, my friends, my home. I proclaimed my vows to my master, Patanjali, and to all the people who came to witness this event. I have lived those vows all this time; twenty years. So you see, I am no longer that person I once was. I no longer have a mother. I no longer have a stepfather. I have no brothers or sisters. I have no aunts or uncles. This is why I did not choose to try to find the people who used to be my aunt and uncle."

"And yet you now call yourself Yeshua once again."

"Yes. Now that I am back in Israel, I choose to call myself by my Jewish name."

"So something you once gave up as part of your vows, you now reclaim?"

Yeshua looked down at the ground. "Yochanan, to be honest with you, I am very confused about many things now that I am back home. How well you know me. Yes, I would like to see my mother above all others. And yet, I feel like I would be betraying all that my master, Patanjali, taught me, if I sought her out. This is why I wish to learn how to survive in the desert. It is here that I will one day come to sort out all of my problems."

"But not today?"

"No, Yochanan. Not today. I first need to feel like I belong once again. This is my home, yet I feel like a stranger. I left it when I was only twelve. Now I am thirty-two. I need to be able to speak my language once again. I need to learn more about my people. I need to see them, as well as my homeland, through the eyes of an adult."

"And so you will remain true to your vows?"

"For now, Yochanan. For now."

59 (Semadar shows feelings toward Yeshua)

It had been many months since Yeshua and Yochanan had returned from the wilderness. Semadar had made good friends with many of the family, and her fascination with Yeshua was evident to all. The two were together all the time. They now spoke in Aramaic to one another. It came back to Yeshua much quicker than Hebrew.

It was several hours before their evening meal. Yochanan was still at the river teaching and baptizing. Yeshua listened to him almost every day, except this time. He and Semadar were gathering wild berries for dinner. They both reached for the same berry. Yeshua found it first; Semadar found his hand. She continued to hold it and looked deeply into Yeshua's eyes. She moved closer to him. Her lips were moist and slightly parted.

Yeshua blushed. "What's the matter, Yeshua?" Semadar asked, somewhat seductively. "Am I doing anything wrong?"

"Semadar, I—I ..." Yeshua broke her grip and turned away from her. "I can't. I can't do this. This is all wrong." He shook his head from side to side, and lifted his shoulders, his palms toward the sky, and then dropped them.

Semadar walked around him to face him once again. "What can be wrong with this? We are attracted to one another, aren't we? We both see that, don't we? So tell me what is so wrong."

In the silence that followed, her demeanor changed. Before she had looked seductive. Then, when Yeshua first broke away, she looked puzzled. Now she looked deadly serious. Yeshua sat and beckoned her to do the same. "It's complicated, Semadar. I suppose I should have told you all this before. It just never seemed like the right time."

Semadar narrowed her eyes, folded her arms, and said. "Yes. Maybe you should tell me, *Yeshua*. Maybe you should tell me this *complicated* thing."

She sat across from him, her arms still folded, her eyes now cold. Yeshua couldn't bear to look at her. He turned his head toward the ground. As best he could, he told Semadar the vows he had taken in India twenty years ago, and all the things he had vowed to give up. The desire for sex and family. The desire for wealth and comfort. The desire for fame and reputation.

When he was done, Semadar was livid. She was almost spitting as she spoke. "And so you led me on all these months, knowing that we could never be together? You couldn't have told me when we first met? What a horrible thing to do to me, Yeshua. What kind of man are you?"

He grabbed her hands, but she forcefully pulled them away. Semadar then got up and began walking swiftly back to the tents. "Semadar, wait!" Yeshua cried out. "Let me explain." She paused for a brief moment without turning around, and cocked her head, as if waiting for him to say more. But when he didn't, she hurried away. He wasn't sure what he would have told her if she had come back. He wasn't sure what he felt.

He sat there for a long time trying to think things through. And then he began to gasp. Before long, his gasping escalated into crying. He lay face down on the ground and cried in anguish for several minutes. Hurting the people he loved was not what he wanted to do. Especially Semadar. It was true what she said. He did have feelings for her, feelings he hadn't felt since he was first in India and met Chitralekha. But he knew from the start that he could not—no, *would* not give up his vows. Had he purposely not told Semadar of his vows when they first met, like she had said? Did he want to keep her close because of his feelings toward her, knowing all the while that they could never be lovers? He was so torn. He felt guilty and ashamed.

Yeshua did not eat that night. He stayed where he was until it was way past dark. Then he got up and went into the tent and fell asleep.

60 (Semadar becomes Yeshua's first disciple)

Semadar and Yeshua avoided each other for two weeks. Sometimes, when everyone was cleaning up after a meal, they would accidentally brush shoulders, or bump into one another. They would both say "I'm sorry" at the same time, much to the amusement of the rest of the family.

On the fifth day of the third week, Semadar made the first move. "Yeshua," she said to him that morning, "let's go somewhere and talk. We can't go on pretending the other doesn't exist."

Yeshua reluctantly followed her to a spot they had gone to often in the past. They sat facing each other, looking directly at each other for the first time since Semadar had walked away from him. "So, Yeshua, do your vows prevent you from being *friends* with me?"

Yeshua was puzzled. "But ... but ... no. I can be friends with anyone. But I thought you said you wanted more than friendship. Didn't you say that?"

This time it was Semadar who bowed her head and looked down to the ground. "I did want that, Yeshua. I am attracted to you, and I know that in spite of your vows, and in spite of what you may say, you are attracted to me. I can't change that. And apparently I can't change you. But I would rather have you as a friend than not know you at all."

"As would I, Semadar. And now I should tell you some more of my past, so that you can better understand me."

She looked into his eyes and waited. He was silent for a moment, and then began speaking. "When I was a child, I was gifted in one thing, Semadar: scripture. Even as a nine-year-old, I understood the meaning behind the words almost as soon as I read them, or they were read to me. It was as if God Himself were helping me understand. And I found it easy to tell the stories of the scriptures in ways that everyone could grasp their meaning.

"But the other children only laughed at me and teased me and even beat me up. My mother had married, but after I was conceived, and before I was born, my father was murdered. That's when she moved to Nazareth. When it was evident that she was with child, nobody in Nazareth believed her when she said that she had been married. They all thought she was a sinner, and many thought she should be stoned to death as it is written in our laws.

"With the help of my teacher; the town rabbi, Rabbi Towbiyah, she was spared. But the whole town still thought that she was a sinner and I was a bastard. They even used her name to call me a bastard. They called me 'Yeshua, son of Mara.' Our whole family was castigated by the people of Nazareth."

"How awful for you," Semadar said. She reached over and found his hands with her own.

"Since that time, I have been almost killed by children in Samaria, almost murdered in Jerusalem, and locked up in prisons in India. I was close to having my tongue cut off once. Things such as these have happened to me all my life. But my master, Patanjali, a great man who lives in India, told me that I would one day become a great spiritual leader. He has this ability to see into the future."

Now Yeshua sat up taller and opened his eyes wide. "And it is real, Semadar. All the way over in India, he was able to see a plot to kill me when I was twelve years old, before he ever knew me, and sent a great warrior to Jerusalem to prevent it from happening. That's how real his powers are."

Semadar stood and beckoned Yeshua to do the same. She wrapped her arm around his, and they began walking, arm in arm.

Yeshua continued. "From the time I was thirteen until last year, when I came back to Israel, I have been studying and teaching the philosophies of India. They are in so many ways identical to what we believe here, although they are worded differently, and their spiritual customs are much different from ours. But the truth is that God's message is the same, regardless of your religion.

"Patanjali told me that I would one day be a great spiritual leader. I believed him when he told me that, and I came back here prepared to begin my mission. But everyone here seems to follow Yochanan. I'm not angry or jealous. I am, however, confused. Sometimes I think maybe Patanjali was wrong in his vision. Maybe he mistook me for Yochanan. Maybe it is Yochanan who is supposed to be the great spiritual leader and my mission is to help him. I just don't know, Semadar.

"And as for my vows; I have followed them for almost fifteen years. They are now a part of me. When I was thirteen, I was attracted to a girl in India named Chitralekha. But—"

Semadar giggled. "You had a girlfriend in India? Yeshua, you never told me that."

Yeshua ignored her playful taunt and went on, "But my master, Patanjali, showed me how to have friendship with women, even with those feelings inside me. Chitralekha became my friend and I rejoiced at her marriage. I was never again attracted to a woman—that is, until I met you." They stopped walking and looked into one another's eyes for a long time.

"What are you saying, Yeshua?"

Yeshua took a deep breath. "Being attracted to someone as an adult is much different from being attracted to someone as a child. The feelings are much stronger—much deeper. In these past few days I have meditated and resolved these feelings. I love you, Semadar, but I love you like I love everyone else, without thoughts of sex or of family. You are, and will always be, special to me. In that one way, Semadar, you are different from everyone else. But we can never be more than friends. Special friends, to be sure, but—friends."

Semadar continued to look into his eyes, and he did not look away. She said, "I have watched you and your amazing healing powers when we go into cities on the fifth day, Yeshua. You are a gifted physician. Yochanan can't begin to do the things you do. I have heard you comfort the sick and the poor with your words. I have listened to you speak at night at the fires. I have listened to those wonderful stories that you tell only to me when we are together. I believe you are already a great spiritual leader.

"These people here—these are Yochanan's followers. They may listen to you, but it is Yochanan whom they follow. That's another thing that can't be changed. But I am a believer in you, Yeshua. And if you will have me, I will be your follower. Think of me as your first follower of many."

When she had said that, Yeshua reached over and held both of her hands in both of his. "I am honored to have you as a follower, Semadar. For now, I will continue to learn from Yochanan. Perhaps in another year I will feel ready to begin my mission. You see, I made many mistakes in India. I don't want to make them here. So I will listen to Yochanan, I will learn all I can from him, and I will plan. Then, when the time is right, I will take myself far away from Yochanan and his followers and begin my own teaching."

Yeshua knew Semadar was unhappy with his decision to wait a year. He could see it in her eyes, in the way she folded her arms suddenly, in the tension in her neck. But he had made his decision, and would not be dissuaded.

61 (Yeshua's decision to leave)

AD 29
Yeshua's age: 32

Over the next year, each night, after everyone went to sleep, Yochanan and Yeshua stayed at the fire and talked of spiritual matters. Yeshua taught Yochanan more about meditation, and in turn, Yochanan taught Yeshua many methods he used when speaking before a large crowd. But mostly they talked of their faith. Yeshua would share with Semadar much of what they had discussed later the next day. She chose not to join them in their nightly discussions so as not to interfere with the close relationship the two men had.

At first, Yochanan and Yeshua rarely disagreed. Lately, though, they were finding differences in their beliefs. This night, they were discussing the Messiah. Yochanan believed, as he had been told when he was with the Essenes, that there would be two Messiahs. The first, the Messiah of David, would be a kingly person who would lead Israel in a war. The Messiah of Aharon, on the other hand, would be a priestly person who would restore the temple at Jerusalem, and it would become pure again. The Messiah of David would lead them in the ultimate war—good against evil. Yochanan truly believed that it would be a war of weapons, and the Romans would be defeated and driven out of Israel. Others among the Essenes felt it would be a war of ideas, and the Sons of Light, as the Essenes often called themselves, would defeat the Sons of Darkness, the disbelievers, through words and ideas alone.

"What do you think, Yeshua? Is a Messiah coming? Are two Messiahs coming?"

"Here is what I believe, Yochanan. As you well know, the Pharisees pick apart our holy scriptures, and have thus far found 456 passages that prophesize the coming of the Messiah. According to them, then, a Messiah would have to meet the requirements of each of these passages. Many of these passages contradict one another. Thus, the Pharisees will never find their version of the Messiah. Of this I am certain.

"So what is a Messiah, really? Our people are starving for freedom. But the Romans are oppressing us. Our people are starving for the true word of God. But the Pharisees are confusing us with their unique interpretations of the scripture. Our people are starving for equality. But the Sadducees are turning their backs on us and conspiring with the Romans. Our people are starving for unity. But the Essenes are deserting us and living apart from us. Our people are starving for peace, but the Zealots are murdering Romans, Greeks, and even Jews who do not agree with them.

"Anyone who can be the bridge that brings *all* of us together might well be called the Messiah by others. This is what I believe. And when I talk of bringing us together, Yochanan, I'm not just talking about us Jews. I'm talking about Romans and Egyptians and Samaritans and Greeks. I'm talking about everyone, Yochanan. Everyone."

Yochanan grew agitated. "No. You are wrong, Yeshua. The Messiahs *are* coming. I just know they are. With them leading us, we will drive our oppressors out of Israel for good. Let the Egyptians and Samaritans and Greeks find their own Messiah. The two I am speaking of are Messiahs for the Jews alone."

Yeshua clasped his hands in his lap and shook back his hair. "Then, Yochanan, I hope you one day find your Messiah, or Messiahs."

Yochanan stood and began to pace. He always did this when he was searching for answers to tough questions. Finally he turned, as if he had found what he was looking for, pointed his finger at Yeshua, and said in a loud voice, "The Romans will never leave of their own accord. They are warrior-like in their ways. Your message of unity will never resonate with them. You cannot defeat them with words."

Yeshua was calm. "No, Yochanan. I cannot defeat them with words. God does not ask us to defeat our enemies. He asks that we love our enemies."

Yochanan glared at Yeshua. "Bah! Where is it written that we must love our enemies?"

Yeshua responded, "Two of our greatest leaders were Moshe and David. Here is what they tell us. First, Moshe, in the scroll of Shemot: If you come upon your enemy's ox or donkey straying, you must return it to him. If you see the donkey that belongs to someone who hates you lying down helpless under its load, you are not to pass him by but to go and help him free it.

"Next, David tells us in the scroll of Tehillim: Malicious witnesses come forward, asking me things about which I know nothing. They repay me evil for good; it makes me feel desolate as a parent bereaved. But I, when they were ill, wore sackcloth; I put myself out and fasted. I can pray that what I prayed for them might also happen to me. I behaved as I would for my friend or my brother; I bent down in sorrow as if mourning my mother.

"When a child misbehaves and says that he hates you, is it better to yell at him and send him away? Or is it better to love him and show him the right way to act?"

Yochanan raised his voice even louder. "The Romans are not children, Yeshua. You know that."

Now Yeshua raised his voice. "We are all God's children, Yochanan. Would you smite someone, knowing he was a son of God?"

The loud arguing of the two had brought many people out of their tents. They nervously gathered by the fire and watched this scene unfolding.

Yochanan began pacing again. "It's useless arguing with you. I tell you we will eventually have to fight the Romans, no matter what you say."

Yeshua scooped up a large stone and placed it in Yochanan's hand. "I am a Roman child. I am seven years old. I throw stones at you because my father tells me you are evil. I believe what my father tells me, because he is always right. I have just thrown a stone at you. What will you do?" Yeshua scooped up a handful of smaller stones and began pelting Yochanan with them, one at a time. "What will you do?" he asked loudly as each stone found its mark.

The crowd grew larger, some rubbing the backs of their necks, others biting their lips. Yochanan was growing angrier. He ducked the latest pebble and suddenly drew his arm back, his hand holding the stone tightly, his eyes wide, his teeth clenched. Then he paused. He stood there like a statue for what seemed like a long time. The crowd leaned forward to see what would happen next. His mouth began to quiver, and then he threw down the stone and brusquely stalked back to his tent, ignoring the crowd. Yeshua dropped what was left of his pebbles. It was over. Yeshua too left. The crowd that had gathered now looked at one another, but not a single word was spoken. Then, one by one, they too went back to their tents.

Yeshua lay in bed and thought for some time that night. He had been living with Yochanan and his family for almost two years. He had taught at the Jordan River some of the time, but the crowds mostly came to hear Yochanan, not Yeshua. Yet he was burning with desire to share his simple message with everyone, and concluded that going away might be the best way to begin. He would start at the Sea of Chinnereth, far away from where Yochanan was teaching. This is where he longed to be anyway. And though they differed in some ideas, like the Messiah, and dealing with Romans, for the most part Yochanan and Yeshua were united in their beliefs.

The next morning when Yochanan awoke, Yeshua was sitting beside him. "Yochanan, I'm sorry for last night. I know how deeply you believe in your quest. I told Semadar when she first came here that you would be my last teacher before I began my own teaching. I think now is that time."

"Fine. Leave me, Yeshua. Go where you will." He rose abruptly and left the tent.

When Yeshua went outside a few minutes later, Yochanan was gone. "Where did he go?" Yeshua asked a family member standing nearby.

"He went down the river to teach and baptize. He said he was not hungry, and would miss our morning meal," Yeshua was told.

Yeshua sought out Semadar. She was with some of the other women, helping prepare the food. "Semadar, can we talk for a moment?" he asked.

Semadar saw that he wanted to talk in private and rose and walked with him, placing her arm inside his. When they were alone he turned to her. "Semadar, it is time. I leave today for the Sea of Chinnereth. My mission begins."

Semadar broke into a smile and embraced him. "Finally! I have waited to hear those words for so long, Yeshua. I will tell the others that I am leaving."

"No," Yeshua said. "I need to spend some time by myself, Semadar. I will first go into the wilderness. I'm not sure for how long. One day? Three days? Perhaps forty days. There are things in my mind I need to resolve. And then, I will make my way to the Sea of Chinnereth. Meet me there, Semadar. We will find one another, I am certain. It will give you time to think things over as well. You must be sure. You are either my follower or you are not. There is no in-between."

"I am more sure than I have ever been before. Have you told Yochanan yet?"

"I think Yochanan does not want to hear anything from me right now. We had a pretty bad argument last night, worse than any we have had before. He was quite angry when he left this morning. I told him I was leaving, but I didn't exactly say when."

"I heard the two of you yelling last night from my tent. But you must tell him, Yeshua. You can't just leave without saying goodbye. Even if he is angry, you owe him that. He has done so much for you. Go to him."

Yeshua threw his hair back. "You're right, Semadar. I *will* go to him. I'll make things right between us before I leave. I promise. You go back to prepare the morning meal. I will go to Yochanan."

"Goodbye, Yeshua. I will look for you around the Sea of Chinnereth. I will wait for you."

He walked the path to the river, wondering what he would say to Yochanan. When he arrived, there was a line of new followers waiting to be baptized. Herod was there too, sitting in his usual spot on his ornate chair, watching for a miracle, no doubt. The followers would wade out to where Yochanan was, and he would ask them if they were ready to truly follow the path of God. They would say yes, and Yochanan would dip each one into the water. Many would be in a state of ecstasy when they were lifted out, which would only add to the excitement of those still in line. Yeshua suddenly knew exactly what he needed to do. He stepped into the line.

Yochanan had baptized seven persons when he saw Yeshua wading out to meet him. Yochanan watched as Yeshua neared. All his anger seemed to disappear in an instant, and he grinned at Yeshua, who grinned back at him. They embraced as the crowd on the shore, many of whom had witnessed the fierce argument of the night before, cheered. Yochanan then faced the crowd, with one arm around Yeshua's shoulder. He spoke loudly and with authority: "I have told you all before that one greater than me would come after me. *This* is that person I spoke of. This is Yeshua. I am not worthy to stoop down and untie the thongs of his sandals, let alone baptize him. I have baptized you all with water, but he will baptize you with the Holy Spirit."

Yeshua quietly said to him, "Yochanan, my good friend, I ask that you baptize me. You are doing great things here. You are bringing our people back to God. I have not yet started my ministry, but you have been instrumental in my training. I have quietly watched you and listened to you. You have inspired me greatly, Yochanan, and I will take with me much of what I have heard you say. Now, please baptize me, my friend."

Yochanan held Yeshua and dipped him beneath the water. As the waters closed around Yeshua, he was filled with rapture, unlike anything he had felt before. It felt as if he was only now beginning his life. He rose, placed both his hands on Yochanan's shoulders, and said, "Goodbye my friend. I will miss you."

"As I will miss you, Yeshua. Safe journeys, my friend." Yeshua walked to the shore as all the people watched him, turned to wave goodbye to Yochanan, and went far away from the crowds.

Herod continued watching from the shore as this event took place. He sensed this was something different from what he had seen in the past. When Yochanan had baptized the last person and came to shore, Herod beckoned to him. "Yochanan, who was that man you gave so much credit to?"

Yochanan bowed and said, "His name is Yeshua, Prefect."

Herod stiffened at being called "Prefect" instead of "King," but he allowed it from Yochanan. Anyone else he might have imprisoned or killed on the spot, or lock them up, but there was something about Yochanan that made him treat the baptizer differently from all the other Jews. "You said he was greater than you. You have spoken in the past of such a person. Is it he?"

"Yes, Prefect. I believe it is."

"How can you be so sure?"

"Because I have seen him perform miracles."

"Miracles? He performs miracles? What miracles? Tell me." Herod's eyes were wide and he was almost trembling.

Yochanan spoke of Yeshua whispering in someone's ear and casting out their demons. He spoke of Yeshua healing sores with a sort of heat that came from his hands. He had used this unusual heat in his hands to burn the wax from people's ears, allowing them to hear once again.

"I must find this Yeshua and have him perform a miracle for me," Herod said.

But Herod would not find Yeshua that day. He was on his way to a wilderness where Herod and his guards would not go.

62 (Into the wilderness and temptation)

Yeshua walked toward the Judean desert. He looked south and found the peak that was taller than the rest, heading toward Yochanan's cave. It took longer than he remembered, but when he got to the mountain, he turned east.

There they are, he thought. *The two mountains that appear to be the same size*. He headed toward the spot between them. It was much hotter that day than it was when he and Yochanan had last gone there, and he was walking much more slowly. Another hour passed, and he still wasn't there. He stood for a moment staring ahead, wondering if he had chosen the wrong mountains to walk toward. It had been a long time since was last there. *No*, he though, *this has to be right. I'll just keep walking*. The two mountains in the distance were now closer than he remembered seeing them before.

And then he saw Yochanan's cave straight ahead. He climbed up into it, sat with his legs crossed, and took a long drink of water. "And now," he said aloud, "I will not eat or drink until my meditation has ended." He set his water skin down and began to focus attention on his throat, because one of the Siddis he had learned was that by performing Samyama on the throat there would be a cessation of hunger and thirst. He wished to be in meditation for a long time, and didn't want hunger or thirst to distract him.

And so he sat for the remainder of the day and into the night. Somewhere in the darkness he began to dream or to have a vision. At first he saw what looked like distant stars, blinking on and off. Then he noticed the many colors of the stars. When he thought of the color red, all the red stars would suddenly come together, whirling and whirling, growing in number, and suddenly rush toward him and through him. When this happened he could feel the color red. He could hear it. He tried another color, this time blue. The same thing happened.

Then he heard a great booming voice. Perhaps the voice of God? There were promises of greatness, and promises of many things. The Siddis he had obtained in India could bring him fame throughout the earth. He could correctly predict future events. He could understand what anyone was saying no matter what language they said it in. He could display the power of an elephant, the strength of the wind. Kings would bow to him, queens would offer him whatever he wished. The Romans would fear him and leave his country, and the rabbis and priests would proclaim him the Messiah, perhaps the Messiah of Aharon.

But Yeshua knew this was not God who was speaking. God would never say such things. God had never spoken to him in words. And so he turned his back and his heart away from the voice, and when he did its volume, as well as its power, diminished. Shortly thereafter, it went away, along with the colorful stars, leaving him in silence and darkness.

When his meditation finally ended, it was afternoon. Was it the next day, or had several days passed? He was not sure. He contemplated what had happened. He knew that his ministry was about to begin, which made him very excited and happy. He knew that he must not make the same mistakes he had made in India. He knew especially that he should not be tempted to use his Siddis to satisfy his ego. This is what Patanjali had warned him about, telling him that most adepts quickly gave up their Siddis just so they would no longer be tempted.

Yet he had not yielded to his temptations, even though they were only in a dream. Maybe this was a sign that he indeed could use them without being tempted by them. He would not give them up, at least not for now.

He also realized something very important about his life up until now. He realized that he had been running away from himself all these years. Whether it was going into the woods or to Samaria as a child to escape becoming a carpenter, whether it was running away from his tormentor Efah or running away to India, whether it was running from the Brahmins and warriors there—all this time, he was running from himself. And it all had to do with his father. Everyone else had fathers; he had a stepfather. Everyone else had legal biological fathers; he was thought to be a bastard. Those words, "the son of Mara," rang through his head whenever he was alone in thought. It made him feel inferior. It was these feelings of inferiority that he was always running away from. But now he knew for certain he had a father. And His name was God!

In India he had been a foreigner. Here in this land he was at home. He was a person not unlike any of the other people in this country. He would be a rabbi, but not like the upper-crust Sadducces, who largely ignored the poor, or the Pharisees, who argued about the meaning of every word of the Torah. He would be a teacher of the poor and of the common people. He would use simple words and simple mashals. He would tell stories that everyone could understand. How many laws had Moshe written? Six hundred and thirteen? How could the poor who could not even read ever remember that many laws?

No, his teachings would be uncomplicated. He would heal the sick, he would cast out demons, but mostly he would teach. In India he had taught some of the Jewish philosophies to the people through his mashals. Now he could teach some of the Indian philosophies to the people of his country in the same way. He felt so strongly that this was his reason for being in this life at this time that it made him calm and self-assured, more so than he had ever been in his life thus far. But though he considered God to be his father, when he walked out of the wilderness he would walk out not as the son of God, but as the son of man.

III. SON OF MAN

The Hebrew expression "son of man" ... appears 107 times in the Hebrew Bible This is the most common Hebrew construction for the singular but is used mostly in Yechezqel (93 times) and 14 times elsewhere. In 32 cases the phrase appears in intermediate plural form "sons of men," i.e., human beings. As generally interpreted by Jews, it denotes humankind generally.

(From Wikipedia, the free encyclopedia)

63 (His ministry begins)

It was a long, slow walk north along the Jordan River. Almost fifty miles to the Sea of Chinnereth, which is where Yeshua was headed. He felt at home among the surrounding cities, and he was sure that this was where he would begin his ministry.

It was perfect weather for his three-day journey: not too cold or hot. He would pause each day and meditate. He was not thinking about what exactly he would tell people. Patanjali had instructed him never to prepare notes or think about what he was going to say before he spoke. This would insure that whatever he said would come from his heart. But he was wondering how he might start.

He had seen Yochanan, but only after word of him had spread. *How did Yochanan start? How does anyone start?* He concluded that he would start with one person, or perhaps two. He would leave the rest to God. If he was going to teach faith, he must first have faith. That was another thing that Patanjali had taught him. You cannot speak with authority about something that you know nothing about. And knowing was much more than reading or hearing about someone else's experience.

When he finally arrived at the Sea of Chinnereth, the first people he saw were two men in a boat coming back from fishing. "Greetings, friends," Yeshua said. "Did you catch many fish?"

The two men were brothers, Shimon and Andreas, from Capernaum. "Not enough," said Shimon. "We have had back luck all this week. Are you a fisherman?"

Yeshua smiled at the two and said, "In a way. But I am a fisherman of men. My name is Yeshua."

Shimon and Andreas looked at each other, puzzled by Yeshua's response. Andreas said to him, "There are a lot more men around these waters than there seem to be fish, but I'm guessing they will be a lot harder to catch!" The two were laughing.

Yeshua said nothing. It was quiet for a moment.

Shimon turned to his brother and said, "The moon is going to be full tonight, Andreas. Last night it was almost full."

"Yes I know," Andreas added, "I love these clear nights we have been having lately."

Yeshua's eyes grew bright. "When did the moon rise?"

Shimon looked back at him and said, "It rose just as the sun was setting. It should do the same tonight."

"Have you ever gone fishing at night?" Yeshua asked.

"Once or twice, maybe," Andreas said, "but not usually."

"If it is a full moon tonight, and if it rises almost exactly as the sun sets, your catch of fish might be improved. In a land far to the east of us called India, they fish for an hour as soon as this happens. This brings them much success."

Andreas and Shimon looked at each other. Yeshua saw doubt in their eyes. "I'll go out with you. You will see," Yeshua said.

They sat and talked as the day moved toward evening.

"What do you do, Yeshua?" Andreas asked.

"I am starting my ministry. I hope to begin teaching in some of the synagogues around the Sea of Chinnereth."

Shimon looked at Andreas, and then back to Yeshua. "You could teach in our synagogue, Yeshua. It's right here in Capernaum, and I could talk to the rabbi. I know him well. But what will you teach us, Yeshua?"

Yeshua replied, "I will teach you how to love."

Shimon and Andreas looked at each other again, and began laughing. "As you wish, Yeshua," Shimon said with a chuckle, "I will speak to our rabbi, and this Sabbath you can teach us how to love. My brother Andreas might want to take notes!" Once again the two began to laugh.

Now the sun was setting and the moon was rising, just as Shimon had predicted.

Yeshua said, "It's time. Let's go."

Although Andreas and Shimon seemed hesitant, they finally lit their lanterns and the three cast off. When they came to the place where they usually fished, they cast their nets out and Yeshua was right. They hauled in great quantities of fish with each casting.

"Over there!" Yeshua would tell them as he pointed to one side of the boat or another. "Look. I can see them, lots of them. Right there. See them?"

"That's amazing." Shimon said. "You learned this in India, you say?"

"Yes, in India. There are two times when they fish at night like this: When a full moon rises as the sun sets, like it happened tonight, and when there is a new moon. But when there is a new moon, they use many lanterns. They place them all around their boat. It seems to attract the fish."

"And whenever these two events happen we fish all night?" Andreas asked.

"No," replied Yeshua. "Only for an hour. The fish are already leaving. Look."

They threw their nets out a few more times, but they hauled in fewer and fewer fish, and heeding Yeshua's advice, they brought their boat back to the Capernaum port and tied up at their pier.

As they prepared to carry their fish home, Shimon asked, "Do you have a place to sleep tonight, Yeshua? It's very late, and if you don't have anywhere to sleep, you are welcome to come to our house."

"That would be nice. I wouldn't want to trouble you, though. I can always find a place to sleep."

"No. You must come with us. It's the least we can do after you showed us a fishing trick that will make us rich."

Shimon and Andreas lived quite close to the pier, and the walk took only a few minutes. After fixing a place on the roof for Yeshua to sleep, Shimon and Andreas went to their own beds.

Andreas said to Shimon, "So what did you think of him?"

Shimon said, "I don't know about you, but I liked him. There was something about him, something very likable. His mannerisms? His gentle voice? More than that. He's somehow different from anyone I have ever met, but I don't know how exactly to describe it. He seems so sure of himself."

"I know. I thought the same thing. And he sure helped us fish tonight."

They left it at that. Shimon would talk to the rabbi, and this Sabbath they would all hear what this new teacher had to say.

***

Capernaum was on the northwestern shore of the Sea of Chinnereth, and the villagers had all been told by Shimon and Andreas that a new rabbi was going to teach there. Some came out of curiosity, others simply because it was the Sabbath. Nobody was prepared for what they were about to hear.

Yeshua came to the front of the synagogue and began preaching to the crowd that had gathered to see him: "Your Pharisees and scribes tell you many things. They tell you how far you can walk on the Sabbath before it is considered 'work.' They tell you what you can say and what you cannot say. They tell you what you can do and what you cannot do. They even tell you what you can think.

"But I say to you all, think for yourselves! Most important, you need to follow two of the commandments handed down to us. First, from Devarim, you should love God. You should love God with all your heart, and all your soul, and all your strength, and all your mind. Second, from the commandments of Moshe, you should love your neighbor as you love yourself. If you follow only two commandments, follow these two. If you remember only two commandments, remember these two.

"We know both of these commandments, but do we *really* know them? How do we love God? Has anyone here actually seen him?" Yeshua held a dramatic pause. "No! We can't see God, or hear God, or touch God, or taste God. So how do we love God? Does anyone here know the answer? By going to the synagogue every Sabbath? By reciting prayers? By following rituals? I say to you, no, no, no! We love God by loving what God has created! And what has God created? Everything! By showing love to everything and everyone that God has created, *without exception*, you show your love for God.

"So the second thing you must do is simply an *example* of the first: love your neighbor as you love yourself. And who is your neighbor? The person who sits next to you in the synagogue today? Yes! The person who lives in the house next to yours? Yes. The person who lives in the town next to yours? Yes. What about a Samaritan? Do you love a Samaritan? Yes! A Roman? Yes, my friends, even a Roman.

"And so the words are quite simple, but to follow them is hard. You must all learn to love those who hate you because God has created them, and because they *are* your neighbor. Let me repeat: you must all learn to love those who hate you."

Everyone was looking at everyone else. Love a Roman? Love a Samaritan? Was this man crazy? This wasn't what they were brought up to believe, and yet, when he said it, it all kind of made sense. Moshe really did say to love your neighbor; it was one of the ten great commandments, but could he really have meant to include neighbors who didn't like us, who hated us?

As they were pondering, a tall, disheveled man with only one eye walked into the synagogue. After listening for a few minutes he stood up and began fiercely shouting, "What do you want of us? Have you come to destroy us? Who do you think you are? Do you think you are the son of God?" Those near him grew uncomfortable and began to move away. Now he began laughing hysterically. Suddenly he began to thrash his arms wildly about, his face turning bright red, and started talking in tongues. He lunged toward the front of the synagogue, and toward Yeshua.

Several men came to him, threw him to the ground, and held him down. But Yeshua had seen this many times in India. He remembered his lessons in the use of mantras from Jnyaneshwar. And he already knew it would work, since he had tried this when he was with Yochanan. He slowly walked over to the man, bent over, held his earlobe, and gently whispered into his ear the mantra he had been taught to remove unclean spirits. The man's eyes immediately rolled up until there was only white showing, and he went into a deep sleep.

There were loud gasps as those closest to the incident turned their heads back and forth from the sleeping man to Yeshua. Some ran out to tell others. Voices began to increase in volume and number. The word "miracle" could be heard amid the growing cacophony of sounds.

Yeshua paid no attention to the crowd's reaction. He sat next to the man he had put to sleep and waited. When the man awoke a few minutes later, he seemed quite normal, apologized for his outburst, and calmly walked out the door.

Again the crowd gasped, and someone asked Yeshua, who was now standing at the door watching the disheveled man leave, "Was he right? Are you the son of God?"

Yeshua said, "What I just did, you can do also if you have faith. Don't call me the son of God, but rather, the son of man."

When Yeshua left the synagogue, the people all ran to tell their friends what they had just seen. Only one man was left. Most of his face was covered. He slowly walked toward Yeshua. "What did you mean when you called yourself the son of man?" he asked.

The two looked at each other, and then the man lowered his head coverings, exposing his bald head. Yeshua gasped, a hand flying to his chest. "Bacha, what are you doing here?"

Bacha replaced his head covering and replied, "I came because I wanted to visit you. I missed you, Yeshua. I asked around in Jerusalem, and they all spoke of a man who had been baptized by Yochanan. So I went to Yochanan, and he told me you had left to begin teaching. I knew you would begin here, because you always spoke with love of the cities around the Sea of Chinnereth. And so after asking around in some of the cities, I learned of a stranger, a new rabbi who was going to teach here today. I knew it had to be you."

Yeshua smiled and answered Bacha's original question. "The son of man simply means, in our teachings, a *common* man. *This* is what I want to be seen as, Bacha. If everyone sees me just as someone no greater or lesser than they, then they can understand that what I can do, they can do too. Remember when we first began learning from Patanjali? The things I do now, I could not do then. The things I do now, many in India have done for thousands of years, and are doing right now. It only requires that you love God unconditionally and have faith."

"But Yeshua, I learned from Patanjali as well. I can't do those things that you can do."

"Try harder, Bacha. If I can learn to fight a bully in Nazareth, you can learn to recite mantras to cast out demons!"

They both had the sudden urge to wrestle on the ground as they had done many years ago, but now that they were adults, it didn't seem like the right thing to do. And so they laughed instead, long and loud.

***

When Yeshua had finished teaching, there was a small crowd of people who began to follow him. Shimon had invited him to his in-law's house to have lunch, and as they walked down the road, the crowd walked a respectable distance behind. Yeshua was not surprised. It had started. Bacha fell back with the crowd and watched his friend from a distance.

When they arrived, Shimon found that his mother-in-law, Kyla, was in bed with a fever. His wife and father-in-law were quite worried. Shimon said, "Maybe my friend here can help. You should have seen what he did in the synagogue." He looked at Yeshua.

Yeshua said, "Bring me to her."

The others were not pleased that a stranger was being asked to tend to her, but they said nothing. Kyla was almost delirious, and one of her other daughters was wiping her brow with a wet cloth. Yeshua asked the daughter to move away and sat on the bed next to Kyla. He took from his tunic the medicine bag that Samik had giving him in India and from it took out a plant from which he asked Shimon to make tea. When the tea was made, he asked Kyla to sip it. He then placed his hand on her head and closed his eyes. She fell into a deep sleep, although she was now sweating profusely—much more than previously.

"What have you done to her?" The daughter who was caring for her asked loudly. "Did you give her poison?"

Yeshua turned toward her, held up his hand, and shook his head. As the minutes passed, the sweating ceased and the fever broke. In a short time, Kyla opened her eyes, and upon seeing a stranger sitting on her bed asked, "Who are you?"

Yeshua replied, "My name is Yeshua. How are you feeling now?"

Appearing puzzled, Kyla sat up and looked around at the group of family members, felt her own forehead, and said, "I feel fine now. Absolutely fine. But how did you do that?"

Yeshua told her, "It was my hand that touched you, but it was God who made you well."

The daughter who was tending her ran outside, where the crowd was still mulling about and shouted, "The stranger has taken the fever away from my mother! He placed his hand on her head, and she was well!"

The crowd began running away to tell their friends. Before long everyone and anyone with an ailment was standing outside Shimon's house waiting for this Yeshua person to come out. "Where is the great physician?" someone in the crowd shouted.

Yeshua looked at the size of the crowd and sighed. So many sick people. This was not what he had intended for the start of his ministry. He had hoped to teach as he had seen Yochanan do. But still, he would not turn them away. Healing the sick was as much a part of his ministry as teaching.

The fever Kyla had must have spread, because many of the sick had the same thing. By nightfall, he had tended wounds, reduced fevers, and restored faith to nearly twenty people. Now he was exhausted. Shimon and Andreas invited him to stay with them in the boat. This is where they often slept on hot nights such as this, and Yeshua accepted. They brought the boat just beyond the breakwater and set down their anchor. The gentle rocking that the waves provided and the cooling breeze were just what Yeshua needed, and he fell asleep almost immediately.

When he awoke the next morning it was still dark, and Shimon and Andreas were still fast asleep. The seagulls circled overhead crying noisily and looking for fish. Yeshua thought this would be a good time to meditate. He swam to shore and walked down the shoreline in the direction of Lake Gennesaret, which was nearby. As he walked, Bacha appeared and walked with him.

"I watched you last night, Yeshua. You were amazing."

Yeshua smiled, placing his hand on Bacha's shoulder. "It's beginning, Bacha. It's truly beginning."

"It seems so, my friend."

"What will you do, Bacha? Will you stay here with me? I would like that very much."

Bacha took a deep breath and sighed. "No. I would love to stay here with you, Yeshua, but my path has also begun. I am teaching Buddhism in Samaria, and now have a small following. I only came to see you and see how you were doing, but now that I have found you and seen you and talked to you, even for this brief time, I feel Samaria calling out to me. I must return, my friend. Maybe you can come and visit me and then we can spend more than a few moments with one another. But it's important that you now continue your ministry without having me as a distraction. I probably shouldn't have come, but I'm glad I did."

"I'm glad you did too, Bacha. And I accept your offer. Once I am able, I will come and find you in Samaria. Peace be with you."

Bacha turned south and began his journey back home to his Samaria. "And with you," he said as he turned to look back and wave.

When Yeshua was quite a distance away, and before he reached the lake, he sat on the western shore of the Sea of Chinnereth facing east. He would watch the sun continue to rise over the sea as he meditated. He wondered if his message of love had been lost in the frenzied healing that he had performed. Would anyone even remember what he had said in the synagogue? But once again, he thought of the faith that he was asking his people to have. He needed to have the same faith.

He sat there watching the sun and was filled with the beauty of it all. The dark of the sea and the inky dark of the clouds above were separated at the horizon by streaks of colors merging from dark to light: purple, blue, red, orange and yellow. Now he could see the red reflection of the sun on some of the waves. And then the sun appeared, at once turning bright white as it burned away the clouds. Yeshua chanted the sound of "*om*" and moved into meditation.

"Yeshua, there you are!" Shimon and Andreas were walking down the shore in his direction. Behind them were two others. Shimon said, "We want you to meet two brothers, Yaaqob and Yochanan. They heard you on the Sabbath, watched you heal people outside the house, and now they wish to become your followers."

Yeshua came out of his meditation and stood. "And now there are four of you. Shimon, Andreas, Yaaqob, Yochanan, come. Let's walk around the sea and into neighboring towns and I will teach my people how to love."

"But what about the people in Capernaum who are waiting for you?" asked Andreas.

"We are moving around the shores of the sea, Andreas. Eventually it will take us back to Capernaum. I need to spread my message to more people than in just one town. Come on, let's go."

64 (Curing the leper and making the lame walk)

"Don't go near him, Yeshua, he is a leper," Yaaqob warned as Yeshua walked toward the man with a disfigured face sitting by the water. What other lesions he might have had on his body were hidden by his robe, but his face was full of them. Yeshua was not afraid. This too he had seen in India, and in the forest near Nazareth as a child.

Instead of turning in terror as others did, he sat next to the man and smiled at him. "My name is Yeshua. Who are you?"

"Why are you talking to me? Can't you see I am a leper?" the man replied as he lips and chin trembled. Yeshua knew that other than fellow lepers, it was likely nobody had actually talked to him in years except for the occasional shouts at a distance for him to go away. Mothers, Yeshua imagined, would gather their children into a tight circle and walk far to the side of the leper to quickly pass him. The children would stare at him as they passed and look at him with horror or would laugh and poke each other after they had passed him by.

Yeshua reached out and placed his hand on the leper's shoulder. Nobody had ever done that to him since he had contracted the disease. Most were afraid of catching it. But Yeshua continued to smile at him. "Don't be afraid of me, my friend. I'm not here to hurt you. I'm here to help you."

Shimon, Andreas, Yaaqob, and Yochanan kept their distance but watched this scene unfold. The leper said, "My name is Yo'el. I have been a leper for three years now. You are the first person, not a leper, who has ever talked to me. What do you mean you are here to help me?"

Yeshua was staring intently into the man's eyes. "I have come to minister to the poor, the sick, and the needy. I see that you are sick and in need, and I offer you my help. Come down to the water with me that I may wash away your illness."

Yo'el eyed Yeshua suspiciously. He told him that his disease could not be washed away with water. He would carry it for the rest of his life. Eventually his limbs would fall off, and he would die a wretched death. Such was the fate of those with this disease. But Yeshua only beckoned him to follow. And so the two of them walked to the Sea of Chinnereth and waded out until they were waist deep.

Yeshua asked Yo'el if he believed in the power of God, to which Yo'el replied in the affirmative. Yeshua held Yo'el as he had seen Yochanan the Baptizer do and brought him under the water and immediately back up. "Your faith in God will make you well, my friend. Come with me back to the shore."

Yo'el had, in the last year, begun to experience muscle weakness, especially in his legs—another cruel outcome of the disease—but he noticed how strong his legs felt as he walked back to the shore. When they got there, Yeshua asked Yo'el to sit. He then reached into his medicine bag and removed some oil derived from the chaulmoogra tree. In India, Samik had given it to him before he left India because they too had their share of lepers and the stigma of leprosy was as great there as it was in Israel. This oil held special properties that often cured leprosy, or at least helped ease its effects. Yeshua applied some to the lesions on Yo'el's body. The look on Yo'els face told Yeshua that it was already helping.

"I will give you some of this oil, and I ask that you apply it to your lesions once a day. After a week, your leisons should begin to disappear. Once most of them are gone, you should then go to your town and seek out your priest. Offer yourself to him for cleansing as Moshe has commanded. Only then will you be accepted back into your society. Continue to apply the oil once a week for a month. Take some to your leper friends as well. I have given you more than enough. Show them what to do as I have shown you."

Lunchtime had passed, and Yeshua and his disciples set out for the next town. Yo'el went in the opposite direction. He did something he had not done in years—he ran! He ran as if he could not wait to tell the other lepers of what had just happened to him.

***

By the time Yeshua and his four disciples had circled the Sea of Chinnereth and reentered Capernaium, the word had spread. The people had all heard about the leper, who had now been accepted back into his hometown, and many had seen Yeshua's casting out of demons firsthand.

The Pharisees and scribes had now all heard about this great physician who could heal the sick, but it was his words that were at issue. They had discussed among themselves whether he was a threat to the people, or, more importantly to them, to their own authority. If Yeshua was a false prophet, he could be brought up on charges before the Great Sanhedrin. They needed to see for themselves what he was saying and doing. And now that he was back in Capernaium, they proposed to do just that.

Word had spread that Yeshua was back, and as the five sought refuge in Shimon and Andreas's home, the crowd closed in. Everyone wanted to see him and hear him speak. But more than that, they wanted to see another healing. The group of Pharisees and scribes had all bullied their way into the house and were among those inside listening to Yeshua speak. Once again he was telling them that they should follow two commandments above all others. This was going against all the laws that the oral tradition of the Pharisees had set forth. One could not just follow two commandments and be blessed. A truly holy man—a son of God—would have to follow all the laws. What was this man trying to make them believe?

Meanwhile, a lame man by the name of Mordecai was being carried by his four sons to the house that the great physician and teacher was in. Mordecai had asked to be brought to Yeshua, and his sons had obeyed. When they realized that the crowd was too thick to make their way through, they devised a plan. They went around to the back of the single-story house and saw that not many people were there. Most were in front trying to listen and perhaps get inside to actually see Yeshua. There was no back door, nor were there windows in the back. But two of the sons climbed up on the roof, and the other two handed Mordecai up to them. Then the remaining two climbed on the roof as well.

They were in luck. The roof of this house was covered in thatch, mud, and straw. They began to dig with their hands between the supporting beams, and soon had a hole big enough for a person to go through. The first son climbed through the hole and landed with a loud thump just a few feet from Yeshua. Everyone inside turned and watched. The sudden falling of the thatch and straw had stopped Yeshua mid-sentence, and he and his group continued to stare as another son came through. Then the paralytic man was lowered by the two still on the roof.

When all five were inside, the last son laid a mat on the ground.

Mordecai was gently placed on it, and he looked at Yeshua with anticipation. The group of Pharisees and scribes were also waiting. They wanted to see what Yeshua might do. "My dear friend, how can I help you?" Yeshua asked as he sat next to the man.

Mordecai began to weep. "Teacher, I am not worthy of your help. My sons have brought me to you because I asked them to after hearing of your great healing powers, but now that I am here, I realize I don't deserve help from you."

Yeshua looked concerned and asked, "What makes you think you don't deserve help?"

"I am an old man. I have raised my sons well, but I am a sinner. I have done something horrible that I haven't even told my sons. This has to be the reason why I was stricken down two years ago. God is punishing me. I don't deserve your help, or anyone's help. It was wrong of me to come here."

In India, Yeshua had seen people who became lame and could not walk for years, only to have the strength in their legs come back, allowing them to once again walk. He knelt sideways to Mordecai, lifted his leg, holding his shin bones parallel to the ground with his two hands, as Samik had once taught him to do, and circled his upper leg bone around his hips. This leg seemed to move without effort, but without being completely limp. During their bouts of lameness, these people in India would have very stiff legs, making it almost impossible to do what he now did to Mordecai. He went around to the other side and repeated this circling with Mordecai's other leg, with the same result. The only thing keeping this man from using his legs once again, Yeshua surmised, was his belief that he would never again walk and his shame for some past deed.

Yeshua placed his hand over Mordecai's heart and said, "Sir, you show sorrow and repentance here in your heart. I can feel it. For that, your sins are forgiven."

As Mordecai closed his eyes and brought both his hands to his heart, on top of Yeshua's, the Pharisees and scribes began to converse loudly with one another. One of them glared and said to the other, "It's blasphemy what he just now said! Did you hear him? Only God can forgive sins. It's blasphemy, pure and simple."

Yeshua stood suddenly and turned to them, saying, "You say that only God can forgive sins, but do you not also say that only God can heal the sick? And of these, which do you think is easier to do? Is it easier for God to say, 'Your sins are forgiven,' or 'stand up, take up your mat and walk?' But I say to you that God works *through* the sons of men. You, me, all of us. The son of man has authority to both forgive sins, *and* to heal the sick. But so you may know that we all have such authority ..." Yeshua now turned toward the paralytic man, smiled at him and said, "I say to you, my friend, stand up, take up your mat, and go home."

Once again, Yeshua faced his accusers and stared at them as Mordecai struggled to his feet with the help of two of his sons. He looked down at his legs, and then back up at Yeshua, who had now turned back around to face him. Mordecai looked puzzled. Each of the two sons held his arms, one on each side. Slowly, looking down at his legs again, with great effort he placed one in front of the other and took the first step he had taken in two years. Then he took another.

His legs trembled, because they were weak, but he remained standing. He stooped with the help of his sons, picked up his mat, and handed it to one of his other sons. He looked at Yeshua once more, then at the Pharisees, and then, along with his four sons, slowly shuffled past the crowd, which moved back to make a path for him, and out of the house. Then he pushed his sons away and walked on his own—very slowly, but of his own accord. As the Pharisees and scribes continued to stare at Yeshua in amazement, and at each other, a chorus of shouts arose from the crowd outside.

The Pharisees and scribes left the house and walked away quickly without saying a word. Those near the front of the crowd were shouting at them as they left: "Did you see it actually happen? Did you see the miracle? What did it look like? Tell us!"

65 (A spy is summoned)

The Great Sanhedrin was the supreme religious body in the land of Israel. It met daily in the Chamber of Hewn Stones in the Temple in Jerusalem except during Sabbath festivals or festival eves. It was led by a president called Nasi, which means "prince." At this time the position was held by Rabbi Gamliel I, the grandson of the great Rabbi Hillel. He was known as Gamliel the Elder, and affectionately called "Rabban," which means "our master."

He listened to the Pharisees and scribes as they told him all that had transpired. Also listening was the vice president of the assembly, called the av bet din, or, "father of the court," as well as the other sixty-nine members.

One of the Pharisees said, "Rabban, it is our opinion that this new teacher is spreading blasphemy and falsehoods. We have seen him apparently heal a lame person, but whether this person was really lame in the first place, we have our doubts. It may have just been a trick to impress the crowd."

"Yes, we have heard of people who do such tricks, but has he truly committed an offence that would warrant him to be brought to trial here?" said Gamliel the Elder, who had his doubts but reserved his judgment.

The Pharisee continued, "Rabban, we feel he is also breaking the laws of Moshe." The other Pharisees and scribes all nodded in agreement.

Gamliel the Elder did not personally subscribe to the many oral laws that the Pharisees had interpreted and set forth as laws of Moshe, but he respected their beliefs. "You say he teaches around the Sea of Chinnereth? Isn't that near Sepphoris?"

"Yes Rabban," one of the group answered.

"There is a former member of the Great Sanhedrin who lives in Sepphoris by the name of Aharon. I will summon Aharon and ask him to keep watch on your problem teacher. He can be very useful to you because he knows what might constitute breaking of laws that he could be arrested for. Then we will all know for sure. Thank you all for coming."

***

Filippos was an up-and-coming lawyer, a sometime adviser to Pilate, and was being trained for membership in the Great Sanhedrin when the next position became available. Filippos was also a friend of Aharon. Aharon had asked him to his house for lunch. Aharon's house was big and immaculate. It had been in his family for three generations, and still looked like it would last forever. "Filippos, I have a mission that has been given me by the Great Sanhedrin. It involves knowledge of the laws of the Pharisees as well as the Sadducees. You are well versed in these laws, so I am giving the task to you. It will go a long way toward impressing the Great Sanhedrin, and along with a kind word or two from me, I'm sure the next position in the council will be yours."

Filippos was eager to do whatever this task might be, but he was also very curious. "What is it I need to do, Aharon?"

"You need to do some spying on someone and keep written records of what you find. He is a new teacher called Yeshua and is teaching around the Sea of Chinnereth. He has several followers, I am told, and their numbers are growing. Your mission will be to get into his inner circle, posing as a new follower. This will get you close to him, where you can watch his every move. Whenever he does something that breaks a law, either of Pharisees or Sadducees, write it down, write down the date, and write down the names of two witnesses. Every two weeks you will come back to Sepphoris and report to me."

"I will do as you ask, Aharon. I can go to Capernaum today and find out his whereabouts. I will see you in two weeks." Filippos left the house and headed east to Capernaum.

Good, Aharon thought. *Now that's done. I will soon be able to please the Great Sanhedrin without lifting a finger! Am I not brilliant? Tomorrow I will go hunting.*

***

Aharon knew the woods like he knew the back of his hand. His love of hunting was matched only by his cunning and skill. He would stalk the woods throughout the year, so he always knew where to find what he was hunting for. His weapon was his bow and arrow. He called his bow "Samael," an angel of death; its meaning is "venom of God." It was a huge bow, much bigger than most, and required considerable strength to pull the string back. But Aharon was very strong and had used this bow for many years. Samael was true to its name, and had killed many animals.

It was early in the morning, and Aharon knew that deer would be coming near the forest's edge where the stream was. They would forage through the bushes nearby, perhaps finding some berries to nibble, and then drink water from the stream.

Aharon knew all the tricks of being a skilled hunter. He had chosen a day where he was upwind at the forest's edge, and he would walk a distance, wait behind a tree for a short time, and then walk some more—slowly and quietly. The clothes he was wearing he had put inside a mattress along with some pine branches for several weeks so it would be harder for the deer to smell him. He knew enough to do everything, even swatting a mosquito, in slow motion so as not to alarm a deer if it was near.

He didn't have to wait long on this morning. A family of deer had come to the water to drink. There was a buck, its mate, and three little ones. Aharon was after the buck. It was much bigger, and therefore had lots more meat. There was another reason he always chose the buck, something more hideous. That would come soon.

He slowly pulled an arrow from his quiver and lifted Samael to the shooting position. His heart was racing as it always did while hunting as he patiently waited for the buck to turn just the right way so he could shoot into the heart-lung area. Everything had to be perfect. Just as he was about to commit to a shot, a flock of birds, startled by who knows what, screamed and flew out of the bushes and into the air. All the deer jumped with the first sound of alarm and ran deep into the woods. "Damn," Aharon said aloud.

But this was how the game was played. And Aharon knew that battles may be lost, but it was the ultimate victor who won the war. And he was going to win the war today. He spent the rest of the morning moving up and down the area he had scouted throughout the year. He knew the deer would come back, or others would come. This was their habit. He was about to move farther up when he spotted it. It was another buck, this time all alone. Although it didn't smell him, it sensed something that made it very uneasy. Aharon stood absolutely still. The buck came toward the stream several times, but kept shying back as if it knew that death lurked nearby. Finally, it came to the water and began drinking. This is when Aharon readied Samael. The deer lifted its head and turned toward Aharon, exposing its chest.

But that was not what Aharon was truly waiting for. He knew it would happen, and then, suddenly, it did. The face of the deer turned into the face of his father! The same father who had beaten him time and time again as a child. The same father who had beaten his mother and his brother. When little, Aharon was never strong enough to fight his father. And when he tried, it only made the beatings worse—much worse. When he was finally old enough and big enough to stop the beatings once and for all, his father died one morning, clutching his heart. One minute his father was standing outside the door of the house with a handful of grapes, and the next he was lying on the ground. Aharon remembered hating that his father had robbed him of the joy of killing him with his bare hands. He had done it in his mind many times over the years, and had vowed to do it the next time his father laid hands on him, his mother, or his brother. Since that time, with each hunt, he killed his father again and again.

He had been holding his breath with his weapon in place so that his body would remain steady, and with self-assuredness, he let the arrow fly. There was always a sense of wonderment in those few seconds where the arrow was loose, the commitment made. There was no turning back. Death was slicing through the air, nearing its target. It was now up to fate whether the buck would move before the arrow reached its mark. The slightest move could cause the arrow to hit the buck's shoulder instead of its midsection or miss it altogether. But it did not move, and the arrow plunged deep into its chest. Its front legs buckled, and then its back legs followed. The deer made a loud thump as it fell onto its side.

Aharon readied another arrow in case the deer was just wounded and began to quickly run toward the downed animal. But when he got there, he saw that a second arrow would not be needed. It was dead, there was no mistake. Aharon smiled triumphantly. He enjoyed the hunt and the kill much more than actually eating the animal, although he enjoyed that too. It made him feel superior to again take the life of his father, even if it only happened in his mind. And it always took away feelings of frustration that had built up inside him from past conflicts. He would eat deer tonight. He would cut his father into pieces, cook him over a fire, and eat him.

66 (Filippos witnesses the sermon on the mount)

AD 30
Yeshua's age: 33

Filippos had no trouble learning the whereabouts of this teacher. Almost everyone around the Sea of Chinnereth had heard of him and was talking about him. He learned that tomorrow, on the Sabbath, Yeshua would be talking in Tiberias, about two miles north of Capernaum. He wanted to speak to all the people around the Sea of Chinnereth, and made it known that he would teach on that day and answer questions. He also chose Tiberias because it had a small hill by the sea that he thought would be perfect as a teaching site. He could stand near the top of the hill, overlooking the crowd. Many would be able to hear his voice.

Filippos carried with him a parchment and an ink quill; he would write down everything he heard Yeshua say that might be contrary to the laws of the Pharisees or Sadducees, and have the notes ready for Aharon in two weeks.

It was quite a spectacle that morning. Thousands of people had gathered to hear Yeshua speak. They had come in the night so that they would have a place near the mountain where he would be speaking, and so that those who lived far away would not be accused by the Pharisees of walking more than a Sabbath day's journey. Since it was forbidden to work on the Sabbath, walking too far would be considered work. And how far was too far? According to the Pharisees, it was two thousand cubits (about a half mile.) They derived this from learning that two thousand cubits was the distance that God commanded the people to keep from the Ark of the Covenant as it was being moved. So they reasoned that this distance would be a Sabbath's day journey.

Yeshua made a rather grand entrance from the sea. Shimon and Andreas took him by boat to Tiberias, and as the boat neared the shore there was cheering that grew louder and louder. Getting off the boat, Yeshua found himself surrounded by those nearest the shore. Some were reaching out just to touch him. Others were trying to ask him questions. A small boy, about four years old, jumped into his arms.

"My name is Tovit," he said loudly. "What's yours?"

"Why, my name is Yeshua. Thank you for coming to see me, my little friend," Yeshua replied with a big grin as he strode to the mountain side. Once there, he handed Tovit back to his mother, and solemnly walked up the side of the mountain. He stood in silence as the crowd continued to cheer. His disciples—he now had eight—also walked up the mountain and sat by his feet. As he raised his hand, a hush came over the crowd. When it was quiet, he began to speak.

> Blessed are the poor in spirit, for theirs is the kingdom of heaven. Blessed are those who mourn, for they will be comforted. Blessed are the meek, for they will inherit the earth. Blessed are those who hunger and thirst for righteousness, for they will be filled. Blessed are the merciful, for they will receive mercy. Blessed are the pure in heart, for they will see God. Blessed are the peacemakers, for they will be called children of God. Blessed are those who are persecuted for righteousness' sake, for theirs is the kingdom of heaven. Blessed are you when people revile you and persecute you and utter all kinds of evil against you falsely on my account. Rejoice and be glad, for your reward is great in heaven, for in the same way they persecuted the prophets who were before you.

The crowd leaned forward to hear every word. Even Filippos was listening with interest, rather than trying to find fault. One of the criticisms he had heard from the Pharisees was that Yeshua was trying to abolish their laws. But Yeshua continued almost as if he had read Filippos's mind:

> Do not think that I have come to abolish the law or the prophets. I have come not to abolish but to fulfill. For truly I tell you, until heaven and earth pass away, not one letter, not one stroke of a letter, will pass from the law until all is accomplished. Therefore, whoever breaks one of the least of these commandments, and teaches others to do the same, will be called least in the kingdom of heaven. But whoever does them and teaches them will be called great in the

kingdom of heaven. For I tell you, unless your righteousness exceeds that of the scribes and Pharisees, you will never enter the kingdom of heaven.

Very clever. He first told the people that they should continue to follow the laws given to them, and then told them that they needed to be more righteous than the scribes and Pharisees! He had countered the argument of the Pharisees that he was abolishing the laws, and insulted them at the same time. Filippos would write this one down. He would have no problem finding two Pharisees or scribes as witnesses.

Yeshua continued to teach and after a time he asked for questions. One by one, people would come to the foot of the mountain, tell one of the disciples their question, and the disciple would, in turn, walk back up the mountain and ask Yeshua. Yeshua would loudly repeat the question, and then proceed to answer it. Each answer was both thorough and thought-provoking. One question was about vengeance, which brought Yeshua back to his discussion with Rabbi Towbiyah many years ago. He remembered it clearly. The rabbi had been challenging Yeshua's displeasure with the laws of Moshe, and asked that if the town bully, Efah, struck Yeshua on his right cheek, would he seek justice, using the laws, or would he simply turn his left cheek as well. All these years later, he now knew exactly what he would do. He said to the crowd, "You have heard that it was said, 'An eye for an eye and a tooth for a tooth.' But I say to you, Do not resist an evildoer. But if anyone strikes you on the right cheek, turn the other also. And if anyone wants to sue you and take your coat, give your cloak as well. And if anyone forces you to go one mile, go also the second mile. Give to everyone who begs from you, and do not refuse anyone who wants to borrow from you."

Nobody was quite ready to do all that, but that was exactly what was being asked of them. The question and answer period went on for the rest of the day. The only thing that Filippos could find that could perhaps be construed as another insult to the Pharisees was when Yeshua said, "Beware of false prophets, who come to you in sheep's clothing but inwardly are ravenous wolves. You will know them by their fruits. Are grapes gathered from thorns, or figs from thistles? In the same way, every good tree bears good fruit, but the bad tree bears bad fruit. A good tree cannot bear bad fruit, nor can a bad tree bear good fruit. Every tree that does not bear good fruit is cut down and thrown into the fire. Thus you will know them by their fruits."

He was smart, this Yeshua, Filippos would have to give him that. But he would soon work his way into the inner circle and gather evidence for Aharon. Filippos was sure he was speaking about the Pharisees just then, but he had not named them, so these words could not be used against him. Yet Filippos could have sworn that as Yeshua talked about those coming to you in sheep's clothing who inwardly are ravenous wolves, he was looking directly at him. But there was no way Yeshua could have known of Filippos's mission. Aharon was the only other person who knew.

67 (Learning mashals and the spy reports back)

Yeshua became accustomed to sitting apart from the crowd when he spoke, either on the side of a mountain with the crowd at the bottom, or in a boat a few feet from the shore with the crowd at the water's edge. Today he was sitting in a boat. Many hundreds of people had gathered. They were now beginning to come to him to hear his words, not just to witness his powers of healing. He stood in the boat with ease as the waves gently rocked it back and forth.

He raised his hands, which brought silence through the crowd and they all sat down. He shared once again his commandment to love God, and to love everyone, especially those who hate you, as you love yourself. Someone in the crowd stood and asked, "Lord, why should we love Romans? They do more than just hate us. They murder us, if it pleases them. They look down upon us—"

Yeshua interrupted him. "Why do you call me 'Lord,' and then don't do what I say? Two men once built a house. One dug down deep and laid the foundation on rock. The other built his house on ground without a foundation. What do you think happened when the floods came? The house that had its foundation laid on rock stood. When the floods came, the torrent struck the house but could not shake it. The moment the torrent struck the second house, the one with no foundation at all, it collapsed and its destruction was complete.

"I'm not looking for your curiosity, or your fascination, or your admiration. I'm telling you what you need to do to become a true follower. And either you follow these words, or you don't. Follow them, and the fiercest flood cannot shake your house because it is built on a foundation of rock. Or don't follow them, and your house will be swept away and destroyed. The choice is yours.

"Here is another mashal. This one I'm not going to explain. I will leave it to each of you to figure it out for yourselves. A sower once went out to sow. As he sowed, some of the seeds fell on the path, and the birds came and ate them. Some fell on rocky ground where there wasn't sufficient soil. These seeds sprang up quickly, but they couldn't put their roots into the ground, so when the sun rose, they were destroyed. Some of the seeds fell among the thorns and were choked, yielding no grain. Ah! But some of the seeds fell into good soil and brought forth grain, yielding thirty and sixty and a hundredfold. Let anyone with ears to hear, listen!"

There was murmuring throughout the crowd, and some were smiling and nodding their heads in understanding,, while others, including the man who asked the first question, were looking puzzled. After a few more mashals came the usual questions and answers. Those that wanted to speak would form a line, and the person in the front of the line would state his or her question. Yeshua would repeat it loudly for all to hear, and give his answer. That person would then sit down, everyone in line would move forward, and the next person in line would pose a question.

Filippos had, over the course of a few weeks, made friends with Yehuda, and they sat together and listened throughout the afternoon. "What do you think, Filippos? Isn't he amazing?"

Filippos made his move. "He is, Yehuda. I would so like to learn from him. What does he say to you, his disciples, in private?"

Yehuda did not hesitate. "Would you like to hear? Come with me when he is done talking. You can hear for yourself. It's all right. You are with me."

Filippos thanked him and they listened until Yeshua turned and signaled Shimon that he was ready to leave. Shimon beckoned the rest of the disciples and they piled into the boat along with Filippos.

This was the first time Filippos had gotten close to Yeshua. Yehuda had invited him to be with the inner circle, and he was congratulating himself on how easy it had been. Now he would hear what Yeshua had to say when he was alone with his disciples. Maybe there would be something that he could use.

They made land a few miles away from the crowd. Yeshua sat on a rock with his disciples sitting around him and asked, "So, did you understand what I just said?"

Andreas spoke for the group. "Master, we would understand better if you just said what you meant instead of using mashals. Some of them we understand, but some of them perplex us."

Yeshua looked at all of them to see if they were in agreement. They all seemed to be waiting for an explanation. "The last mashal I told was both *for* the crowd I told it to, and *about* the crowd I told it to," Yeshua said. "It was meant to separate the devoted from the curious. If they do not understand and simply go to their homes, it means they are not yet ready to hear the true meaning of the mashals I tell. If they do understand, they are indeed ready. But those who come to me later and ask me to explain, then I will gladly explain it.

"As for all of you, I am giving you the secrets of the kingdom of God, don't you see? And you can only learn these secrets if you understand what I am saying. Those on the outside might look but not perceive. They might listen, but not understand. Or it means they are doubters or spies."

Filippos winced at the word "spies," but Yeshua had not made eye contact with him, so he felt safe.

Yeshua continued, "But, I expect more of you. You are my disciples, and you will help spread the word far and wide. It is important that you understand my message, even when I speak in mashals—*especially* when I speak in mashals. Here is what I said to the crowd a short time ago: I spoke of a sower sowing seeds, right? So who is the sower?"

The disciples looked at one another and back to Yeshua.

Yeshua sighed. He rubbed the back of his neck and then threw his hair back. "I am the sower. It is I! So, if I am the sower, what are the seeds I am sowing?"

This time Shimon spoke up. "Are the seeds the words, Master?"

"Yes, yes! Now tell me, who are the people?"

Again they looked around at one another. But Shimon was now understanding. "The people are the paths that you sow the seeds on."

"Again you are correct. So now the rest of this should make sense to you. The seeds that were sown on rocky ground sprang up, but they couldn't put their roots in the ground. There are some people in that crowd who are much like the rocky ground. They hear the words, and are joyous for a time, but when they go back home, they soon forget the message and return to their old ways.

"The seeds that fell among the thorns were choked and yielded no grain. Well, many wealthy people who are consumed with their wealth and power and desires, they are like the thorns. They too were in that crowd. They hear the words, but they aren't ready to give up anything so they choke on the words just like the thorns choke the seeds, and nothing is accomplished. It's only people who represent the good soil who will hear my words and accept them and bear fruit. And yes, they too were abundant in the crowd.

"Learn to think like this, my friends. If you can't understand this simple mashal, how will you ever understand the rest of them? Now I'm worried that you didn't understand any of the others I have told you. Listen with your heart next time, not just with your ears."

His eyes rested on Filippos, a stranger, and he stopped speaking for a brief moment and stared. "Who are you?" he asked.

Yehuda stood and answered for him. "This is Filippos, master. He has been listening to you since you spoke that day in Tiberias by the sea, and is most anxious to learn more from you. I invited him to be with us today."

"And do you understand my mashals, Filippos?" Yeshua wanted to know.

"I do, sir. I find them fascinating. I was once a lawyer and learned many different ways to turn words and bring forth their meaning, but I have never before heard such complex messages told in such simple ways."

"See? He finds them simple!" Yeshua gestured at Filippos to his disciples. "I say to you again, listen with your hearts as well as your ears."

Filippos had listened not with his heart, however, but with his lawyer's mind, and had heard nothing he could use. He also began to see this complex man in a different light. He didn't seem to be the threat that Aharon had made him out to be. He mostly spoke to the poor and the middle class. Thus far, he had avoided the rich and the Pharisees and scribes. It was they who came to him, not the other way around. Aharon was wrong about this man. But Filippos was a good lawyer and was still dreaming about his future position in the Great Sanhedrin. Of course, if Yeshua continually talked in mashals, it would be hard to prove any laws being broken, because their meaning was all a matter of interpretation. No, he would have to find something that Yeshua did rather than something he said.

Off in the distance, Shimon spotted a large group of people coming their way. It was becoming harder and harder to be away from the crowds, because if they just went a few miles away, even by boat, they would be spotted, and before long they would be surrounded by followers. They were now going much farther from the crowds in order to give Yeshua a chance to rest.

They knew of several houses all around the Sea of Chinnereth, owned by friends and family of the disciples, and it was decided that they would seek refuge in one of these houses.

They climbed in the boat and headed for Shimon's mother-in-law's house. Yehuda and Filippos sat together. Filippos found Yehuda easy to manipulate, and he therefore wished to keep up his friendship with him.

Filippos needed some information. "I hear we will be with Shimon's relatives for a few days. Is it true?"

"Yes, our Master will speak on the Sabbath, and word is going out that he will do so. This will give the crowds the time they need to get here, and give Yeshua a chance to rest and 'meditate' as he calls whatever it is that he does by himself where he sits without moving. Why do you ask?"

Filippos siad, "It's just that I need to go back home for a day and tend to my mother. She is quite old now, and I need to buy her enough food to last for some time. I'll be back before the Sabbath, though."

As they got out of the boat, Filippos walked away from them toward Sepphoris, turning now and again to make sure he was not being followed. It had been two weeks, and he owed a visit to Aharon.

***

"Hi Filippos, it's good to see you." Aharon invited Filippos into his home and the two sat at a table. There was a jug of wine, and Aharon offered Filippos a cup.

"So, what do you have for me?"

Filippos shuffled in his chair. "Not much, I'm afraid. Not yet, anyway."

If Aharon was angry, he did not show any signs. "Well, tell me something positive."

"I have managed to get into Yeshua's inner circle. I am now able to hear what he says to his disciples."

This pleased Aharon. He smiled brightly at Filippos, reached across the table, placed his hand on his shoulder, and said, "This is good, Filippos. This is very good. What does he say?"

"That's the problem, Aharon. What he says in private is not so different from what he says in public. Also, he speaks in mashals. Mashals can be interpreted many different ways. He could tell you a mashal about anarchy, and you couldn't use it against him in a court because of its vagueness."

"Does he speak ill of the Pharisees?"

"He doesn't speak about them at all. He insults them to their face, it is true, but he never talks about them in private."

"Then what is your plan? Damn it, Filippos, tell me something good."

Filippos sipped his wine and placed the cup on the table. "There are two courses of action, as I see it. First, I can engage him in conversations about things that I might be able to use in a court, depending on how he answers them, and if there are witnesses around. But if I do that, I would need to be very careful. He is a very clever person, Aharon, and highly intelligent. I have hear the Pharisees and scribes try to trick him, and he is always ready for them. If he suspected that I was trying to incriminate him, I would no longer be welcome in his circle of disciples."

"And what is the second course of action, Filippos?" Aharon leaned forward, listening intently.

"The second one, the one I favor, is to watch what he does and try to find a law being broken by his actions. For example, he seems to have no regard for the law when it comes to working on the Sabbath. Unfortunately, most of the 'work' he does is healing the sick. We would be hard-pressed to make charges on that count."

"Good, Filippos," Aharon said, "good. We don't have anything yet, but I'm certain if anyone can find something, you can. Go back and watch. Come back in another four weeks and tell me what you have learned. I'll give you a piece of advice: whenever I am out in the woods hunting, the animal I am after may escape me the first time, or the second time, or even the third time. But it is persistence, patience, and focus that eventually brings down the animal. Be like a hunter, Filippos. I'm counting on you."

68 (Semadar finds Yeshua)

Yeshua sat in meditation near a spring behind Shimon's mother-in-law's house in the new city of Tiberias, named for the Roman emperor of the same name. It was a beautiful city, developed around seventeen mineral hot springs, and Herod Antipas had made it the capital of his realm in Galilee. The Jews who lived there, however, chose to call it by its traditional name, Yam Ha-Kinerett. Just not in the presence of Herod Antipas.

It had been another exhausting week for Yeshua, filled with teaching and healing, and arguing with the Pharisees and scribes. Meditation brought him both peace and strength. When he opened his eyes, he was looking at the tunic of a woman who stood before him. "I have chosen," he heard her say.

He looked up to see a familiar face. "Semadar!" He stood and embraced her. "You have truly chosen?"

Semadar smiled a recognizable smile to Yeshua, blinked her eyes rapidly, and replied in a teasing voice, "Did you think I would not?"

She was the only woman who could make him blush. He looked down to focus his thoughts, even as his cheeks grew bright red. He finally said, "I didn't know what might happen once you went back to your home. You did go back home, didn't you?" He had lifted his head to face her again.

"Yes, Yeshua. I have been home, and said goodbye to my family. They didn't agree with my decision, but they didn't try to stop me, either. It is what I want. This is where I want to be: with you. I told you before I was your first follower, and I still am."

Yeshua stood and squeezed her shoulder. "I am so pleased, Semadar. Come, I want to introduce you to my other followers. They walked together to the house where he was staying, and sitting outside were his disciples. The five appeared to be quite surprised to see their leader with a woman with whom he was obviously very familiar.

"Andreas, Shimon, Yehuda, Yaaqob, Yochanan, I want you to meet my very good friend, and my first follower, Semadar."

They looked to one another in silence. The silence grew, and began to become uncomfortable to Yeshua. Finally, Yehuda said, "Peace be with you, Semadar." Then, turning toward Yeshua, he continued, "Master, you didn't tell us you had another follower before us."

Semadar's eyes darted toward Yeshua. As he again turned his head downward, she said, "Peace be with all of you. We met near the river Jordan. I was ill, and Yeshua cast the demons out of me, and we lived in a community with Yochanan the Baptizer for several years. He probably didn't tell you about me because I told him I needed to see my family first, and he didn't know if I would stay or come here. Isn't that right, Yeshua?"

Yeshua knew she was angry that he hadn't told anyone about her, but he was pleased that she stood up for him. He felt they needed to talk alone. "Come, Semadar," he said, "let me show you around this city."

***

As they left, the other followers began to talk. "A woman follower?" Yaaqob began. "I don't like it."

"Nor do I," Yochanan said. "Did you see the way they looked at each other? I'm guessing she is more than just his follower."

Shimon broke in. "Let's not make judgments about a woman whom we know nothing about, and whom we have only met for a brief moment. Let's find out more about her. What do you say, Andreas?"

"I'm with you, my brother. Yeshua has not disappointed us thus far. I will not stop following him just because he brings a woman into our group. I trust him, and I trust his judgment."

Shimon now looked at Yehuda. "And what do you think?"

Yehuda weighed his words. "I, too, am not overly fond of having a woman follower among us. But I also agree with you and Andreas. Let's just wait until we know a little more about her."

***

"Semadar, I'm glad you are here. How did you find me?"

Semadar replied, "I told you that I was from Magdala—Magdala Nunayya. It is a short journey north of this city. It is where I was when you arrived here. I was saying goodbye to my family. There was much talk throughout the city about you and your miraculous healing abilities and your powerful teachings. It was rumored that you were here in Tiberias. You should come to Magdala sometime. I would love for my parents to meet you."

"Tell me about them," he said as they strolled slowly along the beautifully paved streets. "You never told me much about them when we were living with Yochanan."

"Well, my father is a very wealthy and well-known fish dealer. He has a fleet of fishing vessels, and his fish are sold throughout Israel and Egypt. I have two brothers, both whom work with my father. I am the only girl. My mother helps with the record keeping, but stays at home. She is a remarkable woman."

"Remarkable in what way?"

"She works in the house, she helps with the record keeping and she watches over both her parents and my father's parents. She teaches some of the girls in Magdala how to read. She does so much, and yet she never seems to be tired. She also believes, as do I, that women should be afforded the same freedom and opportunities as men. Most of the men disagree, but the example she sets has been slowly changing some minds."

Yeshua smiled. "If she's anything like you, I'm sure she is changing some minds!"

Semadar smiled back, and then grew serious. "Yeshua, why didn't you tell your other followers about me? I told you before I would always be your follower."

Yeshua took a deep breath, and slowly let it out. "I'm sorry, Semadar. I know I should have. When I left to go to the wilderness, I feared I was going to lose you, even as I hoped I would not. You mean so much to me. In India, I learned to live in the present moment, and to treat each moment as if it were the last moment I would ever have. So when I was alone, I began to live my life as if I would never again see you. Does any of that make sense to you?"

Semadar softened her eyes and relaxed her body. "You have the strangest way of saying things. Sometimes I don't know if you are complimenting me or purposely trying to make me angry. Anyway, I am now back in your life and have no intention of leaving, so let's live in this present moment once again."

Yeshua nodded his head. "What do you think of my other followers?"

"To be quite honest, I don't think they like me. I'm sure they are just being cautious, but it was obvious that they were not happy about seeing me. I hope I can soon become their friend."

"I'm sure of it, Semadar. They've only just met you. Let's go back and be with them and talk."

***

When they got back, there was another with the five. Filippos had returned. "Filippos, it's good to see you again. This is my dear friend and my first follower, Semadar. Semadar, this is a new follower, Filippos."

Semadar tilted her head slightly and said, "Peace be with you, Filippos."

"Peace be with you, Semadar. The others have just been telling me about you. I look forward to knowing you better."

Filippos's voice had a cautiousness about it, and he avoided looking her in the eyes. *Now I must be more careful than ever. If she remains with us, she will be looking out for him, as only a woman can do. My mission has now become even harder. Perhaps I can convince her that I am Yeshua's friend.* When he glanced at her again, she was staring at him. *No, this is not going to be easy.*

***

It was evening, and they all sat around the fire. "Master," Yaaqob began, "every day we see you sitting still for a very long time with your eyes closed. Are you praying?"

"In a way it is praying. In India it is called meditation. However, instead of *talking* to God, you become *one* with God. It requires much discipline. Perhaps some day I will teach you all how to meditate."

Yeshua waited but no one asked any questions. They were all looking forward to the fun part of the evening. Yeshua had been telling them mashals each night, then challenging them to explain what they meant. After their puzzlement about the rather simple mashal he told the crowd the other day, he wanted to be sure that when he told them in the future, they would understand them.

"There was once a man who went to his friend's house at midnight. He began banging on the door. Finally, the friend yelled out the window, 'Who are you and what do you want?' The man outside yelled back, 'It is I, your friend. A friend of mine is on a journey, and is staying with me. He only now arrived, but I have no food to offer him. Can you lend me three loaves of bread?' The man inside was furious.

'It's midnight. Don't bother me. My doors are locked. My wife and children are with me in bed. Go home and leave us alone.'

"But the man outside was shameless, and kept banging on the door and yelling. He banged and yelled for so long that the neighbors around the house were now being awakened from all the noise. Finally, in order to keep the peace, the homeowner went to the first floor, got three loaves of bread, and gave it to the man."

Yeshua was quiet now, and smiled. It was their turn. Yaaqob began. "Master, I believe your mashal means to tell us that we need to be understanding of other people, especially when asking favors. We may eventually get what we want, but the way we go about it is often wrong. Just like it was wrong for the man to bang on his friend's door at midnight. He eventually got his bread, but at what cost? His friend was mad. The neighbors were mad. We must always be understanding of others."

Yeshua shook his head. "No, that is not what this mashal is telling us. It is true that we must be understanding of others, but this mashal is about something else. Think."

Andreas tried next. "I think we need to look at this mashal from the viewpoint of the man in the house. The man outside was his friend. He should have gotten up immediately and given his friend the bread. Eventually, he did just that, but he was wrong to wait until the man had awakened all the neighbors."

Again Yeshua shook his head. "Yes, we should always give what others ask for, but this mashal is not about that, either."

Filippos seized an opportunity to embarrass Semadar. "Semadar, you are very quiet. As Yeshua's first follower, what do you think?" All eyes turned toward her. They waited to see what this woman would say.

Yeshua sensed Filippos's ploy, but knew Semadar and had great faith in her. "Tell them, Semadar," he said with a half-hidden smile.

"Your mashal is about praying, Master."

The men all looked at one another, and then at Yeshua. Yehuda asked, "Praying?"

"Go on, Semadar. Tell us more." Yeshua looked at the smugness on the men's faces.

Semadar sat up straighter, and looked around. "It was what we were talking about just before the mashal. Don't you all see? When you have need to pray, it doesn't matter if it is early morning, late afternoon, or even midnight. Others may think your acts shameless. God may even test your resolve. God may tell you to pray later, and see what you will do. But if you are in need, you should pray right then and there. Don't be afraid to knock on God's door, even if it is midnight. Be persistent. Now is always the right time to pray."

The six exchanged glances, and then faced Yeshua. "Semadar, as usual, you understand completely," Yeshua said. "If ever you don't understand my mashals, and I am not around to explain them, ask Semadar. She has been with me longer than all of you, and has a great ability to comprehend what I say. She is, after all, my first follower."

Filippos glared. The other men looked into the fire. Semadar quietly lowered her head and smiled.

"Where do we go next, Master?" Yochanan asked after some time.

" Capernaum," was the reply. "Tomorrow we go to Capernaum."

69 (A reunion)

The sun was getting hot by the Capernaum seaside during his sermon, and Yeshua went inside a follower's house to escape the heat. As usual, the house immediately filled up with those closest to it, and the remainder sat outside, crowded around, hoping to hear Yeshua speak.

As he taught, he could see some commotion outside the door, which was open, and someone working his way through the crowd toward him. It was Yochanan. He said, "Master, your mother and your brothers have come and are outside asking for you."

Yeshua's eyes grew wide, and his heart began to pound. He had avoided facing this moment that he knew deep inside him would eventually come. Yochanan the Baptizer had tried unsuccessfully to prepare him. Now he knew he should have listened. His mind raced back to the mashal he had told last night, the one about praying. *Too late*, he thought.

The crowd was silent, and they were all looking at Yeshua, waiting for his reply. He was afraid to look out at them for fear of making eye contact with his mother. Instead, he looked at the ground. *Have I truly given up my family? If so, what do I now tell the people?* Although his eyes were now moist, he rose his head and said, "And who are my mother and brothers?" Then, gesturing to the crowd, he continued, "Here are my mother and my brothers. Whoever does the will of God is my brother; my sister; my mother."

When he was done teaching, the crowd was told to disperse, and they all went back to their homes. All, that is, but one. A lone woman stood outside the door, and Yeshua knew she would be there. "Come in, Mother," he said. Off in the distance, Semadar beckoned the rest of the disciples, and they left Yeshua to be with his mother.

As soon as they were alone, Mara began to cry. "Yeshua! My son, my son!" She wanted to say more, but she could not. Each time she would start with, "Yeshua …" and then she would cry some more. He had buried his past seventeen years ago, but had never until this very moment considered how it might affect his family, and in particular his mother. Now this revelation was causing him more guilt than he had ever in his life felt. He too was crying to the point he couldn't respond to her.

Finally, after several minutes had passed, Mara said to him, "Why did you leave us and not say anything? Why have you been living around the Sea of Chinnereth, so close, and never once came to Nazareth to see your own mother? Your own stepfather? Your own brothers and sisters? Tell me why, Yeshua, why? We are your family, are we not? When we heard of this new teacher everyone spoke so highly of, like everyone else I wondered who he might be. But then when they said his name was Yeshua, I just knew it had to be you. I could feel it in my heart, Yeshua.

"I even traveled to Bethsaida once, just to make sure. I stood in the back of the crowd just so I could see you with my own eyes. And when I did, I knew my son had returned. I was afraid to come to you then, afraid that you hated us so much that you *wanted* to cause us this pain; but I finally gathered the nerve to come here. Do you hate us that much? When you didn't acknowledge us earlier today, your brothers grew angry and went home. But I stayed to find out what has turned your heart. Tell your mother why."

"Mother, there is so much to tell you. I don't know if it will make you understand, but I do owe you an explanation. Come, let's walk along the water. The sun is low in the sky now, and the sea air is pleasant. Come walk with me."

As they slowly walked down the shoreline Yeshua said, "When I sent you that letter those many years ago ..."

"What letter?" Mara looked into her son's eyes.

"Mother. The letter I sent to Uncle Yo'el. The one that said where I was going."

Mara shook her head. "Your uncle received no letter."

Yeshua was silent for a moment, feeling the weight of the implications of nobody knowing where he had gone, and why; nobody knowing for seventeen years where he was. He held his mother in his arms and said, "Oh mother. I had no idea. I wrote a letter to Uncle Yo'el about my going to India, and a young boy, I've forgotten his name, was to deliver it the next day after I left. Kaleb! That was his name. Oh mother, I'm so sorry for what you must have gone through. I'm so sorry."

Mara said, "And so you finally came home. And still you told no one."

He looked to the sky as if searching for the answer in the clouds. Then he told her much of what had happened to him over the past seventeen years. He told her about his experiences in India, and the birth of his ministry here. But he especially wanted her to understand the vows he had taken those many years ago, the vows where he renounced the desire for, among other things, family. She was very quiet as he spoke.

Finally she said with some bitterness in her voice, "So you are saying that we are no longer your family?"

Tears were flowing from Yeshua's eyes. He placed his arms around her. "Mother, what I am saying is that *everyone* is my family now. I love everyone the way I love you. When I look out to the crowds who come to see me, I don't see strangers anymore. I see my mother and my brothers and my sisters. I see my sons and my daughters. These are more than just words, Mother. It is how I feel. I love you with all my heart. That will never change. But I love everyone else now just as much as I love you. Everyone."

"Do you see fathers in the crowd too, Yeshua? Do you love those fathers too?"

Yeshua's reply was quick. "I can have many mothers, but I have only one father. He is my heavenly Father. In India I learned He has many names. One such name is Brahma. In one of the holy teachings over there, which are called Upanishads, they say, 'This universe comes forth from Brahma, exists in Brahma, and will return to Brahma. Verily, all is Brahma.' So you see, there can only be one, without a second."

Mara's eyes grew cold and she said, "Enough. You are just avoiding the obvious. You should know, son, that your family had to move. Your stepfather has lost so much money over the past years that we needed to sell our house and move into a poorer neighborhood. We live not far from where you used to play with your friends when you were eleven. Remember?"

Thoughts of his childhood in Nazareth came streaming back into Yeshua's consciousness. It had always seemed like a prison to him. And his stepfather, Ephrayim, was to him like the prison warden. When he left, he had never looked back. "How is it that he is losing money, Mother? He was a good carpenter. Is it still not so?"

"So, you now admit he is a good carpenter? Of course he is a good carpenter. And you always knew that. It would have been nice for you to tell him that, just once. Your youngest brother Yehuda now helps him. It is just that things keep happening, my son. I can't explain them. It is as if there is a curse over us. He will get a job somewhere, and something will always seem to happen. His tools will be stolen, his project will burn down, the person who hires him will suddenly go back on the deal.

"With each incident, he loses money instead of making money. It has gone on and on like that for all these years, and it has made us poor. Yeshua, you should come to Nazareth and visit. It would mean so much to your sisters and brothers, and yes, it would mean much to Ephrayim. Do it for me, Son. Do it for your mother."

She now looked deeply into her son's eyes. "Yeshua, you need to know something else. That day I went to Bethsaida to hear you, and I saw the crowds around you and heard what they were saying; well, I just want to say that I am very very proud of you. Your father Yosef would have been proud of you too. You are truly a great rabbi, and you have made your mother happy."

Yeshua fell to his knees and wept in his mother's tunic. He didn't realize it when he was a child, but these were the very words he had waited all his life to hear. It was his mother's love that he yearned for. He wept for his lost childhood as if it were a relative who had just died. He wept for all the years of bitterness he had endured. He wept for his own misunderstanding of his mother's need to care for his younger siblings. And he wept with joy on hearing the genuine praise of his mother, and with sadness in thinking about his father Yosef, and what might have been. When it was over, he felt drained and exhausted.

It was now too late for Mara to return to Nazareth, which was a good twenty-mile walk. The owner of the house agreed to let her stay the night, and she and Yeshua slept side by side as they once did when he was a baby.

In the morning, Yeshua agreed to come to Nazareth soon and make amends to his family. Mara kissed him goodbye, hugged him one last time, and began her walk back home, holding his promise in her heart. "Goodbye, Mother, peace be with you," she heard him say.

70 (Seeing Efah and talking to Ephrayim)

The temple of Nazareth was crowded that day. It was filled with townspeople, but it was also overflowing with strangers who traveled with Yeshua. As he began teaching, the local crowd was unaccustomed to hearing stories and lessons that didn't come from the Torah or from the prophets. He told many mashals. While some were mesmerized with these strange and delightful stories, others began to get angry, not so much by the strange teachings but because Yeshua was openly being touted by the strangers in the crowd as a prophet. One person even claimed he was the anointed one, the Messiah.

From across the temple, Yeshua's old nemesis made eye contact. Although they had not seen each other in many years, it was Efah who first made the connection. His eyes lit up. With a cruel smile and a most sarcastic tone, he continued his taunting as if no time at all had passed since they were children. Standing and pointing an accusing finger at Yeshua, he said loudly, "Who is this strange teacher who these people *claim* to be a prophet? I think many of us may know him. A prophet indeed! Is this not Yeshua, the son of ... Mara?"

There was a loud gasp mouthed almost in unison among the crowd, followed by a deafening silence. All eyes turned from Efah back to Yeshua. Some of the older Nazarenes now began to recognize him as well. They began to wonder aloud what he might do. Would fists fly as in the old days? But this time, Yeshua's anger spewed forth in confrontational words only, though words aimed at more than just his immediate accuser. These words were meant for all those who had spoken ill of him in the past, and spoken ill of his family, especially of his mother. He gazed around at the people in the temple and then looked straight at Efah with steely eyes, and after a dramatic pause said, "A prophet is treated with honor wherever he travels, except in his own country, and among his own kin, and in his own house."

Although angry, Yeshua had gained the upper hand. Efah's face turned red, yet he said nothing. He turned quickly and left. Many Nazarenes followed him, but many did not. Yeshua stayed, and continued his teachings.

***

When he saw the house his family was now living in, he was saddened. It was much smaller than the house he had grown up in, and had only one story. His brothers, Yaaqob, Yosef, and Shimon, now grown up, had all left home years ago. Yaaqob was still single, but Yosef and Shimon were married. His two sisters, Miryam and Salome, were also married. Yehuda was now twenty-four and engaged to be married, but he still lived at home to help his father. And so the family of nine was now a family of three.

The years had not been kind to Ephrayim. He looked much older than his fifty-one years, and his hands were withered and wrinkled from the hard work of carpentry. His mother had told him that Ephreyim's joints ached, and sometimes he could not hold a hammer without dropping it several times.

Since Yeshua had not told anyone he would be visiting, Yehuda was the only sibling who was at home. And because he had left home when Yehuda was only five, Yehuda didn't remember him at all. It was a very uncomfortable homecoming.

Ephrayim had very little to say, although he sometimes smiled as Yeshua told them some of his stories of India. Ephrayim had secretly wanted to travel when he was younger, and hearing of these people and their customs drew his interest. Mara said that if he would stay another two or three days, she would let the rest of the family know that he was here. Yeshua agreed to stay.

When Ephrayim went back to his workroom, Yeshua followed. "Ephrayim," he said, "I know we never got along when I was young, and I know I caused you a lot of pain. I would like to make things right between us." He had thought about this a lot since his mother's lecture in Capernaium, and was only now beginning to come to terms with one of the main sources of his internal anger, a barrier to achieving Kaivalya.

Ephrayim was as bitter as Mara was when she first confronted him. "And what would you have me say, Yeshua? Do you want forgiveness? I have none. To be honest, I think I was as happy with you out of my life as you were with me out of yours. Why did you bother to come back?"

Yeshua suspected this would not turn out well, but he had to try. "Ephrayim, Mother asked me to come back. I did it for her. She now wants the peace between us that we never had when I was little. And although we never got along back then, let's at least try to get along for a few days while I am here.

"You may not believe it, but I truly am sorry for all the pain I caused you in particular. I now know how hard you were trying to be a good father to me. You are a good person, Ephrayim, and I only wish I could have understood that when I was little. But we can't change the past. The past is the past. We can't change the future, since it hasn't happened yet. That leaves us with the present. This we can both change. So I would like to be your friend. Won't you please at least let me be your friend, if only for a few days?"

"So, I hear you are a rabbi now?" Ephrayim began to make the first move toward reconciliation. He was looking down at his tools and not at Yeshua, but it was a start.

"Yes I am. It is what I was born for, Ephrayim. This is why I was born. I've never been more certain about anything."

"And I hear good things about you from the people around the Sea of Chinnereth—that is, except from the Pharisees and scribes."

For the first time in their lives, Ephrayim and Yeshua laughed together. It was a true tension-breaking belly laugh.

"No, I don't think they like me very much," retorted Yeshua. He now looked at his stepfather's withered hands and said, "Ephrayim, stretch out your hands."

Ephrayim seemed reluctant, but after a brief moment, he stretched them out. Yeshua gripped them tightly in his own and closed his eyes. Ephrayim could feel the tremendous heat coming from Yeshua's hands, almost a burning heat. And when he let go, Ephrayim was amazed. He felt like he had the hands of a twenty-year-old. He could feel the strength in them that he hadn't had in years. He flexed and opened them several times.

"But how ... how did you just do that?"

Yeshua smiled and gave his familiar reply, "It was my hands that touched yours, Ephrayim, but it was God's hands that healed them."

Ephrayim ran into the house. "Mara, Mara, come look what your son has done to my hands!"

At first alarmed that the two of them were fighting again, Mara rose, but when she saw his hands, she too was in awe.

The cure would be shortlived. Yeshua had simply used heat to ease the pain. By tomorrow, Ephrayim's hands would again be withered and weak. From Samik's teachings, Yeshua knew that the disease he saw in his stepfather was a Vata imbalance. In the Ayurvedic book of medicine called the *Cakara Samhita*, it was said that the sites of its manifestation are hands, feet, fingers, toes, and all the joints. A Vata imbalance established its base first in the hands and feet and then spread through the entire body. There were several cures, but most required plants found only in India. Yeshua remembered that one cure was a course of old barley, wheat, and sidhu wine, which was a wine made from fermented sugar cane. Sugar cane was making its way into Israel from Egypt, and Yeshua guessed that some winemakers were already using it. He would look into it, and then show his mother how to prepare the cure.

Over the next days, one by one, Yeshua's siblings came and visited, along with their spouses and children. There was at last peace and happiness in Ephrayim and Mara's house—complete and total joy. Yaaqob, who had once been a total nonbeliever, was now very interested in hearing of Yeshua's teachings. They had some philosophical discussions about the Torah, and Yaaqob's grasp of religious matters was pleasing to Yeshua. Mara was content to sit in the background and just listen to her children and her husband and her grandchildren, and smile. She had dreamed of these days, and was a very happy woman. Both she and Ephrayim were now resigned to being poor, and Ephrayim no longer had anything to prove to her parents. Besides, they were both now dead. Mara and Ephrayim had each other, and that was all that mattered.

The time came for Yeshua to leave, and he did so with a heart full of joy. "I teach a lot around the Sea of Chinnereth," he said. "It would be nice to see you all from time to time." And with that, he headed northeast, back toward Capernaium.

71 (Efah's uncle)

"Uncle Aharon, he's back, he's back!" Efah was breathless as he ran into Aharon's house.

"Calm down, Efah. Who's back?"

"Yeshua! He's that teacher who everyone is talking about."

Aharon was puzzled. "Yes, I know all about Yeshua. I'm having him investigated even as we speak."

Efah was now catching his breath, and could speak in longer sentences. "You don't understand, Uncle. It's the same Yeshua whom I used to beat up when we were kids. You know. The son of Mara whom you so despised. I don't know where he has been, but wherever it was, he's back now. I know it's him. He as much as admitted it to everyone in the synagogue."

Aharon was now standing up, with his eyes open wide in surprise. "Him?" he shouted. His muscles tightened; he clutched at his chest. "No! He can't be. He's dead!"

"I tell you it was him, Uncle."

Now Aharon's face was turning red. He began pounding his fists on the table and swearing. Efah did not expect this much of a reaction. He was slowly backing away from his uncle. Aharon saw the look on Efah's face and began taking slow, steady breaths. He feigned a smile and said, "Thank you for telling me this, Efah. And don't worry, very soon he will never bother us again."

As Efah left his uncle Aharon's house, Aharon grew angry again as he began to think. *How could he still be alive? I had him killed by two assassins all those years ago. Unless he somehow escaped. But where has he been all this time? It's been, what, almost twenty years now?*

Aharon had many trophies, but the invisible ones that he kept in his heart were the ones he was proudest of. He had overseen the ruin of that bitch Mara's husband Ephrayim. Mara was promised to him many years ago. She was to be his wife. But she rejected him for Yosef, that idiot studying to be a rabbi. Aharon would never let that insult go. Never. He continued, even today, to make sure Ephrayim would be poor, and as a result, Mara as well. She was never able to reconcile with her parents while they lived, and that made Aharon happy.

He had paid someone to kill Yosef, his first act of revenge. Then, when he learned Mara was pregnant, he bribed the government officials to say that they knew nothing about Yosef's death, and that Mara had never been married. This turned her into a sinner, and her son into a bastard in the eyes of the Nazarenes.

Next, he turned to Yosef's son, Yeshua. He taught Efah how to torment Yeshua and beat him up. He spread the rumors to the Great Sanhedrin that made them turn Yeshua away when he was seeking their help in becoming a rabbi.

Finally, when he found out that Mara and Ephrayim had left Jerusalem without Yeshua, he hired two assassins to have him and his Samaritan friend killed. He had paid them good money. And he never heard about Yeshua again for all these years, so he had been sure he was long dead.

Now he needed to act. He needed to take care of this unfinished matter himself. There would be no mistakes this time. How ironic, he thought, that the person he sent Filippos to spy on was the same person he was sure he had gotten rid of so long ago. Now he had to settle the score once and for all. Filippos would continue to be useful, of course, but he would make absolutely sure that Yeshua would be stilled forever—even if he had to kill him himself. Aharon began to make his plans. The hunt was on!

72 (Yeshua brings Leviy the tax collector into his following)

In the center of the town of Genesaret, two Pharisees, Shemer and Nimrowd, who had been present when Yeshua healed the paralytic in Capernaium, were being questioned by the townspeople. "Did he truly heal the paralytic?" one person asked.

"Bah!" Shemer said. "What the crowd saw was a magician's trick, nothing more! Anyone can pretend to be lame, and then get up and walk."

"And what about his casting out of demons by whispering in the person's ear?"

Nimrowd answered that one. "He is able to do that because he himself is possessed by the devil, Beelzebub. Also, he speaks blasphemy. We heard it with our own ears. Jehova will never forgive such a man. Any person who speaks blasphemy can never be forgiven."

The crowd was quiet when Nimrowd made his proclamation, which puzzled him. He was expecting a reaction from them. Instead, they were all turning and looking behind. Then, suddenly, out from behind the crowd came Yeshua himself. Some of his disciples were with him.

"And what blasphemies have I uttered? Tell me." His voice was filled with anger. As he moved closer, the Pharisees took a few steps back.

"Keep away from me," Nimrowd shouted. "You are possessed. It is by Beelzebub, the ruler of demons that you cast demons out!"

Yeshua laughed loudly and sarcastically. "And how can Satan cast out Satan? Why would Satan even do that? Listen to what you say. If a kingdom is divided against itself, it can't stand. If a house is divided against itself, it can't stand. And likewise, if Satan has risen up against himself, he can't stand either. Your statement is absurd."

He now turned his back on the Pharisees and addressed the crowd: "You can say anything you want about a person when he is not there to defend himself. You can call him a magician, a possessed person, or a blasphemer. But remember, if you wish to enter a strong man's house and plunder his property, you must first ..." Yeshua paused and held his two fists close together above his head and then continued, "tie him up."

Now Yeshua addressed the Pharisee's last accusation. "If he is not tied up, it is not so easy, is it? So let me say this to all of you: you can all be forgiven for whatever unintentional blasphemies you may have uttered. Your Father in heaven is a forgiving Father." There were gasps coming from the crowd, and from the Pharisees. He continued, "But there are limits."

He now turned back to face his accusers. "The limits are that if you intentionally blaspheme against the Holy Spirit, you will never be forgiven. Never." Yeshua waited for a response, but there was none. Shemer and Nimrowd turned and walked quickly away. The crowd began to cheer.

He walked toward the Sea of Chinnereth, but the crowds now walked with him. They all wanted to hear more of his teachings. And so he stood at the shore, and as they all sat, he began to teach. After he had talked to them more about love and forgiveness, he asked that he be allowed to walk alone. He wished to be away from the crowd so he could meditate.

More and more Yeshua was beginning to feel that his life was no longer his own. When he turned in one direction, the crowds wanted to hear him speak. When he turned in another direction, there were sick waiting to be healed. When he turned in yet another direction, there were the Pharisees and Scribes taunting him and testing him. It was overwhelming. When he was alone with his disciples it was less intense, but even then, he was constantly teaching them and being asked questions. His only two refuges were his meditation, and sleeping at night. And now it was time for meditation. He sat in his meditative posture, chanted the holy sound of "*om*", and focused on his breath and the sacred silence between the thoughts.

When he opened his eyes again, he felt revived and refreshed. He would walk into town and find his disciples. The road from the sea to the city wound gracefully through the trees, and because it was spring, the scent of flowers filled the air. The birds chattered in the trees above him, and off in the distance he could hear the sounds of children playing.

The town was a buzz of afternoon activity. Away from the rest of the crowd sat a man in a booth. As Yeshua neared, he saw it was a tax booth. No one was in line at this time, and Yeshua had no articles that had been purchased. "Have you come to chastise me?" the man in the booth wanted to know.

"Who is it that asks?" said Yeshua.

"I am Leviy, son of Alphaeus. And who are you?"

"I am Yeshua. And no, I have not come to chastise you."

Leviy was a large man with an unkempt beard and hair, and his clothes had not been washed in quite a while. "So why are you here then?"

Yeshua smiled at Leviy. "You just looked like you could use a friend. May I sit here?"

"As you wish," Leviy replied, beckoning Yeshua to a stool beside his booth.

"So tell me, Leviy, do you enjoy your work?"

Leviy began to laugh. Then he said, "Yeshua, nobody in town likes tax collectors. But somebody has to do it. I am very meticulous in my record keeping, and quite good with numbers. I never cheat anybody. I am very honest. But do I enjoy my work? I've been asking myself that lately. It's not easy being so unpopular.

"You are that physician and teacher that everyone talks about. Do you enjoy *your* work?"

Now it was Yeshua's turn to laugh. "If you love what you do, it's not really work, is it? But yes, I do enjoy what I do."

The two talked for some time and Leviy looked up at the sun, seeing that the day was coming to a close. "Yeshua, would you like to share a meal with me? My house is nearby, and there will be other tax collectors. We often eat together. You see, there is safety in numbers. When we are alone, we never know what might happen to us."

"I would like that very much, Leviy. I would enjoy being with you and your friends."

Leviy introduced Yeshua to his friends when they arrived; some of them had already heard Yeshua teaching. As they ate, Shemer and Nimrowd walked by with some other Pharisees and scribes. Shemer turned to Leviy's house, and seeing Yeshua eating with them called out to him, "You there. You profess to be virtuous, and yet there you are eating with tax collectors and sinners. We all find that very interesting."

Yeshua quickly stood and shouted back to them, "Those who are well do not need a physician. I have come to call the sinners, not those who consider themselves ... *righteous!*"

Another humiliation. They all began talking and pointing back in Yeshua's direction as they hurried away. Leviy was most impressed. He wished to learn more from this person. "Where will you speak next?" he asked. "I would like to hear you."

Yeshua had already looked into this man's heart and knew what kind of person he actually was. "If you wish to hear me, why don't you give up your tax collecting and travel with me. You are just the kind of person I am looking for."

Leviy was quiet for some time, and then said, "If I did that, I would surely be disliked by the Pharisees, as you are. Still, being disliked by the Pharisees is a lot easier than being disliked by the sons of men."

Using that phrase "sons of men" brought a bright smile to Yeshua's face. "Then do what you must to turn your accounts and your money over to your superiors, and follow me. I will remain here for a few more days."

73 (Filippos finds something useful for Aharon)

For once the crowd was small—only thirty or forty persons. Yeshua sat on the ground, and the crowd sat round him. He enjoyed teaching this way much more than standing in a boat and addressing thousands. One of those seated asked, "Teacher, you teach us many things, but we wish to learn the other things. The secret teachings that you share with your disciples."

Yeshua looked puzzled. "*Secret* teaching?" he asked. "Answer me this: When you bring in a lamp, do you put it under the bushel basket or under the bed? Or is it brought in to be put on the lampstand?"

"It is brought in to be put on the lampstand, of course," the asker of the question replied.

"That is correct. My teachings are like that too. There is nothing secret here. I keep no secrets. Whatever I say to you, or to my disciples, is to be brought to light. If you have ears, you can hear anything I have to say. So use your ears and pay attention to what I tell you. Remember, the measure you hear will be the measure you get, and even more so. So for those who hear, they will get more. For those who don't, even what they have will be taken away."

Another asked, "You tell us about the kingdom of God. But I'm not sure where it is, or even *if* it is. I believe in Jehovah, to be sure, but tell us about His kingdom."

There was more than one concept among the Jews of Israel about the kingdom of God. Yeshua knew this. For some, the kingdom of God was in heaven. For others, the kingdom of God was going to be created on earth. This crowd consisted of farmers. Yeshua perceived that most of them likely believed in a kingdom on earth, a Jewish kingdom that the Romans would be driven out of. A violent uprising was not what he wanted to advocate to them. Rather, he wanted them to prepare their own minds and hearts for an earthly kingdom.

Yeshua thought back to his own childhood. "When I was a small child," he began, "I once wanted to watch a seed grow into a stalk of grain. And so I planted it. Two, sometimes three times each day, I would uncover it to see if it had changed. Of course, it died!"

The crowd laughed as he continued, "The next time I tried, I didn't uncover it; I just watched it as it grew out of the ground. You know, I could stare at it for the longest time, yet see no changes in it. And still it changed. Each day brought new changes, but I could never actually see these things happening.

"The kingdom of God is much like this. We sow the seeds, but no matter how closely we watch we don't see anything happening. The miracle happens nonetheless, does it not? Eventually, the seed sprouts, it grows, it produces a stalk, then a head, then it fills with grain. We don't understand how all this happened, but we are only too happy to eat that grain, are we not?"

Again the crowd laughed. "Don't try to understand heaven, friends, because it's beyond your understanding. Just accept that it will happen one day, and enjoy it when it does," Yeshua said.

Yeshua then thought back to his study of the Upanishads, and one in particular: the Chandogya Upanishad. In it, a father asks his child to bring him a fruit from the nyagrodha tree. The father then asks the child to break it and asks the child what he sees. The child sees the seeds and tells this to his father. The father then asks the child to break open the tiny seed and tell him what he sees. The child breaks it open, but sees nothing at all, and tells this to his father. The father explains to his child about the hidden essence within that seed that is able to become a tree, and the spiritual implications of it all.

It was a good analogy to use. Yeshua began, "So what can we compare the kingdom of God to? Well, it is like the mustard seed. It is the smallest seed anyone has ever seen. And yet, when it is properly sown, it grows up and becomes the greatest of all shrubs, and puts forth branches that are large enough for a bird to make a nest in. Is it not so? All of that is contained within that one tiny seed. We can't see it, but there it is. The kingdom of God is like that."

***

Yeshua and his disciples had traveled down the Jordan River and were near where Yeshua had first met Yochanan the Baptizer. It was the fifth day of Sabbath, and many were observing the practice of fasting. It was believed that Moshe ascended Mount Sinai on the fifth day of Sabbath, Yom Chamishi, and that he descended on the second day of Sabbath, Yom Sheini, and so the Pharisees dictated that there should be a fast on those two days.

Among those who were fasting were followers of Yochanan and, of course, the Pharisees. Yeshua sat with his disciples by the river and together they ate fish that Shimon had caught and bread that one of the other disciples had brought. Although not trying to be conspicuous, they were the only ones eating. Many watching began to talk among themselves, and finally, a self-appointed group of Pharisees walked over and confronted Yeshua. Some of Yochanan's followers came with them to hear what Yeshua would say.

"You there! It is the fifth day of Sabbath. Why are you and your disciples not fasting?" one of the Pharisees asked.

Yeshua was not fond of the many rules that the Pharisees brought forth that were not from the Torah but from their own ideology. These rules had nothing to do with following the teachings, and many had exceptions. Fasting was suspended on wedding days, for example. Yeshua used this to try to make a point. "The wedding guests cannot fast while the bridegroom is with them, can they? When the bridegroom is taken away from them, on that day they will fast."

His own disciples had now learned to think the way he had taught them. They knew that symbolically Yeshua was saying that *he* was the bridegroom, and *they*, his followers, were the guests. But the Pharisees and the group of onlookers seemed puzzled. One said, "There is no wedding today."

Yeshua tried a more direct approach. "It is the Pharisees who say we should fast on the fifth day of Sabbath. It is the Pharisees who say this custom can be broken if there is a wedding. And so it has been for many years. But this is a new day. Nobody sews a piece of unshrunk cloth on an old garment."

Still they stared at him saying nothing. Yeshua sighed. "Nobody puts new wine in an old wineskin," he said.

Yehuda looked toward Filippos because he too didn't understand the last two statements. Filippos posed the question, "What happens if you sew a piece of unshrunk cloth on an old garment Yehuda?"

Yehuda thought a moment and then said, "I suppose when you washed it the patch would shrink and tear the garment, making the hole even bigger."

Filippos said, "That's right, Yehuda. And what happens if you put new wine in an old wineskin?"

"Ah! The wine would expand and break the wineskin, right?"

"Again you are right, Yehuda. So, now the most important question, what do those two things have in common?" Yehuda pondered but could not find an answer.

Filippos said, "In both cases, you are mixing something old with something new. Fasting is the old way of honoring the teachings of Moshe. Yeshua told them that this is a new day. He is offering us something new. The new and the old, they don't mix!"

The group of Pharisees understood nothing and returned to discuss what Yeshua had said with the others.

Filippos, on the other hand, made a mental note. *Yeshua is now making his own laws, different from Moshe, different from the Pharisees. Maybe this could be used. There were certainly enough witnesses.* He would approach some of the Pharisees later and get their names.

The Pharisees, after talking among themselves, decided to keep an eye on Yeshua and his disciples. At least three of them would, from this day forward, always be among the group that seemed to congregate around him, and they would watch him carefully from morning until night.

**

Two days passed. It was now the Sabbath, and the sun was just beginning to rise. Yeshua and his disciples found a grain field, and they were all plucking the heads of grain to prepare their meal. One of the Pharisees who was watching ran up to Yeshua and shouted, "You there! It is unlawful to work on the Sabbath. Why are you breaking yet another of our laws?"

Filippos was watching as well. Plucking grain was no more work than scratching an itch, but according to the Pharisees and their many interpretations of the Torah, this was forbidden.

Yeshua was clearly annoyed. "Do you not even *read* the scriptures that you profess to cite as proof of the breaking of a law? Did you not ever read about David in the first scroll of Samael? When he and his companions were hungry on the Sabbath, he went into the house of God, where Ahimelech was the high priest. The only food there was the bread of the Presence. As you well know, only priests are allowed to eat this bread in the house of God. Yet the priest gave him the bread, which he ate, and David, in turn, gave some of that bread to his companions. Why? Was David trying to break a law? No. He did it because they were all hungry and needed food. What does this say to you?"

Before anyone could answer, he answered the question for them. "This says that both David and the high priest understood that the Sabbath was made for humankind, not the other way around. Therefore, the sons of men are lord even of the Sabbath. I will say it louder, in case your two friends behind you didn't hear. The sons of men are lord even of the Sabbath."

Filippos would share this story with Aharon, but he doubted if it could be used. Technically, David and his companions were eating, not working. But the point that Yeshua was making was that whenever something makes common sense, it should be done. It made sense for him and his disciples to pluck grain because they were hungry, just as it made sense for David and his companions to eat holy bread that was sitting on an altar because they too were hungry.

After Yeshua and the disciples had eaten, it was time to go to the temple. Those disciples who knew him best recognized his continuing angry mood, even as they went to observe the Sabbath. Many from the surrounding area had come to hear him speak. He did not disappoint them. His teachings were simple, direct, and understood by all. When he had finished speaking, a man with a withered hand came to him. All of the Pharisees and many scribes were there, including Shemer and Nimrowd, and they watched in anticipation. If he cured the man, they could accuse him again of working on the Sabbath. Once more, Filippos quietly observed. Plucking grain Yeshua had explained away. But what could he say about this? Filippos knew of no story that Yeshua could reference.

Yeshua's face grew red as the man with the withered hand stood before him, and the Pharisees stood blatantly in the front of the crowd. To them Yeshua asked, "Tell me Pharisees, because you understand the laws so well, which of these is lawful: to do good on the Sabbath, or to do harm? To save a life, or to kill a life?" Glancing back at the man with the withered hand, he continued, "To heal the sick, or to let them suffer? Which of these is lawful?"

The Pharisees looked to one another, hoping one would have the answer, but only silence followed. Yeshua dramatically dismissed them with a toss of his hand and a shaking back of his hair, turned his back to them, and said to the man, "Stretch out your hand." The man held out his hand, which Yeshua held in both of his hands. It was a cool morning, and Filippos clearly saw steam rising from the three hands clasped together. Heat was coming from somewhere. When Yeshua let go, the man flexed his hand a few times, dropped to his knees, and wept as gasps came from those who witnessed this event. Yeshua had again snubbed the Pharisees and scribes yet left them little with which to find fault.

But Filippos saw what they may have overlooked. Maybe he could not be accused of working on the Sabbath, but Yeshua had forgotten to give God credit. The law required that every case of miracle-working be preceded or immediately followed with the words "Thus saith the Lord." Yeshua almost never used those words, but usually said something similar like, "It was my hand that touched you, but it was God's hand that healed you." But he had not said anything this time, probably because he was so angry that he was being followed and questioned. Filippos had previously obtained the names of Shemer and Nimrowd, whom he recognized as being in attendance before they left in haste. He now had a legitimate charge, and two reliable witnesses. Aharon would be pleased.

74 (The disciples get new names)

AD 31
Yeshua's age: 34

It is time, Yeshua thought to himself, *to prepare my disciples to teach, just as I was once prepared by Patanjali.* First he wanted to find out who were the real leaders. He took them to a steep and rugged mountain and told them to follow him. Yeshua was an experienced climber, having ascended mountains both in India and on his journey back home, among them, the mighty Himalayans. *This will be the first test*, he thought.

Most of them followed, but as the climbing got harder and harder, some went back down. To everyone's surprise, Semadar was among those who continued to climb. When he got to the top Yeshua turned to those who were still with him and said, "You have all proved yourselves to be good and worthy followers. What I need now are leaders. Those of you who are willing to lead, please remain. Those of you who are content merely to follow, return."

Nobody moved. "Good," he said. "You have all seen me go by myself and meditate. You have all wondered what that word actually means. Today I will teach you how to meditate. You will need to know how to do this because it will bring you peace and calmness in the face of danger. Not long from now you will all know danger.

"This peacefulness I speak of is much deeper than the peace you feel when you watch a beautiful sunrise or sunset. It is the peacefulness of being close to God. Perhaps it is the peacefulness that Moshe once felt long ago on the top of the mountain. It is …" For a moment Yeshua thought of the first lessons he had ever learned from Patanjali: yoga is a stillness of the fluctuations of the mind. He continued, "It is a quietness of all thoughts. First, I will show you, then I will teach you."

They watched as Yeshua sat in a cross-legged straight posture and closed his eyes. They heard him chant the word *"om"*. They looked to each other, then back at Yeshua, but he remained in this position with his eyes closed. They kept waiting for him to open his eyes and begin teaching, but he remained as he was. Nobody said anything. And then it happened: they saw him glow! There was a visible aura around his head. And just like Yeshua had once turned to Bacha to see if he was the only one seeing Patanjali glowing, the disciples looked at each another, and seeing the look in each other's faces, they knew what they were seeing was real.

After some time, Yeshua opened his eyes and quietly began to teach them. He taught them how to sit straight. This was important during meditation, he said. He told them of the many obstacles their minds would place before them, and how to overcome them. He admonished them to sit this way for a few minutes every day for the rest of their lives. It would only be after their daily practice became a routine that their meditation would begin to improve.

There was little food or water at this great height, but there was enough to keep them alive. They stayed on the mountain with him for two weeks as Yeshua continued to teach them some of the many things he had learned in India. He taught them the chant to remove evil spirits and how to hold a person's earlobe and whisper the words into that person's ear. He taught them how to channel people's own faith so that they could heal themselves. He taught them some of the many Ayurvedic cures for illnesses—cures that were not yet known in Israel. They would continue their lessons over time, but for now, he felt had taught them enough.

He remembered how Patanjali had renamed him Issa before sending him out, and he remembered how wonderful it had made him feel. "You who have stayed with me these two weeks, you will become my apostles. You will study my teachings, and soon I will send you out to share what you have learned. I will give you new names to symbolize your new position. My dear and faithful followers, these are more than just new names. Today you will become a totally new person. The person you once were is now dead. He is buried high on this mountain. You will bury your past. You will bury your name. You will bury your family. Your family is now all of mankind."

They all bowed before him, and one by one, he placed his hand on their heads and renamed them. Shimon was first. Yeshua closed his eyes, and then said, "Rise, Cephas." Cephas meant "rock," and Yeshua considered him to be a rock that would always stand by him. Yaaqob the son of Zebedee, and Yochanan, the brother of Yaaqob, he both gave the name Ben-Ragash, which means "sons of thunder."

Semadar looked up to Yeshua in anticipation. A radiant smile formed on her face. Yeshua smiled back at her. "Rise, Miryam. Miryam of Magdala."

"Miryam of Magdala," she whispered to herself as she stood. Leviy became Mattityahu. All the rest received new names.

When he had finished, they all went back down the mountain. The rest of the disciples were still there waiting for them. They all saw a profound change in the faces of those who had stayed on the mountain, and many wished they had not been so quick to give up when they first began the climb. It was getting late now and the air was getting chilly. A fire was built, and they spent the night there at the foot of the mountain. Many of the apostles meditated before going to sleep. Yeshua was pleased.

***

The next morning, everyone except Yeshua and Filippos went to gather food for their next meal.

"Well, have I passed your test?" Yeshua was looking straight at Filippos. His question came out of nowhere. They had been sitting alone for the first time since Filippos broke into his inner circle.

"Passed your test?" Filippos asked.

"You have been observing me since Yehuda first brought you, as if I were on trial. So, have I passed your test?"

"I am not testing you, Yeshua."

"All of my followers call me Master, or Teacher. Only the Pharisees and scribes call me Yeshua."

"I am not a Pharisee or a scribe, I assure you."

"Come on, Filippos. Tell me what's on your mind. If I can help, I am only too happy to do so."

Filippos thought about his last meeting with Aharon. He had the proof of Yeshua's blasphemy by not giving God credit when he healed the man with the withered hand, even the names of witnesses, and yet he'd held it back. He wasn't sure why he had withheld this from Aharon, but he had. Aharon was not pleased with his lack of progress.

"Call me a doubter, Yeshua. When Yehuda told me about you, I wanted to see you for myself. I have now listened to you speak, and I am very taken with what you say. I have seen with my own eyes the healing powers that you possess. I have seen the crowds around you grow bigger each day."

"But?" Yeshua interjected.

"But, I—I just need more time. I feel like I am changing, Yeshua, but I need to understand what is going on inside me."

Yeshua placed a hand on Filippos's shoulder. "When I was in India, I learned a technique called 'watching of the thoughts.' It is as simple as that. You sit very still like you have seen me do. You close your eyes. And then you simply watch your thoughts. You do this without judgment; without attachment. You don't try to stop your thoughts, rather let them come, welcome them. But, you must do this as if you were not the thinker of the thoughts, but rather the watcher of the thinker of the thoughts. It is a very powerful practice. Would you like to learn?"

Filippos was curious. "I would like to learn, yes."

"Very well, Filippos. Meet me tonight after everyone has gone to sleep, and we will begin our lessons."

"Is that what I see you do each morning and evening?"

"No," Yeshua replied, "what I do is called meditation. You can learn that too, but first you need to clear your conscious of things that are bothering you. Maybe you have done something wrong or that you are ashamed of. It will come up during the watching of the thoughts. Maybe there is something that is very important to you but that you keep putting off. It too will come up during the watching of the thoughts. Then, once your mind is clear, you can begin to learn what I do. I will be happy to teach you that as well, but first things first."

The disciples began coming back. "Tonight, then," Yeshua said.

***

Somehow, he knew, Filippos thought. *He said "Maybe you have done something wrong or that you are ashamed of." How did he know I was betraying him?*

His lessons with Yeshua that night went well. He learned how to sit, how to breathe, how to watch the thoughts without becoming involved in them. It seemed so ironic that he was being helped to see his sins by the same person he was sinning against. That was another thing. When he first began his mission, he felt like he was spying on a traitorous person. Now he thought of what he was doing as sinning. How did that happen all of the sudden? Yeshua was right. He had a lot of clearing out to do before his mind was clean enough to practice this thing he called meditation.

The next morning Filippos sat by himself after everyone had eaten, and began to practice what he had been taught. All his thoughts seemed to be directed toward what he had heard Yeshua say since that first sermon he heard him teach, and what he, Filippos, was now doing on behalf of Aharon. *Will these thoughts ever go away?* he wondered. He needed to decide once and for all whether he would continue spying or begin following this strange teacher. Only then would these thoughts leave him.

Yeshua passed by him as he was shifting his position. "How was your first practice, Filippos?"

"It went very well, Master."

Yeshua stood there with his head tilted and a strange smile on his face, as if waiting.

It took a moment before Filippos realized that he had just called him "Master." The decision seemed to have been made. Filippos smiled back, meekly nodding his head.

75 (A storm in the Sea of Chinnereth)

Yeshua taught from Cephas and his brother's big fishing boat for the morning and the better part of the afternoon. The boat took five persons to operate: four oarsmen, and one helmsman. It could hold up to thirteen passengers. By the time Yeshua was finished teaching, his throat was hoarse. They planned to bring the boat to the center of the Sea of Chinnereth and sleep there for the night in order to avoid the crowds. When they left shore the waters were calm, but within an hour the wind was howling out of the west and the waves were sweeping over the boat. Yeshua was exhausted and was fast asleep in the back. Cephas and his brother lowered the small sail in the center of the boat to keep the wind from turning the vessel on its side.

The storm was getting worse when Yaaqob, now Ben-Ragash, shook Yeshua awake.

"Why do you wake me?" Yeshua asked.

"Master, we are about to die! The storm is going to destroy our boat."

The boat was pitching wildly, and the wind was even fiercer than before. But Yeshua looked puzzled. This was nowhere near the storm he had once endured on the Indian Ocean, although this boat was much smaller than the ship he had sailed on. He looked to the sky, then to the water, and then to the disciples. "What do you mean we are going to die? My work is not yet finished. Do you think my Father sent me out here to drown?"

To prove his point, he moved to the small deck in the front of the boat and sat facing the angry waves and the howling wind. He sat in his meditative posture. "But Master," Ben-Ragash pleaded, "the storm is getting bigger!" They were all hanging onto the side of the boat and waiting for him to do something. Miryam and Yehuda were getting sick.

Yeshua turned his head and shouted, "If you have no faith, then gather together and cower in fear at the back of the boat. As for me, I will sit here facing the waves you are so frightened of. I will stay here in full view of this reality of nature." He then closed his eyes and moved into meditation, sitting as the warrior Vijayananda had once done when he and Bacha were so terrified. As each wave struck, the bow of the boat lifted up and then came crashing down. Yeshua too was bouncing, but, just like Vijayananda, he maintained his seat.

The five-man crew struggled to keep the boat from capsizing. Cephas, with the help of his brother, was keeping the boat heading into the wind. During storms like this the long oar-like quarter rudder near the back of the boat took two sailors to keep steady. Visibility was nonexistent, and Cephas had no idea if they were now close to shore or not. The waves were tossing the boat around like a child with a toy. Yeshua had still not moved.

A huge clap of thunder resounded through the boat. "Yeshua!" they all yelled together. Yeshua, having been drawn out of his meditation, turned to face them, then looked up to the sky. As he gazed upward, suddenly the wind began to decrease, and then within a few minutes, almost as if it had never been, the storm passed and the waters turned calm. Yeshua held his hands out to either side of his body, palms face up. "There. Why were you afraid?" he asked. "Have you *still* no faith?"

"You saved us," Ben-Ragash cried out. "You calmed the waters."

"Ben-Ragash, it was not me. Cephas and his brother used their experience as fishermen. Storms in the Sea of Chinnereth come and go, as did this one. You all know that. I did nothing except to have faith in my Father. The storm ended—the waters calmed."

There was an uneasy silence as they all looked to one another. Yehuda said, "But ... but it was when you looked up at the sky that storm went away."

Yeshua ignored his remark, shook back his hair and asked, "Cephas, how long have you been a fisherman?"

"All my life, Master."

"And how often have you encountered storms like this?"

"Many times, Master."

"And have you ever had your boat sink in a storm?"

"Never, Master."

Yeshua stood and said, "There, you see. You had a captain who knew how to act in a storm. You had a teacher who assured you that you would not be drowned. And you had the love of God. With all these things, there was no need to be afraid. God loves all of you. And God will look over you. But you must use the tools that He gave you:

your head, your arms and your legs, and yes, your courage."

Yehuda shouted, "Then let us celebrate the courage of Cephas and Andreas! We are all safe because of them!" Everyone began cheering.

Yeshua was remembering the lesson from the Bhagavad Gita where Lord Krishna was instructing Arjuna in performing actions but abandoning the fruits of action. Lord Krishna says at one point, "Renouncing all actions by using the mind, the self-controlled one sits in bliss in the city with nine gates, neither doing anything nor causing anything to be done." It was an important lesson he now needed to teach.

"Stop this, all of you," Yeshua shouted. "Sit and listen." The celebration ended as quickly as it had begun, and they all sat. Yeshua continued, "Always do what you need to do, what you feel is right, just like Cephas and Andreas did. They had no idea what was going to happen, yet still they did what they had done their whole lives when the storm came.

"But here is the important point I want you all to remember. It may be *your* mind and *your* arms and *your* legs that do the work, but it is *God's* work that is being done. Therefore, never take credit for the good that comes of it, nor feel guilty for the bad that comes of it. It is God's work, and we are not gifted enough to understand His plan. So if we survive the storm, it is God's will that we survive. And if we had truly perished, that too would have been God's will.

"You will all perform acts in God's name in the future and it is important that you remember this lesson. Be like Cephas. Be like Andreas. Do what must be done. Do your work with intelligence and forethought. And then, like a thief in the night, move on quickly. That way you won't be tempted to take the fruits of your actions for yourself if that action caused some good. That way you won't feel sorrow for the fruits of your action if that action caused some bad."

Yehuda was curious. "Master, how can this be? If we do something in the name of God, how could that action possibly cause something bad?"

"Yehuda, if you were to see a small child drowning in the sea, what would you do?"

"I would save him, of course!"

"And so you have done the work of God?"

"Yes."

"Very good, Yehuda. Now what if, when this child grows up, he becomes a murderer and kills one hundred people? Now have you done the work of God? If you had only let him drown, you could have saved one hundred people."

"But how are we to know what a child will become when he grows up, Master?"

"We don't. And that's the point. But very well, Yehuda. Say that you *did* know what he would grow up to become. You knew he would kill one hundred people. Now would you save him?"

"No. I mean ... yes. Wait ..." Yehuda was baffled.

"Did you not hear me before? Let me say it again. We are not gifted enough to understand God's plan. You can never know the outcome of your actions. Some will appear to turn out good, some will appear to turn out bad. This is exactly why I tell you not to become attached to them. Do them and do them to the best of your abilities. But don't become attached to them. Save the child if that is what your heart tells you to do. And then be done with it."

He wasn't sure if they fully understood what he had just told them, but he would repeat it in different ways in the coming years. This was an important lesson, one of many they all had to learn. He looked to them and saw Miryam smiling at him. *At least Miryam understands,* he thought.

76 (Yochanan the Baptizer is arrested)

It was an exceptionally hot summer afternoon by the river Jordan. Herodias and Herod sat in their brand-new elegant arched-top carruca, which was covered with ornate plates of silver and gold and drawn by four large white horses. It was said that the price of this imperial carriage equaled that of an entire farm. Herodias ordered the driver to stop. She turned to her husband and asked, "Isn't that Yochanan the Baptizer; the one who fascinates you so?"

They were nearing the River Jordan, and a man stood waist deep in the water as those on shore lined up and waded out to him, one by one. Herodias pointed at Yochanan. "Yes, it is, precious," Herod said. "Come. Let's go watch. Maybe he will show us a miracle today."

"Oh, must we?" Herodias did not want to spend the afternoon watching Jews. She wanted to be home in her palace where it was cool. It was getting ever hotter, and now she was sorry she had pointed him out.

"Yes, we must. When last I talked to him, he spoke of another Jew who he had seen performing a miracle. Yeshua was his name. We tried to find him, but he had wandered out into the wilderness somewhere. Maybe he is back. If so, maybe he will show us a miracle. Wouldn't you like to see a miracle, my dear?"

Herodias sighed. The two things her husband was most interested in were Yochanan the Baptizer and miracles. She was interested in neither. But she did not want to make Herod angry. When he was angry, he often became mean. And she had been on the receiving end of his anger on more than one occasion.

"Very well," she said to her husband, "let's go see your ... miracle."

They got out of their carruca and walked to the water's edge, each holding a chalice of wine. Usually Herod would wait until Yochanan was finished with his baptisms and then talk to Yochanan. But Herodias wanted to be done with this as quickly as possible. As Yochanan looked in their direction, she beckoned to him. Coming from Herodias, it was a command to any Jew. He immediately came out of the water and approached, lowering his head.

"Yochanan, it's good to see you," Herod said. "Have you met my wife?"

Yochanan was steadfast when it came to marriage. The laws of Moshe were clear: It was legal for a man to divorce his wife. But he and Yeshua had discussed this in depth, and both agreed that to divorce and remarry was the same as adultery. Yochanan had never approved of what Herod had done, divorcing his wife and stealing his brother Filippos's, but he had thus far been quiet about it. Today was different. Perhaps it was the familiar way Herod had always talked to him. Or perhaps it was because he was tired. But for whatever reason, today he replied with frankness. "Yes, I have met her on occasion, Prefect. Where is she today?"

Herodias felt the sting of his insult and threw her chalice at Yochanan, hitting him on his forehead and drawing blood. "How *dare* you?" she said, turning, red faced, to Herod. "Well? Are you going to let a Jew talk like that to me? Well? Do something."

Herod looked surprised at Yochanan's insolence. He hesitated, staring at Yochanan as if waiting for an explanation. Yochanan, realizing his mistake, stood silent, hoping for the best. His head was still lowered towards the ground, but his eyes were looking up.

"Well?" Herodias said again. She had her hands on her waist, and was getting more and more angry.

She's right, Herod thought. This was an insult he could not let pass. He beckoned his guards and told them to arrest Yochanan. The guards immediately threw Yochanan to the ground and bound his hands. They placed a noose around his neck and roughly pulled him up.

The crowd at the water backed away from the spectacle lest Herodias's anger be turned toward them as well. Some of them that were out of Herod and Herodias's eyesight ran back to tell the others.

***

"Yochanan has been arrested," someone shouted. The frightened crowd raced towards those that were still in the camp.

"Arrested? What did he do?" asked someone.

"I didn't hear it, but he said something to Herodias. She threw her chalice at him and then they arrested him. I think they are going to bring him to Machaerus."

One of the women, Noam, said, "If Yeshua were here, he would know what to do. Someone needs to find him and tell him."

Abiyah, one of the younger of the family, volunteered to go find Yeshua and let him know what had happened.

***

Herod and Herodias climbed into the carruca. The opposite end of the rope around Yochanan's neck was tied to the back of the carriage. He would need to keep up to the speed of the vehicle or be dragged by his neck and likely suffocated. Two guards walked on either side of him. Herodias was pleased, and her mood quickly changed. As they marched Yochanan back to Machaerus, Herodias smiled and put her arms around Herod. Finally she was getting rid of this distraction in her life. Maybe now her husband would pay attention to her. She kissed him on his cheek and said, "That's more like it, love. Shall we execute him today, or tomorrow?"

There was a long silence. "Herod. Did you not hear me? I said shall we execute him today, or tomorrow?"

Herod slowly turned to her, but was silent; his eyes vacant. *Damn it!* she thought. *He's not going to execute him at all. This strange Jew holds power over my husband that even I can't match.*

77 (Sending his apostles out to teach)

Yeshua had taught his apostles for many months now. It was time for them to see for themselves what it was like to go out and teach on their own. He remembered the first time Jnyaneshwar sent him out to teach, and how unprepared he felt. It was his ability to heal the sick using the Siddis he had obtained through his studies with Patanjali that first gave him courage. It was only after they had been cured of some ailment, or after seeing someone else being cured, that the people listened to him.

This is exactly why he taught his apostles how to draw out a person's own faith and be healed. They would anoint a sick person with oil, and that person's own beliefs could cure him or her of many ailments. He taught them how to cast out unclean spirits using the mantra he had been given by Jnyaneshwar. He taught them some simple Ayurvedic remedies for common sicknesses he had learned from Samik. And he taught them how to teach his two basic tenents: to love God with all your heart and all your soul and all your strength and all your mind, and to love your neighbor as you love yourself. If they could imprint these two simple messages on the hearts and minds of the people of Israel, he would be content.

Yeshua and the apostles were once again on the top of the mountain where they went to deepen their practice of meditation. It was early in the morning, and the sun was just beginning to vanquish the mountain mist. Yeshua looked at them and began to speak: "Your lessons are nearly over, my friends. This next lesson will be hard, I promise you. It will be one of the hardest things you have done so far. You will all be gone for three months. I will not be with you."

There was a stunned silence. "Where will we go, Master?" Shimon asked.

"You will go east and west, north and south, near and far. I will give you a direction to travel in, and there you will go. I will send you in groups of two. But to find your own faith you must also do this: You will take nothing on your journey except a staff—no bread, no bag, no money. You will wear only one tunic, and you will wear sandals. Nothing more."

"But how will we eat? Where will we sleep?"

Yeshua was surprised at their questions. "Have you learned nothing from me? Do the birds in the field wonder how they will eat? Do the deer in the woods wonder where they will sleep? Even they have faith in God. How much greater is your faith than that of the animals? God provides for them because He loves them. How much greater does God love you?

"You will have faith that these things will be provided to you. This is part of your lessons. When someone invites you into his house, stay there until you leave that town. And if they won't welcome you, and if they refuse to hear you, then you have no further responsibility. You are free to walk away. What have I taught you about ears?"

Yochanan answered, "Let those who have ears to hear, listen."

Yeshua nodded.

"When do we leave, Master?" asked another.

"Right now!"

Yeshua grouped them in pairs, telling them the direction they would travel, and gave them a final blessing. They were surprised. They had expected that there would be more instructions about their journeys. They had all thought that they would not leave until the next morning. They were not prepared to leave their spare clothes, their food, their money—all their possessions at this spot in the mountain.

Of all Yeshua's disciples, Cephas was the strongest and, of the men, the one he felt the closest to. He paired Miryam up with him. She would be looked after, he was certain. He and Cephas exchanged knowing glances, and Cephas nodded his head to show he understood his duty.

As they descended the mountain, Yeshua remained. He would meditate the rest of the morning, pray for his apostles, and then prepare for his own journey. He wished to see his friend Bacha in Samaria. It had been a long time, and he wondered how his friend's Buddhist teachings were progressing.

78 (Aharon's meal with Herodias)

Aharon was pacing the floor once again. He was not used to losing. Yeshua was becoming increasingly popular. His crowds were growing every day, and wherever he went, people were talking about him. *And what of Filippos?* he thought *He reports to me, but he gives me nothing! Is he even loyal to me anymore?*

Aharon needed to take action. This was his way. He would destroy Yeshua the same way he destroyed Yeshua's mother. He would destroy everything that Yeshua loved. By the time he was done, Yeshua would have nothing: no followers, no friends; nothing. And then, when Yeshua was thoroughly defeated, Aharon would destroy him.

It was late in the afternoon and nearing time for Aharon to attend a dinner. As a Herodian, it was his honor to occasionally mingle and eat with the upper echelon of Roman dignitaries. Not all the Romans wanted to be this close to Jews, but after the last uprising, which caused the destruction of Sepphoris, they wished to placate the Jews enough to keep the peace. The city was being rebuilt, and it would be horrible to have it destroyed before it was even finished.

Aharon wore his finest robe and tunic for the feast and walked briskly to the banquet hall. This part of the city was already finished and looked spectacular. Antipas was set on making this a model Roman city, and when it was completed he would rename it Autocratoris in honor of the emperor Augustus. Aharon liked Roman architecture, and was planning to have a new home built in this style.

As he entered the great hall, he was greeted by his friend Marcus Duccius Gallus. "Aharon, it's good to see you. Would you like a cup of wine before dinner?" Aharon accepted and was soon talking with those few Romans he felt would be most beneficial to his status in the city. Off in the distance he saw that Herod Antipas' new wife, Herodias, was present. She was beautiful. She was surrounded by many admirers, and Aharon had no opportunity to get near her. But he kept watching her, and several times, she caught his eye and smiled.

When the feast was ready, the Jews would all be required to sit on one side of the table; the Romans on the other. The Romans would, of course, be served first and take the best portions of food, leaving the rest for the Jews. Aharon acted as if he did not mind this indignity, but secretly he found it repulsive. He found his seat and drank his wine while he waited for the Romans to be served. The seat across from him was empty, but it would soon be filled with—he knew not who. Maybe someone who could be useful to him. He kept thinking about Yeshua, though he scolded himself for doing so. He could not let thoughts of this person ruin his dinner.

And then, to his amazement, Herodias took the seat directly across from him. *What luck*, he thought. They both started to speak at the same time, then paused, then both started to speak at the same time again. They laughed. Aharon was silent, allowing Herodias to begin. "You are Aharon, I've been told. I've never met you before."

Aharon replied, "Madam, of this I am certain. Were it otherwise, I certainly would have remembered."

Herodias blushed. "I understand you have been very useful to my people in the reconstruction of this city. My husband will be pleased to hear that."

"Madam," he began.

She interrupted him and said, "Please call me Herodias."

"Herodias," he continued, "your husband is truly making this city the jewel of this land. I am only too happy to do what I can to help."

Unlike the other Romans, Herodias waited until Aharon had been served before she began eating. This did not escape Aharon's watchful eye. As the evening progressed they talked more and more. After dinner there would be more mingling for a brief time, and then the Jews would leave. The Romans would continue to feast by themselves.

Herodias did not leave Aharon after dinner, but stayed by his side. Some of the Romans did not seem pleased, but it would be foolish for them to step in. "I understand, Aharon, that you know of this person named Yeshua. He has quite a following."

Aharon's posture changed. *Even here I cannot rid myself of talk about this man!*

"Herodias, everyone knows of this person. I personally do not approve of him."

"And why is that, Aharon?"

"He is a troublemaker. Have no doubt about that. He stirs up my people like nobody I've ever seen. I don't mean that in a good way, either! At some point in time he will have to be dealt with, either by my people or by yours."

"Tell me more. What does he do that bothers you so?"

"He shows disdain for the rich. He shows disrespect for the religious leaders. He openly disobeys our laws. Soon he will be disobeying your laws as well. His friends are the poor, the lepers, prostitutes, and thieves. With friends like that, what good can come of it?"

She pressed further. "I have heard that he is good friends with Yochanan the Baptizer."

"I hadn't heard that." Aharon stored that piece of information in his brain. It might prove useful.

"Well, it's true. I heard this from Yochanan himself. They even write to each other. My husband has imprisoned Yochanan because he doesn't approve of my marriage. Perhaps my husband should imprison Yeshua too?"

"Perhaps he should, Herodias, but thus far, he only breaks our laws. He hasn't broken any Roman laws."

Herodias laughed and said, "That has never stopped my husband from arresting anyone, Roman or Jew!" She stared off into space and was quiet. Aharon thought he saw concern in her eyes, but he didn't know what she was thinking.

The wine was having its effect, and she finally told Aharon the whole story. She told him that she was previously the wife of Herod's brother, Herod Filippos I. When Herod Antipas divorced his first wife, Phasaelis, he married her. Yochanan reproved Herod and her publicly, and for this he was thrown in prison.

It was nearing time for the Jews to leave, but Aharon took the opportunity to plant a seed. "Herodias, I have heard that your husband is very generous on his birthday, is it not so?"

"Drunk is more like it! But yes, you have heard right. Last year on his birthday he gave me a palace, just because I told him I liked it. The next morning he remembered none of it. But I was quite persuasive. The palace is now mine."

"If this Yochanan were dead, it would solve your problem, and it might also help solve the problem of Yeshua."

"How do you mean?" Herodias asked.

"Well, if Yochanan and Yeshua are such good friends that they write each other, then the one influences the other. With one gone, maybe the other would think twice before stirring up the people more."

"Perhaps. But my husband will not take that final step. Trust me, Aharon, nothing would please me more." Again she stared off into space.

Aharon struck the blow he had been waiting for. "Maybe if it were his birthday, and maybe if he were drunk, he might be persuaded. Do you think?"

Herodias' face drew into an evil grin. "Maybe you are right, Aharon. Maybe you are right."

It was now time to leave, and Aharon hoped that his suggestion might bear fruit. He knew by the look on her face that she would not soon forget.

79 (Yeshua in Samaria and the woman at the well)

The breeze on his face always felt good to Yeshua. He loved it when he was on the water, because of its unique smell, but still he loved it on land because it carried the scent of whatever was in bloom at the time. It was late summer, and the fragrance of flowers and fruit mingled together in a symphony of delicious music for the nose.

He had not traveled far into Samaria, stopping in Sychar. From there it would be a short distance northwest to the city of Samaria, where he hoped Bacha still made his home. He was thirsty, and seeing a well, he approached it. Sometimes there would be a bucket and rope for visitors to use to draw water, but this well had none. He sat there next to the well, thinking it would be an opportunity to meditate. Because it was nearly noon, surely someone would come by soon with a bucket. He did not wait long before a Samaritan woman neared the well. She was hesitant because Yeshua was a stranger. But Yeshua stood and said, "Good day, woman. May I use your bucket to draw water to drink? I am very thirsty."

"I don't know you." she said.

"My name is Yeshua. I have come all the from Galilee."

She continued to be cautious. "From Galilee, you say? So you are a Jew. And why would you ask such a thing of me, a Samaritan?"

Yeshua saw that she was cautious out of something more than fear of strangers, or of Jews. She was bearing a secret. He began using one of the many Siddis he had learned from Patanjali, who had taught him that "by performing Samyama on the flashing forth of the insight of the soul, one gains the knowledge of things that are subtle, hidden, or at a far distance." He was silent as he moved quickly into meditation, and now saw what she was afraid of.

"Woman, if it were you who was thirsty instead of I, and if it were God standing here with a bucket instead of you, He would have gladly given you water—living water."

"Living water?" she asked. "What is living water?"

Her inquisitiveness became greater than her fear, and she came closer to him. He rose from his meditation seat and said, "Anyone who drinks the water I speak of will never again be thirsty. It will bring them eternal life."

"Eternal life, you say? So where does one get this living water?"

Yeshua replied, "Go get your husband, and I will give this living water to the two of you."

Her eyes turned toward the ground, and her face reddened. "Sir, I have no husband."

"No, you do not. Even the one you have now is not yours, is he?"

Her hand flew over her mouth as she gasped. *How did he know that?* "Sir, you must not tell anyone. The man you speak of and I could both be put to death by stoning."

Yeshua raised his hand and said, "I am not here to betray you, woman. I am here because I am thirsty. May I now drink some water?"

She stood in shock and watched as her hands seemed to rise by themselves to offer her bucket to the stranger.

"My name is Yeshua, by the way," he said as he dropped the bucket down the well and drew it up.

She then began to cry and told him the whole story: She had never intended to fall in love with a married man, but he professed that he was not happily married, and it just happened. He promised her that he would soon divorce his wife, but it had been months and he kept holding off. She was beginning to wonder if she had been made a fool of.

Yeshua agreed to help. The two walked to the temple, and Yeshua went inside to talk to the priest. After a short time, the priest came out and asked the woman to enter. He asked her to confess her sins, which she readily did, and then he forgave her. "This man who brought you here, Yeshua, is a great man. He spoke highly of you, and it is because of him that I forgive you of your sins. But I am surprised you have not heard of him before. It is said by some that soon he will rid our land of all Romans.

"He travels about, mostly in Galilee, but also teaches in Judea and Samaria. He has agreed to stay here for another day, and I have asked him to speak in this temple. Yes, a Galilean Jew speaking in a Samaritan temple. Unheard of, is it not? But they will come, and they will listen. Many have hoped that he might teach here in this city. It is a blessing that you have brought him here."

***

Yeshua taught, as he had promised to do, and the temple was

packed. Many came to hear his message of love while others came just to see this person they had heard so much about. A few avoided his teachings because their hatred of Jews was so great, but neither did they come to the temple to confront him.

As he prepared to leave, he asked the crowd around him if they knew of a person in Samaria named Bacha. One man in the crowd came up and asked, "Are you speaking of the man who shaves his head and speaks about, um, Budd …"

"Buddhism!" Yeshua said with excitement.

"Yes, that's it. Buddhism. Yes, I know him. As far as I know he lives just outside the city of Samaria. He has some followers there, and I think they live out in the forest."

His old house, Yeshua thought *The place where we first became friends.* He knew exactly where to find Bacha now.

He thanked the man, and walked quickly to Samaria.

80 (Filippos leaves Aharon while Yeshua finds Bacha)

"Filippos, come in." Aharon beckoned him inside his house. He was somewhat surprised, since he told Filippos not to come unless he had something useful, and had pretty much given up on him. Maybe he was wrong about Filippos's loyalties after all.

"Hello, Aharon. I have something important to tell you." Filippos was not looking directly at him, and this made Aharon a little suspicious.

Aharon beckoned him to sit, but Filippos remained standing.

Aharon asked, "So tell me. What have you found out?"

Filippos breathed in sharply. "I have found out nothing, Aharon. I only came to say goodbye to you. That's the important thing I came to tell you."

Aharon stared at him and said nothing.

After a pause, Filippos continued. "I will no longer work for you, Aharon. I have found nothing illegal about what Yeshua does. He preaches to the poor, mostly. He takes care of the sick. And I'm not sure why you're trying to spy on him. He's no threat to you, or to anyone else."

Aharon began clenching his fists. "So be it, Filippos. I thought as much about you. He got to you, didn't he? You're now one of ... of them. Of course you realize what you are throwing away, right? You will never be a member of the Great Sanhedrin. But know this, Filippos: You are not my only source of information. I have many spies. I will find out what I need to know. And nobody will stand in my way. In fact, Filippos, I would look over my shoulder often if I were you."

"And now you threaten me? How petty. You can't stop him, Aharon. It's too late. Even as we talk, his apostles are out spreading his message. They are in pairs. They are all over this country. I saw them all leave myself only yesterday. You will never stop him."

Aharon got up and left. There was nothing left to say.

After Filippos left, Aharon sat at his table, clenching and unclenching his fists. "Damn him!" he said aloud. He banged one of his fists on the table and repeated even louder, "Damn him!"

Then a smile crept across his face and he pointed his finger into the air. "Wait a moment. Maybe you gave me something useful after all, Filippos."

He rose and began pacing. "Yes," he shouted. "Yes."

Filippos had just told him that Yeshua's apostles had scattered across the country in groups of two. *A divided army is much easier to defeat. They are in twos and vulnerable now,* he thought. One by one, he would destroy them, leaving Yeshua with no apostles at all. He would send assassins after them. He knew from his other spies who they were. He knew their names and what they looked like. Up until now, they had all been together in one big group. But now they could be easily hunted down and killed.

Then, after he had destroyed everything that Yeshua loved, he would destroy Yeshua. Somehow, with or without the help of Filippos, he would make it happen. He began to make plans. There was much to do.

***

The house Bacha had built all those many years ago had changed. It was much bigger. There were lots of people, some with shaved heads, moving about. Some were bringing in fresh food from the fields, others were sitting in groups talking and laughing, and there were children playing. Yeshua knew he had found his friend.

One of the children ran up to Yeshua and asked, "Are you coming to join our clan?"

Yeshua smiled and knelt so that he would be at the child's level. "No," he said, "I have come to find an old friend. Maybe you know him. His name is Bacha."

"Everybody knows Bacha! Come, I will bring you to him." With that the child, a little girl of about six or seven, took Yeshua by the hand and brought him to the back of the house, where a large group was listening to a talk by his old companion and friend. Bacha was teaching everyone a discourse by Buddha called *The Bhaddekaratta Suta: An Auspicious Day.*

> So don't chase after the past, or make expectations on the future. For whatever is past is left behind. And unreachable is the future. The qualities of the present, however, you can see clearly. They are right there, right there, not taken in, unshaken. And that is

how you develop the heart. Do what must be done today because who knows what comes tomorrow? Perhaps death? No, you cannot bargain with mortality. Whosoever lives thusly both day and night, ardently and relentlessly, will truly have an auspicious day. So said the Peaceful Sage.

When he had finished his discourse, he started back to his house. It was only then that he spotted Yeshua. "Little brother! You are here," he said.

"So it would seem," Yeshua replied with a huge grin.

"And I see you have met Chaya," he said, picking the little girl up and holding her in his arms. Chaya began to giggle.

Yeshua recognized this as a Hebrew name meaning "alive." Bacha was attracting Jews as well as native Samaritans. *Good*, he thought.

In the course of a little more than one year, Bacha had reached out to the people of Samaria, and attracted those who saw in Buddhism the same things that he saw. They created a mini-community, and because they weren't stirring up trouble and kept mostly to themselves, they were left in peace by the people of Samaria. In some ways, it reminded Yeshua of the Essenes, and his friend Yochanan. He had recently written Yochanan, who was now in prison, but had not heard back from him. But these things took time, and as Bacha had just taught, the important moment was the present moment.

Over a meal, the two began to catch up on what had transpired since last they met at the temple when Yeshua had just begun his ministry.

"I hear your name everywhere I go in Samaria, Yeshua. Your followers are growing."

"Yes they are, Bacha."

There was a hesitation in the way he said it that made Bacha ask, "But?"

"But my enemies grow in number as well. I am trying not to make enemies, but they grow nonetheless. I am sure there are spies among the crowds, and especially among the Pharisees and scribes. They test me daily. They accuse me of breaking laws. I must always be alert."

Bacha replied, "It was that way in India too, remember? Over there it was the Brahmins and the Kshatriya."

"Yes, I remember. Looking out for the poor and teaching them seems to upset the well-to-do. It's the same in each country. They seem to need them to remain ignorant.

"Bacha, you have quite a following as well. I'm so happy for you."

"Thank you, Yeshua. When I first came home, I thought I would travel around Samaria, teaching as I went. But I soon found that the ones who embraced what I was teaching wanted to be a community. That's when I decided to build onto my house and make room for them. As the community grows, we add more houses. We now grow enough food to feed ourselves, with some left over to sell in town."

They spent much of the day talking about old times in India and the people who they had met. It was a much-needed respite for Yeshua, and a happy time for Bacha. At Bacha's request, Yeshua would stay for a few days and teach the community. He readily mixed Buddhism with his basic message of love that he taught wherever he went. Everyone was impressed with his speaking abilities and pressed him to stay longer. But he needed to get back to Galilee. His apostles would be returning soon, and he was anxious to hear of their successes and failures.

81 (Mattiyahu and Yehuda face danger)

"We did well, Mattityahu, don't you think?" Yehuda and Mattiyahu had stopped to sit for a while as they journeyed back to Mount Arbel. The sun was still high in the sky, and it was quite hot.

Mattityahu picked up a flat stone and skipped it across the River Jordan. Five jumps! Not his record of eleven, but still a good throw. "Yes we did, Yehuda. The Master will be happy, I am sure. We have brought over a hundred new followers into his fold."

Yehuda looked around suddenly.

"What is it?" Mattityahu asked.

"I don't know. I thought I heard something. Probably just an animal."

They were quiet for a short time, both of them now standing and scanning the surrounding area, and when nothing more was heard, they continued talking.

"I thought I was going to starve to death those first few days."

"Yes, me too. I thought … Shhh! Now I hear it too."

They began backing away from the sound, each with his hand on the other's shoulder. Then it happened. Two men came charging at them from behind the brush, each holding a knife. Yehuda and Mattiyahu turned and ran, but the intruders had the upper hand. They had momentum, while Yehuda and Mattiyahu started from a standstill, and in no time the intruders had caught up to them.

"What do you want? We have no money." Mattityahu was shouting as he tried to push the men away, but neither responded. It was obvious that they were intent on stabbing them, either to hurt them or to kill them.

Yehuda managed to grab the hand with which one of the assailants held his knife, but the man's other hand came crashing into Yehuda's temple. He stumbled backwards and fell onto his back. The assailant seized the opportunity and jumped on him, trying to pin Yehuda's arms with his knees. Yehuda managed to wiggle out from under him, but not before the knife slashed towards him. Yehuda instinctively held up his hand, only to have the knife make a gash across his palm. Now Yehuda's fear was replaced with anger. He threw his fist hard into the assailant's face, making blood pour out of the man's nose.

Yehuda was able to get onto his feet before the assailant did, and as the man struggled to get up, Yehuda kicked him hard between his legs. He howled as he dropped his knife and curled onto the ground with both his hands between his legs.

Yehuda grabbed the knife and threw it far away. He then turned to see Mattityahu's plight. Mattityahu was lying on the ground, his assailant on top of him. Yehuda grabbed the assailant from behind, yanked him up and heaved him into the water. The stranger's eyes widened as he stood waist deep in water and saw his friend on the ground groaning. He got to the shore and then quickly ran away. His partner now rose, still holding his hands between his legs, and ran in the same direction.

Yehuda thought of running after them, but he stopped when he heard Mattityahu groaning. His tunic was covered in blood. He had been stabbed! Yehuda ran to his side.

"Oh this hurts, Yehuda. It hurts bad. Make it stop."

Yehuda opened Mattityahu's tunic to find he had been stabbed low in the left shoulder. The target had probably been his heart, but Mattityahu must have deflected the thrust. In any case, Yehuda needed to stop the bleeding. He tore a long piece of cloth off his own tunic and tied it tightly around his friend's shoulder. Mattityahu groaned as Yehuda tightened the cloth.

"Mattityahu, I know it hurts, but we are going to have to move. We need to get to a city before those two come back. Get up, my friend. I'll help you."

After getting Mattityahu to his feet, Yehuda tore another piece of cloth off his tunic to wrap around his own hand and stop the bleeding. Mattityahu was in great pain and couldn't walk very fast. Yehuda was concerned because once the one assailant told the other that he had wounded Mattityahu, the men would surely come back and it would now be two against one. Yehuda dragged Mattityahu along, heading quickly towards the city of Pella. There would be a physician there, and perhaps a place to stay.

***

Filippos was glad to be rid of Aharon. He had just finished with his "watching the thoughts." He was having fewer and fewer thoughts, and wondered if he should ask the Master to begin teaching him meditation. He stood at the foot of Mount Arbel and looked up. He had never liked being up high, and even the sight of the mountain from the ground made him a little dizzy.

"Filippos, we have returned!"

He turned to see Yehuda and Mattityahu walking towards the fire he had built. They were the first to come back. But something was wrong. Yehuda was helping Mattityahu walk. He ran to help.

"It's okay, Filippos. He'll be fine."

"What happened?"

"Someone tried to kill us, that's what happened," Mattiyahu. And they would have, too, if it hadn't been for Yehuda here. He saved my life."

As they told their story, Filippos became numb. He remembered his conversation with Aharon and immediately knew what had happened. How could he have been so stupid? Aharon was trying to kill the apostles. And he, Filippos, had mistakenly told him that they were all out in groups of two.

"It's okay, Filippos," Mattityahu said, "I'll be fine. The doctor not only helped me, but became a follower as well. We baptized him before we left."

"Yehuda, Mattityahu, do either of you know where the Master went?"

The two looked at each other, then shook their heads. Mattityahu said, "I know he talked about visiting a friend who was with him during his travels, but I'm not sure where he lives. Somewhere in Samaria.?Maybe the city of Samaria. I'm really not sure. Maybe he went there. Why do you ask?"

Filippos did not want to tell them what he had done and so he lied. "The Master said that as soon as the first of the apostles returned, I was to find him and let him know. But he didn't say where he was going."

Yehuda chimed in, "Yes, I'm sure he said he was going to visit his friend while we were gone. Bacha was his name I think."

Filippos had to reach Yeshua quickly and warn him. Then he would have to find the rest of the apostles. He had no idea where any of them had gone, just that they were in pairs. Only Yeshua knew where he sent them. *How did Aharon find some of them so fast?* he thought. *And how will I get to the others before Aharon does?*

He would hire a camel. That would hasten his journey to Samaria. He would begin in the city. Being a Jew, he would have a hard time gaining cooperation, but he reasoned that anywhere near Yeshua, there were sure to be followers. He said goodbye to Yehuda and Mattityahu, then started walking to town to find a camel. As soon as he was out of sight, he started to run. There was no time to waste.

82 (Filippos finds Yeshua)

The camel ride was swift, and Filippos reached the city of Samaria by late afternoon. He had no idea where to begin. Knowing Yeshua's love for the poor, he decided to start asking in the poor section of town. He would ask if anyone knew either Yeshua or Bacha. As in most places, the poor section was outside the main city. As he approached them, many people turned and walked away quickly. *It's the way I'm dressed*, Filippos thought. *Too fine a tunic, even one that is dirty from a twenty-five-mile camel ride.*

"You there," Filippos said as he approached a stranger, "do you know of a person named Bacha, or a person named Yeshua?"

"I know nobody by those names. Leave me alone!" The stranger turned and walked around a corner.

He keep trying. By the time he'd unsuccessfully questioned six more people, someone approached him from across the road. "Excuse me sir, are you looking for the one who shaves his head?"

Filippos's quick mind told him that this would not be Yeshua, so it must be Bacha. "His name is Bacha."

"Yes, I know him. He lives in a community on the other side of the city. If you wish to find him, you must go in that direction." He pointed south. "I could bring you to him for a few coins."

Filippos held out five coins. "Will this do?"

The man snatched them out of his hand and said, "Come with me." He avoided the city, leading Filippos instead around the outskirts. He said nothing more. Filippos wondered if he was being led into a trap, but he had to take that chance. Now he was being led into the woods. Filippos was about to say something to his guide when the man turned and said, "There! Just beyond those trees." He was pointing to a beautiful fig tree. Filippos looked in that direction, and when he turned back, the man was running away. *Have I just been tricked?* he wondered.

But he walked beyond the fig tree, and saw that there was a community of some sort off in the distance. The guide had not lied to him. He approached a garden where several women were picking vegetables. They stood to face him. "Are you a Buddhist?" one asked.

"I am looking for two men, one named Bacha, and the other

named Yeshua."

"You have come to hear them speak? They are both here. I will take you to them," the woman said. Usually, women would be very leery of a male stranger, but this one seemed to have no fear as she led Fillipos further into the settlement.

"Teacher, you have a visitor," she said as she approached two men sitting with their backs to her.

One was a strange-looking man with a shaven head, and the other was Yeshua, who looked at Fillipos with surprise. "Filippos, what are you doing here?"

Bacha stood and placed his hands in prayer position over his heart. "Welcome, my friend. My name is Bacha."

Ignoring Bacha in his haste, Filippos said, "Master, you must listen to me. There is no time to lose. I need to tell you something that I have wanted to tell you for some time."

"You want to tell me that you are a spy, Filippos?"

Filippos lost his balance and fell to the ground. "But how ... how did you know that?"

Yeshua moved to him and helped him up. "Filippos, I have known from the first time I met you that you were a spy. But I also know that you would change. That you have changed."

Filippos looked from Yeshua to Bacha and back again. Bacha smiled knowingly. "He has many powers beyond healing, my friend. He can look into your heart and see what kind of person you truly are. Don't be afraid."

Filippos told them the whole story. He told them of leaving Aharon, of inadvertently giving Aharon information about the apostles, of Mattityahu being stabbed. And then he fell to the ground sobbing. "Forgive me! Please forgive me! I was trying to make things right, Master. Only they went horribly wrong."

Bacha turned to Yeshua and asked with concern, "What can I do to help?"

"Nothing, Bacha, nothing," Yeshua replied. "You continue your mission. I will deal with this. We will leave first thing in the morning.

"Filippos sit and listen to me. I don't know if you know that I have lived in another country for many years. It is called India." Filippos nodded his head. He had heard some of the stories from those closest to Yeshua. He knew that the meditation that Yeshua did he had learned from this faraway land.

"Over the course of the years I was there, I did many things. Some of them turned out good, and some of them bad. I was unclear of my own feelings back then, just as you are now unsure of yours. What you did by mistakenly telling this Aharon person about my apostles, you did with the best of intentions. You were severing your relationship with him. You now wish to be my follower. So be it. I accept you as one.

"As to your mistake, I say to you, don't feel guilty about it. Remember when we were in the boat in the Sea of Chinnereth, and that storm came up? Remember what I told everyone? I told you all to do your duty to the best of your ability, and then neither feel proud for the good that comes out of it nor guilty for the bad that comes out of it. This is what my Master, Patanjali, taught me while I was in India.

"We will return to Mount Arbel and wait for the other apostles. Whoever returns, it is by the will of our Father that they return. Say nothing of this to them. Time will pass, and this will go away."

He seemed so sure of himself that Filippos began to feel more at ease. But he wouldn't be fully content until he saw all the apostles with his own eyes.

83 (Yochanan is beheaded)

It was raining that dark evening outside the prison in Herod's fortress in Machaerus. It was unusual for an execution to take place at night, but the orders were to do it immediately. Four men marched in unison into the courtyard, one holding a lantern and leading the way, one with an axe, one, Yochanan, about to lose his life, and the last at Yochanan's side guiding him. Yochanan was led to the execution site and made to kneel down, placing his head over a tree stump with dark stains and random grooves from many previous beheadings. The chief executioner announced that he was an expert at what he did, and had spent the morning as he did each morning, sharpening his axe. "It will be swift and painless, I promise," he bragged.

"For you it will be swift and painless," Yochanan replied bitterly. The executioner's posture stiffened, and he turned to his assistant and nodded.

The assistant knelt at Yochanan's head, pulling and holding his hair so that his neck would be exposed, his head would be held fast to the stump, and he wouldn't move. The rain clouds had parted, and for a few moments, the full moon lit the gruesome scene below: four men, one about to lose his life. The executioner raised his axe high, his muscles glistening in the moonlight. Yochanan, who could only look down, watched a rat a few feet away, scurrying across the grass looking for food. The rat stopped for a moment, looking up at Yochanan. The two fixed their eyes on each other. Yochanan wondered if it was a male rat or a female. Then he wondered why he wondered that. Yochanan noticed the rat's nose twitching, and it seemed to now look above him. *How odd*, he thought, *that the last thing on earth I should see is...* Whack!

The first blow of the axe was placed perfectly and the head severed completely. The assistant was covered with Yochanan's splattered red blood, holding his head by the hair as it swung back and forth. "Swift and painless," the executioner repeated aloud as he turned and left. The rat scurried away and continued its search for food.

***

When the severed head was presented to Herodias, inside the fortress, her daughter left the dining hall. She had with great reluctance done what her mother requested, asking her father for Yochanan's head as a gift for a dance she had performed for her father, but she did not want to see the end result. Herod stared long at Yochanan's head. The guests at Herod's birthday celebration would not look at the macabre sight, and the once-festive mood turned somber. The only one who seemed to be happy was Herodias. She turned to her husband and smiled and blew him a kiss. Herod arose, his face red, his fists clenched. Then, turning and loudly knocking his chair down on its side, he left the hall in haste.

"Continue eating, everyone," Herodias said to the guests in a melodious voice, but nobody moved. Her demeanor changed abruptly. "That's an order! I command you all to eat and enjoy yourselves!"

They silently obeyed, but the grave mood remained, and nobody wanted to talk. *I will send a letter to Aharon. He will be the first to know*, she thought, drinking a sip of wine as Yochanan's glazed eyes stared at her half-empty plate.

***

Herod sat in his room, staring at the walls. How had he been talked into it? Why would his daughter ask for such a gift? This was his wife's doing, he was sure of that. He had a kind of admiration for Yochanan, but his hand was forced when Yochanan admonished him for his marriage to his brother's wife. This he could not let stand. But now Yochanan was dead. He could still see the grizzly head sitting on a plate.

When he slept that night he had nightmares. In his dream, the head was talking to him. He could see the eyes blinking, looking directly at him, and the mouth moving. Yochanan was again admonishing him for his marriage to Herodias. He woke up in a panic, sweat dripping from his brow. It took a long time to go back to sleep. He resolved that first thing in the morning he would order his guards to return the head to the followers who would come to collect the body. No telling what Herodias might do with it if he allowed it to stay.

***

Yeshua sat with three of his apostles near Mount Arbel in the early afternoon. One of the apostles had just said something funny, and they were all laughing.

Leviy came running towards them from off in the distance. As he neared, he shouted, "Master Master, Yochanan the Baptizer is dead!

I just heard about it in the city from one of the Essenes. He has been executed!"

Yeshua clutched his chest and stared at Leviy with disbelief. "Executed? But why?" he shouted, more to himself then to Leviy.

"I don't know why. His followers are asking for his body so they might give him a proper burial. Everybody in the city is talking about it."

This was the same kind of shock Yeshua had experienced when Bacha killed that guard almost twenty years ago. Only this time, he was able to recognize what was happening and control himself. He sat for a long time, staring at the horizon and breathing heavily. "I need to be alone," he suddenly said to Leviy. "I will climb Mount Arbel. Don't let anyone else come."

Yochanan had been his friend and mentor. He felt almost as close to Yochanan as he did to Bacha. He had written a letter to him only two days ago. Yochanan had said in his last letter to Yeshua that Herod visited him often and they discussed miracles and spiritual matters. It did not sound to Yeshua like Yochanan was in any danger. He was sure Herod would eventually release him. *Why would they execute him?* he asked himself. *Why?*

***

Aharon read Herodias's letter with delight. "She did it! She did it! That will show that bastard Yeshua. Take *that*, you bastard! And I'm not done with you yet. You'll see! First I will destroy everything you love, then I will destroy you." Aharon began dancing around the room and singing as he opened a fresh jug of wine. This was a time for celebration. His first group of assassins had told him that they failed in their task of killing two of Yeshua's apostles, but at least they had injured one. Meanwhile, the other assassins were out scouring the countryside looking for the rest of the apostles. One complete victory, and one partial victory thus far. He would wait patiently for word from them. His plan was working.

84 (Feeding the thousands)

Yeshua spent two weeks at the top of Mount Arbel. At first he could not meditate, although, as he had been taught by Patanjali, he would sit twice a day and try. His mind kept going back to Yochanan. Was this in some way his fault? Then he remembered that the Ayurvedic physician, Samik, had told him that blaming oneself was a natural part of the healing process. It was not his fault, and this feeling would eventually pass. Samik was right.

Yochanan's followers would likely find a new leader, but for now they would look to him, Yeshua, for guidance. Yeshua's flock had just increased, and Yochanan's many followers were disliked by the Pharisees and the Sadducees as much as he was. His life was going to get harder.

But his seventeen years of training and experience in India helped get him through all this, and early one morning he came down from the mountain. All his apostles had returned. Nobody else had been killed or injured in their return journeys. He greeted them all and asked them to tell him stories of their adventures. This would be healing for him as well. He was pleased to see that they had sacrificed so much to do his bidding. Many weighed much less than what they weighed when they began.

While he was on the mountain, he learned, they all taught the crowds of people who had come to see him. Tomorrow more would come, and when they saw Yeshua was back, their numbers would increase even further. He could see the weariness in his apostle's faces. He gathered them together and said, "You all need a rest. Come, let's row the boat into the sea and find a place to be by ourselves."

But the search for isolation did not go as expected. Someone had seen Yeshua and had spread the word that he was back. Knowing he and the apostles were going across the waters, the crowd walked along the shore to where they saw the boat heading, growing in numbers as they went, and were waiting for the boat's arrival. There was more people thanYeshua had ever seen in one place;.those on the boat could not believe their eyes. Yeshua shook his head and smiled. "It looks like our rest will have to wait!"

He taught to them all that day, but as it got later the apostles grew hungry. "Master, some of us are going to go into the nearest village and purchase some food," Cephas said.

"And what of the crowd? Don't you think they are hungry as well? Buy some food for them too."

Cephas replied, "But Master, we don't have enough money to buy food for everyone. Look at how many there are. What would you have us do?"

Yeshua thought back to his experience in India, where he began with a single chapatti and a basket, gave it to the little girl who was hungry, and by the time the basket came back to him, there was more food than he could eat. Of course back then the crowd numbered less than a hundred people. Here there were many thousands. But Yeshua's faith was unshakable.

"How much food do you have right now among all of you?"

After they gathered what they had, Cephas said, "Master, we have five loaves and two fish."

"And how many baskets do we have?"

"We have twelve baskets, Master."

"Good. That should be enough."

The apostles did not know what to think. How could so little food feed so many people?

Someone in the crowd shouted, "Give us a miracle, Master." He rose and addressed the crowd, as he had done in India. "My friends, listen to me! It is time for us to eat together. But we have only five loaves of bread and two fish."

The crowd began to get noisy until Yeshua held his hands in the air. He continued, "We have divided the food into twelve baskets. My apostles will arrange you into twelve groups. Each group will be given a basket. When it is passed to you, if you have nothing to eat, please take some food out, leaving some for others, and pass it to the next person. If you have brought food with you, please put some of it in the basket to share, and then pass it on. My apostles and I have given you all that we have. We now have nothing but faith. When the baskets come back to us, if there is food still in them, we will join you in this meal. You will make the miracle today. Now make it."

As in India, the crowd buzzed with excitement. Yeshua blessed the food before his apostles began distributing it.

It took over an hour for the distribution to take place. A family of five was seated near the back of one of the groups. "This isn't going to work," the father of the family said. "There will never be enough by the time the basket gets all the way back to us."

The mother was not as convinced as her husband. "Let's wait and see, Zevach. Maybe Yeshua is right."

But as the basket got nearer and nearer, there was less and less food in it. Zevach held the basket as it was passed to him, looking down at the little that was left, and then looked at his wife. But the others who were in his group also saw the almost-empty basket. The person nearest Zevach, the one who had first handed it to him, took the basket back and placed half of what he had back in it. Then several other people took the basket and did the same thing. The basket was now moving from the back to the front. Before long it was almost full again. Now it was once again passed to. Zevach held it above his head for all to see, and he and his family all nodded to the crowd.

In the end, the result was the same as in India. The twelve baskets came back to Yeshua filled with food. The apostles looked at each other in wonder as Yeshua held some of the overflowing baskets up for the crowd to see. "You asked for a miracle? The act of compassion and sharing can be seen as a miracle if you look at it correctly. Can five loaves and two fish feed five thousand? Yes it can. And it did. A miracle."

"A miracle!" the crowd cheered loudly.

85 (Aharon tries to turn away Yeshua's followers)

On that same day, back in Sepphoris, Aharon was not happy. He had found out that other than the one who had been wounded, the apostles had all returned safely. This was disappointing, but Aharon always had another plan, just in case. He had gathered in his house twenty-six people who were beholden to him in one way or another. Some were relatives of men who worked for him, others were men looking for work. All of them he judged to be loyal. He would pay them a small amount of money to do his bidding.

"Welcome, friends," he began. "How many of you know of the man called Yeshua?"

They all raised their hands.

"And what do you know about him?"

One of the men answered, "He is a great teacher, Aharon. He's becoming more and more popular every day. Some even say he's a prophet."

"A prophet, you say? A prophet? Bah. How many of you know that he is a bastard?" With this revelation, they all looked at one another in wonderment. "How many of you know that this person regularly breaks our laws?" They continued to look at one another. "Just as I thought! So let me tell you a little more about this person. He has spent most of his life in another country."

"Another country?" one of them asked.

"This is true. He lived in a land called India. So although he was born here, he is not really one of us. He is more a foreigner than a Jew. He regularly speaks with contempt to our religious leaders. He subverts our laws and replaces them with his own. Did you know that? He is often hailed as the son of God. But who is it that calls him that? Only the flocks who follow him. And who might they be? They are the poor, they are thieves and tax collectors, they are whores and drunkards. He once said of the idolatrous Samaritans that they were of greater worth than our own priests. He has angrily denounced entire cities. As for his so-called miracles, many of them are nothing more than magician's tricks.

"So this is where you come in. The truth must be told about him. You will plant yourselves in these crowds, and at every chance you get, you will tell people what I have just told you. When the rich come to hear him, you will tell them that he hates the rich. And he does. You will tell them that he only flatters the poor to make them follow him. And he does. Let them see for themselves the company he keeps. When he speaks ill of the Pharisees or Sadducees, point it out to them.

"While he travels often to Jerusalem and spends time in Samaria, he spends most of his time traveling around the Sea of Chinnereth and teaching there. So it is there that I want you to go. You will space yourselves in the cities around this sea and begin spreading the truth about this criminal. Then, when crowds come to hear him from far away, you will speak to them as well.

"If you find people who agree with you, encourage them to tell all their friends. Gather in groups and spread the word. You will all be part of a movement against this criminal foreigner to our land that will grow person by person. If you see him doing something that you know to be against one of our laws, find a Pharisee or scribe and tell him what you saw. Remember, the more people you tell, the better.

"Here is one more thing. If you are successful in turning people against him; if he is finally arrested and thrown in jail, I will pay each of you five hundred denarii. It's all up to you."

Aharon sent them in groups of three and four, and gave each a specific city to plant themselves in. He was pleased with the effect he had on them. They were certain that they were doing something positive for all of Israel. *Maybe they* are *doing something positive for Israel,* Aharon thought, *but they are also destroying my enemy.* He readily admitted to himself that he was being deceitful, but he felt this to be an admirable trait. He would now patiently wait for the outcome of his efforts.

86 (Yeshua rebukes the Pharisees and scribes)

Some of the Pharisees and scribes who lived in Jerusalem had heard the stories of Yeshua from their peers, but wanted to see for themselves. The stories they heard were of lawbreaking by Yeshua and scorn for Pharisees. Yet this man's popularity was growing daily, and they wanted to see for themselves if the stories of contempt were true. They traveled to the Sea of Chinnereth and began going from town to town inquiring as to his whereabouts. There were seven of them altogether, and they met up with five local Pharisees who said Yeshua was in Capernaum. All twelve headed in that direction.

When they arrived, they were in the midst of a huge crowd of people, all waiting for a chance to hear Yeshua speak. One in the crowd who noticed them was one of Aharon's spies. He and his friend, the other spy, went to them and asked, "Are you looking for the one who breaks our sacred laws?"

The elder of the Jerusalem Pharisees replied, "We are looking for the teacher called Yeshua."

"Follow me. I will show you what he and his disciples and apostles are doing right now. You can judge for yourselves."

He took them to a spot by the sea where several of the disciples had returned from town with food for their meal. The Pharisees watched as the disciples removed pots from the pack the donkey was carrying and placed the food in them without washing either the food, or the pots first. They all sat together and began eating. The man in the center, dressed in a white tunic and a plain outer garment, appeared to be their leader. His hair was long and flowing, and he had a full beard. A jug of wine was brought out, and again, from the donkey's pack, cups were obtained. The Pharisees gasped. These people were not following the tradition of washing their hands before eating, or even washing the food, since it had come from the market. Neither did they wash their cups or pots or bronze kettles. The elder of the group accosted them and shouted, "Why do you and your disciples not live according to the tradition of the elders, but eat with defiled hands?"

A crowd now gathered. Yeshua was simply trying to eat a quiet meal with his disciples and apostles. But apparently the Pharisees were no longer satisfied with harassing him when he taught and were now harassing him when he ate. The anger inside him began to boil to the surface. He stood and walked toward them. They were surprised and took a few steps backwards. The crowd was anxious to see what would happen and moved closer.

"Yesha'yahu prophesied rightly about you hypocrites."

The elder of the group, a tall man, stepped forward. He stood face to face with Yeshua, his eyes wide, his face red, and asked, "You are calling us hypocrites?"

Yeshua stared at him briefly and then said, "It is written in Yesha'yahu, 'These people honor me with their lips, but their hearts are far from me; in vain do they worship me, teaching human precepts as doctrines.'"

The elder was now shaking with anger. He clenched his fists and repeated more loudly, "You are calling us hypocrites?"

Yeshua could not be intimidated and did not back down. Just as loudly, he said, "You abandon the commandment of God and hold instead to *human* tradition. You have a very strange way of rejecting the commandment of God just in order to keep *your* tradition. Moshe tells us, 'Honor your father and your mother. Whoever speaks evil of his father or mother must surely die.' He says nothing more. Just that. And yet you, no doubt, would *starve* your parents unless they first washed their hands! How much greater the evil is that? You Pharisees, you all do so many things like this. You distort the laws and then claim them to be the laws of God."

He then turned his back to them and addressed the crowd. "Listen to me, my friends. Listen all of you and understand. There is nothing *external* to your mouth ..." he then picked up a piece of unwashed fish out of an unwashed kettle, holding it high above his head for all to see, "that can be defiled by going in." With that he dramatically put the fish in his mouth and swallowed it. The Pharisees eyes widened. The crowd began to cheer. Then, turning back to the Pharisees he pointed to his mouth, shaking his finger at his mouth as he pointed, and said, "It is what comes *out* of your mouth that can defile!"

With that the crowd cheered even more loudly, and the group of Pharisees and Aharons spies all left in haste.

The disciples sat back down and continued eating after Yeshua regained his composure. Filippos quietly asked him about what he had said, and two of the other disciples also said they didn't understand. Yeshua looked astounded. His anger grew again, although not as fiercely as with the Pharisees. "Don't you even yet understand what I say? Listen closely. I said that whatever goes into a person's mouth from the outside cannot defile. It doesn't enter the heart, does it? It enters the stomach. But the mouth is not just the entry point for food; it is the exit point for a person to say what he holds in his heart. It is from *there* that evil intentions come from: fornication, theft, murder, adultery, avarice, wickedness, deceit, licentiousness, envy, slander, pride, and folly. All these evil things come from within, and it is *these* things that defile a person. Do you understand now?"

They all nodded yes. It took Yeshua another few minutes to settle his mind.

The Pharisees from Jerusalem said to the local Pharisees that they needed to hear nothing more. They would return to their home and report to the Great Sanhedrin of this public humiliation and disregard for their traditions. Their own anger would grow as they journeyed home.

87 (Making a deaf man hear)

Yeshua's popularity was growing at an ever increasing rate. Using the Sea of Chinnereth as their central point, Yeshua and his apostles and disciples were expanding their circle to the west, all the way to the city of Tyre on the Mediterranean Sea, and then north to another port city called Sidon. From there, they had traveled east into Gaulanitis, turned south into Decapolis, and were now traveling westward back to the Sea of Chinnereth. People came from miles to hear him speak.

It was fall, and the cold air made them all walk just a little faster. As they neared the Sea of Chinnereth, they were met by a small crowd of people who had heard about Yeshua's great healing powers.

"Master, Master," one man shouted as he approached, "please help this man."

Yeshua came toward them and asked, "Who needs help?"

"Him. This man right in front of you. He can't hear you; he's deaf. You can't understand him either. He can talk, but you can't understand what he says."

Yeshua took the deaf man by the arm and said to the crowd, "Please stay here. I will bring this man to a quiet place and help him."

The two walked for several minutes until they were in seclusion. The first Siddi Yeshua had learned from Patanjali was the understanding of all sounds uttered by living beings. He remembered being tested in the center of a city in India long ago. He remembered two merchants talking about business.

He sat with the man and asked, "Can you read my lips?" The man nodded. "Tell me about your illness," he said slowly and clearly.

The man began to talk at a rapid rate, speaking sounds that made no sense at all … except to Yeshua. He clearly understood that the man had gone deaf two years ago after an illness that brought him fever and chills. He had always had a slight speech impediment, but now that he could no longer hear himself, it had gotten worse—much worse. Yeshua looked into the man's ears. At first he saw nothing, but then as he looked further he saw wax deep inside both of them. He remembered one passage from the Caraka Samhita that spoke of the oiling of ears. It said, "Ear disease due to weakened vata, torticollis, lockjaw, hardness of hearing, and deafness are prevented if oil is regularly dropped into the ears." One of the best oils to use was sesame oil, and sesame was widely available throughout Israel. All Yeshua had to do was remove the wax.

Yeshua asked the man if he believed in God. He eagerly nodded his head yes. Yeshua then asked if he believed that God could cure him. The man was still for a moment, and then nodded his head again.

Yeshua cupped his hands over the man's ears and closed his eyes. The heat generated by Yeshua's hands was enough to make the wax in the man's ears sizzle. "Ow!" he cried out. And then came the look on his face that indicated that he had just heard himself say, "Ow."

Yeshua said to him, "God has given you your ears back. Now that you can hear yourself talk, your speech will improve. Over time, everyone will be able to understand you. This will be your work. You must listen to others, and then go home and practice saying those words. God will help you, but you have to help God." Yeshua then told him about sesame oil, and instructed him to place several drops in each ear once a month.

The two walked back to the crowd and the man began to rant about what had happened to him. Yeshua was still the only one who understood all of what he was saying. He told the crowd that God had opened his ears, but it was now up to them to help him speak clearly. Someone behind him, not believing that the man could now hear, said his name, and upon hearing it, the formerly deaf man immediately turned around and said, "Whaa?"

There were no longer any doubters in the crowd. They had all witnessed for themselves that the man could now indeed hear. Yeshua addressed them: "My friends, you have now seen the work of God. I would be grateful if you would be quiet about this. Too many people are giving credit to me for these miracles, and not to God. What I teach and what I do is not about me. It's about our Creator. I am but a lowly son of man, a servant.

His request was, as usual, made in vain. At their very first opportunity, the members of this crowd would tell everyone they knew of the miracle of Yeshua that they had seen with their own eyes. Some would say to their friends, "He asked that we be quiet about this, so don't tell anyone, okay?" And each in turn would tell ten others, saying the same thing.

***

Aharon continued to get reports about Yeshua from his legion of spies. His people were doing their work, trying to spread Aharon's lies among the throngs of people, but the only ones who listened to them were the Pharisees, scribes, and now the Sadducees, who were also paying attention. He was losing again, and he did not like it. But, as in all his endeavors, he knew that winning battles was one thing, but winning the war was still another. He would continue his mission, but it was now time to come up with another plan. He knew that the death of Yochanan had deeply affected Yeshua. He knew that the wounding of Mattityahu had likewise taken its toll. And he knew that the religious establishment was now largely against Yeshua. But try though he might, he could not get the thousands upon thousands of people who followed Yeshua to turn against him. He needed something else. But what?

88 (The Sadducees meet Yeshua)

It was early in the morning in the town of Bethmaus, just east of the Sea of Chinnereth. Bethmaus was a small town of no prominence save for the fact that it was where Enowsh, a Pharisee, lived. He had invited several of his Pharisee friends and a group of Sadducees to his house to discuss Yeshua. The Sadducees and Pharisees normally did not mingle because they had quite different beliefs, but this was beginning to change. Like Aharon, they were trying to bring Yeshua down any way they could, and were starting to realize that they were stronger together than apart. Miyka, a Sadducee from Jerusalem spoke: "You say this man performs miracles? Have you seen them with your own eyes?"

Enowsh replied, "I have not. But several of my Pharisee brothers have."

"Then let us start there. We must see with our own eyes whether what he does is truly miraculous, or the work of a magician. I have seen magicians doing wondrous things, but still they are only tricks. I will know if I am being deceived."

The Pharisees and Sadducees made their way to the Sea of Chinnereth. The Pharisees' spies had said that Yeshua was on a boat and would likely be landing in Dalmanutha. They hurried to the shore of that city, where a crowd had already gathered.

Someone pointed to a boat on the horizon, and the crowd began to grow noisy. "It's the Master! He's coming!"

The boat continued to make its way to the shore, and the Pharisees and Sadducees had worked their way to the front of the crowd. Four of the disciples stood in waist-deep water and held the lines fast. Yeshua stood and raised his hands in the air. The crowd cheered wildly. He waited patiently, and after a time they grew quiet. But before he could say anything, Miyka shouted to him, "It is said that you are a prophet. If you are truly a prophet, show us a sign. Show us a sign from heaven. We all want to see a sign from heaven. Don't we?"

Again the crowd cheered. Yeshua closed his eyes and used a soothing breathing technique he had learned from Patanjali. But his anger would not be stilled. These kinds of confrontations were happening more and more. The scorners would simply not leave him alone. He again lifted his hands to quiet the crowd. "I am not a trained animal that does tricks on command! You will see no such sign." Then pointing at the Pharisees and Sadducees, he continued, "You hypocrites couldn't see them anyway. Perhaps you can look at a red evening sky and say, 'The weather will be fair tomorrow.' And maybe you can look at a red morning sky and say, 'The weather will be stormy today.' Yes, the sky you might read clearly. But signs, you cannot. They can be as close as the noses on your faces and you still can't see them. No, I say you will see no sign today."

Yeshua beckoned his disciples to turn the boat, and they jumped aboard as the boat began to sail toward the direction from which it had come. Miyka, Enowsh, and their group quickly disappeared before the disappointed crowd's anger turned to them. They walked far away from Dalmanutha, and sat on the ground to discuss what had just happened.

"He is certainly contemptuous of us, wouldn't you say?" asked Enowsh.

"Downright humiliating. I've never been talked to in that fashion before. In my opinion, if he really could produce a sign, he would have. This just bolsters my belief that he is nothing more than a magician. He knew that we would see through any of his tricks. And he wasn't prepared to do something that was asked of him. Yes, I am certain he is a magician." Miyka looked to his own group of Sadducees, and they all nodded in agreement.

***

Their plans had been ruined. Yeshua was now in a foul mood, and they were getting hungry. They intended to go into the city and buy food, but now they were out in the Sea of Chinnereth. Mattityahu said, "I think some of those people were from Jerusalem. They sure talked like it."

Cephas replied, "You are probably right. You know what they say: If all the hypocrites in the world were divided into ten parts, Jerusalem would contain nine of them!"

That got Yeshua's attention, and he smiled. "I know we were going to eat a meal in Dalmanutha, but did you all know that when you buy bread you need to beware of the yeast of the Pharisees and the yeast of Herod?"

"What do you mean?" asked Cephas.

"I mean that the yeast being spread by those at the shore asking for a sign is the yeast of hatred. It is not God's yeast being spread, which would otherwise increase the size of that which is good, but the yeast of hypocrites being spread which now increases the size of that which is evil. Those men at the shore—that's exactly what they were spreading."

After a short pause, Yehuda said, "We understand what you say, Master, but in truth we really don't have anything to eat."

Yeshua stood abruptly and shouted, "Why are you talking about having nothing to eat? Do you still not perceive or understand what I teach? Do you not remember when we fed the five thousand? How much food did we have then?"

Yehuda looked down at the bottom of the boat, not at Yeshua, and replied, "Master, we had five loaves and two fishes."

"And how many baskets did we have?"

"We had twelve, Master."

"And did anyone go hungry that day?"

"No, Master."

"Why, Yehuda?"

Yehuda was silent. Yeshua spoke louder and more forcefully. "*Why* Yehuda?"

"Um ... because many of those people had food. They just needed to be prompted to share what they had with others."

Yeshua now stared at them in silence. They all looked to one another and their faces turned red with embarrassment. One reached in his tunic and pulled out half a loaf of bread he had brought with him. Another pulled out a handful of figs. One by one, they began nervously reaching inside their tunics and bringing out food. Yeshua's eyes grew wider, looking at the food as its quantity grew larger and larger. His mouth was completely open, just like he remembered Bacha doing whenever Bacha wanted him to laugh. And it had its desired effect. The tension was broken, and everyone began laughing.

They placed all their food in a basket and passed it to Yeshua. Then, after Yeshua blessed the food, they ate. The seagulls landed in the water and noisily circled the boat waiting for food scraps as they drifted in the still waters.

89 (Aharon's plan, and Yeshua's experience on Mount Tabor)

Aharon woke up and jumped out of bed. Every night when he went to bed he was consumed with how to sway the thousands of people who believed in Yeshua to his way of thinking. He would dream about it. He would ponder it all day. But last night, sometime in the middle of the night, his mind had unconsciously worked on the problem and arrived at the logical answer. When he woke up, there it was waiting for him. He was jubilant.

The people who idolized this impostor would be part of the solution, not part of the problem. He realized that he couldn't turn them against Yeshua. But now he didn't want to. He wanted to do just the opposite. He would use them to destroy Yeshua. It was all too good to be true. Why hadn't he thought of it before? There was a certain crime that the Romans would convict someone of, and the punishment was execution. He knew about a particular Roman law known as lex Julia Majestatis, and it defined treason as: "An insult to the dignity or an attack upon the sovereignty and security of the Roman State."

Aharon's spies had reported hearing some people proclaiming Yeshua "Christ the King." Being proclaimed as Christ, or the anointed one, the Messiah, would convict him of blasphemy by the Jewish laws, and being proclaimed king would convict him of high treason against Caesar by the Roman laws. A death sentence to be certain.

Aharon's new plan was to gather his twenty-six spies and give them new instructions. They would now spread the word that Yeshua had openly proclaimed himself Christ the King. They would bow down before him and call him by that name and tell others to do the same. This would be easy. Most of the Jews already half believed it anyway.

Aharon lifted his arms over his head, shaking his fists, and began shouting to an empty room, "I've got you now, son of Mara. You are all mine. I will see you hang on the cross!" He prepared to travel to the Sea of Chinnereth and gather his spies. He sang to himself as he walked out the door of his house.

**

On that same morning, Yeshua was with three of his most

trusted apostles: Cephas, Yaaqob, and Yochanan. He had taken them to Mount Tabor, the mountain where Moshe was said to have received the commandments from God. This is where he would teach them more of what he had learned in India. These three had meditated daily for almost two years, unlike the others. They were ready to learn more. The other apostles would continue to heal by drawing out the faith of the sick. But Cephas, Yaaqob, and Yochanan would learn how to heal by touch, as Yeshua had once learned.

He asked them to sit with him in meditation. They all sat in a circle and closed their eyes. The mountain was alive with power that morning. They were all feeling something different from what they had ever felt before. The could almost hear a buzzing inside their heads. Suddenly Yeshua broke their meditation, saying, "You must move from this spot, now! Quickly, go sit by that rock over there."

As they rose and moved, they looked back at Yeshua, who sat in his meditation posture, with the sun behind him, and he appeared to be glowing with a blinding light. They had all seen him glow during meditation before, but never like this. They became frightened and clung to one another. It was as if he no longer had a body, and it was almost too bright to look at. Then a huge cloud came rolling in and filled the top of the mountain with a thick fog. It was so dense they could no longer see one another, only the light that was Yeshua. Cephas was certain that he saw not one, but three lights. The apostles lay on the ground, face down, fearfully waiting for their fate, afraid to look. Their fear turned a few seconds into a few minutes.

Then, as suddenly as the cloud had come, it disappeared. They looked up and Yeshua was now standing. His hair and beard had turned snow white. There was still a faint glow around his entire body making his tunic also look white. He seemed taller.

"What just happened?" Yochanan asked.

When Yeshua spoke, his voice echoed as if he were in a cave. "This is a very holy place we are in. I am standing on the very spot where Moshe once stood. I could feel it. I could feel him. I could feel the prophets. I could feel the presence of God."

They had come up the mountain for further training, but there would be no training today. Yeshua began slowly and quietly walking down the mountain, almost gliding with each step he took, and Cephas,

Yaaqob, and Yochanan followed. As they neared the bottom, he turned to them to say, "You must not tell anyone what you saw. Not now. Maybe some day, but not now."

They nodded. Over the next two days, most of the color would return to Yeshua's hair and beard, but leaving him with visible streaks of gray.

90 (Yeshua struggles with the concept of a Messiah)

It had been six weeks since that episode on Mount Tabor. As they walked to the next town Yeshua asked some of his disciples, "Who do people say that I am?"

Cephas replied, "Some say you are the incarnation of Yochanan the Baptizer, others say Elijah, or Jeremiah, or one of the other prophets. Many say you are the Messiah. Many are now saying you are Christ the King."

"But I constantly call myself the son of man. Do they not understand?"

"Master, they are simply voicing what their hearts tell them."

Yeshua was quiet for a moment, pondering what had been said. "But what about you, Cephas? Who do *you* say that I am?"

Cephas said, "Master, I side with the others. I truly believe you are the Messiah. I saw what happened on Mount Tabor. You are the true Son of the Living God."

Yeshua said nothing. More and more, the crowds of people, as well as his own apostles and disciples called him the Messiah. Yeshua walked in contemplation. *Am I just the son of man, as I set out to be, or a prophet, or even one of the Messiahs? Is someone born a Messiah, or is it a title bestowed upon them later in life? Can someone be the Messiah, yet not know they are the Messiah? What if I am? Was God Himself proclaiming me so on Mount Tabor? I just don't know. What if I am the Messiah to some people but not to others? Could this work the same way miracles of faith worked? For those who believe I am the Messiah, I am. And for those who don't, I am not. How can I know the truth? If Patanjali were here, he could tell me. Maybe the answer is back on Mount Tabor. I must go back there for meditation and prayer.*

***

Yeshua climbed the mountain early in the morning, asking Cephas to keep the others from following him. He needed to be alone.

It was now late afternoon "Is he still up there?" Yaaqob asked.

Cephas answered, "Yes. He is so puzzled by the reaction of his own followers. To be honest, I'm a little puzzled too. It has only been in the last few weeks that so many are bowing before him, calling him Christ the King. You know he has always admonished people not to call him that. He cures their sicknesses, then asks them—begs them sometimes—not to tell anyone what he has done. He always refers to himself as the son of man."

"Do you think he is the Messiah we have been waiting for?" Cephas wanted validation for his own belief.

"I don't know, Cephas. I know he is more than just an ordinary son of man, as he calls himself. I have seen with my own eyes how he lays his hands on the sick, and the heat that comes from his body. I've seen the steam coming from his hands on cold days. I've seen the lame get up and walk. I've seen the deaf get their hearing back, and the blind able again to see. He is truly a worker of miracles. But a Messiah? To me a Messiah is someone loved and respected by the religious leaders as well as the people. He will be, after all, our king. But you have seen, as I have, how he scorns and disrespects the Pharisees and scribes. The other day in the boat he even was shouting at the Sadducees. To me a Messiah will chase the Romans out of Israel once and for all. Yeshua all but ignores the Romans. I have never seen him stand up to any of them.

"I'll give you this, Cephas, I think he might be a prophet. And as to the religious leaders, I think those he has yelled at had it coming to them. But I just can't see him as the anointed one, the one we have been waiting for."

Cephas was disappointed but did not want to argue with Yaaqob. "We had better gather some wood for a fire. Who knows how many days we will have to stay here before he comes back down?"

"You need not gather wood. I have returned." They turned around to see Yeshua standing before them. How much of their conversation he had overheard, they didn't know. There was a faint glow about him, but not like that day that his hair and beard turned white. He looked very peaceful and content. He looked like a man who had just found the answers he was looking for.

"Where to, then, Master?" Yaaqob asked.

"To Jerusalem. It is time for Passover. We will stop first in Jericho."

Cephas continued to press him for an answer. Everyone was there, and this was not the first time they had talked among themselves about this subject. "Master," he began, "are you the Messiah?"

Yeshua replied, "If others say that I am, so be it. If you think that I am, so be it. I only ask you—and I ask all of you—that you not openly call me the Messiah again. Will you do this for me?"

Cephas's question had not really been answered. But this was as close as he was going to get to Yeshua proclaiming himself the Messiah. They all nodded in agreement.

91 (Yeshua raises the dead)

It was a sunny day in Jericho. Yeshua enjoyed being in this place because it was near where he first met Yochanan the Baptizer. Although some time had passed since Herod had him killed, the thought of him being gone still saddened Yeshua. As he and his disciples sat by the River Jordan and talked, a stranger came up to him and asked, "Are you Yeshua, the teacher?"

Yeshua replied that he was.

"Then you must come at once to Bethany. Elazar, the brother of Miryam and Martha, is very ill. They heard you were here and asked that I come get you. They are very concerned."

Cephas said, "Master, you can't go now. You promised the people of Jericho that you would teach in the synagogue on the Sabbath, tomorrow. There are many who have come a long way to hear you."

Yeshua pondered a moment and then asked, "How ill is Elazar?"

The man said, "I don't really know. I was only summoned to come and get you."

Yeshua thought some more and then replied, "Tell Miryam and Martha that I will be there the day after the Sabbath. I have already promised to speak here in Jericho. And tell them ... tell them not to worry. Elazar is going to be just fine."

After he left, Cephas turned to Yeshua and said, "Master, you know you have enemies in Bethany. Maybe it's not such a good idea to go there. They have been known to stone people to death whom they dislike."

Yeshua did not answer Cephas. Instead, he and Miryam of Magdala left the other disciples to walk and talk in private. It was not uncommon for them to do so. She was, after all, Yeshua's most trusted disciple. As they found solitude in the surrounding hills, Miryam turned to him and asked, "You seem troubled, Master. What is it?"

Yeshua looked up to the treetops, spotting a solitary sparrow, preening its feathers. He continued to watch it as he answered. "It's more than just Elazar. It's all this talk of my *enemies*, Miryam. Before it was just the Pharisees and scribes. But now it's more. And they seem to grow in number each day. Every crowd I speak to now has its distracters. Don't they see that I love them? Why do they hate me so?

Everywhere I turn, they are waiting for me."

Miryam was quiet. She seemed to know that he wasn't talking to her; he was talking to himself.

Yeshua continued, "When I was a young child, my fiercest enemy was a boy named Efah. He used to beat me up. I avoided him as much as I could. When Bacha and I were in India, I had enemies there too. My teachers all advised me to avoid them whenever possible. And now, I am being advised by the other disciples to avoid going to Bethany. What do you think, Miryam?"

"Yeshua, I say this to you as your friend as much as your disciple. First of all, you have already promised to go there the day after Sabbath. You can't go back on your word. And your friends, Miryam and Martha, are counting on you. Elazar is ill and needs you. Second, all those people who look up to you do so in part because of the way you stand up to your enemies. Your enemies are their enemies as well."

The sparrow had flown away, and Yeshua was now looking at Miryam. He said, "Part of standing up to them is but show. When I was a child, I always wanted to be right. The other children hated that I was right all the time, but I was just—I don't know—stubborn. And so I would go out of my way to let them know that I was right and they were wrong. That's why I often stand up to the Pharisees and scribes, Miryam. They are simply wrong. And I want them to know that they are wrong. I can't help myself. Just like my bursts of anger. They just come out. Maybe I should try to hold my tongue more. Maybe there is a better way."

"Yeshua, you aren't a child anymore. And confronting falsehoods with truth is more than just being stubborn. What you do when you stand up to them is important. It says who you are. It speaks of your character. I say, go to Bethany, help your friends, heal Elazar, confront your enemies, and above all else, don't doubt yourself."

Yeshua put his arms around her and said, "Miryam, what would I do without you? You always know what to say to me. Were it not for my vows ..."

"Shhh," Miryam said as she placed her finger over his lips. Yeshua blushed and smiled at her, but noticed her moist eyes and a far-off look that he had seen in her before.

When they returned, Yeshua said to his other disciples, "It is decided. We go to Bethany the day after Sabbath." He saw disappointment in some of their faces, but his mind was now made up.

***

The synagogue was full that Sabbath, and Yeshua spoke about loving your enemy and praying for those who persecute you. After his talk with Miryam, he spoke with more conviction. This was a hard message to get across, and harder still to follow. Loving those who loved you back—now, that was easy. But loving those who hated you? It was just a difficult concept to understand. However, as he spoke, they all listened.

That night Yeshua did not sleep well. He sensed something was wrong. He was restless all night, and arose early the next morning. He awakened all his disciples and said, "We must go to Bethany now. I need to be there."

It was less than a day's journey, and they made their way quickly to the house of Elazar and his two sisters, Miryam and Martha. As he walked down the path, Miryam came running up to meet him with tears in her eyes. "Yeshua, come quick. I think he is dead. Hurry."

Yeshua ran inside the house and found Elazar lying on the floor. Elazar was huge. His belly was bigger than a pregnant woman's with twins inside her. His wrists were thicker than Yeshua's legs. He appeared not to be breathing, but when Yeshua put his head close to Elazar's nose, he thought he heard a faint breath.

"Quickly, get me some honey!" he shouted. If this was what he thought it was, honey just might save Elazar. Martha brought it to him, and he smeared it under Elazar's tongue, and on top. At first nothing happened, then, he appeared to swallow. Yeshua applied more. He continued for a moment, and then, Elazar began to blink and open his eyes.

"You have brought my brother back to life! Oh, thank you, Master." Martha began crying.

He turned to her sister, Miryam, and said, "Miryam, bring me some tea. Not too hot. Make enough for two or three cups."

Miryam left, and Yeshua turned back to Elazar. He lay there with his eyes opened, but he appeared confused. "Just rest, Elazar. You are going to feel better in a few minutes."

He then turned to Martha. "Tell me what happened."

"He was sick for many days. He was weak and dizzy all the time. He just lay in his bed and moaned. Just before you came, Elazar got up and began to shake all over. He was sweating and said he needed to eat something. Then he vomited. He tried to tell us something, but couldn't seem to talk right. He looked very confused, and then he fell. He looked dead, and we couldn't hear him breathing. We were sure he was gone. That's just when you came."

Yeshua held Elazar's hand between his own two hands and continued talking to Martha. "I have seen this same thing in India. Over there, they make a wooden cup from the bark of a tree called Vijaysar. By placing water in it and leaving it overnight, the water changes to brown. The person with this disease drinks it, and then fills the cup up for the next morning. They must continue to drink this brown liquid each morning for the rest of their lives."

Miryam returned with the tea. Yeshua put the rest of the honey in it and tasted it. It was sickly sweet. "Elazar, can you sit up?"

With difficulty, he did so. "Drink as much of this as you can," Yeshua said.

While Elazar drank the sweet tea, Martha asked, "Is there such a tree here in our land?"

"No, Martha. But a different diet can help. I will write down those things that your brother should eat. He must become smaller. Not so big and heavy. You must then keep him from getting big again. Don't let him eat anything that I have not written down."

Elazar was now more alert. "I like this tea. Should I drink it every day?"

"No, Elazar, you shouldn't. This was just to bring you back from the sleep this disease put you in. If it ever happens again, your sisters will do as I just did." He looked at the two of them, and they nodded. "In fact, you should avoid eating all sweet foods, Elazar. Eat only what I will write down. It is important. If you don't follow this way of eating, you will die."

Yeshua wrote down an Ayurvedic diet specific for this disease. The two sisters were happy to have their brother back, but Martha was convinced that Yeshua had raised him from the dead. Yeshua could not dissuade her.

92 (A dream within a dream)

It was the middle of the afternoon, and Yeshua craved solitude. He wished to meditate. He left the house and walked into what looked like a remote area. It was overcast, so the afternoon was quite bearable. He found a cave along the side of a hill, and sat just inside. The air was even cooler where he sat.

As he tried to meditate, thoughts kept appearing in his head. *Pharisees, scribes, enemies, confrontation, death, near-death.* It was all he could think about. Finally, knowing meditation would not come, he lay down his head and slept.

***

It was foggy. Everything was a gray hue. He saw himself walking toward Miryam and Martha's house, his disciples all around him. Martha came out of the house, crying when she saw Yeshua. "You're too late. Elazar died two days ago. Why didn't you come when I asked you to? You could have saved him, Yeshua." She sat on the ground and cried.

He too began to weep. He had never wept over the dead before, at least not that any of his disciples had ever seen. He asked Miryam to take him to the place Elazar was buried. It was a cave with a stone lying against it. He then asked to be left alone. Whenever he was troubled, he would meditate and find answers. But try though he might, he was not able to move beyond his feelings. Each time he closed his eyes, he would begin to choke up with emotions which would keep him from his meditation.

It had been overcast all that day, and now storm clouds were gathering as he sat in front of the tomb continuing to weep. He still could not explain his own feelings. Suddenly, the storm let loose with a fury. The rain came down in torrents and there was a continuous volley of thunder and lightening echoing up and down the river. Yeshua was soaked. And then along with the rain came hail. It pounded down on him. The only refuge was the cave Elazar was buried in. Yeshua pushed away the rock with some difficulty and climbed inside. The stench was almost unbearable. He looked down at the wrapped body of his friend's brother and began to feel dizzy. Maybe it was from the putrid smell, or the sight of a dead man, or perhaps the chill he was feeling from his wet clothes, but he passed out, falling to the floor.

I am standing over the body of Elazar. I slowly unwrap his death shroud. Everything is happening as if time has slowed down. Why am I unwrapping it? I don't want to continue. I know what I am going to see. Stop! Stop! No, I can't stop. As I unwind the cloth, more and more of the dead man's face is appearing. I give it a final yank. I'm afraid to look; knowing what I will see, but I slowly turn my head downward. It's me! It's me lying dead in a tomb. What is happening? I must leave this place. I run as fast as I can. But the faster I try to run, the slower I go. I am being dragged back to the cave. The rain and hail are pounding down upon me. Now I slip on a rock. I hit the ground hard. My head has hit another rock. My head is bleeding. My foot is bleeding. And now I am looking at my hand. There is a sharp stick protruding all the way through it. I can feel the pain. I can taste the blood from my head as it drips down. My heart is pounding. Everything is turning dark. Darker, darker, and now, at last, blissful silence. It is finished.

Now it was nighttime, too late to return to Miryam and Martha's house. He would have to spend the night here. The storm had lightened somewhat, and so he slept near the opening where he could still breathe fresh air, and be away from the stench of the body of Elazar. He was afraid to go to sleep, but it finally overcame him.

***

He awoke the next morning, stiff from having slept on the cold damp ground and arose. He turned one last time to look at the body of Elazar, but . . . it wasn't there! *What could have happened to it?* he thought. He ran outside the tomb and looked around. Maybe a wild animal had carried it off. He could find nothing. He frantically searched in ever-increasing circles around the tomb, but there was no trace of the body of Elazar. He had vanished. Three days had gone by since the death of Elazar, and now the tomb was empty.

Now he would have to tell Miryam and Martha that their brother was gone. He still felt confused and a little dizzy. As he reached the house, Elazar came outside with his sisters. "There you are, Yeshua," Elazar said, "We were worried about you in the storm. Where have you been?"

"You have risen after having been dead for three days? How is that possible?"

"Dead?" Martha asked.

***

Yeshua awoke and sat up suddenly. He was back inside the cave along the side of the hill where he had gone to meditate. *What just happened?* he thought. He remembered trying to meditate and finally falling asleep. And then? *It had all been just a dream. But it was also a dream-within-a-dream.* That had never happened to him before. It was now late in the afternoon, and he needed to go back to the home of Elazar and Miryam and Martha.

When he arrived, Yeshua said nothing to anyone of his dreams. Miryam of Magdala, his most trusted disciple, sensed his unease, but knew he would not want to talk about what troubled him until he was ready.

93 (Yeshua foresees his death)

A week had gone by, and Yeshua was now ready to talk. He sat with Miryam by the River Jordan.

"Miryam," he began, "my life is near its end. I am now sure of it."

"How is this possible?" Miryam asked.

He shared with her his dream, and his dream-within-a-dream from Bethany. He waited for her reaction.

"It was just a dream, Yeshua. You were consumed with thoughts of enemies, remember? We talked about it before we left to go to Elazar. And then you saw a man who looked as if he were dead. All these thoughts and worries and confusion blended together into a dream, or, in your case, into two dreams. But it wasn't real, Yeshua."

He reached over and held both of her hands in his own. He often did this when he had something important to say to her. "When I ended my training with Patanjali, I obtained powers, powers that I have used to help people. He called them Siddis. One of these powers is the ability to see the past and the future. This was more than a dream, Miryam. It was a Siddi. I was seeing the future, my future. Only it was a future I was not prepared to see at the time. And so it was disguised as a dream.

"Some time soon I will give up my powers. Patanjali told me I would. And shortly after that, I will die. I don't know how much time I have left, but I must not leave this earth without making sure my message will live on. It needs to live for all eternity. I have so much work left to do."

Miryam stared at him in disbelief. She had no arguments to offer because she knew he was right. She knew, because she knew Yeshua. When he talked like this, with so much conviction, he was *always* right. She knew of his great powers and of his special relationship with God. All she could do was hold his hands while tears ran down both of their cheeks. "But why must you give up these powers? They have helped you help others."

Yeshua pondered, then said, "Patanjali once explained to me that the Siddis are subtle experiences. They are attained, seen as an obstacle, and set aside with nonattachment. By giving up these powers, the seed of evil is destroyed and liberation follows."

"The seed of evil? You have none."

"Miryam, it is very complex. All these powers are simply manifestations. They are no better than dreams. As long as there is a mind, they can be understood. But the goal of total liberation is a goal even beyond the mind. The mind is the source of the seed of evil. So one may not be evil, but the seed is there, nonetheless. By setting aside, with nonattachment, these powers, there will be nothing left. I have already set aside all else. With this final act, the seed of evil will have been destroyed. Liberation will follow."

With a quivering voice, she said, "I will spread your message, Master. All of us will."

"I am depending on it, Miryam."

94 (The money changers at the temple)

AD 32
Yeshua's age: 35

It was Passover in Jerusalem. Yeshua and many of his followers had each brought two doves to the Temple Mount as their ritual sacrifices. They had checked them in, gone to the mikveh to ritually bathe and purify themselves, and had picked them back up afterward. According to the scroll of Leviyticus, if anyone could not afford a lamb, they were to bring two doves instead, one for a sin offering and the other for a burnt offering.

As they were heading to the Huldah gates, they noticed a number of people coming back, each with doves in their hands. One of them said, "Don't bother bringing your doves upstairs. They are telling everyone that their doves can't be used. You have to buy them here, and they are very expensive this year, more than three times what they were charging last year. And that's nothing compared to what the money changers are charging."

"What will you do, then?" asked Yeshua.

"There is nothing we can do. We can't afford the prices, so we will leave."

Yeshua became very agitated. The priests upstairs in the Court of the Gentiles would often examine and find marks on sacrificial animals, making them not worthy of sacrifice. This was so that the visitors would be forced to purchase one of the vendors' animals at a marked-up rate. The priests would take part of the money collected by the vendors in exchange. Normally many of those who brought their own animals got through because there were plenty of people who came without. This year was different.

Yeshua and his followers climbed the massive stairs that went up thirty feet, and passed through the Huldah gate into the Court of the Gentiles.

There were lots of people enjoying the festivities and listening to the music. But Yeshua saw many people coming back from the money changers looking unhappy, and leaving. The money changers also had a good deal going for them. Jews were not allowed to coin their own money, and Roman currency was considered by them to be an abomination to the Lord. So the only thing to do was to exchange Roman for Tyrian money. The rate of exchange was usually determined by the high priest, in this case a man by the name of Chanan. It was usually a fair price, but not this time. It was four times as much as last year, and Chanan was making a huge profit.

Yeshua stood in the background and watched. He watched the money changers; he watched the sellers of doves; he watched the sellers of sheep, and he was starting to shake. Many had never seen him in such a state. More and more people were leaving because they could not afford the prices being charged this year. And then, quite suddenly, he snapped. His face was turning bright red.

Anger greater than Yeshua had ever felt before coursed through his body. He was breathing faster and faster. He was no longer even thinking. He looked about with wild eyes, suddenly spotting and picking up some cords off the ground. He quickly strung them together into a whip. Before anyone could stop him, he stomped towards the tables of the money changers and vendors. First he grabbed some of the dove cages, tore them open, and freed the birds to the protest of the vendors. Then he violently threw the table of the money changers on its side, smashing the table with a loud bang. Coins were scattered everywhere on the ground.

He grew angrier still and began to lash his whip in the air towards the money changers and vendors, shouting at them, "Get out! All of you! Get out of here! My Father's house is a house of prayer, but you have all turned it into a den of thieves! Get out I say, and don't come back!" He continued lashing his whip towards them, and many of them grew frightened and started running away. He shouted at the remaining ones as a crowd started to gather.

Some of his disciples were grabbing at Yeshua, pulling him back, but the damage had been done. It was enough of a disturbance to cause the guards to work their way towards the commotion. Filippos and one of the other disciples saw the guards coming and pulled Yeshua back to the stairway just in time. They quickly ran through the gate and down the stairs.

***

"What just happened here?" shouted Chanan, as he furiously charged his way to the overturned table.

The money changers, the vendors, and the crowd all started talking at once until Chanan silenced them and asked one of the money changers to explain. "It was that ... that teacher called Yeshua. The one everyone is talking about. He freed most of the doves, he scattered our money on the ground, and he was thrashing his whip at us. I was afraid he might kill us. He was yelling at us about what we had done to his father's house. *His* father's house? Who does he think he is? The son of God?"

Chanan was not going to let this go. He would see the Great Sanhedrin and have Yeshua arrested. Nobody was going to embarrass him while he was the high priest. He would go there immediately. He entered the temple and found Rabbi Gamliel the Elder, the Nasi—the head of the Great Sanhedrin—and told him what had just happened. "Is this so? Were there witnesses?" Rabbi Gamliel seemed very concerned.

"Of course there were witnesses," Chanan replied. "The vendors and the money changers, to name just a few."

"Then at long last we can have him arrested," Gamliel said. "We will search the city and find him. Chanan, we have been waiting for just such an opportunity. This Yeshua has been a thorn in our sides for some time, flouting many of our laws, and now it looks like we can finally deal with him. Go back to the court now, and we will let you know when we have him in custody. Have your witnesses ready." Rabbi Gamliel summoned his friend Aharon and sent him to find Yeshua.

***

"Where is the teacher? Have you seen the teacher called Yeshua? Which way did the teacher go?" Aharon was asking everyone and anyone. Nobody knew. He had several men searching the city, and others searching the roads leading out of Jerusalem. To the east, through the Susa Gate, were the roads to Bethany and Jericho; to the west were the roads to Emmaus and Joppa; to the north, through the Fish Gate and the Sheep Gate, were the roads to Samaria; and to the south was the road to the Sea of Salt. All of these roads were filled with travelers coming and going.

If Yeshua wasn't found soon, it would be dark, and then Aharon would not find him at all. But which gate would he choose? He could be going almost anywhere. Sometimes he would wander through Samaria, going as far west as Casarea, and sometimes he would travel northeast into Peraea and Decapolis. If he was hiding in the city, he would be found. But Aharon did not hold out hopes of that happening.

***

As Filippos guided him out the Susa gate, he noticed that Yeshua no longer seemed angry. But that anger was replaced by confusion. He kept shaking his head. Then he would furrow his eyebrows, narrow his eyes, and open his mouth, but say nothing. Right now, it was important to keep moving. Fortunately, Yeshua was also docile and easy to lead. Filippos instructed the others to spread out so as not to be seen together, and to meet in Jericho.

The elevation of Jerusalem was much higher than that of Jericho, and it was a difficult, mountainous winding road connecting the two cities. Filippos and Yeshua moved off the road, climbed higher up the mountain, and sat by a tree and watched quietly. Filippos knew that Aharon's men would be out looking for Yeshua, and Filippos knew what most of these men looked like.

There were three of Aharon's moving through the crowd, along with two Roman guards, asking if anyone had seen Yeshua. Filippos recognized them immediately. They could cover a lot of distance, because it was a downhill road. But knowing human nature, Filippos concluded they would not go far. Going back to Jerusalem would now be an uphill climb, and the further they went towards Jericho, the longer and harder it would be to come back. And indeed, they were soon trudging up the mountain road, returning to Jerusalem. Once they were out of sight, Filippos and Yeshua slipped back down to the path and headed to Jericho, where they would join the other disciples and spend the night.

Yeshua was unusually silent during the journey. Normally he was quite talkative when walking, and Filippos enjoyed being close to him and listening. Why had he become so angry back at the temple? And what was wrong with him now? But this was not the time to ask. It was obvious that Yeshua needed to be alone with his thoughts, so they walked as if they were total strangers drawn together only by the narrowness of the road.

They slept at an Inn in Jericho, and in the morning, when Filippos arose, Yeshua was gone. He knew he had probably gone out to pray or meditate, and that he would likely be back. Filippos waited patiently.

**

Yeshua got up early in the morning and walked around the city, trying to make sense of it all. *What just happened to me back at the temple? Why was I so angry? And why do I feel so strange now?* He closed his eyes for better focus, but still the answer would not come to him. And then ... it did. His eyes opened wide, he felt goosebumps on his arms, and he began to gasp. Although his mouth was open, it was also in a half smile. *Did it happen? Did it really happen? Yes! It's true.*

With that fiery outburst at the temple, Yeshua had finally and completely rid himself of all the anger that once burned inside him. Patanjali had told him that would happen. He began to remember more fully the last conversation he had with Patanjali. He remembered Patanjali telling him that he still had anger that needed to be burned and one day soon it would. So, Yeshua reasoned, the event at the temple was in itself not so extraordinary, it was just the means by which to burn his anger. He now knew for certain that this is what was different. That anger was all gone. It was such a tremendous feeling of liberation.

The only thing left in his heart now was love. Patanjali had also told him that once he rid himself of all his anger, he had one last task to perform in order to reach Kaivalya. He must willingly give up his Siddis—his powers. That time was now. There was no turning back. He would no longer heal the sick using his Siddis. But he had taught some of his disciples how to do this through faith, through the mantras he had taught them, and through the knowledge of Ayurveda that he had passed on, so his work would go on. He would no longer see the future, but he already knew what was awaiting him. He would no longer know what people were saying, even if they were speaking in a different language, but he had no further need for that power either. In fact, he had no further need for any of his Siddis.

He went into deep meditation for a long time. And when it was over, it was nighttime. His powers were gone. He sensed their absence because they had given him a great strength throughout his last few years which was no longer there. And yet ... he was complete!

95 (Yeshua's transformation)

It was early morning in the city of Ramoth-Gilead, far to the east of the Sea of Chinnereth. It had been several months since the incident at the temple. Myriam and Cephas watched as Yeshua sat on the ground with a sick child of about three or four on his lap.

"Am I going to die?" the child asked.

"No, child. I'm going to help you. What is your name?"

The child replied, "Daniyel."

Daniyel's mother stood close by and watched.

"What's wrong with you, Daniyel?"

Daniyel rested his head on Yeshua's shoulder. "My head hurts. Please make it stop."

Yeshua stroked the child's head and gently whispered a mantra into his ear. The boy immediately went to sleep. Yehsua cradled him in his arms and gently rocked him back and forth.

He looked to the mother and asked, "His head hurts?"

"Yes. He's been like this for a week. You made him go to sleep so easily. Even I can't do that. Are you a physician?"

Yeshua smiled and replied, "I know some things about such matters. Please, sit here by me and tell me more."

As the two talked, Cephas turned to Myriam. "The change in our Master is quite remarkable, is it not? He no longer confronts the Pharisees and scribes. There is no more anger in his voice. And he spends his days," Cephas gestured to Yeshua, Daniyel, and Daniyel's mother, "doing this. And have you noticed that smile on his face? That perpetual smile?"

Myriam nodded her head yes. "He is at peace, Cephas. At long last he is completely and totally at peace."

***

The change in Yeshua was indeed remarkable. He now visited new places, places he had never been to before. He wandered far beyond the Sea of Chinnereth. This thirty-five-year-old teacher who used to walk so quickly from one place to another walked slowly now, like an old man. Everyone noticed it. Even his sermons, although he was now repeating much of what he had said over the past two years, were delivered much more slowly and were filled with a quiet peacefulness. He seemed to enjoy being in smaller groups now, teaching as few as four or five at a time. He would question his listeners to make sure they understood what he had said. He asked about their families. He was a totally different person.

And it was *this* person to whom everyone was drawn even more deeply than before. Before there had been a lot of flash and grandeur as he openly and loudly confronted the establishment and spoke to his people of hope. He had always spoken of love, but when he first began, it was a new kind of love that nobody had ever considered: the love of your enemy. It *needed* to be proclaimed loudly, because it was such an alien concept. He had chastised the Pharisees and scribes loudly and openly at every opportunity. Again, it was something that needed to be done, because people needed to understand that the spirit of the law was more important than the law itself. But now, all that shouting had turned to almost a whisper. And the love he previously spoke of was now so eloquently shown in the way he lived rather than in the words he chose.

"Where do we go next, Master?" asked Myriam.

Daniyel and his mother had left. Yeshua had given her instructions on helping her son with his headaches. "Home," he replied quietly. "We haven't been back to the Sea of Chinnereth in quite a while."

Yeshua's disciples and followers all saw that he needed this time to teach in his own way, and at his own pace, and they complied. They no longer went from town to town in advance, proclaiming his arrival. Instead, they went quietly with him, often arriving at night. Yeshua might teach in the synagogue on the Sabbath, but more often he would sit wherever small groups of people congregated and simply converse with them, and in the process teach them. Many didn't even know who he was. But they were attracted to the aura of peacefulness that this holy man seemed to exude from his very being.

***

"Damn it, where is he hiding?" An angry Aharon prodded Zevach, one of his spies.

Zevach answered, "We continue looking for him, Aharon. Occasionally we hear stories about someone we think might be him, but when we go to that place, he is not there."

Aharon's plan had been working so well. He had half of Israel calling Yeshua Christ the King, and then … gone! Almost a year, and he was not to be seen anywhere; at least as far as his spies could find out. Was he going to disappear for another seventeen years? Or did he find out about Aharon's spies and was now in hiding?

But Aharon was not a quitter. It was not in his nature. He would go to Jerusalem, stir up the Sadducees, and make plans just in case Yeshua showed up for Passover.

***

Much of the time when he was not teaching, Yeshua returned to the place he loved the most, the Sea of Chinnereth, spending his spare hours sitting in solitude on its shore, just looking across the waters for hours on end, listening to the splashing of the waves and the sounds of the birds, enjoying the smell of the air and the feel of the warm golden sun on his skin. He remembered the excitement of going over the sea to India as a child. He remembered the colorful people there, and his own master, Patanjali who had taught him so much. He remembered all that was taught from this great master about Kriya Yoga. He remembered the teachings of the Vedas from Jnyaneshwar and the teachings of Buddhism from his teacher Munish. He remembered all that Yochanan the Baptizer had taught him. All different, yet all very much the same. They all blended together into a seamless tapestry of great spiritual knowledge with which he taught. He thought about the past few years, and how his ministry had grown.

***

The year went by quickly—almost too quickly—and soon it was time for the Passover celebration in Jerusalem once again. Yeshua said he needed to be there, although his disciples were reluctant to take him to a place where he was so disliked by the religious authorities.

It was a few days before the festival, and they stayed at the house of Shimon the leper in Bethany. The women there were always excited to see Yeshua, and as usual they began to fuss over him and groom him. One of them had prepared a bowl of warm water with spices in it for him to bathe his feet in after his long journey. Afterwards, she would massage his feet. As he sat there enjoying her kindness, another woman opened an alabaster jar that contained some rather expensive ointment and began to comb it into his hair.

Andreas said to her, "It's nice that you are being so kind to our Master, but you really didn't need to use such expensive ointment. It might have been more appropriate to use a less expensive ointment and sell this one instead. You could have gotten at least three hundred denarii for it and then used the money for the poor. Isn't that right, Master?" Andreas was hoping to impress Yeshua with his focus on the poor.

Yeshua put one arm around the woman, and the other around Andreas. "Andreas, don't say that. I know you mean well, my friend. But you should never refuse or belittle a gift that someone gives you out of love. Not a three denarii gift, not a three *hundred* denarii gift. The true gift is that it comes from the heart. The poor will always be with us, Andreas, and we can always help them. We don't even need money to do it. The people whom we know, however, our friends and our family, we never know how long *they* will be with us."

He then turned to the woman and continued, "My dear, you have just done a good thing, and I thank you for it. You don't know it yet, but you have just done something very special that people will talk about for a very long time: you have prepared me to leave."

She looked puzzled, but Yeshua did not explain further.

***

Yeshua and his followers began their journey to Jerusalem early in the morning. He seemed very quiet, which was unusual. Normally he would teach as they walked, and they all tried to be as close to him as they could to hear what he had to say. But this morning he seemed to want to look around and see the faces of those coming with him. As each made eye contact, he would smile that gentle, forgiving smile that could tame a lion with a single glance.

As they neared their destination, they paused to sit and eat. Because Yeshua was so quiet, the crowd around him likewise was silent, but it was not an uncomfortable silence. It was a silence of sharing. Whatever it was that he was feeling, his followers seemed to feel it too. It was a union of spirit that was almost audible, like a faint buzzing.

From the outside of the crowd, a lone rooster ambled up to Yeshua. The two looked at each other, and Yeshua tore a piece of his bread into tiny crumbs and fed them to the bird. Everyone seemed amused at the sight and waited for a lesson from the Master.

"There you are!" came a voice from the back of the crowd. An elderly man appeared from the same place the rooster had come from and neared Yeshua. "I hope he didn't beg too much. He is an expert at begging the crowd for food."

Yeshua picked the rooster up and stroked him gently before handing him to the stranger. "Did he get out of your pen?" Yeshua asked.

"He doesn't live in a pen," the stranger answered. "He is free to leave anytime he wants. His wings are not clipped, and he sometimes flies into nearby trees, but as with most roosters, he is not a very good flier. We—that is, my wife and I—have always let our chickens and roosters roam freely. Some left us and probably were eaten by wild animals, or maybe taken in by others for their eggs or food, but most of them stay. Are you all on your way to Jerusalem for the Passover?"

They all nodded in the affirmative. Yeshua asked, "And you? Care to join us?"

"Not this year, my friends. My wife and I are getting too old. We have celebrated enough Passovers in Jerusalem. Besides, something doesn't feel right this year. I can't explain it, but it just doesn't seem to invite us as others have. No, we will stay at home. But thank you just the same."

"My name is Yeshua," he said to the man as he left with his rooster.

The man turned to reply. "And mine is Nadav. May you all have a meaningful Passover."

Yeshua grew even quieter as he watched the man disappear into the distance. After a long silence, he rose up and said, "Let's complete our journey."

IV. COMPLETION

com·ple·tion

Noun

The action or process of finishing something.

The state of being finished.

Synonyms

consummation - conclusion - perfection - fulfillment

96 (Aharon springs his trap)

AD 33
Yeshua's age: 36

As the mayor of Sepphoris, former member of the Great Sanherdrin, and personal friend of both Herod and Herodias, Aharon wielded a lot of political power. This year he intended to use it.

It was two days before the feast of the unleveaned bread when the meeting took place at the house of Caiaphas, early in the morning. Aharon had arranged for Rabbi Yochanan ben Zakkai, who was the Av Beit Din (father of the court) of the Great Sanhedrin to be there. Being second in command, the rabbi presided over the Great Sanhedrin whenever it sat as a criminal court. Aharon was glad to have him. He was a Galilean, and sided more with the Pharisees than the Sadducees. This would go well with Aharon's plans, since it was the Pharisees who so despised Yeshua and since the laws he broke were, for the most part, laws handed down as part of the oral tradition that the Pharisees followed, but the Sadducees did not. Chanan was also there, still angry about the incident last year with the money changers when he was high priest. And finally Aharon had gathered several priests, elders, and scribes.

Aharon addressed the group, saying, "Thank you all for coming. I think you all know why we are here. It is my belief that Yeshua will be present at this year's Passover. I not only want to be ready for him, I want to make sure he won't escape again. It won't happen this year, I can assure you. I have five hundred Roman soldiers at my call to surround the city and arrest him on a moment's notice. I need only give the word.

"I had a spy whom I placed in Yeshua's inner circle some time ago, and he brought me documented proof of Yeshua's disobedience of the laws. And I have witnesses. It is my understanding that two witnesses are required for each charge being brought against him. Is that correct?"

The scribes all nodded their heads in the affirmative, although Aharon was well aware of the procedure.

Rabbi Yochanan then said, "Aharon, we have heard of his

disobedience of the laws, and it is good that you have witnesses, but since it is capital punishment you are looking for, that we are all looking for, we must have more than that. The specific laws that we could have him executed for are doing work on the Sabbath, blasphemy, witchcraft and sorcery, and being a false prophet. It is my understanding that he done all of these things."

Aharon said, "The Pharisees and scribes tried to accuse him of witchcraft and sorcery, but he twisted their words around, and my spy did not think he could find witnesses willing to testify against him on that count."

Rabbi Yochanan said, "What about working on the Sabbath? I hear there are many claims that he did that."

"He cites examples of David doing the same," Aharon said. "He twists words around so that nobody can question him. Especially when the 'work' he does is healing people. The Pharisees, many of them, would welcome being a witness to these transgressions, but not the people. Also, his arguments are quite sound, and would not stand up in your court, I'm afraid."

Rabbi Yochanan thought a minute and said, "Yes, I have heard from the Pharisees in great detail how he turns things around. Therefore, the only two things we could still have him executed for are blasphemy and being a false prophet. And since we have no proof of these transgressions, it would be best if we could trick him into committing them when he arrives here. I have enough members to confront him, and if we all focus on that goal of forcing him to commit blasphemy or doing something that would allow us to be able to accuse him of being a false prophet, we stand a chance in my court and ultimately the Roman court. I only say this: if we try to do this during the festival, there are enough of his followers here that it would cause a riot. So let's do what we can, but, Aharon, don't arrest him until *after* the festival or, if you can, *before* the festival."

***

Yeshua had arrived, much to Aharon's delight, and Yeshua knew his enemies would come and test him. Some of the people remembered him, and gathered around him as he stood just outside the temple walls. Sure enough, some members of the Great Sanhedrin came out of the temple and walked toward him. They were going to try to get him to proclaim himself a prophet, and if he did, they would have their conviction.

"You are the teacher Yeshua, are you not?" one member of the Great Sanhedrin asked.

Yeshua smiled at the dignitaries and gently said, "You know that I am, or you would not have asked the question."

"We have heard that you cast out demons and give sight to the blind. Some have claimed that you even raise the dead. Tell us, by what authority do you do these things?"

There was a small crowd around him, and they all awaited his answer. Yeshua spoke. "If you first answer my question, I will answer yours."

The priests, scribes, and elders sensed victory. "Then ask your question," one of them said.

Yeshua asked, "Who baptized Yochanan the Baptizer? Did his baptism come from heaven, or was it of human origin?"

Yeshua's interrogators stepped away from him and huddled together to ponder his question. It was a brilliant question. If they answered that Yochanan's baptism was from God, then Yeshua would say, "Then why did you not believe Yochanan when he told you this?" Yochanan was another person who was not well liked among the Pharisees and Sadducees, even in death. But if they said that his baptism was of human origin the crowd would riot, because they all believed that Yochanan was a prophet. They feared they might even be stoned to death if the crowd got angry enough.

Finally, after much arguing, one of them said to Yeshua, "We cannot tell you this."

Yeshua had never stopped smiling. He shook back his hair, outstretched his hands, and said, "And so, neither can I tell you by whose authority I do these things." And with that, he turned and walked away from them, with the crowd gleefully following him.

The Pharisees tried to trap him next. The crowd was getting bigger now, and they joined it and worked their way to the front. One of the Pharisees asked, "Teacher, we all know how sincere you are, and that you treat everyone equally. We know that you teach the ways of God in accordance with truth. So tell us, is it lawful to pay taxes to the emperor?" They reasoned that if he said tribute should be given to

Caesar, he could be charged with being an enemy of the Jews, but if he said it was wrong to pay taxes, he could be charged with sedition under the Roman laws.

Yeshua easily saw through that one. He said to the Pharisees, "Do any of you have a denarius that I can hold in my hand?" Several of them tried to hand him coins. He took one and asked, "Whose head is this, and whose title?"

The Pharisees were silent, but one of the crowd said, "It is the head of Tiberius Caesar, and he is emperor."

Yeshua handed the coin back to its owner and said, "Then I say to give to the emperor the things that are the emperor's," and then turning his back to them, facing the crowd and stretching out his hands, he continued, "and give to God the things that are God's."

The crowd laughed and shouted as the Pharisees sulked and walked away. It was going to be hard to trick him, of this there was no doubt.

***

It happened in the early afternoon. The crowd that followed him was getting larger. They stood near the front steps of the temple. A woman was commenting on how large the stones were that the temple, and indeed the entire city was made of. Before he gave up his Siddis, Yeshua had once looked into the future and seen the destruction of the entire city of Jerusalem. He told the woman, "Do you see these great buildings?" Yeshua held up his hand and gestured all around him. "Soon not one single stone will be left standing. Everything will be thrown down. This entire city will be in ruins."

"Even the temple?" someone else in the crowd asked.

"Even the temple," he answered. "But if the temple that is made with hands is destroyed, in three days' time I will build another *not* made with hands."

One of the Pharisees overheard the whole thing and ran to Aharon to tell him what had happened. Aharon, in turn, quickly gathered Caiaphas and Rabbi Yochanan and said, "We have our proof! He just now claimed that the temple would be destroyed. He also claimed that he would raise it up again in three days. We have our false prophet. We can't wait any longer. We have to arrest him now. Tonight. Tomorrow we will have him tried and executed. And it will all be done *before* the feast of the unleavened bread. I will set his arrest in motion. Caiaphas, we will bring him to your house tonight, and rabbi, we will bring him to you and the rest of the Great Sanhedrin in the early morning. We have him now!"

97 (The arrest of Yeshua)

It was now evening, and Yeshua sat in silent meditation, in a state of perfect Kaivalya. Here, in Jerusalem, in the Garden of Gethsemane, he moved into the ultimate state of meditation. Although he had given up his powers, the radiance coming from his face almost lit up the star-studded night and turned it into daylight.

He opened his eyes to see a familiar face, one he had not seen in some time. "Bacha! What are you doing here?"

Bacha had been running, and was still somewhat breathless. "Yeshua my friend. It is time for us to go. No time for talk. I'll tell you later what this is about. Get up and follow me quickly."

Yeshua did not move. "There is plenty of time to talk, Bacha, because I am not running anywhere. Now sit and tell me what this is all about. Why have you come all this way in the middle of the night?"

"Yeshua, Yeshua, they're coming for you! I saw them. Roman soldiers. Hundreds of them. We have to leave now." Bacha looked behind, then back at Yeshua.

Yeshua was in such a state of calm that everything that transpired felt as if it was happening in slow motion, as if in a dream. "I always knew that they would come, Bacha. I have seen it in my meditation many times now. Patanjali taught us to see the future, remember?"

Bacha remembered, but his abilities had never come close to Yeshua's. He could no sooner see the future then he could see a black stone on a moonless night. "Yeshua, I have made all the arrangements. We can travel with a group of merchants. This time we will *walk* to India. We will be in a place that is not ruled by the Satavhanas. We will be welcome. You can continue your ministry there. But we have to go now."

Filippos now arrived, also breathless, which woke up Shimon, who had been sleeping with some of the other disciples near where Yeshua sat. Yeshua looked at the three of them and then said to Shimon, "I asked you and the rest of the disciples to sit with me as I meditated. Could you not stay awake even for an hour?"

Filippos said, "The soldiers, the soldiers! They will be coming over the Mount of Olives any minute! We have to leave now!"

Yeshua said to the three of them, "The time for running is past, my friends. I ran as a child. I even ran as an adult. I will run no longer. This is where I belong, you see. These are my people. Let them do to me what they must. I have already witnessed it. And remember what I have said to you many times. We are not the body. We are not the breath. We are not the mind. We always were. And we always will be. This is not the end, my dear friends. This is not the end."

Yeshua calmly closed his eyes in meditation once more as Shimon, Filippos, and Bacha looked at one another and wondered what to do next. Do they pick him up and carry him? Yeshua opened his eyes, stood, and said, "They are here. Now go before they arrest you too."

The sound of Roman boots was unmistakable. Aharon had arranged for five hundred soldiers to come. This was going to be done right. Yeshua would not escape. About four hundred of them surrounded the garden and stood guard at the top of the hill; the remaining hundred came for the arrest. The *tromp tromp tromp* of their boots came closer.

As they marched down the hill towards him with lanterns in hand, Yeshua quietly walked towards them as if he were greeting a group of followers. He placed his hands in prayer position over his heart and smiled. "Greetings. And who have you come to see on this beautiful evening?" he asked.

"We seek Yeshua of Nazareth," the head soldier replied.

"Then you have found him. The others who are here, let them pass. They have done nothing wrong."

The crowd who came with the soldiers stepped back in fright, expecting violence. There was none. The head of the soldiers grabbed Yeshua by his right hand and forced it behind his back and up between his shoulder blades. At the same time he ground his boot into Yeshua's bare foot. Yeshua hunched over and gasped in pain. A noose was placed around his neck, and the other end was tied tightly around his right wrist. The same thing was then done with his left hand. Any move in an attempt to undo the knots would only tighten the noose. It was the perfect way to hold a prisoner.

Most of the disciples ran. But some of them stayed, including Miryam and Filippos. Bacha, too, stayed. As the soldiers marched Yeshua out of the garden, those who remained walked quietly behind them. Filippos whispered to Bacha, "They'll probably take him somewhere for the night. If they are arresting him for a capital crime, it's illegal for them to do it at night."

The house they brought him to was lit up from the inside. Most of the others around it were dark. Out of the front door came Chanan, the father-in-law of the High Priest Caiaphas. Filippos stared at him and thought for a moment. And then he remembered. "Chanan!" He said to Bacha, "He was the high priest at the temple when Yeshua threw the money changers out. Why are they bringing him here?"

Chanan had been terribly embarrassed by that incident and almost lost his position as a result. He had been high priest for seventeen years, and this was the only black mark on his legacy. Shortly after that event, the position had been passed on to his son-in-law, Caiaphas.

The soldiers now stood in a circle around the crowd. Chanan walked up to Yeshua and shouted, "Give me the names of all your disciples, and tell me what secrets you have been teaching them." Chanan was strutting before the crowd like a proud rooster. He was showing off, and his lips formed a cruel smile.

Yeshua replied, "Every word I have ever spoken, friend, was out in the open. I have taught openly in the synagogue, and I have taught openly in the temple. I have *never* taught secretly. True, I have spoken to my disciples in private, but I tell them nothing I would not tell you right now. But don't take my word for it; ask those who have heard me. Some of them are here. Ask any one of them."

Whack! An infuriated Chanan backhanded Yeshua as hard as he could as he said, "I am *not* your friend." The blow almost knocked Yeshua off his feet, but he did not back down. He looked straight at Chanan with his gentle blue-gray eyes and said, "If I have said anything evil or offensive, then I surely deserve your blows. But if I have only spoken the truth, kind sir, why are you now striking me?"

Chanan answered by throwing his closed fist into Yeshua's nose, then again into his mouth. The blood poured out of Yeshua's nose, but because his hands were tied, he could do nothing to stop it. His lips, too, were puffy and bleeding.

"Stop it, stop it." shouted Miryam. Filippos was holding her for fear she might run to him and be arrested as well.

Chanan took delight in Miryam's shout and looked to the rest of the crowd for approval. There was none. Some of the crowd looked down to the ground, some turned and walked away. And those people who did look at Chanan had horror and disgust written on their faces.

"Take him to Caiaphas!" a humiliated Chanon shouted to the guards. Chanon and Miryam for a moment made eye contact.

Filippos now realized that nothing lawful was going to happen tonight. He must get to the Great Sanherdrin and hope that some of them were still awake and at the temple. He would tell them about this illegal nighttime arrest. "Bacha, you and Miryam stay close to Yeshua. I will be back." The two had never met before this night, but they looked to one another and nodded.

The guards led Yeshua away, blood still dripping from his nose. As they followed with the crowd, Miryam turned to Bacha and said, "Bacha, Yeshua has spoken of you often. How did you know to come?"

Bacha replied, "I came to Passover because I believed Yeshua would be here. It was to be a surprise. We haven't seen each other in many years. But when I saw him from a distance being challenged by some of the religious authorities, while others—the scribes and Pharisees—whispered to one another and pointed to him, I knew something was wrong."

Miryam narrowed her eyes and tilted her head. "What did you do, Bacha?"

Bacha replied, "I discreetly followed two of them and overheard them talking about having Yeshua executed."

"Executed? They are going to execute him?" Miryam was trembling. "Oh Bacha, why didn't you do something right then?"

Bacha stopped walking and held her firmly by her shoulders, looking directly into her eyes as the rest of the crowd walked around them. "I did. I quickly found some merchants who were traveling to India and made arrangements for Yeshua and me to go with them. It took the rest of the afternoon to do that.

"As I was returning, I saw a great number of Roman soldiers gathering, and as I neared them, I heard talk of having the 'Jewish troublemaker' arrested. I had no idea it would happen so quickly. That's when I ran to find him. I asked several people of his whereabouts. Nobody knew where he was. Finally I saw Filippos, who I met some time ago in Samaria. He told me where Yeshua was, and that's when I ran to him and told him about the soldiers."

98 (Filippos plots to save Yeshua)

Yeshua was taken to Caiaphas. They took him to his house, not the council chambers.

Yeshua was ordered to stand before the rather tall man. To Caiaphas's right were the twenty-three members of Jerusalem's lesser Sanherdrin, and to his left were a group of witnesses. Caiaphas turned to the witnesses. "Tell us what you heard him say."

One man said, "We heard him say that he would destroy this temple and within three days would build it back, but without using hands." But there was disagreement among the group if he really said those words. Some heard him say, "I *could* destroy this temple," but others heard him say, "I *will* destroy this temple." Still others weren't sure what they heard. Caiaphas was smart enough to know that this testimony was worthless. He needed two witnesses who agreed. But he tried to use the testimony anyway. He said to Yeshua, "Well? Do you have nothing to say for yourself? Which of these persons is telling the truth, and which is lying?" Yeshua was silent.

Next he tried another tactic: "I command you, to tell me, *in the presence of the Living God*, are you the Christ, the Son of the Blessed?"

Legally, a question asked in this manner required an answer, and Yeshua knew it. Yeshua looked intently into Caiaphas's eyes and said, "When it is your turn to die, Caiaphas, you will see the son of man sitting on the right hand of power."

Caiaphas grabbed Yeshua's robe and tore it. This was done because according to the Talmud, if a moderator hears what he perceives to be blasphemy, he shows that he disagrees by tearing the blasphemer's garment. As far as Caiaphas was concerned, Yeshua had just admitted to being Christ. Then he turned to the Sanhedrin and said, "I don't think we need to hear any more, do we?"

The eldest member of the Sanhedrin stiffened and replied, "No, we do not." The other members nodded their heads in approval.

If Filippos had been there, he would have told Bacha and Miryam that in a legal proceeding, there would have to be a vote, taken from the youngest to the oldest so that the younger members would not be in any way influenced by their elders. Also, they would all have to go to their homes and be separate from each other for at least one day and think about all they had heard. They were supposed to, according to their code, "Eat like food, drink like wines, sleep well. And once again return and hear the testimony of the accused. Then, and only then, shall you render a vote."

But Filippos was not there. After arriving at the temple he guessed that the Great Sanherdrin were likely part of this travesty of justice. He instead turned and made his way to Herod's Praetorium, where he knew Pilate would be. He waited for Pilate to awaken. Now he had a plan!

**

Filippos knew that Pilate was an early riser. Most of Filippos's meetings with him years ago, when he was Pilates' adviser on Jewish matters, took place shortly after the sun rose. He was hoping that the guard stationed outside Herod's Praetorium was one that he knew. But Filippos had no such luck. As he approached, the guard bristled, his hand moving to the handle of his sword. "Who goes there?"

Trying to make it as official as he could, Filippos said, "Filippos the lawyer. Jewish council and adviser to the prefect."

The guard replied, "State your business here."

Filippos was having doubts that he would be successful, but he would try. "Sir, I have come a long way to speak with the prefect, on a matter of urgent business."

"Is he expecting you?"

"Sir, I have only yesterday arrived. He is not expecting me, but he will see me once you tell him my name."

The guard was not convinced. "Pontius Pilate does not see anyone who is not expected, especially a Jew. Especially at this time of day."

Filippos, being a good lawyer, tried a new tactic. "This matter is most urgent, and important, and something that he needs to know right now. If he finds out that you have turned his adviser away, it will not go good for you, I can promise."

The guard was still not convinced, but decided not to be too foolish. He called a second guard and said, "Go and tell the prefect that there is a Jewish lawyer here by the name of Filippos who requests an audience. He says he has urgent news."

Filippos smiled. The first guard glared. The second guard

disappeared.

After what seemed like a long time, the second guard returned. "The prefect says he will see you."

Filippos could not believe it actually worked. Neither could the first guard. He continued glaring, but reluctantly stepped aside. Filippos was led into the Praetorium, down a hallway, and into a room where Pilate was already drinking tea. "Filippos, it is nice to see you after all these years. I have been told that you have some very important news for me."

This was it. Yeshua's life now depended on this crucial meeting. He had to convince Pilate of Yeshua's innocence. Pilate avoided the Jewish population as much as possible, preferring instead to surround himself with fellow Romans, or the occasional Sadducees. Filippos knew that Pilate likely was not familiar with Yeshua's exploits. Anyway, they had mostly stirred up the priests, not the Romans. It was only the incident with the money changers that Pilate may have known of.

"Prefect, I have come to tell you about a horrible injustice about to unfold by the Great Sanhedrin, one that will surely involve you."

He had said the right thing. Pilate did not much like the Great Sanhedrin. They were, in his opinion, a group of Jews with far too much power. If he gave them what they wanted, they only wanted more. If he refused what they wanted, they complained to higher authorities. He had already been summoned to Syria once to stand before the governor, Vittalius, for not being "sensitive" to Jewish customs. He was sure that the Sanhedrin had their fingers in it. And although he originally hated Herod's insistence that he learn more about Jewish customs from a Jewish lawyer, he had grown to actually like Filippos, who was well spoken and polite and never presumed too much when they met.

"It was right of you to come. Sit and tell me more, Filippos."

As best he could, Filippos laid out the case of injustice being done against Yeshua by the Great Sanhedrin: the false charges, the illegal trials, everything. When he had finished, Pilate said, "What you have told me is mostly of Jewish matters, and this concerns me not in the least. But if they are bringing criminal charges against him, Filippos, charges that mean execution, I am obligated to see him and judge him. And if the evidence is powerful, I will have no choice but to condemn him."

Filippos smiled. "But I have a plan, Prefect. It's one that the Great Sanhedrin will not approve of, but one they will have to abide by."

Now it was Pilate who was smiling. "Tell me more, Filippos."

And so Filippos told Pilate of his plan. When he was finished, Pilate was elated. "It could just work, Filippos. It could just work. Thank you for bringing this matter to my attention."

Filippos had planted his seed. Now he would see if it would grow.

99 (Pilate agrees to judge Yeshua)

It was now daylight. Yeshua, having had no sleep, having been slapped, beaten, and mocked by his accusers, was bleeding and tired. But his journey had not yet ended. His unofficial trials were about to make way for his official trials.

The guards now marched him to the Hall of Hewn Stones, just inside the temple. The Great Sanhedrin were all assembled, sitting in their seats and waiting for him. Caiaphas stood at their side. Rabbi Yochanan ben Zakkai, the Av Beit Din, sat in the center seat. He arose and approached Yeshua, but before he could speak, Yeshua said, "Why are you all here? I have done nothing wrong. Untie me and let me go."

Ignoring his demands, the rabbi asked, "Are you the Christ? The Son of God?"

A weary Yeshua sighed and answered, "When I tell you the truth, you don't believe me. When I ask you a question, you will not answer me. I have done nothing wrong, rabbi, and you know it. Yet when I ask you to let me go, you will not. Why?"

"What did you tell Caiaphas?"

Yeshua began to see the conspiracy being brought against him. He turned to look at Caiaphas as he replied, "I have told him that the Son of Man will sit on the right hand of the power of God."

"And so you now openly admit that you claim to be Christ, the Son of God?"

"No, it is *you* who have said that I am. I claim to be the son of ..."

Caiaphas interrupted, "No! It was *you* who said that you were. I asked you, and you answered so." Then, turning to the others he gestured toward Yeshua and said, "See his torn tunic."

Rabbi Yochanan stood, faced his assembly and proclaimed, "What do we need any more witnesses for? We have the only witness we need. The high priest who heard his blasphemy coming from his own mouth. Members of the Great Sanhedrin, deliver your verdicts."

This time, the vote was done in a legal manner; from the youngest to the eldest. Nicodemus was the only one who voted no. The rest all found him guilty of blasphemy, and voted to take him to Pilate. Aharon had paid Nicodemus to say no. If everyone immediately voted Yeshua guilty, the charges would be thrown out because unless the defendant had at least one advocate and one vote, the verdict would be deemed invalid. But he didn't have to bother with that formality. Much of this trial was not being done legally. There was to be no waiting a day for deliberation. The verdict was going to be announced right now.

Aharon was not a lawyer, but he knew that a single charge of blasphemy would not be enough to convince Pilate. He took Rabbi Yochanan to the side, away from the others, and told him that he would need more charges.

"What do you suggest?"

Aharon thought a moment and then said, "Didn't Yeshua throw the money changers out of the temple last year?"

"Yes. The kind of thing that gives us all a bad name among the Romans."

"And didn't he today claim he would destroy the temple? Isn't that a threat of treason in Roman law?"

"Caiaphas could not find witnesses who were in agreement about that."

Aharon said, "And would Pilate know that?" Rabbi Yochanan narrowed his eyes, and stroked his beard. Then his eyes opened and a slight smile formed on his lips. Aharon continued. "Rabbi, you *must* add the charge of treason to your original charge of blasphemy. First of all, Yeshua is claiming to be king. Caiaphas heard him say that. Secondly, he is threatening to tear down the temple. And last of all, he is guilty of stirring up our people in an attempt to overthrow the government. That speaks of both treason and sedition. Pilate will hear such a case."

Rabbi Yochanan and the rest of the Great Sanhedrin immediately headed off to Herod's Praetorium to request an audience with Pilate. Aharon walked behind them. He would wait outside and make sure that everything would be done right.

As they neared the Praetorium, Aharon noticed someone walking away from the direction they were headed. The figure quickly darted down a side street upon seeing them. Something was wrong. Aharon just didn't know what it was. He had a feeling, nothing more. *Wait*, it suddenly occurred to him, *that was Filippos! I know it was him. What was he doing here?*

Rabbi Yochanan and one of the elders announced themselves and requested an audience with Pilate. Because it was Passover, they could not enter a Gentile court, or they would be considered unclean. They therefore asked that Pilate come outside and talk to them. Aharon would now have to leave. There was bad blood between him and Pilate, and he didn't want to jeopardize the meeting if Pilate recognized him. But he would stay nearby in case he was needed. All the better. He needed the time to consider what Filippos might have done.

Pilate greeted them and asked what their business was. "Prefect, we have a man named Yeshua who we wish to bring before you for judgment."

Pilate winced when he heard Yeshua's name, but it went unnoticed. "What accusations have you brought against this man?"

Rabbi Yochanan replied, "Prefect, these are more than accusations. If we hadn't already found him guilty, we wouldn't be here."

Pilate first tried to avoid the conflict altogether. "If he is guilty, as you say, than take him and judge him according to your laws."

The Av Beit Din replied, "But Prefect, it is not lawful for us to put any man to death. And that is the punishment that treason demands. Yeshua has claimed to be king, another Caesar. We call that treason! And he has done other treasonous and seditious acts which we will put forth to you."

Pilate then realized that Filippos was right about the charges, and trumped-up or not, he needed to proceed with the official judgment. "Very well. Send Yeshua to me."

100 (Sending him to Herod)

Pilate had stayed outside. It was a nice day, and the Jewish council would be back with Yeshua soon enough. No sense in making two trips. He had tea brought to him and sipped it as he waited. He did not have to wait long. Down the street they marched. It was his first up-close look at Yeshua. This bearded man had both a strong and gentle look to him. Even through his beaten face Pilate could see that. Yeshua's nose was caked in blood and misshapen. Both his eyes were bruised. His lips were puffy and split. His entire tunic was covered in blood. And yet, he stood undefeated.

Pilate came straight to the point. "You have been accused of many crimes, Yeshua. Blasphemy does not concern me. But treason is an entirely different matter. So let me begin with this. Do you claim to be king?"

Yeshua answered, "Is it you, Prefect, who is asking this of me, or is it something that others have told you about me?" Yeshua turned and looked back at the rabbi.

Pilate was not used to being spoken to in an accusatory manner, especially by a Jew. "Do I look like a Jew? Do I? It is *your* nation, and *your* priests who have brought you before me. You will answer the question."

"My kingdom, Prefect, is not of this world. If it were a worldly kingdom, then my servants would even now be in great battle against those who brought me to you. But no such battle is taking place. Is it not so? My kingdom is not of this world."

"Still, you *do* claim to be a king?"

In a tired voice, Yeshua answered almost in a whisper, "People say that I am a king. I do not deny that they say so. I can only attest to you that for *this* I was born, and for *this* cause I came into the world: that I should bear witness unto the truth. Any person who is of the truth will hear my voice."

"Hmm. And what is truth?" Pilate asked.

Filippos was right, Pilate thought, *this man is not a threat.*

"I find no fault with your accused," Pilate said in an official voice. "He does not claim to be a king of any land here on this world. I see no treasonous offense here."

Rabbi Yochanan now said, "But Prefect, he has threatened to

tear down the temple. He has claimed he could build it back in three days. He once chased our own money changers out of the temple. He is stirring up the people, making them rebellious, teaching rebellion against the Romans all the way from his own Galilee to here."

"Galilee you say? Is he a Galilean?"

"Yes, Prefect," the rabbi replied hesitantly.

Pilate was elated to hear this news. Now he would not have to deal with the matter at all.

"I wish you would have said so sooner. Galilee is not in my jurisdiction. Send him to Herod. It is his jurisdiction, and it is he who needs to judge him."

***

King Herod was staying in the palace of the Maccabees on the slope of Zion, his official residence when he came to Jerusalem to oversee the Jewish festivals. He had spent the night happily with one of his concubines, and now planned to spend the day with his favorite wine. He had consumed some of his first jug, and was already feeling light-headed.

One of the guards approached him and said, "Your majesty, Pilate has sent a prisoner to you for judgment. This person is a Galilean by the name of Yeshua."

"Yeshua? The person who performs miracles for the Jews? The person I tried to see only two years ago? That Yeshua?"

"The same, your majesty."

Instead of being upset for having his day interrupted, Herod was happy to see Yeshua. He had heard all about his miracles and had long wanted to see one for himself. He also misread Pilate's sending Yeshua to him as a favor, and perhaps a game.

"Very well. Bring him to the Hall of Judgment, and I will judge him."

Herod had one more cup of wine before he went to the hall. Looking at the floor by the window, he saw a dead bird. Herod had no idea how it got there, but it gave him an idea. He placed it in a cloth bag and took it with him. Yeshua was already there when he arrived.

"Ah! It is the miracle man. I have long wanted to meet you. Show me a miracle, miracle man." Herod took a protracted look at the person that stood before him and waited. "Have you nothing to say?"

But Yeshua was finally through talking. After standing before Pilate in this mockery of justice, he chose to say no more from that moment on. He kept his head bowed, never once even looking up. He also smelled wine on Herod's breath and knew he would only be mocked.

Normally insolent silence would have enraged Herod, and Yeshua would have been quickly condemned. But the wine put Herod in a particularly happy mood. He slowly walked in a circle around Yeshua. "I have heard you can make the blind see, miracle man. Is this true? If I bring you a blind man, will you show me this trick?"

Again, Yeshua said nothing. "I have heard that you can even raise the dead. Look here. Here is a bird I found. You can see for yourself it is dead." He tossed the dead sparrow he had brought in the bag at Yeshua's feet and gestured towards it. "Make it come back to life for me."

Yeshua thought of his own pet sparrow from years ago. He remained silent. But Herod was now thoroughly enjoying himself, seeing that this man could actually do nothing. He didn't even seem to be able to talk. Herod asked, "What is this man being accused of?"

Rabbi Gamliel told him that he was being charged with blasphemy and treason, and that he claimed to be a king. "A king, you say? Miracle man, who can't seem to perform a single miracle, are you truly a king? Should I bow to you?"

Yeshua continued his silence. Herod said, "Very well. Pilate apparently cannot make up his mind if you are a king or not. So I hereby proclaim you king! King of the Jews! Guards, dress this mute man up in his rightful kingly robe and send him back to Pilate. Here, carry this sign in front of him." Herod wrote something on a piece of parchment and handed it to the guard.

King Herod truly thought Pilate was playing a game. And Herod was ready to play along. Now it was time to send him back to Pilate and see what *he* would do. Herod hoped that Yeshua would be sent back to him yet again. And he couldn't wait. This game could go on for the entire day.

As they left, Herod went back to his wine and waited.

101 (Pilate's plan fails)

Pilate was about to go to his pool. A swim always refreshed him in the afternoon, and after a morning of dealing with the Jewish council, he was ready to turn his mind to other things. Outside the Praetorium, he could hear a crowd getting louder and louder. What could it be this time?

He went to the outside courtyard to see Yeshua being led back. This time Yeshua was draped in a gown of some sort. What had Herod done to him? Why was he back? In front of him was a guard carrying a sign that said "King of the Jews." Behind him were the seventy members of the Great Sanhedrin with the Av Beit Din out in front. And behind them was a crowd of a few hundred people who had seen this strange procession and followed to witness what was happening. Scattered throughout the crowd were Aharon and all the people he could round up. At the opportune time, on a signal from Aharon, they would all yell, "Crucify him." Aharon was going to make sure Yeshua would die. He was counting on the crowd to listen to the loudest voices and join them.

Pilate sighed and went out to take care of the situation. *Why are these people bothering me yet again?* he wondered. He truly wanted to be in his pool, and the quicker he resolved the situation, the quicker he could return. Since Herod had sent him back, Pilate assumed that he too found no fault in Yeshua. No doubt they wanted a final verdict from him. Very well, he would give it to them.

As he walked outside the noise of the crowd grew louder and louder. He lifted his right hand over his head, and the noise subsided. Yeshua stood at Pilate's side, a guard on either side of him. Pilate addressed the Great Sanhedrin, "I have told you that I found no fault with this man, but you were not satisfied. You have now brought him to Herod. Herod has also found no fault with this man. Yet you are still not satisfied. Very well. This I will do: I will have Yeshua chastised and beaten and then released."

A loud "No!" arose from the Jewish council. Rabbi Yochanan stepped forward. He replied, "This man who you would free is guilty of treason, Prefect; A crime that *demands* crucifixion. This man who you would free has already stirred up many people and turned their hearts against you and the Roman Empire. This man who you would free is being proclaimed a king by many of his followers, and he himself does not deny it. He has threatened to tear down the temple. His numbers, Prefect, will continue to grow unless you stop him here and now. You don't consider him to be a king. We don't consider him to be a king. But the people do."

Bacha, Miryam, and Filippos stood near the front of the crowd. Miryam was hoping Yeshua would make eye contact, but his head was stooped and he didn't lift it up. Filippos looked around, searching for familiar faces. Off to his left, he suddenly found himself staring at Aharon, who was intently staring back at him. Aharon was smiling. *What is he up to?* Filippos thought.

Filippos turned back to Pilates. *Come on, Pilate, remember my plan. Remember my plan. Please. You have to remember it.*

Pilate thought a minute. Insurrection he could deal with. If Yeshua ever really did threaten him, he could swat him down like a fly. This did not worry him. He did not like the Great Sanhedrin very much. They always asked too much of him. And now they had boxed him into a corner, and he especially didn't like that. He needed to show superiority over them, but without stirring them up enough to go and complain to Vitellius, the governor of Syria. One more such complaint just might rob him of his title. *Filippos,* he thought! *It is time for Filippos and his idea!*

He would use Filippos's plan, but he added a clever new twist of his own that would both free Yeshua, and remove any blame from him. It was perfect! Pilate was very pleased with himself. He couldn't wait to see the faces of the Great Sanhedrin when it happened. "Guard!" he shouted. "Bring me Barabbas. On the double." The guard quickly left for the prison. The members of the Sanhedrin looked to one another and at Pilate in puzzlement. "Soon you will have your justice, I promise you," Pilate said with a smile. *Give the stupid crowd of Jews a choice between a real criminal and a person whose only crime was to threaten the authority of the Great Sanhedrin,* Pilate thought, *and they will surely choose Barabbas. And by giving them the choice, not the Sanhedrin, it will be the* people who set Yeshua free. Let the Sanhedrin be angry at them, not me!*

Shortly thereafter, the guard returned with Barabbas. Pilate stood him next to Yeshua, where everyone could see, and made his final proclamation: "As many of you may know, it was once the custom of one of my predecessors that on Passover a prisoner would be released."

Pilate rose his right hand in the air and said, "I hereby reinstate this custom." A resounding cry of approval came forth from the crowd.

Filippos turned to Bacha and Miryam. "See? That was my plan. I told him about that custom early this morning. He's now going to free our Master." The three of them locked arms and waited in anticipation.

"But what is that other person doing there?" Miryam asked, unlocking arms and pointing to Barabbas.

Filippos was wondering the same thing.

Pilate continued. "I have here two prisoners. The first is Yeshua, a first-time criminal, who has been found guilty by *your* people of blasphemy and treason. The second is Barabbas, a lifelong criminal who has been found guilty by *my* people of murder and insurrection and sedition. I now give the choice to you. One of them will be executed and one of them will be set free. Whom shall I execute and whom shall I set free?" Pilate had arranged for a basin of water to be present, and he symbolically washed his hands as he smiled at the assembly of Yeshua's accusers.

"No, no!" Filippos said. "He's changing my plan. He's not supposed to do that."

The crowd was now quiet. They looked to one another, waiting for someone to say something.

Aharon thought quickly and he seized his opportunity. It was that one single, poignant second of silence between question and response, between inhalation and exhalation. It was the silence Aharon always felt between the time his arrow was correctly targeted on a deer in the forest and when the arrow was loosed into the air. It was that precious moment he had experienced time and time again when hunting, where fate hangs in the balance.

Before anyone, including Filippos, could say anything, Aharon set his own plan into motion. The first step was to be seen. He quickly made two of his friends get on their hands and knees, making a platform that Aharon stood on. He could now clearly be seen by the crowd, including his allies. He was facing the crowd, not Pilates. Shaking his fist in the air he began, "Free Barabbas! Free Barabbas! Free Barabbas!" He was shouting it at the top of his lungs. He had cleverly chosen not to use the words, "Crucify Yeshua," because freeing someone on Passover would be more popular with the crowd than crucifying someone. Strategically scattered throughout the crowd, his allies took his cue and joined in, likewise shaking their fists. "Free Barabbas! Free Barabbas!"

Filippos, Bacha, and Miryam, on hearing the chant, all began to shout together, "Free Yeshua! Free Yeshua!" But they were too late. Their voices were already being drowned out by the crowd who were now joining Aharon and his allies in their chant.

Those in the back of the crowd who only had come to see what was happening heard the cries of others and simply joined in: "Free Barabbas! Free Barabbas!" Others, caught up in the frenzy added their voices, as did the Great Sanhedrin. Hundreds of fists shaking in unison, hundreds of voices shouting in unison. The swell grew louder and louder, like a great thunderstorm echoing through the desert. The Great Sanhedrin, all seventy of them, all with smiles on their faces, now turned toward Pilate.

Pilate and Yeshua momentarily looked at each other, their eyes exchanging what their voices did not need to say. Pilate had no more tricks. He had nothing against this man, but it was at last done. Soon he would be in his pool, and that thought made him happy. Anyway, he was tired of dealing with Jewish laws and customs, and now the matter had resolved itself. Filippos might be disappointed, but that bothered him not in the least. He did try, as he promised he would. He shrugged his shoulders, then looked at his guards and gestured towards Yeshua.

As Yeshua was being led away, the crowd continued its unholy chant for a long time. The very last Yeshua heard of the crowd was the sudden cheering that replaced the chanting as Barabbas was untied and walked through the crowd, a free man. Off in the distance Yeshua thought he could hear Nadav's rooster crowing.

Miryam was now shrieking like she once did before she met Yeshua and was possessed. Bacha and Filippos could not console her.

Aharon smiled victoriously.

102 (Bacha and Miryam console one another)

Miryam was now screaming at Bacha and Filippos: "Do something. Do something."

Filippos said, "I'll try to see Pilate again. Maybe he'll listen to me."

"I'll go with you," Miryam said.

"No, Miryam. You can't. He will only see me. You two wait for me outside the courtyard. I'll find you after I've talked to him."

Bacha and Miryam left the courtyard and sat against the side of a building. It faced the courtyard, so they would be certain to see Filippos when he returned.

"What do we do now?" asked Miryam.

"Be present," Bacha answered.

"I have never met you before today, Bacha, but Yeshua has told me many stories about you. 'Be present' is the last answer I would have expected to hear from you. I have heard stories of your bravery and of your strength."

"Have you also heard that I am now a Buddhist? When I ran to your Master in the garden and begged him to run away with me, that was a mistake. I know that now. It goes against my teachings."

Miryam was sobbing. "Bacha, you must do something. You are talking about your friend and companion. You are talking about the man I ... I ... follow."

"'Love,' you meant to say. The man you love. I can see it in your eyes, Miryam. Well, I love him too. Not in the same way you do, but just as much. So do others. We all love him."

Miryam stood and shouted, "Then we must do something!"

Bacha, too, stood, and placed his hand on Miryam's shoulder. "Miryam, sit."

"There isn't time, Bacha. We have to act!"

"Miryam, sit." He said it with more emphasis this time.

She looked shocked, but she did as Bacha asked. Still, her mind was not yet in the present. Bacha sat facing her. "He said to me in the Garden of Gethsemane that he had seen this event in his meditations. Surely he said as much to you?"

Miryam's mouth was open, but no words came out. She was remembering something that had happened more than a year ago, something she had put out of her mind. Then she told Bacha about the dream within a dream Yeshua had about Elazar, and everything that transpired.

Bacha was nodding his head as she talked. "Yeshua knew a year ago that all of this would come about. He knew he would die, and now it has come to be. Miryam, let me tell you some things that Buddha tells us.

"Nobody can escape death. We are dying from the moment we are born. No one knows when it will come. It comes to us in an instant. The only thing that separates us from death is a single breath. Therefore, the only thing we can do is practice our beliefs here and now. There is no time to waste. We cannot prevent the death of our dear friend. We can't, Miryam. He will suffer and he will die. This is truth, irrefutable truth."

Miryam interrupted him. "But Filippos is ... is ..."

Bacha shook his head no and continued. "And when he is gone we will continue, but only for a time. How many people are alive in the world today, Miryam? Millions? And yet, one hundred years from now, every person that is alive today will be dead. "I say again, we must practice our beliefs here and now. What do you believe, Miryam?"

Miryam had stopped crying for a moment. She was thinking. "I believe what the Master has taught us. He would say to us, his closest friends, something about not being the body or the breath—"

Bacha smiled. "We are not the body. We are not the breath. We are not the mind. We always were, and we always will be."

"Yes. That's it. It sounded so comforting when he said it. But he gave us a message and a commandment to spread throughout the land. It was a simple message, really: To love God with all your heart, and with all your soul, and with all your mind. And to love your neighbor as yourself. Above all, love those who hate you. This is what I believe, Bacha. This is what I will tell others as long as I live."

"Then Yeshua has chosen a worthy disciple, Miryam. You must be strong now. You need to be strong for the other disciples, and you need to be strong for him. He expects it of you. He expects it of both of us."

Miryam knew he was right. But now she needed to cry. And Bacha's shoulder was just the place. Although he looked completely different from Yeshua, with his bald head and stocky build, he was similar to Yeshua in other ways. He was kind, like Yeshua was. And he seemed almost as sure of himself as Yeshua was. He embraced her as she cried, and then he too began to cry. They held each other, comforting one another, for a long time.

***

It was the same guard that Filippos had come to before when he approached the door to the Praetorium, so he felt encouraged.

"What do you want this time?" the guard asked.

Filippos replied, "I must see Pilate. I must see him now. Please, you must tell him I'm here."

"Not this time, Filippos. Nobody disturbs Pilate when he is in his pool. Those are my orders."

Filippos saw by the look on the guard's face that he would get nowhere by insisting an immediate audience. "And when he is done? Will you tell him then?"

The guard sighed. "All right. When he is done I'll tell him that Filippos the lawyer is here to see him."

"Can I wait here?"

The guard snarled, "You can wait in the courtyard, but over there." He pointed to the corner farthest away from him.

Filippos walked to the place where he was instructed to wait and sat in the hot sun. He faced the guard and assumed a meditation posture. The guard stared at him for a while, then turned away.

What will I tell him? Filippos thought. But nothing came to mind. The longer he sat, the more anxious he became. And the more anxious he became, the less able he was to think. He had what he thought was the rest of the day to see Pilate. He was certain the execution would take place on the following day.

The sun was climbing higher and higher into the sky. Finally, after a very long time, Filippos saw a second guard approach the first. They exchanged words, and then the second guard left. The first beckoned Filippos. He jumped to his feet. He practically ran to the front door.

"Does your request to see Pilate involve the criminal, Yeshua?"

"Yes it does."

The guard's voice was softer than before. "You are too late, friend. He has already been flogged, and is right now on his way to Golgotha to be crucified. I'm sorry."

103 (Final victory)

AD 33
Yom Shishi (Friday), 14 Aviv (April 3)
Yeshua's age: 36

The process of crucifixion was public knowledge if one cared to read or hear about it, but not many wanted to know. Yeshua had no reason to learn about this barbaric practice, so although he knew he was about to be executed, and he knew it would cause pain, he had no idea of just how much pain he was about to be put through. No one was allowed to be there that morning. At the insistence of the Great Sanhedrin, this was to be a private execution. They were fearful of an uprising by the followers of Yeshua and had convinced Pilate that this would be the prudent course of action.

It began in the courtyard of the fortress Antonia with all Yeshua's clothing being stripped away and his hands tied to a post above his head. Then one of the Roman legionnaires stepped forward with a flagellum in his hand. The whip was quite short, with several heavy leather thongs. Attached to the end of each thong were two lead balls. Yeshua looked back at him once and then turned away and closed his eyes, tensing his body.

The legionnaire, who was bulky and muscular, used his full force to whip across Yeshua's shoulders, back, and legs. Yeshua had never felt such pain. He cried aloud as each blow was struck. At first the leaded thongs only cut through his skin, but as the whipping continued they began to cut deeper and deeper into muscles, until his entire back was nothing more than ghastly hanging ribbons of skin and tissue, oozing with blood.

The centurion in charge of the execution sensed that Yeshua was already almost dead and ordered the beating to be stopped. There was greater pain to be inflicted on Yeshua, and it was the centurion's duty not to deprive the prisoner of that pain. The ropes binding his hands were cut, and Yeshua fell to the cement floor in a heap.

A bucket of cold salty water was thrown on him and the combination of the cold water against his face, and the salt on his hideous wounds abruptly shocked him into consciousness. He was dragged to his feet. Next, the patibulum was tied to his bloody shoulders. It was the cross-arm of the cross and weighed about 110 pounds. Yeshua was forced to carry this burdensome weight a full 650 yards from the fortress Antonia through the Sheep Gate to Golgotha. Each time he would stumble, he would earn another stroke of the flagellum. This would reopen wounds that had just begun to scab over and bring extreme pain to Yeshua.

Golgatha, a word meaning "place of the skull," was on the city's northwest side, near a highway that ran from east to west. It was at the bottom of a cliff that, from a distance, looked very much like a skull, hence its name. It was, according to the Romans, the perfect place for crucifixions. They wanted passersby to see up close what happened to those that defied them. The sight of the skull in the background only added to the place's gruesome flavor.

Having finally arrived at Golgotha, Yeshua was forced down onto the ground, facing up, his shoulders and arms on top of the patibulum. One of the four legionnaires felt his wrist for the space between the two arm bones and drove a square wrought-iron nail through his wrist deep into the wood of the patibulum, taking care to not pull his arms too tight but rather to allow for just a bit of flexibility. This would help increase the pain yet to come. Yeshua was too much in shock to respond to this new kind of pain and merely moaned, half unconscious. The legionnaire repeated the nailing on Yeshua's other wrist, and then the four legionnaires lifted the patibulum up, with Yeshua hanging from it, and hoisted it onto the stipes. The stipes was the seven-foot upright portion of the cross, and was permanently in place for executions past and executions yet to come. At the top of the stipe was a notch, upon which the patibulum was placed. The Greeks referred to it as the Tau cross, as it resembled the Greek letter Tau, or the letter "T." Hanging by just his wrists, Yeshua began to scream and writhe in pain.

Next, the legionnaire pressed the sole of Yeshua's left foot against his right. Both his feet were extended, and both his toes were pointing down. Another square nail was driven through the arch of each foot, leaving his knees just a bit flexed. Yeshua was only semi-conscious, but this would not last long. As he began to sag down, it put more weight on the nails in his wrists, inflaming the nerves inside the wrists. With this, he felt an excruciating pain exploding inside him. He screamed again. But as he pushed himself up to lessen the pain in his arms, he was now placing his full weight onto the nails through his feet. The nerves in his ankles sent pulses of pain through his body just as great as the pain in his wrists he was trying to lessen. This, then, was the reason for the somewhat loose arms and flexed knees. He could choose his agony.

***

Yeshua and Miryam ran out the gate and towards Golgotha, but were stopped a hundred feet or so from the execution spot. Guards had completely surrounded the area. No witnesses were allowed to be present. They could see the cross behind the guards in the distance, but the legionnaires had hung Yeshua so that he was facing the cliff, so they only partially saw Yeshua's back.

"This is as close as you can get!" one guard shouted to them angrily. "Don't try to get past me."

Bacha could not see his lifetime companion, but he could hear his screams of pain. He didn't know what to do.

Oh Yeshua! We could have been on our way to India by now. Why did you think you needed to stay? Why did you do it? You knew, and yet you stayed. Bacha was for the moment not thinking like a Buddhist. He stiffened with each scream he heard. Most of the apostles and other disciples had fled for fear they too might be rounded up by the Romans. On the request of Bacha, Filippos was on his way to Nazareth to give the sad news to Yeshua's mother and stepfather.

The two guards turned their backs to Bacha and Miryam for a moment, and Bacha took this opportunity to shout as loudly as he could in the direction of Golgotha, "Yeshua! Little brother! I am here! I am with you!"

The startled guards turned and one said, "Quiet you! If you yell like that again, you will spend the night in prison. Be glad that I let you be this close." Both guards stood and stared at Bacha until they were sure he would be silent. He did not want to leave this place and so he sat passively and was quiet as instructed. Miryam held his arm tightly in hers.

***

When Bacha cried out, Yeshua lifted his head and turned it around as far as he could in the direction of Bacha's voice. When nothing else was said, he hung his head down again. The agony was excruciating. How long had it been? The minutes on the cross felt to Yeshua like hours, and the hours like days. But he was consoled by hearing Bacha's affirmation. *Bacha is with me!* he thought to himself through his pain. *Who could have asked for a better friend than Bacha?*

As his arms grew weak, a new torture made itself known. He was overcome with wave upon wave of cramps moving through all his muscles tightening them into painful knots, one by one. They contorted his body into strange, grotesque shapes, and as they cramped even more, he was no longer able to push upward. Hanging now by just his arms, his chest muscles began to paralyze and his ribs were unable to move. Thus he was able to inhale air into his body with some effort, but he could not exhale. Every so often, the cramps would lessen, just a bit, and he could momentarily push himself up with much effort in order to exhale and then inhale fresh air into his body. He could take one or maybe two breaths, but then the cramps would begin anew, pulling him back down.

With these cramping moments of agony systematically increasing in length between each breath, he knew he could not live much longer. Again he thought of Bacha. With his next inhalation, he quite suddenly yelled back to his friend in a painful, staggering voice, "We ... are not ... the body!"

The four startled legionnaires stared at him in disbelief. It was the eighth hour of the day, and he was almost dead. How could he yell so loudly?

"Shall we pierce his heart and be done with it?" one of the legionnaires asked.

"No," said another. "I've attended enough crucifixions to know that it won't be long now. Some last for days, but not this one. He won't last beyond the ninth hour. You'll see."

***

Behind the guards, Bacha, who heard the start of his friend's familiar teaching, smiled through his tears. *We are not the body! He knows I am here,* he thought with a bittersweet joy. *Even in death he teaches!* The two guards were just as taken aback with Yeshua's shouting, as were the four legionnaires. They looked at each other with puzzlement written on their faces and then looked back to Bacha, who was still smiling. He squeezed Miryam's hand and she squeezed back. She too was smiling. Bacha closed his eyes and began to reminisce about the times the two had shared together, almost as if his friend was already dead. He remembered fondly his own decision to become a Buddhist, and how happy Yeshua was for him. He thought of earlier times and wrestling with him in the grass by his home in Samaria. He thought of all their adventures in India.

The next scream of agony brought him back to the present. "Oh God, Miryam. He's dying a cruel death and there's nothing I can do to change it." Bacha buried his head into Miryam's shoulder. "I would do anything to change places with you, Yeshua. How can I live without you, little brother? How can I ever live without you? Ahhh, ahhh." Bacha sobbed in helplessness and in grief.

Now it was Miryam who was consoling Bacha. "Be strong, Bacha. Remember?"

"Be strong," he said back to her in almost a whisper.

***

Filippos was riding a camel back to Nazareth, weeping as he rode. *I only hope it is over by now*, Filippos thought. *I hope his suffering was not too great.*

He retraced the last few hours in his head. Aharon had defeated him. He had succeeded in overseeing the execution of the greatest person Filippos had ever known. Filippos's plan, even with Pilate's clever addition had been thwarted. Aharon had seen Filippos as he prepared to leave and had come over to him in order to gloat. "This is only the beginning, Filippos," he had said. "Within ten years I will make sure that nobody ever remembers your friend. Ten years, Filippos. Mark my word. You will never hear his name again."

Filippos had replied with controlled anger and an unshakable conviction, "His name will be remembered long after you and I are gone, Aharon. An unstoppable movement has already begun. Soon you will see. But as of this day, as of this very moment, I will never say *your* name again. It is *you* who will be forgotten in history, not Yeshua."

Aharon said something back to him, but Filippos did not hear his words.

***

It was almost over. In those last moments on the cross, Yeshua realized that his life was now at its end. He thought about his enemies, his unknown enemies who had brought this event about. *Of course* they were physically stronger than him, and of course they would win *this* battle. They already had. But the greater battle had always been for the hearts and minds of humankind. And in that battle, he would reign supreme. He had no doubts about that. He realized that his simple message would endure throughout the ages. He remembered vividly saying these words for the first time years ago in a synagogue by the Sea of Chinnereth, "Above all others, you need follow two of the commandments handed down to us. First, from Devarim, you should love God. You should love God with all your heart, and all your soul, and all your strength, and all your mind. Second, from the commandments of Moshe, you should love your neighbor as you love yourself."

In that ninth hour, Yeshua suddenly became aware of something he had not yet done himself, almost as if his old teacher Patanjali were whispering it in his ear. His message that he gave to others meant that he, Yeshua, needed to love the Pharisees and scribes and Sadducees who he had once scorned, and even the Romans who now crucified him. They were, as he had once preached, his neighbors. He needed to love the Great Sanhedrin. He needed to love Pilate. He needed to love Herod, who had beheaded his dear friend Yochanan. He needed to love the Brahmins in India who had thrown him in jail. He needed to love all those throughout his life who he had rebuked. He had never hated them; he had never hated anyone. But had he truly loved them? No! He must do that before he died. And … he did.

With his very last breath, he felt a universal love that in a split second overcame all pain, all agony, all doubt. *I love you* all, he said to himself with the firmest of convictions, tears flowing down his cheeks. He felt it with every fiber of his being. All his pain was now completely taken away from him, and then, as if being granted a final gift, an unasked-for Siddi, he once again achieved Kaivalya—no, something even greater than Kaivalya. For a brief second his whole body glowed with a beautiful shimmering translucence, and he dwelt in that incredible ecstasy that is beyond description. "It is finished!" the four legionnaires heard him utter. And with that, Yeshua breathed no more.

Epilogue

The sun was just beginning to rise over the hills of Nazareth, changing the landscape to beautiful shades of crimson and yellow. A majestic eagle circled the deep green forest, looking for its next meal, but the only creatures it saw far below were Aharon and his nephew Efah sitting on the trunk of a fallen tree. They too were out hunting.

As they rested, Aharon was thinking about his victory over the woman who had once spurned him. He had taken everything of significance away from her. Yosef was dead, and had been for many years. That was his first victory. Mara and her remaining family would forever be poor. He would continue to see to that. Ephrayim, the fool, still didn't realize that his misfortunes were not of his own making. But the sweetest victory of all, his proudest accomplishment, was his ultimate conquest over that damned troublemaker, Yeshua, the last living link to Yosef, the favorite son of Mara, the bastard who dared to stir up the people whom he now governed. Nailed to the cross as a common criminal. How it must have saddened Mara. How it must have shocked Yeshua. *Yes*, Aharon thought, *I have won. I have totally and completely won.*

The eagle slowly circled once more just to make sure there was nothing there to eat.

Aharon continued in his silent self-admiration. *Ten years from now*, he thought, *nobody will ever say the name "Yeshua" again. No one will even know who he was. He will be forgotten in time. Ten years at most, perhaps only five. It is finally finished.*

He laughed aloud at this last thought, putting his arm around Efah's shoulders. Efah looked up and smiled uncomfortably at his uncle but said nothing.

It is finally finished, he thought once more. *How ironic. One of the four guards that stood by him as he died told me that those were his last words as well: "It is finished." At the end, I think even he must have realized how totally he had lost.*

The hungry eagle now turned towards the northeast. It was a good ten miles or so, but by the Sea of Chinnereth it would find fish—lots and lots of fish.

The skin on his arms began to turn to goosebumps, as Aharon eerily sensed a presence nearby, something that made him feel uneasy. He ever so briefly looked up to where the eagle once had been, but saw only blue sky.

The End

About The Author

Douglas Thompson has been teaching yoga for over twenty years. As part of his training, he needed to gain knowledge in Eastern philosophy. He found the philosophies of the East so interesting that he continued studying them, and reads about them to this day.

This knowledge led him to write his first novel *Fully Human: The Story of a Man Called Yeshua*, in which he shares, through the character Yeshua, (a.k.a. Jesus,) some of the principles of Eastern philosophy.

Douglas owns a yoga studio where he teaches seven days a week. When he is not writing or teaching yoga or Pilates, Douglas enjoys playing classical guitar. He has been playing guitar on and off for over half a century.

He and his wife of forty-eight years live in Hyattsville along with their two rescue beagles.

Made in the USA
Columbia, SC
28 November 2018